THE ASBDA CURRICULUM GUIDE

A REFERENCE FOR SCHOOL BAND DIRECTORS
compiled by
The American School Band Directors Association

COMPILED BY

Donald W. McCabe, Project Chairman

Paul R. Austin
Joe Graves
Harry H. Haines
Rollie Heltman
Fred Wiest

J. Raymond Brandon, Coordinator

International Standard Book Number: 0 - 913650 - 00 - 5

Library of Congress Catalog Card Number: 73 - 75694

Printed in the United States of America

foreword

The American School Band Directors Association, Inc., organized November 21-22, 1953, is comprised of professionally trained, experienced and certified conductors and teachers of bands, whose aim is to advance and improve this important phase of music education — particularly instruction of students engaged in the study of band instruments. It is the earnest desire of the Association to cooperate with school administrative officials and educational organizations to provide a rewarding experience for all students of instrumental music.

To achieve this goal the American School Band Directors Association is pledged to the fulfillment of the following objectives:

1. To develop a comprehensive band program that will be of musical and educational benefit to school band directors and their students.
2. To foster a spirit of friendliness, fellowship and cooperation among the band directors in the elementary and secondary schools of America.
3. To provide a common meeting ground and clearing house for an exchange of ideas and methods that will advance the standards of musical and educational achievement for the school bands of America and stimulate professional growth among school band directors.
4. To work in close cooperation with school administrators as representatives of their individual schools, and through their respective administrative associations, promote a standard of musical progress and achievement which will be of cultural benefit to the student in his school life and in his adult life.
5. To recognize and emphasize the basic and lasting values of a sound instrumental music program, rather than diversionary activities, the value of which are, at best, transitory.
6. To recognize and encourage the obligation of the school band to participate in school and community functions in the dual role of concert and marching band.
7. To serve as an authoritative means of liaison between the largest group of instrumental music teachers in the United States — the school band directors — and music publishers, musical instrument manufacturers, band uniform companies, school architects and suppliers of school building materials and equipment.
8. To encourage a genuine spirit of professional ethics and maintain a highly professional attitude in all meetings and functions of the Association, in keeping with the prestige and importance of an organization which is national in scope.
9. To cooperate with existing associations whose demonstrated purpose is the further improvement of the band as a worthwhile medium of musical expression.

This book is an attempt to establish a basic understanding of what a quality band program should provide; guidelines for the band director, experienced or inexperienced, as to goals and objectives; procedures and materials; and an evaluation scheme for future band programs in America.

preface

The school band movement in America has grown substantially since its inception in the early twenties. It is now firmly established as a vital force in modern education.[1] The majority of junior and senior high schools in the nation now have bands, with literally thousands of students participating in this important aspect of music study. The American Music Conference reported in a recent statistical review that approximately 7.7 percent of all high school students (1,557,000) participated in marching or concert bands in 1970.[2] Recent surveys have indicated that too few school band programs have firm roots within their individual curricula, with the result that programs which are not organizationally sound are placed in jeopardy. Educators agree that most of the academic subject areas have developed well-defined and well-structured programs, with levels of achievement which are substantially the same throughout the nation. In contrast to this, it has been observed that the school band course of study is generally unrelated in curriculum content from school to school and lacks specific goals and procedures.

Since its inception in 1953, the American School Band Directors Association has given itself to an intensive study of the school band program in an attempt to set standards for improvement. Numerous surveys have been conducted, papers prepared and reports presented concerning all phases of the school band program. Through this concerted effort, the lack of "courses of study" or "guides" to indicate the place of instrumental music in the school curriculum has become evident. Thus, leaders in the Association began planning a compilation to fill the need.

The methods for attacking the problem have been as varied as the melodies one hears played by the bands themselves. One of the earliest was to investigate the most evident avenues of instrumental music education and thereby derive criteria that could be followed by band directors throughout the country. For example, reports were prepared on such topics as "Solo and Ensemble Literature," "Methods and Materials," and "Acoustical Design and Construction of Music Rooms." Others are also in existence, each providing a solution for a specific problem, rather than a compilation of suggestions as offered in a course of study.

Members of the ASBDA Research Committees arrived at the conclusion that *one* work could and should be made available to all interested parties. — a work containing all necessary data to provide a well-rounded instrumental music program. One hundred sample school band programs were selected, representing all fifty states and all sizes of enrollment. Selection was based on the recommendations of hundreds of qualified musicians and laymen. Programs chosen for study do not necessarily represent the top echelon among our schools, but rather those most significantly qualified to be studied and evaluated in the effort to produce a useful source book.

A detailed listing of "evaluative criteria" was sent to each of the chosen schools, requesting complete program information. This evaluative instrument, along with additional relevant material, has been carefully studied by a corps of evaluators and prepared for publication in this book.

---

[1] Leeder and Haynie, *Music Education in the High School* (Englewood Cliffs, N.J.: Prentice Hall, Inc., 1958), p. 100.

[2] Based on a survey for the *"1970 Review of the Music Industry and Amateur Music Participation"* made by the National Opinion Research Center, University of Chicago, for the American Music Conference.

contents

chapter 1

Philosophy

INTRODUCTION

One of the most notable of all the changes that have transpired in education during the past fifty years has been the rapid growth and development of instrumental music in the public schools. Today there are more bands in existence than any other school instrumental music organization. Many figures have been quoted as an estimate of the number of performing school bands that exist at present in the United States. Suffice it to say there are very few secondary schools in the country without a band, and we are told by The American Music Conference that the number is growing every year.[1]

We are, in a sense, many steps removed from the bands of the early twentieth century. During the first two decades of this century professional and military bands were at their zenith, meeting many of the musical needs of the people for concert and marching music. Military and professional bands were organized primarily for entertainment and/or military functions, and they still help fulfill these aspects of music performance. In the early thirties the school band movement mushroomed into prominence, not only in secondary schools, but in colleges as well.

Today's school bands furnish music for entertainment purposes as well as provide an opportunity for participation in a group activity as a social outlet. Students in marching bands even derive some aspects of physical skills and exercise. However, band directors can no longer expect school administrators to accept these as primary reasons for the band's existence in the school curriculum. Indeed, the immense amounts of time, energy, and investment require that justification go far beyond that of entertainment or group activity. In addition, new ideas in scheduling, curriculum planning and other organizational changes spell out the necessity for the directors of bands to reorganize their thinking of the band as an entity in the educational system. A significant majority of directors of school bands has taken for granted the security of the band program in the curriculum. As a consequence, they have merely busied themselves — status quo — without taking the time (neither individually nor as members of band organizations) to plan and organize the work into a course of study. The question of accountability in education must be recognized. Those who are looking at the "frills" of education are reasonable people, charged with the responsiblity of accounting for the use of public money and the direction of the education of young people. They must question the educational validity of each program.

Recent times have witnessed innovations in band literature (challenging music, aptly fitted to the modern band), improved quality in instrument design, and the availability of clinicians and conductors for special help and advice in the techniques of performance. These factors, combined with the perseverance, diligence, and preparation of the director and his will to achieve, have spelled success for many band programs, and the quality of performance of bands all across the nation has improved markedly.

---

[1] Theodore M. McCarty, *1970 Review of the Music Industry and Amateur Music Participation* (Chicago: American Music Conference).

In a sense, the band program has been operating on "borrowed time" within the framework of the educational system. Now more must be done to bring the program in line with the academic subjects. The band's value must be derived not alone as a group activity, but, more essentially, as a musical activity. The school band program must be genuinely involved with the aesthetics of music: the appreciation of music through performance, repertoire, interpretation, trained hearing and response.

The public school music instructor responsible for teaching band music must be a "jack-of-all trades." Not only must he be an excellent musician, able to play and teach several of the wind instruments creditably, but also he must be a good conductor, organizer, administrator, public relations expert, and a diplomat with students, other members of the faculty, principals, administrators, school board members, parents, and the community at large. He must be adept at preparing charts for marching procedures. He must know how to diagnose student problems, maintain uniforms, repair various instruments, have a knowledge of stage craft and be familiar with acoustics. He is responsible for thousands of dollars in equipment, facilities and materials. It is amazing what the competent band director-instructor accomplishes. For the dedicated ones — of which there are many — the joy of hearing young people create music of lasting beauty and watching young members of the band become leaders in their society are satisfactions worth the effort.

The incentives and motivations of the band movement which have proven so attractive to so many students are as many as there are students. Some enter the band program because of the glamour of the uniforms, the group activity, the trips the high school band will take, the desire to be a part of the success of an on-going organization, having a "buddy" in the band, or because their parents recall a pleasant and satisfying experience as band members in their youth. At a more advanced level of achievement, the music festivals attract much attention and motivation for outstanding musical performances. Band and other school music festivals are highly organized at the local, county, and state levels, with a few regional festivals which reach across state lines.

The American school band movement is truly a phenomenon. Its pattern and design can be understood only after intensive study of the whole as well as its infinite parts.

MUSIC AND THE GOALS OF EDUCATION

It is generally agreed that the overall objective of modern education is the transmission of cultural heritage, knowledge, skills, attitudes and ideals to create a responsible citizen. The development of skills in critical thinking and problem solving will enable the student to solve not only the problems he meets today, but also those not yet posed for tomorrow's world.[2]

Today almost every community in America is faced with the difficulty of finding ways for bringing divergent groups together for the purpose of reaching common goals of living. In view of the racial and political turmoil gripping the nation, it must be realized that something else is needed beyond a job and good housing. A job and good housing alone do not make a being *human.*

There is much evidence that a student's conception of himself and his abilities is a major factor in *achievement.* Self-image and achievement are directly related. Self-image is the product of all socio-cultural forces interrelating within the personality of the individual.

The band program can involve the learner emotionally through personal production, and provide additional experiences and learning opportunities for the less verbal students.

In the democratic structure, education belongs to all members of society. Ideally it should help

---

[2] John Dewey, *Experiences in Education* (New York: Macmillan Co., 1938-63).

students to develop skills of discrimination and judgment, and to refine attitudes, patterns of thought, and actions. Each child is entitled to an opportunity for self-realization in an environment favorable to artistic creation and aesthetic experience.

The harmonious development of all the individual's powers has been one of the themes in the philosophy of education developed under the democratic ideal. Pestalozzi believed the purpose of education was the training of the hand, the head, and the heart. The first of these includes artistic skills as well as physical culture. He also urged that education of all three sides of our nature proceed on common lines in equal measure for the sake of the "unity of our nature and the equilibrium of our powers."[3]

One of the watchwords of education for Herbart was "many-sided interests." Education was to concern itself with all six types of interest found in human nature—empirical, speculative, aesthetic knowledge, and socially in its individual, civic, and spiritual aspects.[4]

Froebel likewise included the arts as a major division of the curriculum, the aim being to secure the full and all-sided development of each human being.[5]

In *School and Society* John Dewey included artistic expression among the human impulses that he regarded as "the natural resources, the univested capital, upon the exercise of which depends the active growth of the child." He believed that aesthetic expression grew out of two impulses—communication and construction.[6]

Dewey defined the prime function of literature, music and the visual arts in education as for the enhancement of qualities that make any ordinary experience appealing, appropriate—capable of full assimilation—and enjoyable. Such experiences serve the purpose of fixing taste and forming standards for the worth of later experiences.[7]

Why should music be included in the school curriculum? Why should the band program be a part of the school curriculum?

Music has been included in the curricula of schools from the beginning of recorded history, and for widely different purposes. Many of the uses of music in the curriculum have been for the extrinsic values derived, and it was considered that participation in music achieved ends which were essentially non-musical. Plato, for example, held that the great value of music lay in its social values. The Romans included music as one of the seven liberal arts because of the mathematical aspects of music. During the Renaissance and the Reformation, Protestant elementary schools used music to reinforce religious worship. Children sang songs for religious objectives. Music was used in the eighteenth and nineteenth centuries for nationalistic purposes. The extrinsic values of music have also been emphasized in the American music education program — from Lowell Mason to the present day.

Will a subordination of extrinsic values weaken music's position and leave it unsupported in the competition for curricular time? Certainly not. In fact, when the positive extrinsic values showing the unique role of music in education are emphasized, the position of music is strengthened. For example, whereas the basically intellectual aspects of child growth are mainly satisfied through the school's

[3] Robert R. Rush, *The Doctrine of the Great Educators* (New York: St. Martin's Press, 1965).

[4] *Ibid.*

[5] *Ibid.*

[6] Dewey, *op. cit.*

[7] *Ibid.*

academic program and parental guidance, ethical behaviorisms lend themselves to natural realization through the group (social) experiences of music, and, through aesthetic experience, the child achieves self-realization in terms of insights into life values, cultural significance, and a personal satisfaction in the basic need for creative experience.

That human beings respond emotionally to music is a universal fact.

The role and place of music education in the school curriculum may be justified on the tenets of philosophy concerning music education:[8]

1. Art is the result of man's need to transform his experiences symbolically.
2. Aesthetic experience is the source of man's highest satisfaction in living.
3. All human experience is accompanied by feeling. Music is the tonal analogue of the emotive life.
4. Music is expressive of life in all of its alternatives—even death.
5. The importance of music is not fixed; it is subjective, personal, and creative in the best sense of the word.
6. Music attains significance only through its expressive qualities.
7. Every person has the need to transform experience symbolically, and music satisfies that need.
8. The only sound basis for music education is the development of the natural (musical) responsiveness that all persons possess.
9. Every child has a right to develop his aesthetic potential to its highest possible level.
10. Music education should be cosmopolitan, giving recognition to the values in all kinds of music.
11. While no type of music can be ignored in the music program, major attention should be given to providing musical experience that is educative and leads to an aesthetic experience.
12. All musical material should be instructional in the highest sense; all teaching should have as its primary objective the illumination of the art of music and should emphasize musical values, not extra-musical values.

GOALS OF MUSIC EDUCATION

Assuming the goals of modern education to be: 1. the transmission of cultural heritage, 2. the acquiring of knowledge, skills, attitudes and ideals desirable in order to become a responsible citizen in society, 3. the development of skills in critical thinking and problem solving to enable him to solve not only the problems of his society, but of those posed by tomorrow's world, then the goals for students in the instrumental music program may be stated —

1. To demonstrate, to the extent of his capacity, intense involvement in and response to personal aesthetic experience in music.
2. To think, feel and act creatively with music materials.
3. To develop manipulative and organizational skills in band music and performance, appropriate to his abilities.
4. To acquire a knowledge of man's heritage in great works of music.
5. To develop a set of values for discrimination, leading to effective living.

---

[8] *Ibid.* pp. 100-101.

Building a philosophy and goals gives direction to the music curriculum, its content, objectives and value. Some basic concepts in building the content of the music curriculum include:

1. Music is a basic expression of human beings.
2. Music is a means of self-expression and can be "good therapy."
3. Music is a means to creativity, imagery, and auditory acuity.
4. Appreciation of music is a result of aesthetic experience through active or passive participation.
5. Man's need for cultural expression has produced music.
6. Music components are: tone, melody, rhythm, harmony, and form — in a great variety of arrangements.
7. Music is a means for enriching one's life.

Often the instrumental music program in a school is the result of a teacher moving in and going to work with the ideas familiar to him. He develops the usual type of organization and activities, schedules concerts and performances using musical materials and procedures familiar to him. Even what appears to be a well-rounded program is no guarantee that the objectives of the program have been competently met.

The music program is a body of knowledge and experience which, when applied to the individual, provides an aesthetic experience that in some manner changes behavior. The successful growth and development of an instrumental music program is dependent on the plan of the overall program. A foundation plan for a band program consists of a statement of philosophy and a set of objectives stated in behaviorable and measurable terms.

A statement of philosophy has been explored in the preceeding pages. It is generally agreed that music is worthy of being in the curriculum of the school for the sake of its own values. Developing the band program for music education is a complex task. For far too long the music teacher has felt that general statements of philosophy and objectives were too idealistic or not applicable to his situation. It may be that many music instructors simply do not understand the role of philosophy and objectives as a basis for a successful band program.

"The search for objectives must be based upon an examination of musical needs, both individual and social."[9] Pertinent areas of psychology, sociology and educational practice can be made to yield a picture of the musically educated person. "Mueller points to the fact that popular taste is a new force on the music scene with which to be reckoned."[10] The new forces of popular musical taste are exerting tremendous influence due to the mass technological reproduction of music, changes in standards of living, increased leisure time, and the saturation of television. The schools must accept the responsibility of producing intelligent consumers of music. Graduates should be able to select and purchase quality instruments, recordings and equipment, to help bring fine professional performers to the community, and to support the community and school musical activities. If objectives are to be of practical value in the band program they must be precisely formulated.

The framework for writing objectives should consider the following points:[11]

---

[9] Robert House, *Basic Concepts in Music Education,* the Fifty-Seventh Year Book of the National Society for the Study of Education, Nelson B. Henry, ed. (Chicago: University of Chicago Press, 1958), pp. 242-243.

[10] *Ibid.* p. 243.

[11] *Ibid.* pp. 244-245.

1. <u>Objectives should be stated in terms of a particular context.</u> Preparation for a performance skill or career, for various musical understandings and all the cognitive aspects of music are unique and require specific identification.

2. <u>Objectives must describe definitive knowledge, understandings, attitudes and appreciation, skills and habits.</u> Communication failures or misunderstanding often causes poor achievement. Precise identification and descriptions of the elements of the program will establish a basis for evaluation. All human endeavor includes evaluation and recycling of understandings for better achievement.

3. <u>Objectives must embrace a comprehensive and balanced pattern of musicianship.</u> It is very often the case that the band program emphasizes only the area of performance. Many students, after a very successful membership in the band, upon graduation lay the instrument away never to be played again. Perhaps their band program objective was only performance. There are many other values to be derived from the band music program.

4. <u>Objectives should be reduced to an ordered pattern.</u> It is all well and good to speak of developing broad tastes, worthy use of leisure time, an appreciation of beauty, or a musically literate person. Such broad and lofty goals only provide direction. What is needed is to identify and describe the activities, procedures, materials, facilities and the many other necessary elements of the instrumental music program.

chapter 2

Function and Objectives

OF THE INSTRUMENTAL MUSIC PROGRAM IN THE EDUCATIONAL SYSTEM

FUNCTION

It is the function of the instrumental music program to develop musical standards and to impart a basis for value judgments, resulting in the encouragement of sensitive musicianship with breadth, depth and permanence. To foster the kind of music appreciation and understanding that will be effective in the life of the student, a school band instrumental program should seek to give the student something of intrinsic worth through contact with an extensive repertoire, representing the best of the world's music, balanced by attention to theory, skill development, and listening. The music experienced through participation must be of a standard that imparts lasting values. A school instrumental program based upon less than respect for music as an art which imparts aesthetic, moral and spiritual values will fail to realize its real mission — that of enriching life.

OBJECTIVES

One objective of instrumental music is to develop in the student the ability to work effectively through the acquisition of such traits as industry, persistence, and eagerness to grow. Opportunities shall be given students for self-expression in music, a respect for and an appreciation of outstanding cultural developments. Through music education the student will acquire knowledge, skills, and attitudes which will help to make him a more desirable member of society. The knowledge, skills and attitudes desired can best be imparted through a program which is based upon general and specific goals throughout a graded progression.

The following is a listing of major topic areas with emphasis and outcomes as they may be applied to a two-year elementary program:

BEGINNING BAND

Emphasis	Outcome
Care of Instrument	
1. Cleanliness.	Proper mechanical operation of instrument.
2. Lubrication.	
Holding the Instrument	
1. Finger and hand position.	Continuous growth and development of muscular
2. Angle of instrument.	facility.

7

Tone Production

Development of characteristic sound.

1. Proper embouchure.
2. Use of tongue.
3. Breathing.
4. Posture.

Music Reading

1. Letter names of staff.
2. Letter names of notes.
3. Meter, key signatures.
4. Note values.
5. Fingering.

1. Induce sensitivity to pitch, melodic line, dynamics, tone quality, phrasing, rhythm.
2. Development of eye habits.

Awareness of each individual's responsibility to the group:
    a. Attendance.
    b. Conduct.
    c. Preparation of music.

Group Attitudes

Progress through teamwork.

INTERMEDIATE BAND

<u>Emphasis</u>

<u>Outcome</u>

Care of Instrument

1. Cleanliness.
2. Lubrication.

1. Development of proper care.
2. Awareness of sound due to reeds, mouthpiece and quality of instrument.

Holding the Instrument

1. Finger and hand position.
2. Angle of instrument.

Continuous growth and development of muscular facility.

1. Proper embouchure.
2. Use of tongue.
3. Breathing.
4. Posture.

Tone Production

Development of characteristic sound.

1. Letter names of staff.
2. Letter names of notes.
3. Meter, key signatures.
4. Note values.
5. Fingering.

Music Reading

1. Induce sensitivity to pitch, melodic line, dynamics, tone quality, phrasing, rhythm.
2. Development of eye habits.
3. Greater emphasis on dynamics, phrasing and key signatures.
4. Development to the point where simple standard band literature can be played.

8

Group Attitudes

Awareness of each individual's
responsbility to the group:
  a. Attendance   Progress through teamwork.
  b. Conduct
  c. Preparation of music

This same type of listing may be applied to a junior high program when beginning and intermediate classes are offered at that level. The following is a listing of expected outcomes as related to ten selected aspects of instrumental music training:

1. Breath Control

Year one: Understanding of correct breathing procedure.
Year two: Be able to start a tone at fortissimo and decrescendo to pianissimo.
Year three: Be able to start a tone at fortissimo, decrescendo to pianissimo and crescendo to fortissimo.
Year four: Be able to start a tone at fortissimo, decrescendo to pianissimo and crescendo to fortissimo throughout the range of the instrument.

2. Chromatic Scale

Year one: Play chromatic scale in quarter notes at MM 120.
Year two: Play chromatic scale in eighth notes and triplets at MM 120.
Year three: Play chromatic scales starting at varying levels in sixteenth notes at MM 120.
Year four: Play chromatic scales in all rhythms throughout the range of the instrument.

3. Scales

Year one: Play from memory one octave scales in keys of C, G, F, Bb, Eb, Ab major, and relative minors in natural form.
Year two: Two octaves from memory in keys of C, F, Bb, Eb, Ab, G, D, A and E major, and relative minors in natural form.
Year three: Two octaves from memory in keys of C, F, Bb, Eb, Ab, Db, Gb, G, D, A, E and B major, and relative minors in natural and harmonic forms.
Year four: Two octaves from memory in keys of C, F, Bb, Eb, Ab, Db, Gb, Cb, G, D, A, E, B, F♯ and C♯ major, and relative minors in three forms for all except F♯ and C♯.

4. Articulation

Year one: Correct attacks and releases. Be able to play natural attack, slur, staccato and legato.
Year two: Correct attacks and releases. Be able to play accent, slur 2—staccato 2, staccato 2—slur 2, slur 3—staccato 1, staccato 1—slur 3.
Year three: Be able to play natural attack, slur, staccato, legato, accent, forte-piano, slur 2—tongue 2, tongue 2—slur 2, slur 3—tongue 1, tongue 1—slur 3.
Year four: Additional variety of combined articulations in varying rhythms and tempi.

9

5. Rhythm

Year one: Recognize and play note values in "eight" and "quarter" time. Be able to write whole, half, quarter, eighth and sixteenth notes and rests.

Year two: Recognize and play varied rhythm patterns in all time signatures and be able to write rhythm interpretation in beats and subdivisions.

Year three: Understand rhythmic concepts and their basis in time signatures and note values. Be able to write dictated rhythms in proper notation.

Year four: Be able to play and write all different rhythms.

6. Posture and Embouchure

Year one: Good sitting position when playing the instrument. Demonstrate formation of a good embouchure.

Year two: Correct posture. Demonstrate importance of correct embouchure as applied to complete range of instrument.

Year three: Continue above with correct embouchure as applied to the complete range of the instrument.

Year four: Continue the above.

7. Scale Patterns

Year one: Work on whole and half steps. Review key signatures.

Year two: Be able to write key signatures for C, F, B♭, E♭, A♭, D♭, G and D.

Year three: Write key signatures for all major keys and scales of all major keys on the staff.

Year four: Be able to write all major and relative minor scales in natural, harmonic and melodic forms.

8. Sight-Singing and Ear Training

Year one: Be able to tell major from minor and recognize wrong intervals in major scale patterns.

Year two: Be able to recognize and identify a major third, perfect fifth and perfect octave.

Year three: Be able to hear a perfect fourth, major second and major sixth. Be able to write a simple melodic dictation.

Year four: Be able to hear all intervals of a major scale and recognize any alterations. Increase skill in melodic dictation.

9. Transposition

Year one: Understand basic principle of transposition of own instrument and be aware of differences in other instruments of the band.

Year two: Be able to transcribe folksongs from concert key to key of own instrument and understand transposition of all instruments of the band.

Year three: Be able to transcribe a duet or trio for mixed instruments using correct transposition for another instrument.

Year four: Transcribe for quartet or quintet giving transposition for other instruments.

10. Conducting

Year one: Learn basic beat patterns of $\frac{4}{4}$, $\frac{2}{4}$ and $\frac{3}{4}$.

Year two: Use good posture; hold baton properly and demonstrate preparatory beat; beat patterns of $\frac{4}{4}$, $\frac{2}{4}$, $\frac{3}{4}$ and cut off.

Year three: Learn to use and make a fermata, ritard, accelerando, crescendo and diminuendo.

Year four: Use of student conductors—ability to conduct an instrumental group.

A good instrumental music program provides for the development of sequential learning and skill. A further formula that is used in achieving the goals of the strong music program is the following:

Wind Instruments

Level One

Suggested minimum attainment for beginning students before advancement to an intermediate group:

1. Three major scales (one octave).
2. Chromatics through middle range of instrument.
3. Good practice procedures.
4. Understanding of rhythmic study in connection with literature used.
5. Understanding of embouchure, breath control and tone concept.
6. Use of articulated attacks and releases, legato and staccato.
7. Beginning of simple lip slurs for brasses.
8. Understanding of musical terms in connection with literature used.

Level Two

Suggested minimum attainment for intermediate students for advancement to a regularly constituted intermediate performance group:

1. Two additional major scales (one octave) plus tonic arpeggios in all five scales thus far used.
2. Chromatic scale (one octave).
3. Understanding of rhythms beyond basic units of meter in literature used.
4. Development of concepts of tone production with emphasis on breath support and embouchure.
5. Introduction of vibrato where applicable.
6. Continued articulation development, including introduction to multiple articulation where applicable.
7. Continuation of lip slurs for brasses.
8. Understanding of concert pitch as related to own instrument.
9. Introductory experience with small ensemble and solo literature.

Level Three

Suggested minimum attainment for students before promotion to the advanced performance group:

1. Two additional major scales in extended range (where possible).
2. Tonic arpeggios and exercises of the seven major scales in varied patterns of articulation.
3. Increase range of chromatic scale.
4. Familiarity with and understanding of the following units of beat, note values and rests in simple and compound meter:

11

5. Continued study of tone quality, embouchure, vibrato and breath control with relation to the recognition of intonation problems and adequate tuning.
6. Introduction to trills and grace notes, as well as alternate fingerings, as required in the literature studied.
7. Continuing lip flexibility studies for brasses through extended lip slurs.
8. Recognition and demonstration of simple conducting patterns as encountered in the music studied.
9. Introduction to simple structure in music, including elementary harmonic principles and simple form, as represented in the music studied.
10. Sight reading of simple materials.

Level Four

Suggested minimum attainment for graduation from the instrumental programs:
1. Two additional major scales memorized, with all to be performed at quick tempo.
2. Tonic and dominant arpeggios in same major keys.
3. Extension of range with chromatic scale through complete range at quick tempo.
4. Understanding of complex rhythmic patterns in simple and compound meters as required in the study of band literature.
5. Continued improvement in tone quality, embouchure, vibrato and breath support.
6. Ability to tune instrument precisely, without assistance.
7. Continued study of trills, grace notes, and alternate fingerings as required in the literature.
8. Greater facility with lip slurs for brasses.
9. Introduction to minor scales and arpeggios.
10. Beginning of simple interval studies.
11. Continued study of musical terminology in literature.
12. Extensive solo and ensemble experience from selected lists.
13. Advanced study of structure in music.
14. Addition of more advanced sight-reading material.

Level Five

Suggested sequence for continuing development:
1. Two additional major scales in varied articulation, bringing the total to eleven.
2. Study of tonic and dominant arpeggios in all keys.
3. Memorization of the chromatic scale throughout the practical range of the instrument.
4. Increased emphasis on the study of alternate fingerings and slide positions.
5. Continued study of rhythms and rhythm concepts in simple and compound meter.
6. Continued study of embouchure, breath control, vibrato and tone quality.
7. Continued concentration on more accurate intonation, with attention to intonation peculiarities of each instrument.
8. Advanced lip slurs and flexibility studies in range.
9. Practical application of transposition.
10. Studies in double and triple tonguing.
11. Interval studies in varied patterns of rhythm and articulation.
12. Thorough study of enharmonic tones and transposition.
13. Study of minor scales and arpeggios.

14. Extensive study of solo and ensemble materials (repertoire which is more advanced technically and musically).
15. Advanced study of structure in music, including harmonic principles and form as represented in literature.
16. Advanced sight-reading materials.

Level Six

Suggested level of attainment for superior students:
1. Memorization of minor scales in all three forms.
2. Advanced study of arpeggios in all keys, including major, minor, diminished and augmented arpeggios.
3. Continued study and refinement of embouchure, breath control and tone quality, including vibrato.
4. Development of ability in transposition characteristic to the student's instrument.
5. Complete study of lip flexibilities and alternate fingerings and positions.
6. Varied articulation studies in all intervals, including the ability to recognize intervals by sight and sound, as well as to reproduce intervals vocally and with the instrument.
7. Advanced studies in double and triple tonguing to attain speed and accuracy, where applicable.
8. Thorough knowledge of musical terminology.
9. Study of musical structure in its many forms in literature of all periods.
10. Regular study of solo and ensemble literature.
11. Ability to conduct ensemble rehearsals through knowledge and understanding of conducting patterns and music scores.

Percussion Instruments

Level One — Snare Drum

1. Hand and stick positions (concert: conventional, and "double grip" — where the left stick is held like the right; marching).
2. Proper height and angle of drum; care of drum (head tension, snare adjustment, etc.).
3. Stick bouncing (double strokes) at various but unchanging speeds.
4. Single- and double-stroke rolls.
5. Flam, accented triplets, and flam accent.
6. Care of the instrument.
7. Practice in reading and counting $\frac{2}{4}$, $\frac{3}{4}$, $\frac{4}{4}$, and $\frac{6}{8}$ time; ¢ time; whole note, half note, quarter note, eighth note reading, and application of rolls to fit notation.
8. Other understandings where applicable to Level One for wind instruments.

Level Two — Snare Drum, Bass Drum, Traps

1. Continue work on single-stroke and double-stroke rolls, flam, and flam accent; introduce long roll — open and closed; latin percussion instruments and rhythms; introduce drag and four stroke ruff.
2. Bass drum: Tuning; where to strike drum; mallets.
3. Simple melodies on mallet instruments, and chromatic and three major scales.

4. Triangle, tambourine, castanets, and gong technics.
5. Other understandings related to Level Two for wind instruments.

Level Three — Cymbals, Timpani, Latin Percussion

1. Three additional major and three minor scales on mallet instruments, plus facility practice in mallet control; arpeggios in all keys studied.
2. Cymbals: How to hold; where and how to strike; suspended cymbal technics.
3. Timpani: Stick position, tone production, elementary tuning; theory of music, including major and minor triads and perfect fourths (both pitch recognition and the ability to sing the intervals).

Level Four

1. Mastery of all essential snare drum rudiments: single- and double-stroke rolls, flam, drag, four-stroke ruff, five-, seven- and nine-stroke rolls, flam accent, flamacue.
2. Additional scales and arpeggios on mallet instruments, and sight reading of melodies.
3. Chimes.
4. Continuation of theory for use in timpani tuning; ability to sing major and minor thirds, fifths, and major and minor sixths.
5. Timpani tuning of fourths and fifths during short measures of rest within a composition.
6. Introduction of stage band trap set concepts.
7. Other understandings related to Level Four for wind instruments.

Level Five

1. All scales and arpeggios for mallet instruments; sight reading of more advanced material and study of mallet techniques.
2. Sight reading of very advanced snare drum literature and exercises.
3. Advanced study of timpani, including use of three and four drums; pitch recognition and ability to sing major and minor thirds, fifths, major and minor sixths, and tune these intervals.
4. Experience with all members of the percussion family as required in the literature played.
5. Other understandings related to Level Five for wind instruments.

Level Six

1. All rudiments for snare drum.
2. Mastery of all scales and arpeggios on mallet instruments; sight reading of difficult mallet instrument material; work with four mallets.
3. Advanced timpani techniques, including rapid tuning changes.
4. Advanced performance with stage band set.
5. Increased proficiency with all percussion instruments.
6. Other understandings related to Level Six for wind instruments.

The following listing is related to fundamentals of instrumental technic (wind and/or percussion) in a sequential, ungraded pattern:

1. Introduction to the instrument; care and maintenance.

14

2. Developing correct playing position.
3. Forming the embouchure.
4. Tone production; articulated attack.
5. Developing concepts of tone quality and intonation.
6. Studying technic from an approved band method.
7. Developing proper practice habits.
8. Variation of articulation with addition of marcato and legato tonguing.
9. Introduction to musical phrasing.
10. Beginning use of alternate fingerings and positions.
11. Addition of staccato to articulation.
12. Addition of varied articulations in patterns.
13. Extended development of range.

Next is a listing related directly to music fundamentals in a sequential, ungraded pattern:

1. Introduction of staff and note names.
2. Quarter, half, whole notes and their rests.
3. Dotted half notes.
4. Basic time signatures.
5. Time and note value counting.
6. Musical terms.
7. Rhythm counting.
8. Introduction of harmony.
9. Eighth notes and rests.
10. After-beats.
11. Dynamics.
12. Tempo.
13. Dotted quarter and eighth note groups.
14. Chromatics.
15. Key signatures.
16. Major scales.
17. Minor scales.
18. Flats and sharps — in order of use.
19. Style.
20. Basic conducting patterns.

The follwing music fundamentals should be accomplished by the end of the second year:

1. Rhythm counting, with a knowledge of rhythm patterns containing sixteenth notes, dotted eighth notes, triplets and syncopation.
2. Knowledge of all common musical terms.
3. Knowledge of basic time signatures: $\frac{2}{4}$, C , $\frac{4}{4}$, $\frac{3}{4}$, $\frac{6}{8}$, $\frac{3}{8}$, and $\mathnot{C}$.
4. Knowledge of the construction and aural relationships of the I, IV, V and V_7 chords.
5. Ability to recognize intervals of the major scale.
6. Knowledge of the different dynamic levels: *pp*, *p*, *mp*, *mf*, *f*, *ff*.
7. Knowledge of major (and relative minors) scales and arpeggios in the keys of B♭ , E♭ , F,

15

A♭, C, D♭, and G.

8. Knowledge of the various tempo markings and changes of tempo.

Teaching the fundamentals of technique begins with every student from the first instant he comes in contact with the instrument, and continues throughout his tenure in instrumental music. There can be no isolation of one principal of technique from all others, and there can be no channeling of thought from all other considerations to one. Every teaching minute is involved with all fundamentals and, no matter how hard we try, we cannot introduce techniques one at a time with 100 percent concentration of effort. We must emphasize an area of importance but cannot ignore what is being done to, or is happening to, other techniques. Those fundamentals which are involved at all times and which will receive emphasis at various stages in the development of a student are as follows:

1. Position.
2. Embouchure.
3. Articulation.
4. Breath control.
5. Tone quality.
6. Technique.
7. Intonation.
8. Phrasing.
9. Style.
10. Theory.

Perhaps, if we could divorce one fundamental from all others and teach one at a time, this might be a preferred sequential listing. However, one area might become a problem of immediate concern and require concentration of effort and cause all other areas to be ignored. Each director must reach a decision as to the teaching sequence he prefers and establish his curriculum and choose his materials to fit that decision. It would be an over-simplification to say that the first five should receive major effort during the first year with the next five to be added the second year. However, a sequence of emphasis following that pattern through the first two years should properly prepare students for work in junior high school. At the junior high, and, eventually, the senior high level, training of students for effective participation in the concert band is a continuing process in all areas of technique, with each refinement contributing to the ultimate in <u>musical</u> <u>performance.</u>

In addition to the music fundamentals which should be mastered by the student by the end of the second year as listed above, the following are appropriate criteria for accomplishment by members of a typical concert band of symphonic proportions:

A. Music Fundamentals

1. Knowledge of those elements of notation that are used in the repertoire of the group.
2. Knowledge of the meanings of all musical terms used.
3. Ability to write and recognize signatures for the following keys: C, F, B♭, E♭, A♭, D♭, G♭, G, D, A, E and B.
4. Ability to write and recognize relative melodic-minor scales in the above-mentioned keys.
5. Sight singing and ear training ability; recognize and sing these intervals: unisons, major and minor seconds, major and minor thirds, perfect fourths, perfect fifths, major and minor sixths, major and minor sevenths, octaves.

6. Ability to sing major and melodic minor scales, and sing a solo or in an ensemble.

7. Ability to recognize and conduct basic conductor's patterns for $\frac{2}{4}$, $\frac{3}{4}$, $\frac{4}{4}$ and $\frac{6}{8}$; conduct fermata, and indicate preparatory or cue beat.

B. Fundamentals of technique

1. The emphasis is upon continuing technical development, aimed at producing a musically sensitive and expressive performance. Special exercises and studies should:

  a. Stress good posture and correct playing position.

  b. Develop correct embouchure.

  c. Maintain good habits of proper breathing and breath control.

  d. Stress production of characteristic tone quality for each instrument, with control at all dynamic levels from *pp* to *ff* throughout practical range of the instrument.

2. Students should be able to:

  a. Play, from memory, two-octave scales and arpeggios in all keys that are used in their repertoire.

  b. Play, from memory, the chromatic scale — ascending and descending — throughout practical range of the instrument.

  c. Demonstrate and use various kinds of articulation: marcato, legato, staccato, double and triple tonguing.

  d. Read at sight, in acceptable musical fashion, easy to moderately difficult material.

  e. Transpose simple material for their own instrument.

C. Instructional techniques (for conductor)

1. Rehearsals.

  a. All rehearsals need preliminary planning and should adhere to sound teaching principles. Do not put the most difficult material at the end of the rehearsal when students are tired. Conclude with the most enjoyable material.

  b. Employ cooperative yet well-disciplined procedures.

   1. The concertmaster may conduct the tuning, and principal players in the various sections may mark the music as determined by the director.

   2. The director should keep extraneous conversation at a minimum — his own as well as the students'. Playing should be done at the direction of the conductor and at no other time during the rehearsal.

  c. Encourage students in such a manner that self-respect and confidence will be built.

  d. The score must be well prepared. Carefully note and/or mark all cues, dynamics and tempo changes.

Evaluation of Rehearsals:

At the conclusion of the rehearsal period, there must be an evaluation of its results. This evaluation may take the following general form:

a. Summary and self-evaluation of your own work.

 1. Did you accomplish what you set out to do?

 2. How effectively did you get your points across to the students?

 3. Which procedures used were effective?

 4. Which procedures need improvement?

      b. Summary and evaluation of students' work.
1. Were they interested?
2. Did they apply themselves effectively?
3. Were there any discipline problems?
4. What particular things did they do best or showed the greatest improvement?
5. What are some of the weaknesses that need to be stressed at the next rehearsal?

      c. Preparation for the next rehearsal.
1. What are the next logical steps?
2. What technical improvements must be planned for?
3. What musical ideas need stressing?

2. Intonation.

      a. This problem requires constant work. Careful listening calls for continuous attention and should become a habit.

      b. Develop an awareness of the relationship of whole and half steps according to their organization in scales, of the pure and consonant harmonic sounds of the various intervals, triads, and other chords, and of the necessity of raising or lowering the pitches of scale tones to conform to desirable and differing characteristics of melody and harmony.

      c. Make intonation the prime factor in choosing and purchasing an instrument. Among the woodwinds, improve it as much as possible by adjusting pad clearances, sizes of tone holes, etc., and in valve brasses, by the correction and/or adjustment of lengths of valve slides. Then become aware of intonation tendencies of the instrument that still must be overcome while playing, either by alternate fingerings, movable slides, or by "lipping."

3. Tone Quality.

      a. Quality must remain consistent throughout all registers of the instrument.

      b. Correct posture encourages correct breath support.

      c. Starting with the middle register of the instrument, work up and down, emphasizing the open, relaxed throat.

      d. Work for individual tonal development as well as for the total sound of the section.

      e. Work for dynamic change without changing or distorting the tone quality.

4. Balance.

      a. Achieve balance among the individual chairs of the band.

      b. Do not permit chairs or sections to overpower in relation to the total sound.

      c. Deficiencies in group balance are due to: multiplicity of types of sound, lack of chordal balance, unclean rhythms, and poor development of phrases.

5. Dynamics.

      a. All dynamics are relative.

      b. The melodic material must dominate the dynamic level.

      c. In rehearsing, it may pay to exaggerate all dynamics, although, in actual performance, good musical taste is dictated by the musical requirements.

      d. Ascending passages usually crescendo; similarly, descending passages usually decrescendo.

      e. Do not play all notes with an attack followed by a diminuendo.

6. Analysis of Interpretation.
   The following questions may be of help in self-analysis, and a guide to solutions:
   a. Have I adopted the dynamic level best suited to the music? Do these levels portray the intent of the composer, and do they fit into the period, style, and form of the composition?
   b. Am I using a well-developed crescendo and diminuendo? Do the climaxes give a sense of perspective to the selection? (Many performers use a series of similar climaxes that add nothing to the flow of the composition. Exaggerated use of climaxes robs a selection of its rhythm and form. An anemic climax robs a selection of the richness and brilliance it deserves.)
   c. Is the ensemble sonority balanced with care? (There are groups in which individual instruments or sections of instruments predominate, thereby creating a false sense of perspective. It is the duty of the conductor to disclose all melodic contour, both primary and secondary, to the listener. No single element of vertical structure may be obscured, yet the vertical structure must not hinder the phrase flow.)
   d. Are attacks and releases precise and in style? (The beat preparation must describe the precise moment of attack, the tempo, the dynamics, and the style of attack. Ragged releases usually are the result of a vague termination of the beat, relaxing of the embouchure, slowing of articulation at the phrase end, or not watching the beat. Notes must have spacing proper to the intent of the music. This spacing will vary from staccatissimo to legato.)
   e. Is the phrase well defined? (Inflections in music are as important as inflections in speech. Phrase content is usually indicated by use of the cadence, but care should be taken that the flow of the composition does not stop with each cadence. A sequence of phrases will use varying dynamic levels, depending upon the rise and fall of the sequence.)

7. Interpretation.
   a. Establish a spatial concept of interpretation, observing major climaxes and secondary climaxes.
   b. Anticipate climaxes, cadences and tonal effects. They should be well-defined in performance.
   c. Vary repetitions, and always maintain a forward movement, regardless of speed.
   d. Do not merely sustain a melodic long tone; keep it active by doing something with it dynamically — increase or decrease intensity.

8. Listening.
   a. An important part of the music program at any level is the cultivation of the ability to listen for pleasure as well as to develop understanding. Listening activities must be planned, and students must be encouraged to listen to fine music both in and outside of class. All listening experiences of students tend to broaden musical choices.
   b. Students should be aware that there are many ways of listening. One can listen to music for its intrinsic value, for mood, for tone color and quality, or for sheer beauty. Planned listening activities will assist pupils in selecting listening experiences best suited to their musical responsiveness at any given time.
   c. Listening activities should be a part of each element of music taught. A good listening

19

program seeks to acquaint pupils with varied repertoire, to build standards of discrimination, and to emphasize the importance of listening carefully, whether for study or enjoyment.

D. Evaluation of Instruction

The following questions are guides to improving the director's own instructional activities:

1. Does instruction in music contribute to the school's objectives?
2. Is instruction directed toward clearly formulated, comprehensive objectives in music?
3. Is instruction constantly concerned with the improvement of the quality of the musical experiences involved?
4. Is there evidence of careful planning and preparing for instructional activities?
5. Is instruction related to the musical interests and needs of students?
6. Are differences in emotional development recognized in determining the type and degree of participation by individual students?
7. Is appropriate drill used?
8. Are opportunities provided for students to plan, conduct and evaluate music activities?
9. Is instruction in music coordinated with courses in other subject fields?
10. Are efforts made to create and maintain attractive music rooms?

E. Evaluation of the Instrumental Music Program

A restatement of the objective of our instrumental music program which says that "The student will acquire knowledge, skills, and attitudes which will help to make him a more desirable member of society" requires us to ask the question "Is this being achieved in the existing program?" Progress in instrumental music is observed in four general ways:

1. Skill Development.
   a. Have music reading and sight reading skills been improved?
   b. What improvement has there been in performance ability?
   c. What are strong points with respect to performance technique?
   d. What are areas that need improvement?
   e. What evidence is there that listening skills have been developed?
   f. To what extent can students recognize and be sensitive to nuances of dynamics, quality, and pitch?

2. Knowledge of Theory.
   a. Does the student recognize the elements of music found in the repertoire he performs?
   b. To what extent does he recognize the function of harmony and harmonic progressions, and the use of counterpoint?
   c. To what extent have ear-training skills been developed?
   d. Can the student recognize and sing at sight the material he plays on his instrument?

3. Knowledge of Music Literature.
   a. To what extent is the student aware of the elements of style of the various composers whose works he performs?
   b. To what extent does he understand the contributions that various composers have made to the development of musical ideas and forms throughout the ages of Western music, including the contemporary scene?

4. Attitude toward Music.
   a. Does the student seek out musical activities outside the school?
   b. Does he attend concerts?
   c. Does he collect records?
   d. Is he developing "taste"?
   e. Does he show particular preference for certain kinds of music and musical experiences?
   f. Do his musical activities influence his leisure time activities?

chapter 3

Social Implications of the Band Program

The role of the band in building good citizenship, self-confidence and poise cannot be overestimated. Many directors come to believe that these are by far the most important contributions the band can make in the lives of its members. Students gain a deep and lasting sense of satisfaction in accomplishment, therefore they enjoy the respect, acclaim and esteem of their fellow students, their parents, and the citizens of the community.

Regardless of the location of the school, whether it is in a metropolitan area or has rural surroundings, it is a rare community that does not hold its school band members in highest regard. Band members become acquainted with community leaders and civic organizations, and work with them in promoting local band activities. Not to be overlooked in the social structure of the band is the honor and prestige attached to being elected to a position of responsibility on a well-organized and respected student staff or band council. This is an honor of the highest order, and the band members know it. Regardless of the task of each member, the various staff duties provide a rewarding opportunity for the development of leadership qualities, maturity, and initiative, while assisting in the administration of the program.

By working together, as well as forming lasting friendships through common interests and objectives, the band affords an unusual means for its members to gain self-respect and a feeling of belonging. A great number of students seek the prestige, guidance, discipline and involvement found in this wholesome activity, and then feel strongly that these are the most compelling reasons for taking part. Often this accomplishes their mission of finding their role and place in the school environment. In many schools the band ranks as the most outstanding organization to which a student can belong. In others, especially the larger metropolitan schools, the band fills the need for a social "home base."

The consensus of the directors participating in this study can be summarized with the following observations:

1. Every student should be given an opportunity to participate in one of the groups of the band program regardless of level of proficiency.
2. The band should develop good citizenship and democracy by teaching students emotional stability, self-control and dependability.
3. The band should build poise and social ease by its members performing in recitals, concerts and contests.
4. In many instances the band becomes something of a family where everyone is accepted as an equal. Surveys of representative bands throughout all parts of the country have emphatically proven that there is complete acceptance of all students regardless of their scholastic, ethnic, racial, religious or socio-economic background.

5. Many youngsters enroll in the band program for no other reason than that their best friends play in the band. However, the reverse is also true. Research has shown that this has been identified as the prime reason for the same students dropping out.

6. In many schools there is a strong "in-group" feeling due to the fact that a sizeable majority of the more popular students and higher scholastic achievers are enrolled in the band.

7. Many band graduates come away with a real comprehension and love for music and make music a life-time part of their cultural interests. It becomes a worthy use of leisure time.

8. Band members contribute to the community arts by helping to raise the aesthetic values of the people through the music they perform.

9. Meeting and making new friends in honor bands on the local, district, state and national level; participating in all-American touring groups; hosting touring musical organizations; attending band picnics, parties, excursions, etc.; enrolling in summer music camps — these are some of the activities that contribute to the social growth and maturity of the students.

It is generally agreed that out-of-town trips by youngsters at this impressionable age (especially in the company of others sharing common interests — such as band membership) have a longer-lasting effect than trips taken at any other time in their lives.

chapter 4

The School Administration

The relationship between the school administration and the school band program is of vital importance. No program can succeed without the whole-hearted support of the board of education, the superintendent, and the principals. The administration which recognizes its responsibility for the comprehensive educational development of each child realizes the importance of fully supporting the music education program. It is, then, their obligation to be conversant, if not active, in the following areas:

1. Teaching Personnel
   a. Hire sufficient music department personnel.
   b. Provide adequate salaries in order to attract highly skilled teachers.
   c. Assign reasonable class loads.
   d. Provide for in-service training, workshops, etc.
   e. Work closely with music supervisors in the coordination of the program in all schools throughout the system.
   f. Give personal recognition for work well done.

2. Course of Study
   a. Seek close cooperation with the music staff in formulating a course of study for the entire band program.
   b. Print an Instrumental Music Teachers' Handbook.

   A survey of representative bands throughout the United States has shown that most such publications are drawn up by the music staff and submitted to the administration for approval. Due to the complex and specialized training necessary to undertake such an endeavor, it is obvious that this is the only logical way to establish procedures for accomplishing the aims and objectives of the music department. Some departments work out the written plan over a period of years and periodically submit an up-dated guide for administrative approval. The record shows that after the superintendent and the principal have checked over the changes, the Board of Education readily gives its approval.

3. Scheduling of Classes for Promotion of the Program
   a. Schedule band classes in such a way as to insure maximum student participation.
   b. Help in the coordination of class schedules among schools in the system when teachers must travel from school to school.
   c. On the elementary level, schedule a minimum of two class periods a week (at least 30 minutes each), with classes meeting daily on the junior and senior high level. (See Chapter V.

      d. Promote class enrollment by assisting the band director in establishing good relationships with students, teachers and parents.

      e. Aid in the continued scheduling of band classes for students promoted from elementary to junior high and from junior high to senior high.

4. Equipment
      a. Furnish sufficient funds for the purchase of new instruments and for replacing old ones which are beyond reasonable repair.

      b. Provide adequate funds for instrument and equipment repair. (See Authorization form in appendix.)

      c. Provide suitable instructional facilities.

      d. Provide an adequate budget for instructional supplies, new music, audio-visual equipment, uniforms, etc.

The enthusiastic administrator realizes the part the band plays in the life of the school and the community. He attends as many concerts and activities as possible. By his presence he indicates to the director, the students, the classroom teachers and the parents that he is interested in the program. He also seeks to prevent excessive and unreasonable demands on the performing groups. He assists in promoting youth concerts by professional groups, such as visiting concert bands, opera companies, and symphony orchestras, thereby enriching the cultural development of the students. An effective administrator recognizes the importance of competition festivals and encourages the participation of as many students as possible. He also recognizes the importance of band parent groups, and in cooperating with such groups, helps promote a wholesome relationship between the schools and the community.

The foregoing has concerned itself with the role of the administration in supporting the band program. It would naturally follow that if the band program is to succeed, the music staff likewise has a role in supporting the administration. It is imperative that the superintendent and principals be kept informed about what is being done in the band program—they must feel that they are very much a part of the picture. They should be consulted constantly for advice and recommendations in all matters that concern policy and administrative procedures. Failure to do so can only result in numerous difficulties, some of which can grow to such proportions as to permanently affect the entire program. It has been said many times over that regardless of the importance of the skill of the band director, the school principal is the key person in the success or failure of the band program.

In addition to a well-coordinated relationship with the administrative staff, the band director must also recognize his responsibilities in the total school educational program. This requires that he understand the proper balance of the band program in the overall curriculum and that he foster a spirit of cooperation with the classroom teachers.

chapter **5**

Organizing the School Band Program

RECRUITMENT. In elementary music the term recruiting simply implies encouraging students to participate in the band program. The successful band program begins by recruiting students of talent, ability and interest into the beginning class. There are no best ways of recruiting; there are only effective and ineffective ways. The unique characteristics of each community demand that recruiting procedures vary, and the band program must be geared to meet requirements of the locality. Each teacher should determine what recruiting practice is most effective in his situation. This decision should be based upon the school's philosophy, the teacher's personality, the community's economy, and the general attitude toward the band program. A good recruiting procedure

1. Offers all students the opportunity to participate.
2. Determines the aptitude of interested students.
3. Allows students freedom of their choice of instrument, with advice and guidance.
4. Encourages continued participation.
5. Informs parents of their role in the program.
6. Helps guide families in securing good, quality instruments.
7. Presents the director and the program favorably.
8. Incorporates personal contact with parents.
9. Receives publicity in the school and community at the time of introduction.
10. Yields results which are desirable.

Recruitment may be limited to the selection of only the most promising students in those communities where interest in a successful program is traditional; or it may require great concentration of motivational effort and time in order to inject a sufficient number of students into the beginning class to maintain the program. Motivational techniques used to arouse interest without regard to aptitude might include the following: instrument demonstrations; use of students to interest and instruct prospective students; films and/or filmstrips; flyers which describe the music program; student experimentation with instruments; parent-teacher interviews; and music store displays and demonstrations. One or all of these might be used in initial recruiting where the band has not held community interest. Recruiting in a community which has an established program would likely require only minimum effort and be limited to screening techniques, such as: orientation and experimentation with pre-band instruments; testing of aptitude and talent; interviews; classroom teacher and/or administrative recommendations; and use of the cumulative record data.

Testing materials used in this phase of the band program might include the following:

Kwalwasser-Dykema
  Carl Fischer, Inc.
  56 Cooper Square
  New York, New York 10003

Seashore
  Psychological Corporation
  304 East 45th Street
  New York, New York 10017

Follett Music Aptitude
  Follet
  1010 W. Washington Blvd.
  Chicago, Illinois 60607

Tilson-Gretsch
  Gretsch Manufacturing Co.
  1801 Gilbert Ave.
  Cincinnati, Ohio 45202

Conn
  C. G. Conn, Ltd.
  Oak Brook, Illinois 60521

Selmer
  Selmer, Inc.
  Box 310
  Elkhart, Indiana 46514

LeBlanc
  Le Blanc Corp.
  Kenosha, Wisconsin 53141

Holton
  Frank Holton & Co.
  Kenosha, Wisconsin 53141

Olds
  Chicago Musical Instrument Co.
  7373 N. Cicero Ave.
  Lincolnwood, Ill. 60646

Gaston
  O'dell's Instrument Service
  2515 Arkansas Street
  Lawrence, Kansas 66044

One comprehensive method of reaching all students in a school system requires use of a pre-band instrument such as tonette, recorder, flutophone, etc. The elementary instrumental teacher visits all the classrooms at a selected grade level (preferably grade four) and presents the training instrument to be used. The time spent in each classroom is from 15 to 20 minutes. The teacher displays the instrument, plays a melody for the children to identify, and selects one student from the class to demonstrate a brief orientation lesson. Then each student in the class is given a letter to take home which explains the purpose, scheduling and cost of the program. Most school systems furnish this pre-band instrument as part of the music program.

The teacher sets a date for the return of a consent form which is a part of the letter and a date for the first class session.

_____ Public Schools

Dear Parents:

We would like to call attention to the Instrumental Music Program which is a regular part of the curriculum of the _____Public Schools. No tuition fee is charged for this instruction.

Instruction in instrumental music begins with class work in the fourth grade on a pre-band instrument called the tonette. Instruction on all regular band instruments will be given in the fifth and sixth grades. Pupils enrolling in tonette or beginning instrument classes are expected to complete the course of instruction which continues throughout the school year.

Your son or daughter has become acquainted with the tonette in our class demonstrations. Now this letter comes to you so you may help make the decision regarding your child's participation in the first stage of our instrumental music program.

If your child enrolls now and purchases a tonette and the method book, he will participate in class_____times per week for_____minutes. Cost of the tonette and method book through our local music store will be approximately $_____.

We urge you to consider very carefully the enrollment of your child in the tonette class, for it may lead to educational possibilities that might otherwise remain undeveloped. May we remind you that these values are inherent in the type of activity we are offering your child:

Music builds character.
Music develops wholesome companionship.
Music develops personality.
Music promotes discipline.

If you wish to enroll your child in the tonette phase of our program, we request your cooperation in filling out the information below and returning it to school by_____ .

Name_____ Date_____

Home Address_____ Phone _____

School_____ Room No. or Teacher _____

Students participating in this first year training program accomplish various important objectives: proficiency in fingering the instrument; development of proper articulation and breath control; knowledge of a good musical vocabulary; knowledge of key signatures, time signatures, and basic rhythm concepts; and, the ability to perform at least twelve songs, with from four to six of them committed to memory.

With or without a pre-band program, continuing recruitment takes many forms, but should include display and demonstration of instruments. Perhaps the most effective method of orienting parents and students with band instruments is clinic-demonstration. The initial procedure is to contact administrators and classroom teachers in order to schedule a time to speak to each room at the selected grade level (preferably grade five) during the first week of the school year. At that time, posters of band instruments may be shown to the class for identification, and all students in the class are given a letter to parents, explaining the school's instrumental music program, scheduling of the clinic, and registration procedures.

_____Public Schools

Dear Parents:

      We would like to call your attention to the instrumental music program which is a regular part of the curriculum of the _____Public Schools. Instruction on all the band instruments is available to students in grades five and six. There is no tuition fee for these lessons. Students enrolled in the beginning classes will be expected to complete the course of instruction which will continue throughout the regular school year.

      This letter is sent to you because you play a great part in making the decision regarding your child's participation in the school band program. We hope this information will help you in making your decision.

      Training is offered on all band instruments, including clarinet, flute, oboe, bassoon, saxophone, French horn, cornet, trumpet, trombone, baritone, tuba, and percussion. Students must furnish their own instruments for beginning instruction. Instruments are available through music dealers on rental-purchase plans at reasonable rates. This affords an opportunity for a trial period on the instrument of the student's choice, and the amount for this service can later be applied toward the purchase of the instrument.

      To assist you in selecting an instrument for your child, a clinic is to be conducted for parents and students at_____ on _____ at 7:00 P.M. At this time, demonstrations will be given on many of the instruments. Instruments will be available for your child to see and try, and we will give advice where needed and answer any questions you may have.

      If you wish to enroll your child in a beginning instrumental class, we request your cooperation in filling out the information below and returning it to school by_____. Thank you.

Sincerely, _____

Name _____ Date _____

Home Address _____ Phone _____

School _____ Grade _____ Rm. No. or Teacher _____

      I am interested in learning to play the_____this year. My parents and I would like to have help in choosing an instrument and will attend the clinic on _____ for that purpose.

Signed _____
                      Name of Student

Signed _____
                      Name of Parent

The clinic proper consists of a brief discussion of each instrument family, a short demonstration on each instrument by a staff member or competent student, announcement of details necessary to complete the clinic, followed by individual sessions with each student and his parents. In individual sessions each student is permitted to indicate instrument preference and, after brief instruction, to attempt to produce sound on that instrument. At this time the teacher studies physical features which may make it inadvisable for a student to proceed on one particular instrument and recommends another when it is deemed necessary. Parents and students showing interest are given information concerning the availability of instruments, the cost of an instrument considered to be adequate for a beginning student, and the date by which time an instrument must be procured. As the clinic concludes, each student who intends to proceed with purchase of an instrument is registered for a beginning class.

As indicated at the beginning of this chapter, recruiting practices will, of necessity, be varied. Many things may preclude the possibility of offering instrumental training to all students at one grade level, including staff limitation or inadequate physical facilities. Because of socio-economic peculiarities in one situation or because of inherent education and intelligence levels in another, it may be highly undesirable to be all-inclusive in offering instrumental music training. It might possibly be necessary to be highly selective through intelligence and music aptitude tests in one community and mandatory to be all-inclusive in another. One system which is in use in the Missoula, Montana grade school program consists of five basic steps. (Grade five is the beginning level, and students are admitted to the program on the basis of their interest, music aptitude and scholastic ability.) The five steps are:

1. Students in the fifth grade are tested for musical aptitude during the month of September.
2. Students with above average musical aptitude and average or better grades in school are then invited to join pre-band classes for the purpose of learning fundamentals, getting acquainted with the band instruments, and finding out what instruments they are best suited to play. Pre-band classes are conducted in each school twice weekly for a period of from four to twelve weeks.
3. At the close of the pre-band period, parent meetings are held for the purpose of describing the beginning band program, explaining the rental and/or purchase of instruments, etc. Also, a report is sent to the parents of each pre-band student with a recommendation for their child. This report indicates whether or not the child should play an instrument, and, if so, what instrument he might be best suited to play.
4. Beginning classes are then organized in each school, meeting weekly during school time.
5. After six to eight weeks of instruction, students are selected for the beginning band. If selected at this time, rehearsals are in addition to their regular beginning class in school, with rehearsals held on Saturday or after school.

In a system that does not use a clinic-demonstration, a simple letter such as the following from the Springfield, Oregon Public Schools (which establishes a personal interview for interested parents and students) can be very successful in recruiting:

Springfield Public Schools
School District No. 19
Springfield, Oregon

Dear Parents:

Sixth year students may participate in band. The school lessons are free. The student must, however, furnish his own instrument, with the exception of the larger and more expensive ones. These instruments are available for a rental fee of $_____ for the school year, after the student has been given a careful tryout to determine his musical ability and his potential.

Please indicate your interest and the student's choice of instrument on this form and return it to the school. The band director will contact you later for a personal interview and help choose the instrument for your child.

Please do not rent or purchase any instrument until after your conference with the band director.

I would (would not) like to have my child participate in the school band.

Student's Name _____ Parent's Name _____

Address _____ Telephone No. _____

I have (have not) had piano lessons. If affirmative, how long? _____

I am interested in playing (indicate 1st, 2nd and 3rd choice)

( ) Flute   ( ) Clarinet   ( ) Saxophone

( ) French horn   ( ) Cornet or Trumpet   ( ) Baritone

( ) Trombone   ( ) Tuba   ( ) Percussion

Previous musical instrument lessons student has had: _____

Additional Comments: _____

Whatever the recruitment procedure selected by the director, it must be consistent with the needs of the school and its basic philosophy. The needs of the school and of the band program may sometimes dictate that the director use his powers of persuasion to achieve the desired balance of instrumentation in beginning classes. Agreement is almost unanimous that a child with strong desire to begin study on one particular instrument should not be forced to change. But a student who shows promise can many times be convinced to begin study on one of the more difficult instruments (difficult from the standpoint of filling the chair as much as difficult from the standpoint of performance), and others most certainly can be directed toward choices which will achieve a working balance in instrumentation. The following instrument quota guide in use at Temple High School in Temple, Texas is useful in establishing percentages or ratios for beginning instrument classes in other systems:

BEGINNING BAND INSTRUMENTATION QUOTA GUIDE
Temple Independent School District

Instrument	Class of 35	Class of 28	Class of 25	Class of 20
Flute	5	4	4	3
Clarinet	8	7	7	5
Saxophone	3	3	2	2
Cornet	5	4	4	3
Trombone	3+	3+	3	2
Baritone	2+	1+	1	1
French horn	3+	2+	1	1
Bass*	3	2	1	1
Percussion*	3	2	2	2

+ In larger classes, director may increase quota of lower brass.

* Quota for school-furnished instruments is low due to short supply. Band director may increase quota for such instruments, particularly baritone, French horn or bass, if student furnishes own horn.

Another suggested quota guide is one recommended by J. Raymond Brandon, Supervisor of Music in the North Little Rock Public Schools, Arkansas:

RECOMMENDED INSTRUMENTATION FOR A BEGINNING CLASS OF 36

Flute	5
Oboe	1
Bassoon	1
Clarinet	12
Saxophone	2
Cornet-Trumpet	5
French horn	2
Trombone	3
Baritone-Euphonium	1
Tuba	2
Percussion	2
	36

NOTE: Necessary transfers are a factor in the formulation of this guide.

SCHEDULING. Innovations in education are making inroads into the traditional classroom organization and scheduling, with the result that a wide variety of schedules has been created. Concepts of team teaching, differentiated staffing, periods of different lengths, and flexible class groupings (as in modular scheduling) are a few factors influencing programming and scheduling. As with all change, controversy has developed over benefits to the band program in new scheduling situations. For example, some directors in schools which have adopted modular scheduling feel that the change has been very beneficial to their programs, while others find it difficult to find any advantage in the system. The following modular schedule is one that has been very beneficial:

WESTSIDE HIGH SCHOOL MODULAR SCHEDULE
Darwyn Snyder – Director
Omaha, Neb.

		A	B	C	D	E
7:00	1	W–Tubas & Baritones–9	Sax Quartet–4	Sectional–6–10 R–Band–64 →	Woodwind Quintet–5 W–Saxes–7 →	W–Alto & Bass Clar.–6
8:30	2					
	3	R–Percussion–8 →	W–Percussion–7 →			W–Cornets–7 →
	4					
9:30	5		W–Trombones–6 →		R–Cornet/Horns–8 →	
	6	R–Baritones & Tubas–6	R–Flutes–9 →	W–Flutes–7 →		W–Horns–7
10:30	7					
	8					
	9					R–Clarinets–8
11:30	10	R–Flutes & Saxes–10	W–Clarinets & Flutes–10 →	Weekly Meeting Instrum. Instruc. →	W–Cornets & Horns–7 R–Trombones–7 →	
	11					
	12					
12:30	13	W–Double Reeds–4 →				
	14					
	15		R–Band–64 →	R–Cornets–8 →	R–Band–64 →	
1:30	16					
	17					
2:30	18	W–Band–75 →	S.H. Cafe–150	W–Band–75 →		W–Band–75 →
	19					
	20					
3:10	21		Con. Jazz Band–17	Clarinet Choir–10	Brass Choir–13	Pep Band–24

Total students = 635 per week
Total hours = 27 per week

Two elements of scheduling are obviously involved in a successful program, regardless of the basic program in vogue at one given time — length of period and frequency of meeting. There is no argument with the fact that in a successful program both of these elements are most important at the elementary level. Great variety can be found in the class period allotted to beginning instruction and the number of meetings per week. Responses from selected schools in this survey furnished information for the following two graphs—No. 1, the number of minutes per week scheduled for beginning instruction in instrumental music, and No. 2, the number of class meetings per week:

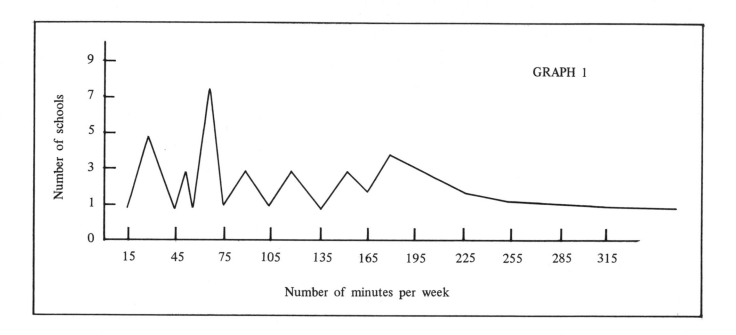

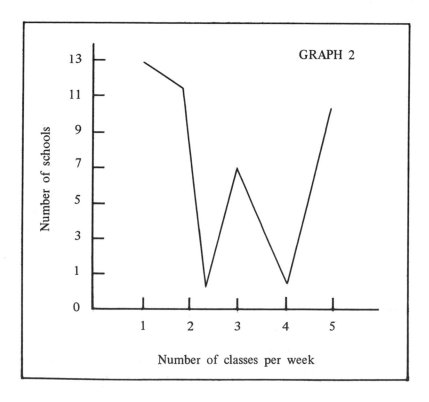

The foundation beginners receive is in direct correlation to the adequacy of the schedule. Ideal scheduling for maximum learning at the elementary level is probably not attainable with the demands of the modern curriculum. However, choices that can make instruction more effective for beginning classes may be possible. Interpretation of the above two graphs would indicate that the average amount of time allotted for instruction in the responding school systems is approximately one hour per week, with the number of classes per week averaging 2.8. From the standpoint of effective teaching, when a choice must be made between a long period at infrequent intervals or the same amount of time divided into more frequent intervals, frequency must be the choice. For example, if the above schools are limited to one hour per week, two periods of 30 minutes each would be more valuable than one period of an hour. If further choice of frequency were permitted, three periods of 20 minutes each would gain more advantage. This would seem to be characteristic of the schools included in the two graphs.

In order to have any sort of successful schedule for instrumental music, it is necessary to have complete cooperation between the school administrator, the classroom teacher and the music teacher. Good scheduling is important in promoting both student and parent interest in the school music program. Fewer dropouts will occur if the music schedule is in accord with other subjects. When instrumental music is accepted into the curriculum, it is necessary to provide sufficient time for instruction. The classroom teacher and the administrator must realize that teachers of instrumental music have an unparalleled problem in instructing students from several grade levels during a given period; therefore, careful consideration of scheduling must be shared by all.

Traditional scheduling in the junior high school precludes choice in the matter of length of period and, quite probably, in frequency. Choice may exist when hours outside of the regularly scheduled day are used for music classes. The daily meeting of large groups, including band, has won almost universal acceptance in schools with successful programs. The length of each period is varied, but only to a minor degree, with 55 minutes per day fairly standard. Differences in scheduling at this level exist in the amount of time available for ensemble or sectional rehearsals in addition to the daily class period. Additional time in small group or individual instruction in junior and senior high school is of value in proportion to the actual time involved. The talented and involved student finds great benefit in instruction outside of the large group situation. Adequate staff at the junior high level permits class offerings for students of various levels of ability and interest. Instruction certainly becomes more meaningful when advanced, intermediate and beginning ability grouping is possible. A complete program makes division into these three groups possible and allows for ensemble training in addition.

Discussion of scheduling in junior high, with daily class periods and the length of the period fairly standard, applies also to senior high scheduling in the traditional situation. Many schools with established programs offer three levels of band in senior high, with variety existing only in the names assigned to these groups. Symphonic Band, Concert Band and Prep Band might be the choice of titles, but the purpose of including three groups in the schedule and the value of ability grouping in this manner is obvious.

Many changes and choices are possible in the flexible schedule situation. Advocates point out that the best students in their bands actually gain in the amount of time allotted to music in their schedules, even though the large group may not meet as such as many times in a one-week period. More freedom of choice is possible in organizing ensembles, sectional rehearsals, individual lessons and individual practice time for the musically involved student. Schools which have adequate staff for private instruction for every band member are rare, but modular scheduling makes this rarity possible. The following are schedules typical of elementary, junior high and senior high schools with complete programs:

ELEMENTARY — Boise, Idaho

Time	School	Mon.	Tues.	Wed.	Thurs.	Fri.
9:00 to 9:30	Mt. View 6th	24		24		24
9:30 to 10:00	Mt. View 5th	24		24		24
9:00 to 9:30	Koelsch 6th		24		24	
9:30 to 10:00	Koelsch 5th		26		26	
10:40 to 11:45	Fairmont Brass	22	22	22	22	22
12:20 to 1:15	Fairmont 7th	28	28	28	28	28
1:20 to 2:10	Fairmont 7th	28	28	28	28	28
2:15 to 3:05	Fairmont Concert Band	49	49	49	49	49

JUNIOR HIGH — Russellville, Arkansas

Time	Class	Mon.	Tues.	Wed.	Thurs.	Fri.
8:00 to 8:30	Beginning Band	57	57	57	57	57
8:30 to 9:30	Preparation					
9:30 to 10:30	Cadet Band	87	87	87	87	87
10:30 to 11:00	Activity period and following period					
11:00 to 12:00	Varsity Band	119	119	119	119	119
12:30 to 1:30	Training Band	42	42	42	42	42
1:30 to 2:30	Beginning Band	17	17	17	17	17
2:30 to 3:30	Conference					

SENIOR HIGH — Ouachita Parish High, Monroe, Louisiana

Time of Period	Class	Mon.	Tues.	Wed.	Thurs.	Fri.	Sat.
7:45 to 8:40	Music Theory	21	21	21	21	21	
8:45 to 9:45	Planning	—	—	—	—	—	
9:45 to 10:45	Symphonic Band	106	106	106	106	106	
10:45 to 12:25	Ensembles	35	35	35	35	35	
12:30 to 1:25	Orchestra	35	35	35	35	35	
1:30 to 2:25	Concert Band	50	50	50	50	50	

ENSEMBLES, twice weekly: Brass, Clarinet Choir & Woodwind Quintet

MIXED SENIOR HIGH AND ELEMENTARY
Don Corbett — Hutchinson, Kansas

Period	School	Monday	Tuesday	Wednesday	Thursday	Friday
8:20–9:20	Hutchinson High School Band	Hutchinson High School Band	Hutchinson High School Band	Hutchinson High School Band	Hutchinson High School Band	Hutchinson High School Band
10:50–11:20	Elementary Schools·	Roosevelt Elem.	Morgan Elem.	Roosevelt Elem.	Morgan Elem.	Planning
11:20–11:50	Elementary Schools	Roosevelt Elem.	Morgan Elem.	Roosevelt Elem.	Morgan Elem.	Planning
12:45–1:15	Elementary Schools	Roosevelt Elem.	Morgan Elem.	Roosevelt Elem.	Morgan Elem.	Planning
1:30–2:00	Elementary Schools	Allen	Wiley	Allen	Wiley	Planning
2:05–2:35	Elementary Schools	Allen	Wiley	Allen	Wiley	Planning
2:40–3:10	Elementary Schools	Allen	Wiley	Allen	Wiley	Planning
3:25	Hutchinson High School	Hutchinson High School	Hutchinson High School	Hutchinson High School	Hutchinson High School	Hutchinson High School

MIXED JUNIOR HIGH AND GRADE SCHOOL
Charles Higdon — Clovis, New Mexico

Period	School	Monday	Tuesday	Wednesday	Thursday	Friday
8:00–9:10	Clovis High School	Band Class	Band Class	Band Class	Band Class	Band Class
9:31–10:22	Marshall Jr. High	Varsity Band Class	Varsity Band Class	Varsity Band Class	Varsity Band Class	Varsity Band Class
10:26–11:16	Marshall Jr. High	Cadet Band Class	Cadet Band Class	Cadet Band Class	Cadet Band Class	Cadet Band Class
1:00–1:30	La Casita Elementary	6th Grade Band		6th Grade Band		6th Grade Band
2:00–2:25	Highland Elementary	6th Grade Band	6th Grade Band	6th Grade Band	6th Grade Band	6th Grade Band
2:30–3:10	James Bickley Elementary	6th Grade Band	6th Grade Band	6th Grade Band	6th Grade Band	6th Grade Band

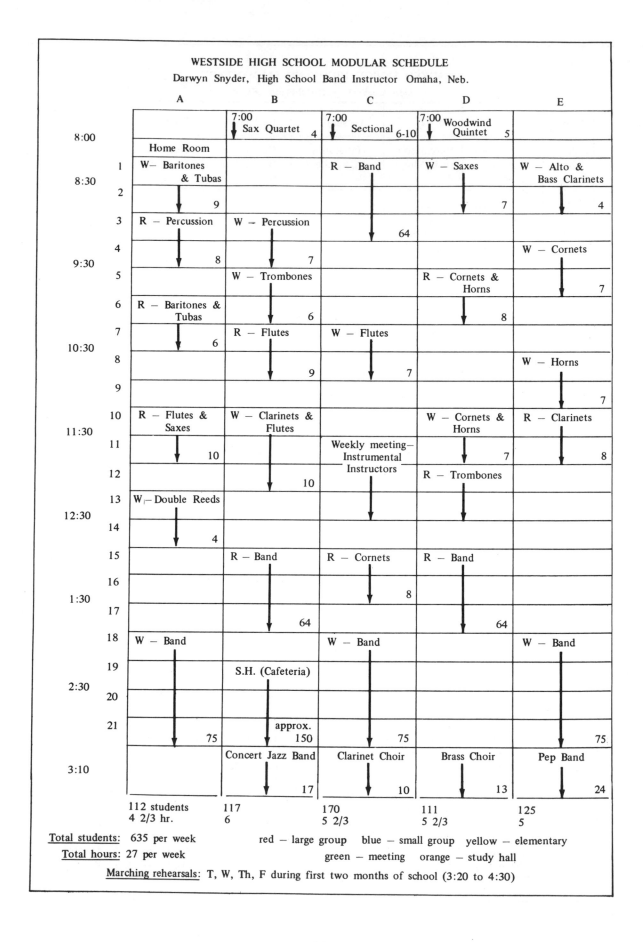

WESTSIDE HIGH SCHOOL MODULAR SCHEDULE

Darwyn Snyder, High School Band Instructor Omaha, Neb.

	A	B	C	D	E
8:00	Home Room	7:00 Sax Quartet 4	7:00 Sectional 6-10	7:00 Woodwind Quintet 5	
1 / 8:30	W— Baritones & Tubas		R — Band	W — Saxes	W — Alto & Bass Clarinets
2	9			7	4
3	R — Percussion	W — Percussion	64		
4 / 9:30	8	7			W — Cornets
5		W — Trombones		R — Cornets & Horns	7
6	R — Baritones & Tubas	6		8	
7 / 10:30	6	R — Flutes	W — Flutes		
8		9	7		W — Horns
9					7
10 / 11:30	R — Flutes & Saxes	W — Clarinets & Flutes		W — Cornets & Horns	R — Clarinets
11	10		Weekly meeting— Instrumental Instructors	7	8
12		10		R — Trombones	
13 / 12:30	W — Double Reeds				
14	4				
15		R — Band	R — Cornets	R — Band	
16 / 1:30			8		
17		64		64	
18	W — Band		W — Band		W — Band
19 / 2:30		S.H. (Cafeteria)			
20					
21	75	approx. 150	75		75
3:10		Concert Jazz Band 17	Clarinet Choir 10	Brass Choir 13	Pep Band 24
	112 students 4 2/3 hr.	117 6	170 5 2/3	111 5 2/3	125 5

Total students: 635 per week

Total hours: 27 per week

red — large group   blue — small group   yellow — elementary

green — meeting   orange — study hall

Marching rehearsals: T, W, Th, F during first two months of school (3:20 to 4:30)

NORTH LITTLE ROCK (ARK.) SCHOOL DISTRICT

INSTRUMENTAL MUSIC

Ron Bryant, North Little Rock High School

SCHEDULE AND ENROLLMENT (Please indicate nature of class.) Name of Staff Member _____ Date _____

Time Block	Monday	Tuesday	Wednesday	Thursday	Friday
1 8:40–9:35	Brass	Brass	Brass	Low Brass	Ridgeroad Jr. Hi. Brass
2 9:45–10:50	Woodwinds	Preparation	Percussion	Woodwinds	Jefferson Davis Jr. High
3 10:55–11:50	Preparation	Central Junior High (all 7th grade)	Preparation	Central Junior High (all 7th grade)	Office
4 11:55–1:05	Symphonic Band	Symphonic Band	Symphonic Band	Symphonic Band	Symphonic Band
1:05–1:40	L	U	N	C	H
1:50–2:30	Levy Elementary	Office	Levy Elementary	Office	Office
2:45–3:30	Office	Burns Elementary	Office	Burns Elementary	Office

TEACHERS: FILL OUT TWO COPIES OF THIS REPORT. Send one to: INSTRUMENTAL INSTRUCTORS (at junior high school).

Give one to: 7th GRADE COUNSELOR.

(Note: It is the responsibility of the teacher receiving this report to have a conference with the counselor to make certain that students are correctly programmed.)

COORDINATION OF INSTRUMENTAL ENROLLMENT

TO _____ (instrumental instructor) at _____

_____ (counselor)

The following students are being graduated from this school at the conclusion of this term and should continue instrumental music classes. Please make every effort to enroll them.

NAME	INSTRUMENT*	RATING**	REMARKS AND RECOMMENDATIONS

*Use "X" to designate that student has his own instrument.

** 1—excellent; 2—good; 3—average

INSTRUMENTAL TEACHER _____

SCHOOL _____

(Oakland, Calif.)

NORTH LITTLE ROCK (ARK.) SCHOOL DISTRICT
INSTRUMENTAL MUSIC

Travis Beard

SCHEDULE AND ENROLLMENT (Please indicate nature of class.) Name of Staff Member

Time Block	Monday	Tuesday	Wednesday	Thursday	Friday
8:00–8:30	Jefferson Davis Jr. Hi. Clarinets, Flutes	Jefferson Davis Jr. Hi. Cornets, French Horns	Jefferson Davis Jr. Hi. Saxes, Woodwinds	Jefferson Davis Jr. Hi. Percussion	Jefferson Davis Jr. Hi. Low Brass
1 8:45–9:45	Jefferson Davis Jr. Hi. Advanced Band	Jefferson Davis Jr. Hi. Advanced Band	Jefferson Davis Jr. Hi. Advanced Band	Jefferson Davis Jr. Hi. Advanced Band	Jefferson Davis Jr. Hi. Advanced Band
2 9:50–10:50	Preparation	North Little Rock High School Woodwinds	Preparation	North Little Rock High School Woodwinds	Preparation
3 10:55–11:50	Central Junior High (All 7th Grade) (Team teaching — five staff members)	North Little Rock High School	Central Junior High (All 7th Grade) (Team teaching — five staff members)	North Little Rock High School	North Little Rock High School
4 11:55–1:05	North Little Rock High School Concert Band	North Little Rock High School Concert Band	North Little Rock High School Concert Band	North Little Rock High School Concert Band	North Little Rock High School Concert Band
1:05–1:40	L	U	N	C	H
2:00–2:45	Lincoln Elementary	Jefferson Davis Jr. Hi.	Lincoln Elementary	Jefferson Davis Jr. Hi.	Jefferson Davis Jr. Hi.
3:00–3:30	Jefferson Davis Jr. Hi. (Prep.)	Jefferson Davis Jr. Hi. (Prep.)	Jefferson Davis Jr. Hi. (Prep.)	Jefferson Davis Jr. Hi. (Prep.)	Jefferson Davis Jr. Hi. (Prep.)

41

MIXED SENIOR HIGH, JUNIOR HIGH AND ELEMENTARY						
Norvil Howell — Clovis, New Mexico						
Period	School	Monday	Tuesday	Wednesday	Thursday	Friday
8:00–9:30	Clovis High School	Concert Band	Concert Band	Concert Band	Concert Band	Concert Band
9:30–10:20	Marshall Jr. High	Concert Band (Team Teaching)	Concert Band (Team Teaching)	Concert Band (Team Teaching)	Concert Band (Team Teaching)	Concert Band (Team Teaching)
10:20–11:15	Grattis Jr. High	Concert Band (Team Teaching)	Concert Band (Team Teaching)	Concert Band (Team Teaching)	Concert Band (Team Teaching)	Concert Band (Team Teaching)
12:30–1:30	Yucca Jr. High	Concert Band (Team Teaching)	Concert Band (Team Teaching)	Concert Band (Team Teaching)	Concert Band (Team Teaching)	Concert Band (Team Teaching)
1:00–1:30	Parkview Elem.	Beginning Band	Beginning Band	Beginning Band	Beginning Band	Beginning Band
2:30–3:00	La Casita Elem.	Beginning Band	Beginning Band	Beginning Band	Beginning Band	Beginning Band
2:15–3:15	Clovis High School	Ensembles & Sectionals	Ensembles & Sectionals	Ensembles & Sectionals	Ensembles & Sectionals	Ensembles & Sectionals

MIXED SENIOR AND JUNIOR HIGH						
James Decker — Greensboro, N.C.						
Period	School	Monday	Tuesday	Wednesday	Thursday	Friday
8:15–8:40	Kiser Jr. High	Alto Clarinets	Bass Clarinets	Flutes	Clarinets	Make-up
8:40–9:30	Kiser Jr. High	Clarinets	Clarinets	Flutes	Flutes	Flutes
10:00–11:00	Grimsley High School	Planning	Clarinets	Flutes	Woodwinds	Planning
11:00–12:00	Grimsley High School	Ensembles	Woodwind Trio	Ensembles	Ensembles	Bass Clarinets
12:00–1:00	Grimsley High School	Oboes	Ensembles	Clarinet Choir	Clarinets	Clarinets
1:30–2:30	Grimsley High School	Clarinets	Clarinets	Flutes	Clarinets	Clarinets & Oboes
2:30–3:30	Grimsely High School	Woodwind Ensemble	Woodwind Ensemble	Woodwind Ensemble	Planning	Planning

JUNIOR HIGH
Duane Miller — Lincoln, Neb.

Period	School	Monday	Tuesday	Wednesday	Thursday	Friday
1	Millard Lefler Jr. High	Ensembles	Ensembles	Ensembles	Ensembles	Ensembles
2	Millard Lefler Jr. High	Advanced Band	Advanced Band	Advanced Band	Advanced Band	Advanced Band
3	Millard Lefler Jr. High	Orchestra	Orchestra	Orchestra	Orchestra	Orchestra
4	Millard Lefler Jr. High	Strings Lunch	Strings Lunch	Strings Lunch	Strings Lunch	Strings Lunch
5	Millard Lefler Jr. High	Planning	Planning	Planning	Planning	Planning
6	Millard Lefler Jr. High	Prep Band	Prep Band	Prep Band	Prep Band	Prep Band
7	Millard Lefler Jr. High	Intermediate Band	Intermediate Band	Intermediate Band	Intermediate Band	Intermediate Band

SCHEDULE (for Ray Fixel) — Oakland, Calif.

Period/Time	Monday	Tuesday	Wednesday	Thursday	Friday
8:45-9:15	Parker GS Beginning Winds	Sobrante Park GS Advanced Orch.	Sobrante Park GS Advanced Orch.	Stonehurst GS Advanced Band	Sobrante Park Advanced Orch.
9:15-9:45	Beginning Winds II	Beginning WW I	Beginning WW I	Beginning Brass	Beginning WW I
9:45-10:15	Beginning Brass	Beginning WW II	Beginning WW II & Int. WW	Beginning WW	Beginning WW II & Int. WW
10:35-11:05	Int. Winds	Beginning Strings	Beginning Strings	Beginning Drums	Beginning Strings
11:05-11:35	Int. Brass	Int. Strings	Int. Strings	Int. WW	Int. Strings
11:35-12:05	Beginning Drums	Beginning Brass	Beginning Drums	Int. Brass	Beginning Brass
	Stonehurst GS		John Marshall GS	Parker GS	John Marshall GS
12:55-1:25	Advanced Band	Song Flutes	Int. Brass, Drums	Beginning Winds I	Int. Brass, Drums
1:25-1:55	Beginning Brass	Beginning Drums	Beginning WW	Beginning Winds II	Beginning WW
2:05-2:35	Beginning WW	Int. Drums	Beginning Strings	Beginning Brass	Beginning Strings
2:35-3:05	Beginning Drums	Int. WW	Int. Strings	Beginning Drums	Int. Strings

STRUCTURE. The scope of the program in instrumental music for a school system should include the following:

Elementary School	Junior High School	Senior High School
Pre-Band Class	Beginning Band Class	Concert Band
Beginning Band Class	Intermediate Band	Varsity Band
Advanced Band	Advanced Band	Wind Ensemble
Solos/Ensembles	Marching Band	Marching Band
	Stage Band	Stage Band
	Solos/Ensembles	Rock Groups
		Solos/Ensembles
		Pep Band

As we have seen in the past section on scheduling of classes, the primary concern of the band program structure is a proper sequence of learning experiences, beginning with the pre-band instrument class and continuing through fulfillment in the top wind ensemble of the school. The sequence of class work by grade level, as defined above, permits the student to progress from the pre-band class in grade four to beginning band in grade five, advanced band in grade six, a progressive class level in each grade of junior high, and another progressive level in each grade of senior high.

The objective of the pre-band class — beyond its use as a recruitment method — has been stated as a basic orientation in instrumental music, with proficiency in fingering, knowledge of key and time signatures, a degree of capability in the areas of embouchure, articulation and breath control, and the performance of selected songs as additional benefits of the program. The objectives of the first year of instrumental music instruction are designed to firmly establish the fundamentals of good performance and a general knowledge of music as an art form. The learning experiences should be immediate, meaningful and pleasurable. Objectives through the second year should follow the general objectives of the first. The intermediate level of band is designed for the student who already has a playing knowledge of his instrument. Emphasis is placed upon further development of the individual in order to prepare him for the advanced band. This level may be achieved early in the school life of some individuals, necessitating a flexibility of class membership throughout the junior and senior high school class offerings. The talented student who is properly motivated will by-pass some classes available at different grade levels. Perhaps he will spend one year in intermediate band at the junior high level, go directly into the advanced band for two years, and eventually perform with the top high school group for three years. Whatever the circumstances for individual advancement may be, the intermediate level of band should develop the kind of musicianship that is desired by including fundamentals of music, thorough technical training on instruments, extensive repertoire, and good rehearsal techniques.

ENSEMBLES/CHAMBER MUSIC. Concert band instruction is augmented in most school systems by training in three other types of groups. The marching band and stage band are both discussed at length elsewhere in this book, but another important area of instruction is that of small ensembles or chamber music. The gap between individual practice and large band playing can most effectively be filled by the use of such ensembles. The organization and development of ensemble activities is essential to the instrumental program and is a major responsibility of the instrumental music instructor.

The full band rehearsal routine is more general than specific. For example, when a large group plays together, the individual student may be inclined to forget the essentials of good musicianship.

Chamber music performance helps to correct this tendency by bringing to the fore such common faults as bad intonation, poor tone quality, poor phrasing, incorrect dynamics and lack of harmonic balance.

The advantages of this phase of the training program can be summarized as follows:

1. It makes for greater accuracy, independence, and poise in the performer.
2. It trains the student in ensemble cooperation.
3. It broadens and deepens the player's general musicianship, having unexcelled artistic possibilities.
4. It promotes a more rapid musical growth.
5. It develops, both in the performer and the listener, a more sensitive appreciation and enjoyment of music as an art.
6. Public appearances of chamber groups open up a wider field for the use of music. Thus, music can be integrated more effectively into home and community life.
7. It acquaints the player with another field of music literature.
8. It has definite recreational value.

What groups should be organized? The number and availability of students will determine what types of chamber music groups should be in existence, and many different combinations are possible. Ensembles for which substantial literature exists should be organized — and organized on a continuing basis. In some schools ensembles only function around competitions, i.e., festival time. This is not a good practice. For if the students are to develop ensemble skill and musicianship, they must work together regularly throughout the school year. Groups in a variety of sizes should be organized.

Good music is of the utmost importance in conducting an instrumental ensemble program. Fortunately, a great many publishers are now marketing a large variety of good ensemble literature to keep up with the growing popularity of ensemble playing. In selecting new music for ensemble groups, the following points should be carefully checked before selection is made:

1. It should be well printed, on a good quality paper. An attractive page is more interesting for the student, and some ensemble literature is very poorly printed.
2. Interesting, moving parts are very important in small ensemble literature.
3. The director must make certain that each part is playable by the students involved. A cursory examination is not sufficient. Often there will be a few measures in one part or another which exceed the ability of the average group, rhythmically, technically, or in range, thereby making the entire number impossible to complete satisfactorily.
4. Try to approach the average ability of the ensemble in grade level.
5. The groups should be as homogeneous as possible in ability, interest and age, so that the music selected is a challenge for each but not impossible.
6. Make sure that the music has educational value rather than merely entertainment value. A program of popular instrumental entertainment has its place, but not in the small ensemble program. It is a matter of education — bringing students and audiences to appreciate the difficulties involved in making a well-polished presentation of good music literature. Only students with a serious approach to music will fit into a well-run instrumental ensemble program. It is the director's task to stimulate such an attitude.

MOTIVATION. Most plans for motivating interest in music employ many psychological principles. Many motivating devices which are psychologically sound have been devised by band directors. The following are suggestions to develop interest and to maintain it at a high level:

1. Develop a performing group of such excellence that it will carry a prestige factor for its members.

2. Recognize individual work through chair position, solos and ensembles, officers, student administrative staff, and student conductors.

3. Make possible varied opportunities for public performance. This capitalizes on youth's desire to perform in public. Listed here are areas of performance that can be used for motivation:

   a. School assemblies.
   b. Evening concerts.
   c. P.T.A. meetings.
   d. Patriotic and religious programs.
   e. Parades.
   f. Solo and ensemble festivals.
   g. Graduations.
   h. Talent shows.
   i. Musical productions.

4. Participate in contests.

5. Conduct festival-clinics.

6. Maintain small ensembles.

7. Organize concert band ensembles.

8. Have available merit and service awards.

9. The educator's attitude should mirror approval. The music conductor-educator should look for and appreciate good work. It is possible to maintain high standards without constant destructive and negative criticism.

10. Present audio-visual experiences; recordings made by groups for playback purposes; television appearances; radio appearances; movies of groups on trips or on the field, and still shots.

11. Prepare a handbook.

12. Make use of bulletin boards.

13. Prepare student progress charts.

14. Make use of trips, exchange concerts, athletic events.

15. Music educators should continually strive to maintain harmony and purpose within the group. An efficiently managed organization permeated with a spirit of cooperative effort will supply motivation within itself.

16. Music is an art which naturally expresses itself through group activity. In bands, orchestras, and choruses, we are naturally availing ourselves of group motivation.

17. A carefully planned and well-conducted rehearsal is of paramount importance. Students are quick to sense and resent weaknesses in organization and mistakes made in managing people and affairs.

18. The fairness, honesty, and sincerity of the music educator in dealing with problems serves as a form of motivation. A firm and fair discipline should be fostered. The idea is prevalent among some teachers that students resent too firm a discipline, and that the so-called "easy" teacher will be the most popular. Studies have proved otherwise. From a student's point of view, the most popular and the best teachers are those who establish and maintain a firm discipline and a business-like atmosphere in the classroom.

STUDENT EVALUATION. The evaluation of students in the band program is generally limited to two forms, the Merit-Awards system and Grade-Report Card system. These two forms serve to provide recognition for participating students in completely different ways. The Merit-Awards system is valuable in recognizing the achievements of deserving students before the school and community, and the Grade-Report Card system is part of the necessary communication with parents concerning student progress and development. If this communication is to have value, it must be based on valid evaluative criteria, must be realistically related to the potential of each student, and must be the product of serious effort on the part of the instructor.

Several guiding principles might be observed in evaluating students:

1. The immediate performance is not the goal of band instruction.
2. There is something available in the band for every child.
3. The modern democratic "opportunity for every child" philosophy is one criteria.
4. All children make at least some contribution and progress in band, but there are individual differences in their rate of progress.
5. In evaluation, mere intelligence is not the only basis of judgment, since some slow learners — less scholarly, but more emotional, aesthetic or expressive — may be the core of the organization.
6. Grading is done on the basis that the purpose of band instruction is not to produce a professional or commercial attitude toward music, but to expose the child to an activity where he can make a contribution, and derive some knowledge, skill, enjoyment, and aesthetic values in the process.

With these principles in mind, it is apparent that the grading process is based on a *ratio of potential to performance*. The sensitivity and discrimination of the director are inseparably important factors in all grading. A system of evaluation which feeds information concerning individuals to the director must be established before he can make realistic judgments. Some factors involved in establishing an evaluative criteria might be:

1. Valid testing used to discover the degree of latent musical talent. (Refer to Talent and Aptitude Tests at the beginning of this chapter.)
2. Placing emphasis on the attainment of appropriate goals by the individual, based on latent musical talent.
3. Evaluation as an integral part of instruction.
4. Evaluation covering such aspects of individual playing as: Intonation and tone quality; technique—including precision, breath control, articulation and reading; interpretation—including tempo, style of articulation, rhythm, expression and phrasing.
5. Records of student performances.
6. Student assistance in evaluation of their own and group performance.
7. Testing procedures consistent with teaching procedures.

Talent tests are available from LeBlanc, Holton, Olds, Selmer, Conn and Hall-McCreary. The director does not usually have either the responsibility or freedom of choice in determining grade reporting procedures. Reports vary widely from a simple numerical or letter grading system indicating high or low achievement to simple or involved check lists which permit comprehensive communication with parents and students. The larger school systems, most of whom are on data processing and computerized reporting procedures, handicap the director to the extent that his reporting may not be as comprehensive as he desires. If this is true, he must then find or establish other means of communication. Following are examples of check list grading forms which may be of use to directors in determining reporting preferences:

WESTSIDE COMMUNITY SCHOOLS
Instrumental Music
Progress Report

Dear Parent:

     Being an instrumental music director affords me the opportunity to observe your child at work in a rather unique classroom setting. The following is a report on your child's current progress. It is hoped that this will aid you in guiding your child toward meaningful achievement.

_____

Instrumental Music
Westside Community Schools

Student _____

Evaluation System: 1 — outstanding
    2 — good
    3 — showing some improvement
    4 — definitely needs improving
    X — inconsistent

Conduct in Class	
Attitude toward band and/or orchestra	
Attitude toward classmates	
Attention to directions	
Application of practice methods	
Consistent in handing in practice records signed by parent	
Total minutes practiced each week	
Achievement record (memorized scales and pieces)	
Poise gained from performance in class	
Consistent progress shown on the instrument	

Remarks:

    The Instrumental Progress Report was designed to keep parents well informed and is sent at least once during the year and more often when necessary.

PROGRESS REPORT IN INSTRUMENTAL MUSIC
Brooklyn Center High School

This is an effort on the part of the Instrumental Music Department to give you parents a more complete and understandable picture of the progress your child has made on his chosen instrument. The letter grade can be better understood in terms of progress toward successfully playing his instrument if you follow the check marks and become familiar with the information that they represent. Pupils are not graded by comparison one to another, but on the manner in which they develop their individual ability to perform on their chosen instrument.

Your assistance at home can be most helpful in assuring your child's success or failure in the instrumental music program at our school. Only with your help and encouragement at home can we work together in giving your child the best musical education. Feel free to call or see me at the high school to discuss any questions you might have.

"Since Music has so much to do with the moulding of *Character,* it is necessary that we teach it to our children." —Aristotle

----

A — Superior   This grade is reserved for the pupil who can play his part well and who shows evidence of practicing.

B — Good   This grade indicates that the pupil plays his part well and does some practicing.

C — Average   This pupil experiences trouble at times in playing his part because he cannot read the music and cannot finger the notes properly. He probably needs parental help in planning his practice time and in being encouraged to improve himself and his playing.

Below C   This grade is given to pupils who play very poorly, though they may be capable of doing average, good or superior work. These pupils tend to slow the band's progress to better performance and learning more music because of the extra time they must be given and because of their lack of attention to good practice habits.

Parent's Signature

1. _____   3. _____

2. _____   4. _____

I would appreciate any comments you might wish to make.   R. E. Papke

Comments:

1st Quarter   3rd Quarter

2nd Quarter   4th Quarter

Student _____ Class _____

1. Outstanding 2. Excellent 3. Very Good 4. Good 5. Average
6. Below Average

	1st Qtr.	2nd Qtr.	3rd Qtr.	4th Qtr.
Attendance				
Required Practice Time (30 minutes daily)				
Attitude				
Work or Progress				

X – Work needed   XX – Much work needed   XXX – Very poor, much work needed or will be dropped.

	1st	2nd	3rd	4th
To improve TONE:				
Practice in front of mirror and watch the embouchure carefully.				
Correct breathing and control of tone and proper breath support.				
Solfeggio exercises (singing intervals).				
To improve TECHNIQUE:				
Learn to count and feel the basic beat.				
Correct improper tonguing; practice exercises daily.				
Study rhythmic patterns and exercises.				
Learn regular and optional fingerings.				
Work method book harder and prepare lessons better.				
Regular daily practice (30 minutes daily).				
Fingers—work finger exercises and chromatics.				
Intonation—careful ensemble listening.				
Posture. PERCUSSION				
12 Scales. Speed in rudiments.				
Playing postion. Stick and hand position.				
Phrasing. Long roll.				
Range. Single stroking.				
Vibrato. Work method book harder and prepare lessons better.				
Legato tonguing. Keep steady time.				
Lighter attack. Counting rhythms.				
Expression. Cadences.				
Key Signatures. Reading.				
Dynamics. Other:				
Other:				
Improve attention and cooperation in band.				
Come with instrument always clean and in repair, folder in order.				
Give close attention to the director and his instructions.				
BAND GRADE				
Band Director's Comments:				

Same on p.297

ANN ARBOR PUBLIC SCHOOLS
Elementary Instrumental Music Report

NAME _____ SEMESTER, 19 ____

SCHOOL _____ CLASSROOM TEACHER _____

GRADE _____ CLASS: Beginning _____ Advanced _____

MUSICIANSHIP

The check in the first line of squares indicates the student's performance in relation to the entire class. The check in the second line shows the teacher's estimate of the student's ability in music. The check in the third line shows the student's progress in relation to this estimate of his musical ability.

Comparative
Performance   Poor ☐   Fair ☐   Average ☐   Good ☐   Superior ☐

Estimate of
Ability   Poor ☐   Fair ☐   Average ☐   Good ☐   Superior ☐

Performance
vs. Ability   Poor ☐   Fair ☐   Average ☐   Good ☐   Superior ☐

For each ability used in playing an instrument a letter shows the student's achievement in relation to his own musical capacity: G (good) for achievement at the level of his capacity, F (fair) for achievement somewhat below his capacity, P (poor) for achievement seriously below his capacity.

_____ Tone quality   _____ Sense of pitch

_____ Knowledge of fingerings   _____ Breath control

_____ Reading of note names   _____ Playing position (position of hands, instrument, embouchure, posture)

_____ Sense of rhythm

CITIZENSHIP

The comments below indicate the student's attitudes and cooperation in instrumental music.

_____ Preparation of lessons   _____ Courtesy

_____ Attention in class   _____ Cooperation

_____ Response to instruction   _____ Promptness

_____ Care of equipment   _____ Attendance with instrument, music

A conference with the parent is
always welcomed.
                                     _____
                                     Instrumental Music Teacher

                              Phone: _____

Additional comments, if any, on reverse side.

Whatever grade and reporting system is finally selected by the director or administration of a school system, it must be used seriously and responsibly as an integral part of the overall instruction process. Importance of evaluation accuracy to both the student and the band program cannot be overemphasized.

Merit systems can also become an important part of evaluation and eventual rewards for students participating in a band program. Recognition of achievement by fellow students and by the community through an awards system is important in terms of motivation for the exceptional and outstanding students in direct proportion to the emphasis placed on the system. If the system is kept "low-key" and publicized primarily for benefit of the members of the band, motivational benefits will also be "low-key." If the system is widely publicized through school news and through community media, greater importance will be attached to the awards with greater motivational benefits and greater pressures on students. The director must determine the value a merit-award system can give to his program and set the tone of the program.

The following will demonstrate some factors which should enter into merit tabulation and, perhaps, the relative value of certain activities in that tabulation. This particular set of values has been established by the North Little Rock High School Band, North Little Rock, Arkansas:

Points	Activity
20	Playing a solo from memory.
35	Playing a solo from memory in public.
50	Playing a solo in State Festival.
20	Each parade.
10	Each concert performance.
5	Three hours of practice per week outside of school time.
20	Each football game performance.
10	Playing in stands for football but not assigned to marching.
50	Each 10 private lessons (listing of private teachers available).
50	Participation in Region Clinic Bands, workshop band.
100	Participation in All-State Clinic Band (chosen from region clinic).
5	First chair in section for six weeks.
25	Attending band camp during summer.
25	Trying out for Region Clinic Band.
5+	Doing special assignments or detail work (approved by director).
20	Each six weeks as principal officer (Captain, Lieutenant, Head Librarian, Head Quartermaster, Property crew).
15	Each six weeks as secondary officer (Librarians, Publicity, etc.).
50	Drum Major during football season.
10	Rank leader six weeks of football season.

There is an activity variation in different geographical locations. The importance attached to those activities, and personal preference as to performance values on the part of the director will be factors in determining how many points may be awarded for one phase of participation. The number of points assigned to each activity and the frequency of these activities will also determine the number of points which must be reached for the various awards to be presented at the end of the season. The director can establish point values and point totals by examining activities of the past year and participation by students and deciding what percentage of the band members should receive each type of award. For example, one point total may be selected which is within range of achievement for 30 percent of the members in an average year, with these students receiving a Band Letter. Another higher point total which is within range for 15 percent of the members may be established for a Band Pin. Another still higher point total may be established for the highest award, the Band Key, and be within range of the top 5 percent only. Names of the awards, their values, and the number which should be awarded are all a part of the mechanics of the program and must be decided in each individual situation. The importance attached to the awards and the publicity given to them will determine their effectiveness. Demerit systems are occasionally used in conjunction with merits and become a part of point total tabulation. Again from North Little Rock, the following demerit values:

Points	Infractions
15	Uniform hung incorrectly.
10	Uniform worn incorrectly (shoes not shined, etc.).
10	Folio out of place.
10	Instrument out of place.
10+	Carelessness with instrument.
5	Failure to pass instrument inspection.
15	Conduct unbecoming to a band member.
15	Tardy for a performance without reasonable excuse.
10	Missing sectional rehearsal without reasonable excuse.
10	In library or quartermaster's room without permission.
10	Personal belongings out of place.
5+	Infractions detrimental to department.

To conclude discussion of merit systems, suffice it to say that the director must assume the responsibility of the details in the organization and administration of the system if it is to be a positive factor in the band program. Band members should be consulted in the organization of the program and can be very useful in administering the time-consuming mechanics of the system.

STUDENT STAFF. The band director who has organized a comprehensive band program in his system will often find that the mechanics of administering that program occupy an increasing share of his available time. It is possible for details to become so cumbersome that teaching effectiveness is impaired. One solution for this problem may be the addition of a student staff. Responsible, dedicated and totally involved students in our band programs are capable of handling much of the administrative work — if they are organized to do so. Student leadership may relieve the director of many time-consuming details, while at the same time developing a sense of pride in group accomplishment, cooperation with other individuals, and that nebulous "esprit de corps."

A student staff should include two classifications of officers—those elected by fellow students and those appointed by the director. Names of the offices to be held will vary according to the wishes of the school system, students, and director, but duties will be fairly consistent. Elective offices usually number four or five, with appointive offices involving another ten to fifteen students.

In Temple High School, Temple, Texas, the elected officers are President, Vice-President, Secretary-Treasurer, and Reporter-Historian. These officers are elected in May to serve the following school year and have the following duties:

President

Call and preside at business meetings.

Appoint special committees.

Preside over Band Council meetings.

Take charge of tuning and warm-up with the assistance of the concertmaster or appointed student conductors.

Supervise duties of subordinate officers.

Appoint judging committees for challenges.

Vice-President

Assume the obligations of the President in his absence.

Assist with challenges.

Secretary-Treasurer

Record minutes of all business meetings of band and Band Council.

Accept and record payments of fees.

Reporter-Historian

Report all news events to school paper and local paper.

Handle band publicity.

Maintain a band scrapbook.

Appointed officers consist of Drum Major, Assistant Drum Major, Majorettes, Librarian, Manager, and Squad Leaders. All duties of the appointed officers will not be listed here, since some of these are obvious and others will vary from school to school. However, some of these duties include serving on the Band Council, helping plan social activities, assisting with discipline, and fostering "esprit de corps."

INVENTORY. Administration of the band program involves inventory of three types of equipment: instruments, uniforms and music. Since each of these three areas involves substantial expenditures of school district money and the investment of band program funds, the inventory system should be organized, simple and accurate. Certain basic information must be contained on inventory forms, and a system established for checking out and returning equipment.

Instrument inventory can be maintained as a simple listing or on a series of inventory cards with the following necessary information concerning each instrument:

Make	School Number (if assigned)
Model	Purchase date
Serial number	Repair record
Description	Present value
Equipment included	

(See sample card from Oakwood School, Dayton, Ohio in appendix.)

Instrument check-out and check-in must be handled accurately. Parents should understand the responsibility involved and indicate their acceptance of that responsibility by signing a form to be retained by the school. (See instrument check-out form from Oakwood School, Dayton, Ohio in appendix.)

Uniform inventory may also be maintained as a simple listing, although some directors may wish to keep a separate card for each uniform. (See sample form in appendix.) The basic inventory should contain information on each item, including number in stock, purchase date and present condition. The end of the year inventory could be more detailed and should include replacement needs. Further detail work with uniforms includes check-out to students, periodic inspections, and signing of bonds or "agreement forms" by students and/or parents. (See sample form used by Lenoir, North Carolina in appendix.)

Library maintenance and inventory is very important to the success of a band program. Time can be consumed wastefully by director and students if the work is not organized and handled efficiently. A master ledger may be used to record each piece of music purchased, with pertinent information on each number. However, a cross filing system is recommended for efficiency. Information on file cards should include: title, composer, arranger, publisher, classification and grade of difficulty. (Sample file cards for Tucson public schools and Westside community schools are included in the appendix.) A numbering system will simplify the identification and location of music. Naturally, the library set up will depend on physical factors, but adequate space, proper arrangement of files, work tables and the like are necessary for optimum efficiency. Worn and torn music should be repaired before filing, and a "re-order card" can be used to indicate replacement needs where music has been lost. Before filing (or re-filing), every piece of music should be arranged in score order and the parts checked against the parts listed on the jacket cover.

COURSE OF STUDY OUTLINES
Elementary School

I. Fundamentals
   1. Correct posture and principles of breath control.
   2. Formation of embouchure and tone production peculiar to the various instruments of the band.
   3. Proper instrument position and fingerings.

II. Basic Musicianship
   1. Recognition of notes by pitch names.
   2. Sequential presentation of meter (time signature).
   3. Sequential presentation of major key signatures.
   4. Understanding of notation (recognition of note values in "eighth" and "quarter" time).
   5. Preliminary training in recognition of enharmonic tones.

III. Class Teaching
   1. Teaching of rhythm through mental and physical response. Establishment of class rhythmic impulse by use of the foot beat, mark time, etc.
   2. Group practice routines.

IV. Individual Teaching
   1. Teaching of rhythm. (See above.)
   2. Individual practice routines.

V. Printed Materials for Use in:
   1. Pre-band classes (song flute, tonette, etc.).

2. Elementary band classes.
   a. Heterogeneous instrument groupings.
   b. Homogeneous instrument groupings.
   c. Individual instrument instruction materials.
      (See the complete course of study for every instrument of the band in the high school band office. This includes basic books on all levels of instruction, supplementary books on all levels of instruction, solo materials of all grades, collections of solos of all grades, and educational recordings dealing with advanced solo materials for all band instruments.)
   d. Solo and ensemble materials (see band library for complete listings).
   e. Other supplementary materials: band books, simple selections in various arrangements, etc.

Junior High School

I. Fundamentals
   1. Continued training in breath control, embouchure control, and tone production.
   2. Continued development of technical proficiency.
      a. Sectional rehearsals when possible.
      b. Full band rehearsals daily.
      c. Individual or group instruction.

II. Basic Musicianship
   Continued training in:
   1. Recognition of notes by pitch names.
   2. Notation.
   3. Time signatures.
   4. Key signatures (major and minor keys).
   5. Enharmonics.

III. Music Reading
   1. Continued training in physical and mental response, to establish an even rhythmic pulse.
   2. More advanced study of notation.
   3. Recognition and playing of more advanced rhythmic patterns.
   4. Training in phrase recognition.

IV. Intonation Studies
   1. Ear training, critical listening.
   2. Matching tones, listening for "beats."

V. Development of Style
   1. Understanding periods of music:
      Baroque, Classic, Romantic, Contemporary.
   2. Playing in various styles.
   3. Use of recordings (disc and tape) to illustrate style.

VI. Materials
   1. Heterogeneous class method books.
   2. Homogeneous class method books.
   3. Individual method books.
      (See the complete course of study for every band instrument on file at the senior high school band office. This includes basic books on all levels of instruction, supplementary books on all levels, solo materials

of all grades, collections of solos of all grades, and educational recordings dealing with solo materials for all band instruments.)

4. Band repertoire: overtures, suites, marches, etc.
5. Tape recordings, records.
6. Electronic aids.

Senior High School

I. Teaching Techniques and Rehearsal Procedures
1. Further emphasis on proper breath control.
2. Continuation of intonation studies at more advanced levels.
3. Continued study of phrasing.
4. Further development of technical proficiency.

II. Further Extension of Basic Musicianship
1. Continuation of work done in junior high school, but on a more advanced plane, and with the addition of transposition for all instruments.
2. Some training in chord recognition.

III. Further Training in the Proper Concept of Tone Quality for Individual Instruments and for Production of Fine Quality of Band Tone

IV. Intonation Studies
Continuation of studies outlined for junior high school, but at more advanced levels.

V. Further Development of Style
1. More detailed study of periods of music.
2. Playing in various styles.
   a. Use of tapes and disc recordings as aids in developing maturity of style.

VI. Materials
1. Band Repertoire.
   a. Overtures.
   b. Suites.
   c. Marches.
   d. Miscellaneous.
2. Supplementary materials.
   a. Books—additional unisonal scale studies, harmonized scale studies, chorales, etc.
3. Small ensemble materials for various combinations of instruments.
4. Solo materials for all instruments.
5. Individual method books for all instruments.
   (See the complete course of study for every band instrument in the senior high school band office. This includes basic books on all levels, supplementary studies on all levels, solo materials of all grades, and educational recordings of all grades.)
6. Electronic aids.
   a. Phonograph.
   b. Stroboconn.
   c. Electric metronomes.

chapter 6

Fundamentals of Music

Although it is generally acknowledged that band programs have become an important part of school curricula all over the nation, most directors and many leaders in the school music field agree that something more than specialized training in the mechanics of playing the instrument must be offered if the student is to realize complete musical development. The band student should be an informed person as well as a performer. Knowledge and familiarity with the vital elements of music will add perspective to his total musical development.

The understandings and skills which are outlined in Chapter II in this book will serve as learning by-products of the instruction received in instrumental music. In the instrumental music program where special effort is made in theory-oriented activities, these understandings and skills will be comprehensive. Attention to this phase of the music program will help satisfy the demand for a general education.

A wealth of material which may be used in teaching basic understandings in the area of music history and appreciation has been available for many years, and the supply of material designed primarily for use in the classroom is increasing steadily. These materials can be incorporated as a separate entity in the daily rehearsal schedule, or used in conjunction with music being rehearsed at the time, or scheduled for separate class instruction. It is the responsibility of the individual director to determine which method would work best in his system, how comprehensive the instruction should be, which materials to use, and how much time should be devoted to this instruction.

For an example of incorporating the teaching of theory, history and appreciation into the daily rehearsal schedule, refer to Chapter Seven — "Teaching Procedures and Techniques." The daily rehearsal program used by Richard Papke in Brooklyn Center High School, Minneapolis, Minnesota, is a good example of a complete rehearsal activity program. Among other items listed in his Concert Band Curriculum Outline are such items as: monthly "music discovery" team projects; monthly Music 300 (musical form); daily, weekly, monthly listening assignments and activities; monthly quizzes; yearly term papers; conducting — all seniors conduct at pep fest; composition encouraged (all band members); and a performance test (the Watkins-Farnum performance test is given every fall and spring).

The remainder of this chapter will be devoted to a brief outline history of musical events and personalities which may be of use to the director in determining a sequence of teaching materials and procedures, plus a reference list of materials.

Outline of Music History

I. Antiquity to c. 200 A.D.
  A. Egyptians.
    1. Development of harp and lyre family, probably used for ceremonials.
    2. Also used lutes.

B. Greeks.
1. Established science of sound.
2. Pythagoras (c. 582-c.500 B.C.): philosopher who established a certain acoustical principle based on the laws of proportion (the relation of the length of a vibrating body to its pitch).
3. Plato (427-347 B.C.): philosopher who held that music developed and fortified the personality and soothed the emotions.
4. Used letters of the alphabet to represent tones.

II. Middle Ages (600-1450)

A. Styles and Forms of Music.
1. Monophony: single melodic line; sacred and secular.
2. Gregorian chant: chants of the Roman Catholic church, sung in unison, without accompaniment.
3. Polyphony: counterpoint in several parts.
   a. Organum — vocal music of two or three and sometimes four parts (melodies) sung simultaneously and in parallel motion, with specific intervals between parts (usually a fourth or fifth).
   b. Counterpoint — two or more melodies heard at the same time.
   c. Canon — theme repeated in different voices, starting at different times and sometimes at different pitches.
4. Rise of secular music.
   a. Troubadours — poet-musician nobles of southern France.
   b. Trouvères — poet-musicians of northern France.
   c. Minnesingers — aristocratic German singers of love-songs.
   d. Meistersingers — middle class German poets and singers (trades people).

III. The Renaissance (1450-1600) — Humanism (the feeling or regard for the value of every person as an individual.)

A. Style of Music.
1. Clear, well balanced, moving along in a steady, flowing beat without accents.
2. Instrumental music composition refined.
3. Beginning of homophonic texture.
   a. Accompanied melody.
   b. Chorus singing a melody with instrumental accompaniment.
4. Addition of a bass part.
5. Imitation — canon; round.
6. New concern for lyrics.

B. Forms of Music.
1. Motet — music for choruses, written to sacred texts and intended for church use.
2. Mass — a musical setting of the formal worship service in some churches, without scenery, drama or costumes.
3. Oratorio — a religious narrative set to music and intended for concert or church use (without sets, drama or costumes).
4. Madrigal — setting of non-religious text for ensemble of mixed voices.

C. Composers.
 1. Giovanni Palestrina (1525-1594).
    a. "Adoramus Te."
    b. "O Bone Jesu."
 2. Claudio Monteverdi (1567-1634).
    a. Early composer of opera.
       1. *Orfeo.*
       2. *Coronation of Aeneas.*
    b. Link between Renaissance and Baroque periods.

IV. Baroque Period (1600-1750).
 A. Styles of Music.
    1. Homophonic — accompanied melody.
       a. Figured bass.
    2. Polyphonic — a new form with rich ornamental lines.
       a. Passing tones and suspensions.
    3. Compositions of greater duration.
    4. Larger orchestras and choruses.
 B. Forms of Music.
    1. Opera development.
    2. Madrigal.
    3. Oratorio.
    4. Sonata.
    5. Concerto.
 C. Composers.
    1. Henry Purcell (English) — *Dido and Aeneas.*
    2. Antonio Vivaldi (Italian) — recognized for development of concerto.
    3. Jean Lully (French).
    4. Johann Sebastian Bach (German).
       a. Well-Tempered Clavier, Brandenburg Concerti, B Minor Mass, Toccata and Fugue in D Minor, *St. Matthew Passion.*
       b. Fugue, concerto, suite and cantata development.
    5. George Frederick Handel (German).
       a. Oratorios: *Messiah, Judas Maccabeus.*
       b. The Water Music.
    6. Arcangelo Corelli — violin virtuoso (Italian).

V. Classic Period (1750-1825) — Age of Enlightenment.
 A. Style of Music.
    1. Strict adherence to form.
    2. Simple melodies.
    3. Contrasting dynamic effects.
    4. Logic and order.

B. Forms of Music.
1. Symphony.
2. Concerto.
3. Sonata.
4. Overture.

C. Composers.
1. Franz Joseph Haydn (Austrian).
   a. Father of the symphony.
   b. "Surprise" Symphony, oratorios (*The Creation* and *The Seasons*).
2. Wolfgang Amadeus Mozart (Austrian).
   a. Operas (*Don Giovanni, The Magic Flute* and *The Marriage of Figaro*).
   b. The Requiem Mass.
   c. Symphonies.
3. Christoph Gluck (German) — opera (*Orpheus and Euridice*).
4. Ludwig van Beethoven (German).
   a. Piano music.
   b. Symphonies.
   c. Concerti.
   d. Chamber music.
   e. Vocal music.

VI. Romantic Period (1820-1900).

A. Style of Music.
1. Importance of melody.
2. Personal and emotional music.

B. Forms of Music.
1. Program music — tells a story or suggests a picture by sounds only.
2. Leitmotif — helps tell a story by thematically identifying someone or something in music.
3. Grand opera — words, music and drama.
4. Enlargement of the symphony orchestra.

C. Composers.
1. Richard Wagner (German).
   a. Unity of music and drama.
   b. *Tannhauser, Tristan and Isolde, Lohengrin, The Ring.*
2. Giuseppe Verdi (Italian) — operas (*Aida, La Traviata, Othello*).
3. Georges Bizet (Spanish) — opera (*Carmen*).
4. Frederick Chopin (Polish) — wrote music mainly for piano.
5. Giocchino Rossini (Italian) — overtures and operas, including *Italian in Algiers, The Barber of Seville,* and *William Tell*.
6. Felix Mendelssohn (German).
   a. Oratorios (*St. Paul* and *Elijah*).
   b. Overture ("Midsummer Night's Dream").
   c. "Songs Without Words."

    7. Peter Tschaikovsky (Russian).

      a. Symphonies which are indicative of this period (No. 6, "The Pathetique," for example).

      b. Other forms: "Romeo and Juliet" (overture-fantasy), "1812 Overture," *Nutcracker Suite*.

D. Nationalism.

  1. Style.

    a. Music based on folk music or music indicative of the country (nationality) of the composer.

    b. Harmonies characteristic of folk music.

  2. Composers.

    a. Alexander Borodin (Russian) — opera (*Prince Igor*).

    b. Modest Mussorgsky (Russian) — opera (*Boris Godunov*).

    c. Bedrich Smetana (Bohemian) — opera (*Bartered Bride*).

    d. Antonin Dvorak (Bohemian) — "New World" Symphony.

    e. Rimsky Korsakov (Russian) — *Scheherezade* (orchestral suite).

    f. Jean Sibelius (Finnish) — *Finlandia* (tone poem).

VII. Modern or Contemporary Period (from 1900) — including Impressionism.

A. Style of Music.

  1. Few clear melodies.

  2. Shifting and changing rhythms.

  3. Disappearance of key center.

  4. Unusual organization of chord patterns.

  5. Fleeting expression of a scene.

  6. Suggestions rather than statements.

  7. Creation of a mood or atmosphere.

B. Forms of Music.

  1. Atonality — music in no set key.

  2. Polytonality — music in several keys simultaneously.

  3. Twelve-tone music.

    a. Arnold Schoenberg.

    b. Anton Webern.

    c. Alban Berg.

  4. Electronic music.

C. Composers.

  1. Claude Debussy (French) — "Clair de Lune."

  2. Igor Stravinsky (Russian) — ballets (*The Firebird, Petroushka, The Rite of Spring*).

  3. George Gershwin (American) — *Porgy and Bess* (opera), *Rhapsody in Blue, American in Paris*.

  4. Aaron Copland (American) — ballets (*Billy the Kid, Rodeo*).

  5. Leonard Bernstein (American) — production music ("Westside Story," "Fancy Free," "On the Waterfront").

D. Composers shaping the music of "today."
   1. Paul Creston.
   2. Samuel Barber.
   3. William Schuman.
   4. John Cage.
   5. Benjamin Britten.
   6. Norman Dello Joio.
   7. Morton Gould.
   8. Vincent Persichetti.
   9. Milton Babbitt.
   10. Leonard Bernstein.
   11. Leon Kirchner.
   12. Lukas Foss.
   13. Peter Mennin.
   14. Karlheinz Stockhausen.

DEVELOPMENT OF MUSICAL STYLES*

by Paul Torgrimson

Development of Musical Styles: Primitive—Middle Ages

Period	Rhythm	Melody	Harmony	Form	Color	Texture	Instruments	
Primitive	Free rhythms and dances	Word—born Passion—born Melody—born	Heterophony Parallelism Drones	Question and answer phrases to form periods	Voices Instruments	Antiphonal Responsorial	Whistles Flutes Trumpets	Drums Xylophones Cymbals
Oriental	Long and short note patterns	Pentatonic Scales Quarter-tones	Heterophony Drones	Psalmody and chanting	Voices Instruments	Monophony Simple polyphony	Natural horns and trumpets Flutes Drums	Reedpipes String instruments
Greek-Hellenic[1] (675 B.C.-100 A.D.)	Poetic meters	Greek modes Whole steps Half steps Quarter-tones	Magadizing (parallel octaves) Heterophony	Hymns	Voices Instruments	Choral Monophony	Lyres Harps Aulos (early oboe)	Hydraulis (early organ)
Middle Ages[2] (100-1400)	Based on text Note against note Poetic meters	Medieval modes Syllabic and melismatic styles	Organum strict (4ths and 5ths) Discant (3rds and 6ths)	Psalmody Plain chant Mass Motet Liturgical drama Poetic types Round, Catch, Ground bass Instrumental dances	Voices Instruments Variable combinations of the two	Antiphonal and responsorial 2 and 3 voice polyphony Similar, oblique and contrary motion Imitation	Monochord Recorder Shawm (oboe) Clavichord	Organ Cross flute Snare drum Harpsichord

1. Representative composers of the Greek-Hellenic period were Terpander, Auchilochos, Phyrnis, and Euripedes.
2. During the Middle Ages important composers were Hermanus Contractus, Leonin, Perotin, Machaut, Landini, and the Goliards, the Troubadours, the Trouveres, the Jongleurs, and the Minnesingers.
"Dynamics" is not listed in this part of the chart. Historians have no positive knowledge of this aspect of musical style until the middle ages. During this period the dynamics were dictated by the nature of the text of the music and depended upon responsorial contrast.

* *The Instrumentalist* (August, 1962), 1418 Lake St., Evanston, Ill. Used by permission.

Development of

PERIOD	RHYTHM	MELODY	HARMONY	FORMS	COLOR
Renaissance (1400-1600)	Macro rhythm (basic meter) Micro rhythm (agogic accent)	Modal Musica Reservata (It.) and vers mesure (Fr.) (the music follows the meaning and accent of the words)	Triads, first inversions and non-harmonic tones on a polyphonic base	Mass Motet Frottola Chanson Madrigal Canon Toccata Ricercare Fantasia Passamezzo Ground- Branle variations Ayre Masque	Vibrato and Pizzicato on string instruments
Baroque (1600-1750)	Bar line regularity Simple and compound meters	Development of major and minor tonalities Development of instrumental character	Thorough-bass Dominance of major and minor tonalities Functional harmony, triads Seventh chords Modulation to closely-related keys	Opera Ballet Oratorio Sinfonia Cantata Overture Chorale Choral- Fugue Prelude Concerto grosso Suite (binary form)	Instrumental Beginnings of orchestration
Rococo (1725-1760)	No new developments	"Style galant" Affektenlehre (portraying typical emotions)	Rameau's theory of fundamental bass and inversion	Development of binary form	All parts scored Decline of improvisation Ornaments
Classic (1750-1825)	Bar line regularity Dominance of simple meters	Diatonic lines in major and minor modes Tuneful, singable melodies	Triads Seventh chords Chromatic alteration Modulation to foreign keys	Development of Sonata form Sonata Trio Quartet Quintet Concerto Symphony Opera Oratorio	Standardization of instrumental combinations
Romantic (1815-1915)	Bar line regularity Simple meters with misplaced accents (hemiola) Exploitation of ritardando and accelerando	Diatonic and chromatic lines in major & minor modes Singable melodies of a more emotional character	Emphasis on seventh, ninth and eleventh chords Chromatic progressions	Traditional forms Art song Character piece Music drama Symphonic poem Leit motif Cyclic form	Development of the possibilities of each instrumental and vocal type Rise of the virtuoso
Modern (1900-____)	Syncopation Mixed meters Polymeters Asymmetric meters	Whole tone scale Modes Synthetic scales Serial technique Micro-tones Angular melodic lines	Impressionism Polytonality Atonality Changing tonalities Chords of 4ths and 5ths Added notes Tone clusters Denial of functional harmony	Forms from all previous periods Arch form Jazz	Exploitation of instrumental and vocal color

Musical Styles

by Paul Torgrimson

TEXTURE	DYNAMICS	INSTRUMENTS	COMPOSERS		
3 to 6 voice polyphony Imitation Polychoral style	Contrast in number of voices *mf, p, f* in the bar form of the Mastersingers	Sacbut (slide trombone) Slide trumpet Timpani Bassoon Cup mouthpiece Polish geige (viola) Bass trombone French horn Oboe Circular horn	Dunstable Dufay Ockeghem Josquin Tavener Tye Cabezon Lassus Vittorio Hassler	Binchois Obrecht Willaert Milan Tallis Palestrina Byrd Marenzio Gabrieli Frescobaldi	
Vocal and instrumental contrast Development of a distinctly instrumental style	Contrast of large & small groups, loud and soft instruments, loud and soft keyboards	Violin Flute (transverse) 2-Key oboe 3-Key bassoon 2-Key clarinet Cello Pianoforte	Monteverdi Schutz Froberger Corelli A. Scarlatti Vivaldi Bach	Gibbons Carissimi Cesti Lully Purcell Couperin Handel	
Homophony	Crescendo and diminuendo Sudden changes	Pedal harp Glockenspiel	Rameau D. Scarlatti C. P. E. Bach Mannheim School	Telemann Zipoli Galuppi Pergolesi	

Homophony
  Solo quartet
  Trio quartet
  Quintet
  Symphony
  Concerto
	From *pp* to *ff*
	Crescendo and diminuendo
	Sudden changes
		Double bass
		Keyed trumpet
		Valve horn
		Valve trumpet
		English horn
			Gluck
			Haydn
			J. C. Bach
			Andre
			Cimarosa
			Viotti
			Cherubini
			Paganini
				Sammartini
				Hopkinson
				Peter
				Billings
				Mozart
				Clementi
				Beethoven
				Weber	

Fuller orchestras Larger choral groups Larger combinations of voices and instruments	From *ppp* to *ffff* Crescendo and diminuendo More sensitive changes	Albert system clarinet Piccolo Alto and Bass clarinet Heckel system bassoon E♭ Bass Saxophone BB♭ Bass Boehm system flute and clarinet Modern oboe Machine-tuned timpani Alto flute Celesta Contrabassoon Mellophone Marimba	Czerny Schubert Chopin Verdi Gounod Bruckner Wieniawski Mussorgsky Faure Puccini	Spohr Berlioz Schumann Heller Vieuxtemps J. Strauss Tchaikovsky Dvorak Sousa Mahler	Rossini Mendelssohn Liszt Wagner Franck Brahms Grieg Rimsky-Korsakoff Elgar Albeniz
From monophony to huge masses of sound Renewed emphasis on polyphonic style	From a whisper to the extreme possibilities of loudness	Complete families of wind instruments. Electronic instruments	MacDowell Sibelius Schoenberg de Falla Stravinsky Berg Honneger Sessions Gershwin Barber	Debussy Vaughan-Williams Holst Bloch Webern Villa-Lobos Milhaud Thomson Copland Menotti	R. Strauss Ives Ravel Bartok Griffes Prokofieff Hindemith Hanson Shostakovich Schuman

SUGGESTED REFERENCE MATERIALS

THEORY

Adams, Ethel G. *Introduction to Musical Understanding and Musicianship.* Belmont, California: Wadsworth Publishing Co. Inc., 1966.

Andrews, Maxson and Lotzenhiser. *Music 200.* New York: American Book Co., 1967.

Apel, Willi. *Harvard Dictionary of Music.* 2nd ed., rev. and enlgd. Cambridge, Mass.: Harvard University Press, 1969.

Dallin, Leon. *Foundations in Music Theory.* 2nd ed. with programmed exercises. Belmont, California: Wadsworth Publishing Co. Inc., 1967.

Harder, Paul. *Basic Materials in Music Theory: A Programmed Course.* 2nd ed. Boston: Allyn and Bacon, 1965.

Hindemith, Paul. *Elementary Training for Musicians.* Associated, 1949.

Orem, Preston Ware. *Harmony Book for Beginners.* Bryn Mawr, Pa.: Theodore Presser.

Peters, Charles and Yoder, Paul. *Master Theory*, books I through VI. Park Ridge, Ill.: Kjos, 1964.

Schanke, David. *The Music Arts: Volume I — Music Fundamentals.* Music Arts Publishing Co., 1966.

Ibid., Volume II — Music Harmony.

Smith, Ralph. *Elementary Music Theory.* Oliver Ditson Co.

EAR TRAINING

Arkis, Stanley and Schuckman, Herman. *An Introduction to Sight Singing.* New York: Carl Fischer, 1967.

Curtis, William. *First Steps to Ear Training.* Berklee Press, 1963.

Jersild, Jorgen. *Ear Training.* New York: G. Schirmer., 1966.

Thomson, William and DeLone, Richard P. *Introduction to Ear Training.* Belmont, California: Wadsworth Publishing Co. Inc., 1967.

MUSIC HISTORY

Berger and Clark. *Music in Perspective.* New York: Sam Fox, 1968.

Brown, Robert B. and Troth, Eugene W. *Music 100 Series: Introduction to Music History.* New York: American Book Co., 1967.

Davison, Archibald T. and Apel, Willi. *Historical Anthology of Music.* Volumes I (1949) and II (1950), rev. ed. Cambridge, Mass.: Harvard University Press.

Dorian, Frederick. *The History of Music in Performance.* New York: W. W. Norton, 1943.

Hoffer, Charles. *The Understanding of Music.* 2nd ed. Belmont, California: Wadsworth Publishing Co. Inc., 1971.

Wold, Milo A. and Cykler, Edmund. *An Outline History of Music.* Dubuque, Iowa: Wm. C. Brown, 1966.

LISTENING

Copland, Aaron. *What to Listen for in Music.* Rev. ed. New York: McGraw-Hill, 1957.

Feinberg, Saul. *Blueprints for Musical Understanding.* Series 1—3. New York: M. Witmark and Sons, 1966.

Hoffer, Charles. *The Understanding of Music.* 2nd ed. Belmont, California: Wadsworth Publishing Co. Inc., 1971.

Machlis, Joseph. *The Enjoyment of Music: An Introduction to Perceptive Listening.* 3rd ed. New York: Norton, 1970.

Moore, Douglas. *Listening to Music.* Rev. ed. New York: Norton, 1960.

Ulrich, Homer and Jordan, Bryce. *Designed for Listening: Assignments in Music.* New York: Harcourt-Brace-Jovanovich, Inc., 1967.

AESTHETICS

Philipson, Morris. *Aesthetics Today.* New York: World Publishing Co., 1961.

Schwadron, Abraham. *Aesthetics: Dimensions for Music Education.* Washington, D.C.: Music Educators National Conference (MENC), 1967.

Sessions, Roger. *The Musical Experience of Composer, Performer, and Listener.* New York: Atheneum, 1962.

chapter 7

Teaching Procedures and Techniques

The techniques discussed in this chapter are practical by their very nature and, in the hands of a competent teacher, could be applied quite successfully to almost any type of class situation. In any discussion of class teaching procedures and techniques, the question frequently arises as to whether a particular technique might be more applicable in a homogeneous as opposed to a heterogeneous grouping of instruments, or in a large as opposed to a small class setting. The small class situation can be advantageous in terms of amount and concentration of attention per individual, but the large class can sometimes be more advantageous in terms of teaching various techniques pertaining to the listening processes of intonation, balance and blend. It should be kept in mind that whatever activity the class is undertaking, whether it be practicing a difficult passage or tuning a chord, the procedure and technique used should point in some way toward the ultimate goal: to increase the level of aesthetic response and musical growth in each student. At this point we should emphasize that there is no substitute for the hours of practice necessary to learn an instrument. Real progress requires effort and dedication on the part of the student, and it is up to the teacher to inspire this devotion.

The director must always strive for *musical* rather than mechanical solutions to problems. Unfortunately, there are no solutions to some problems other than those that are termed mechanical. Then it is up to the director to insist on a musical and a sensitive approach. Practicing a scale pattern or an arpeggio, for example, must have more meaning to the student than just pushing keys or "musical calisthenics," so to speak. Too often the band director only points out the "how's" of technical development without explaining the "why's." The result can only be a kind of musical "robot" who goes through the motions, instead of a maturing musician who views and understands his technical development as a means toward an *artistic* end.

With these thoughts in mind the director is ready to proceed to the actual implementation of various teaching techniques. These techniques, applied in an imaginative way through a series of sequential learning experiences, should lead the student to an ever higher level of musical enjoyment through performance.

BEGINNING TECHNIQUES. The initial problems confronting the beginning student are assembling and caring for his instrument. Instruction can be handled in several ways and need not present any serious complications. Generally, information is disseminated through some form of lecture-demonstration. Very good pamphlets are published for each instrument, and include pictures and explanations.[1] Pamphlets can

---

[1] Available from How-To-Company, 8130 Surrey Lane, Oakland, California 94605

be conveniently carried in the instrument case and provide the student with a ready reference at all times. Film strips on the care and maintenance of instruments are also available.[2]

It is advisable that parents be encouraged to attend the first few lessons in order to be informed on how to help with practice at home. The following steps are recommended as a means whereby parents can assist in building a good beginning band class:

1. Provide the child with a good instrument in good playing condition.
2. Provide proper equipment for above: good mouthpiece; music stand; woodwind players need cleaning cloth and swab to clean out all moisture after playing, and, in addition, reed players need six good reeds; brass players need a cleaning cloth and valve oil.
3. Provide a safe place in which to keep the instrument.
4. Arrange a regular practice time, and stick to it. *Parents* need to do this most of all. Daily practice is important.
5. Home practice:

    The only way to progress is through a *regular, definite schedule*. Thirty minutes daily is recommended. This can be split into two fifteen-minute sessions for beginners. Perhaps more important is to select some arbitrary number of **repetitions** (perhaps 8 to 12) for practicing each portion of the lesson assigned for that week. The exact amount of time is relatively unimportant. What is important is *daily* practice — not for a set amount of time, but for a purpose: progress. It is suggested that the regular, daily practice time should not take the student from his favorite activity or household duties. When a student begins to study a musical instrument, the problems are many. There are very few students who will forego a favorite activity for a new and difficult task.
6. Provide a quiet place for practice with good light and a music stand.
7. Parent interest:

    Show an interest in the child's musical progress, but never make fun of the strange sounds he may produce. Lend an occasional ear to his practice, offering words of encouragement. The parent need not be musical — the teacher will correct the mistakes. Be interested and willing to listen. Just as children must be reminded to "Wash your hands" or "Brush your teeth," parents must say "This is your practice time — let's go . . . now!" (Not later or tomorrow.) The successful student does not usually come from the home of the parent who says, "You wanted to take this instrument, now it's up to you to do your practicing. I am not going to keep after you to practice. If you don't do it on your own, you will have to quit." This is not the interested parent speaking.
8. Help him to remember his instrument on lesson or band days.
9. Private lessons:

    Once a student has acquired a little success, his interest will be renewed. In the study of a musical instrument, we all reach certain plateaus where the next step upward comes with difficulty. Understanding, patience and encouragement will help the student over these plateaus. Private lessons go hand in hand with the school class lessons, and they are highly recommended.
10. Musical success needs three ingredients: *parents, pupil* and *teacher* — all working together.

---

[2] Available from Encyclopedia Brittanica, Inc., 425 N. Michigan Avenue, Chicago, Illinois

Next, a few check points for parents on how to help with home practice:

1. Set a daily practice time, and stick to it.
2. Posture.
3. Embouchure and mirror. (Check often for firm corners, chin down.)
4. Breathing. (Blow steady, sometimes soft, long tones. Increase length daily.)
5. Position. (Check proper finger, hand and arm positions.)
6. Start with mouthpiece only each day. (Brass players buzz lips first.)
   a. Check embouchure in mirror.
   b. Blow long and steady tones.
   c. Work for clear tones.
7. Assemble instrument with care.
8. Practice tone-holding with a clock. (Start with three to five seconds, then increase daily to twenty seconds or more. Work for full, steady, clear, pleasant tones.)
9. Practice from method book. (Use four steps of practice for each example.)
   a. Count and tap.
   b. Name notes and tap.
   c. Sing note names and tap.
   d. Play and tap.
   (Be sure to count steadily and evenly, in a sharp, concise manner.)
10. Go slowly and work daily for better *tone, embouchure, position, breathing,* and *counting.*

The first lesson is one of the most important lessons the student will ever take. The *first* experience is usually the most significant for any individual. The teacher must strive to continually provide "first" experiences for his students. This is one of the keys to sustaining interest. The ability of the teacher to provide sequential experiences, small as well as large, is one of the most significant factors relevant to successful teaching. The goals to be accomplished should be spelled out in detail so that the student knows exactly what is expected. The following material is provided as an example of how the first lesson might be approached — it is not intended to be the *only* good way but one which might be adapted to various situations:

FIRST LESSON: Mouthpiece Alone

   I. Form correct embouchure without mouthpiece:
      A. Teacher explains and demonstrates the correct embouchure formation.
      B. Let student
         1. Watch embouchure formation carefully.
         2. Form the embouchure and *observe in a pocket mirror.*
         3. Blow air through the embouchure.
  II. Compare correct embouchure pictures in available books.
 III. Teacher places the mouthpiece on student's lips and helps form an embouchure.
 IV. Then, student takes mouthpiece.
         1. Forms embouchure with it.
         2. While watching in mirror, blows through mouthpiece without changing embouchure.
         3. Takes mouthpiece off and repeats whole operation.

V. Points to observe while building an embouchure:
1. Hold corners of the mouth firmly in place.
2. Point the chin down.
3. Relax the throat, and blow through mouthpiece as though polishing glasses or panting like a dog.
4. Do not use the tongue yet!
5. Be patient. Forming the correct embouchure is the most important part of learning how to play an instrument.

FIRST LESSON: Correct Breathing
(also known as Proper Diaphragmatic Breathing and Support)

Step One: Hands at sides, bend over until weight hangs on hips. Fill lungs to capacity, and then hiss the air out slowly.

Step Two: Hands behind head—elbows out. Inhale suddenly—exhale slowly—(over and over).

Step Three: Lie face up on the floor. Next breathe deeply and notice what happens, i.e., what parts of the body move while breathing and how they move. Notice the feel of breathing while in this position. Take a deep breath and exhale. Do this ten times, *slowly*, and stay as relaxed as possible.

Step Four: Stand up. Think of the lungs as a balloon. Fill up the balloon completely, and softly say "Hup" so you fill your mouth also. Then hold for an instant, think of the note you are to play, aim, then release. (The diaphragm should have the feeling of grunting as its pressure is used to move the air steadily.) Check daily: with hands on hips, try to fill up all around the waist.

Step Five: Take a pocket-size mirror, open the mouth and throat *wide* and watch closely in the mirror while inhaling. Now do the same thing when exhaling, and try to get the same feeling.

Step Six: Take a deep breath through the mouth (the same manner as when lying down on the back), and then exhale very *slowly* through the lips for about 15-20 seconds. Then take another deep breath and repeat exhaling slowly through the lips. All breathing while playing an instrument should feel exactly this way.

Step Seven: Next take a deep breath and blow a small stream of air against the back of the hand. A stream of cold air suggests inadequate support, and this is wrong. A warm air stream usually means good support. (To obtain a warm air stream, think of trying to moisten glasses to polish them, etc.)

Step Eight: Take a thin sheet of paper (small piece), place it against a wall or the middle of a music stand, and practice blowing air through the lips toward the paper, and see how long the paper will stay on the wall or music stand with this air pressure.

Step Nine: Try to whistle, sustaining the tone as long as possible.

Step Ten: Swim often—especially underwater!

THINGS TO AVOID:

    Avoid tightening the throat, chin or tongue.

    Avoid raising the chest and shoulders when breathing.

    Avoid pulling in or drawing in the stomach when inhaling.

    Avoid leaning back.

    Avoid poor posture—the worst enemy of correct breathing.

PRACTICE CORRECT BREATHING ALL DAY, ALL NIGHT, EVERY DAY, EVERY NIGHT.

Once the mechanics of the first lessons have been mastered, ensuing lessons become a blend of drill on what has been introduced previously and introductions to new experiences and challenges. Proceed slowly and thoroughly in the beginning stages. Patience is the word! The following is a suggested approach in the teaching of beginning trumpet players:

A. The First Lesson:
1. Embouchure should be formed first — without the mouthpiece or instrument.
2. Lip buzz to help form the embouchure, but avoid overtightness.
3. *Have mirrors available.* Very important.
4. Important points about the embouchure:
    a. The muscles that produce a smile should work against those that produce a pucker.
    b. Teeth parted, jaw in relaxed position.
    c. Chin firm and pointed down, corners set downward.
    d. Lips should be moist.
5. Opening of lips for air to come through should look like the end of an oboe or bassoon reed.
6. Place mouthpiece on the embouchure.
    a. Teacher will place the mouthpiece while the student is blowing air through the embouchure.
    b. Approximately 1/2 upper lip and 1/2 lower lip. Strive to keep away from red of the lips.
7. Student continues to blow air through mouthpiece until a pitch is attained.
    a. Try for a concert F, then work down to B♭.
    b. Work up from F to B♭.
8. No tonguing in the initial stages.
9. Familiar tunes can be played on the mouthpiece.
10.. Encourage home practice in front of a mirror.
11. It is recommended that the student use only the mouthpiece until a free buzz (with some degree of pitch control) can be mastered.
12. The student should be given the instrument only after reasonable progress has been made on step No. 11.
13. Demonstrate good playing position as soon as the instrument is given to the student.

B. The Second Lesson:
1. Begin with a review of the first lesson.
2. Introduce tonguing.
    a. Have student say "too."
    b. Tongue with mouthpiece, using tones produced most easily.
    c. Check to be sure that the embouchure is not changed with addition of tonguing.
3. Show student the book he will use, and discuss rhythm and notation.

C. The Third Lesson:
1. Begin with review.
2. Continue each lesson with some time on mouthpiece alone.

D. Conclusion:
1. First lessons are very important, and it should be emphasized that the embouchure formed now will be very permanent.
2. Try not to give student more than one problem to solve at any one time.

One observes that procedures are spelled out in great detail with this approach. Similar procedures for each instrument should be drawn up in detail. Procedures should be adapted to various groupings of instruments using this type of approach. Obviously, the application of any procedure must always be vigorous, enthusiastic, optimistic, and geared to the overall capability of the particular group. Procedures must also be systematic. The teaching technique used for developing a specific skill should always be repeated in *exactly* the same way as it was originally presented to avoid confusion on the part of the student and to get complete benefit from drill work. One of the basic principles in developing a skill is that repeated actions become reflexes, and reflexes become habits. Once repeated action has progressed to a habit, it is extremely difficult to break. Close surveillance can help assure that these repeated actions are the desired actions for positive results.

Positive results can only be obtained through proper practice. Two things should be remembered concerning practice: 1. The student must know what is expected concerning practice requirements; 2. He must be guided in the development of proper practice habits. The following examples illustrate an approach to answering these questions:

PRACTICE REQUIREMENTS FOR BEGINNING BAND MEMBERS

1. Practice requirement: 15 minutes daily.
2. Total practice weekly: Total of 105 minutes weekly.
3. Practice record must be signed by parent weekly.
4. Only excuses for not practicing are: a. Sickness. b. Instrument in for repairs.
5. Keep practice record in case at all times and put practice time on record (in minutes only).
6. Band members may go over the required time if they wish.

- -

Tear along dotted line and return to:

(Director) _____

I have read the above requirements for band practice on my instrument and will fulfill those requirements daily and weekly to the best of my abilities.

Student _____ Parent _____ Phone _____

SUGGESTIONS ON HOW TO PRACTICE
For Beginning Band Members

PRACTICE PROPERLY — on the assigned exercises. Don't try to see how *loud* or how *high* you can play.

1. Count aloud and tap all exercises.

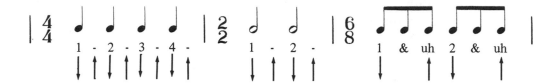

Raise the foot at *exactly* the right time. Use an evenly divided beat: "down-up, down-up, down-up," etc. The foot stays down as long as it stays up. Do not "bounce" the foot. Count and tap, strict and even — like soldiers marching.

2. Breathing exercises.
   a. Breathe deep.
   b. Breathe in for four slow counts, hold it for four slow counts, then breathe out for four slow counts.
3. Embouchure and Mirror.
   a. Firm corners, chin down.
   b. Check in mirror.
4. Mouthpiece and Mirror. (Brass players buzz lips first.)
   a. Check embouchure in mirror.
   b. Blow long, steady tones.
   c. Work for clear, pleasing tones.
5. See how long you can hold mouthpiece tones.
6. Practice the above five items fifteen minutes daily.
7. Ask Mom or Dad to help.

OTHER IMPORTANT ITEMS.

1. Posture: Sit tall, practice standing sometimes.
2. Position: Check proper finger, hand, and arm positions.
3. Assembly: Put instrument together *with care.*
4. Practice in method book:
   a. Four steps of practice for each exercise:
      1. Count and tap.
      2. Name notes and tap.
      3. Sing note names and tap.
      4. Play and tap.
5. Go slowly.
6. Work daily for better tone, embouchure, position, counting, breathing and tonguing.

This type of procedure has the advantage of offering something specific and systematic that will fulfill the two objectives mentioned earlier.

No mention has been made of published method books that are available to the present day band director for use with the beginning band program. The question here is not really *what* book to use but rather *how* to use a book to the greatest advantage. An attempt has been made to provide the director with an approach to teaching that will provide favorable results with any number of good books.

INTERMEDIATE AND ADVANCED TECHNIQUES. The general concept of teaching band instruments at the intermediate level seems to be one of polishing and refining playing techniques and habits (with concentrated effort on fundamentals), plus widening the musical experiences. A majority of the intermediate band programs throughout the country seem to be oriented toward the training-concept idea rather than performance. This indicates that time is spent on technical studies, rhythm exercises, intonation, and scales, through a general corrective approach. Fundamental habits and skills must be reviewed to be maintained.

The concept of ensemble playing should be developed further. At the intermediate level most students are at least acquainted with some combination of solo, ensemble, and full band experiences. Due to the lack of opportunity for individual lessons for a majority of students, it becomes imperative for the director to use techniques that will produce positive results and may be applied to a group situation. One way this may be accomplished is through an effectively structured warm-up.

The warm-up should include long tones, scales, arpeggios, and rhythm patterns. Emphasis should be placed on tone quality, intonation, balance, blend, attacks, releases, and hand positions, with their associated fingering problems. Daily work on lip slurs for brasses should also be a part of the warm-up. The warm-up should be extremely concentrated—not lengthy to the point of boredom. It should set the tone, both mentally and physically, for the rest of the rehearsal. A well-planned approach is the key—one that will always serve to get the most from the time available.

The accompanying warm-up is designed for full band but could easily be adapted to smaller classes and even to individual study.

BAND WARM UP

Norman, Oklahoma Public Schools

Ex. 1—Two Breath Impulses Per Beat   Ex. 2—Three Breath Impulses Per Beat
(Explanation of "Breath Impulse" found later in this chapter.)

Ex. 3—Four Impulses Per Beat   Ex. 4—Six Impulses Per Beat

Ex. 5—8-5-1 Slurs, Two Impulses Per Beat

Ex. 6—5 - Note Slurs

5 - Note Slurs, cont.

Ex. 7—Third Slurs

Third Slurs, cont.

Third Slurs, cont.

Third Slurs, cont.

Ex. 8—Tonguing

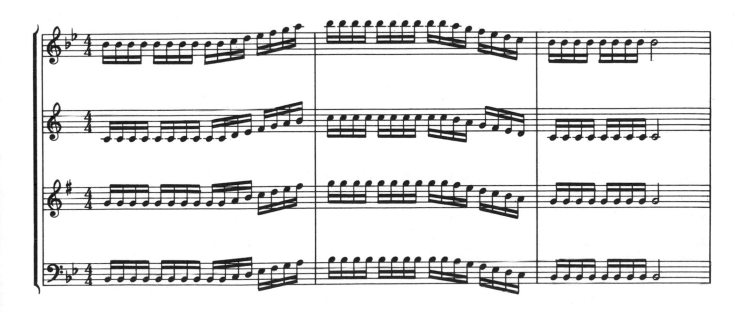

Tonguing, cont.

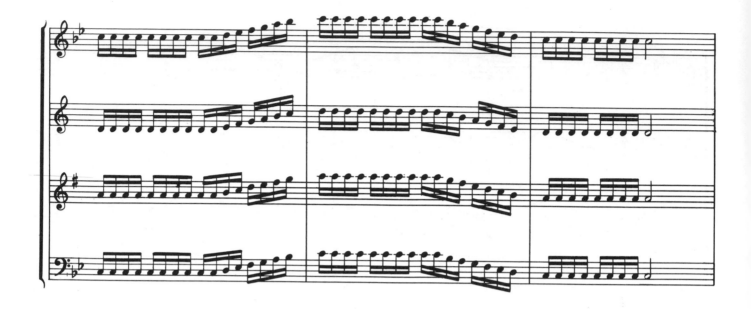

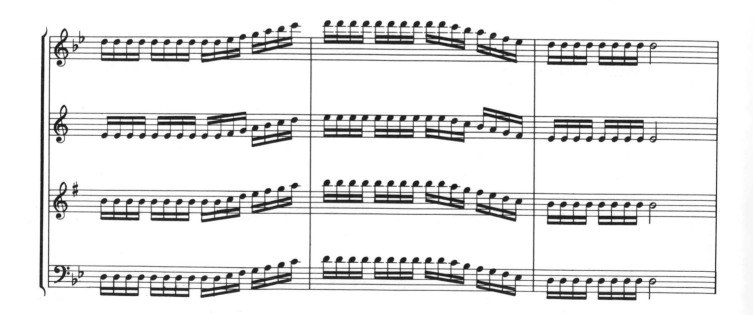

Tonguing, cont.

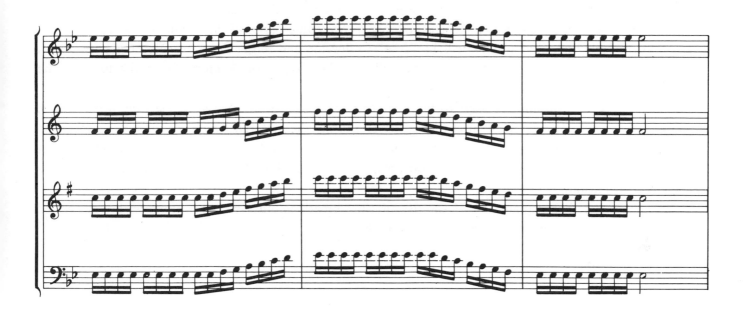

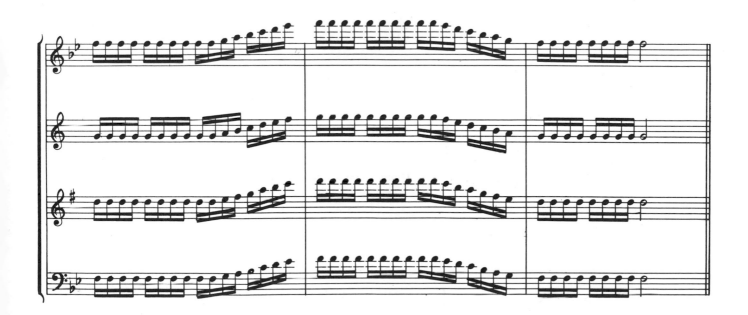

At this point some mention should be made concerning an approach to the teaching of rhythm. Accurate and rapid rhythmic interpretation, along with playing correct notes, is a great help in the development of technique. Technique is really the fundamental upon which so much depends. If a student is forever struggling to play the right note at the right time, the chances are small that he will ever advance in any great degree in the areas of tone, phrasing, and intonation. Even more important, his ability to contribute artistically to the ensemble is practically non-existent because of his weakening effect on the precision of the group. If it is possible to overcome basic rhythm problems within the first year or two of playing, the student will be "free" to develop and refine those aspects of playing which contribute to an artistic performance . . . he will then be able to think more about the music as he plays, and less about mechanics.

There are any number of ways to teach rhythm. The key to the successful teaching of rhythm is in a detailed, systematic and sequential process of presenting the material which is intended to solve the problem. Techniques that demand physical involvement are invaluable in the solution of rhythm problems. Counting out loud, tapping the foot, clapping, and the breath impulse are all valid techniques that deserve attention.

A more detailed explanation of the use of the "breath impulse system" along with a system of counting is presented here for consideration at this time.

1.
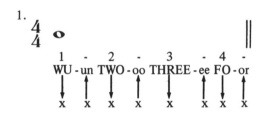

x = indicates breath impulse

↓↑ = indicates foot tap

Count out loud.   WU—un   TWO—oo   THREE—ee   FO—or

Tap steadily while counting.

Play throughout the range of the instrument, eight impulses per whole note, while simultaneously tapping foot.

2.
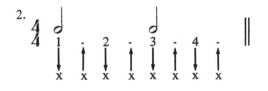

Same as above, except for articulation.

(Four impulses per half note.)

3.
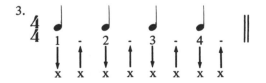

Same, except for articulation.

(Two impulses per quarter note.)

4. 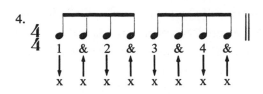 ONE and, TWO and, THREE and, FOUR and

(One impulse per eighth note.)

5.  ONE—ee—and—uh, TWO—ee—and—uh, etc.
(No impulse in this pattern.)

It is important that the foot is raised and lowered at exactly the right time with a sharp movement.

Like this: ⌐‾‾⌐‾‾ ; not like this: ∿∿∿ . In other words, the foot must
1 ee & uh 2 ee & uh   1 ee & uh 2 ee & uh
remain down on "ee" and remain up on "uh." (The breath impulse can be used in subdivision a little later by simply giving twice as many impulses on a whole note, being sure that the foot taps precisely.)

The same principle can be applied to triple meter as follows:

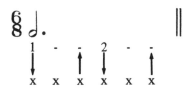 Played with six impulses. Raise foot precisely on the *third part* of the beat.

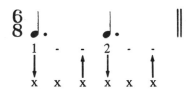 Same as above, except for articulation. (Three impulses per note.)

 No impulse. Raise foot precisely on third part of beat.

 WU-un-uh TOO-oo-uh   Two impulses per quarter note. Raise foot precisely on "uh." Tap steadily.

85

The breath impulse idea can be developed from this framework into all rhythmic combinations and meters. The mechanics of the impulse are the same as the "panting dog" principle. A sudden thrust of air is emitted from the lungs by contraction of the diaphragm. This is a device that would be used primarily in beginning and early intermediate stages or until the student has a definite "feel" for rhythm. It would be presented sequentially, taking care to give the student one problem to solve at a time.

The breath impulse is especially effective because it allows the student to play the instrument and, at the same time, to be physically involved, to a great degree, in the rhythmic process. The breath impulse has the added benefits of teaching proper diaphragmatic breathing and establishing a basis for the development of vibrato. The breath impulse is an excellent device to help the student feel the subdivision of beat at an early stage of development. The lack of a feeling for the subdivision of beat is no doubt responsible for a multitude of rhythmic errors.

The breath impulse system, as presented here, is not intended to be more than an outline. These basic ideas would have to be enlarged and applied by the imaginative director in a detailed and sequential manner. Initially, the mechanics would be the most important thing to get across. In the early stages, the breath impulse will sound rhythmic and even mechanical, but it will evolve gradually into an artistic sound as the impulse becomes a free diaphragm vibrato. (For instruments where vibrato is not usually part of the characteristic tone, as in the case of French horns and clarinets, the vibrato concept is discarded.)

It is not important whether the breath impulse system or some other system is used to teach rhythm. What is important is the fact that *some* definite system must be employed to produce the desired result.

The fact that in many school band programs most rhythm problems can and are being solved within the first two years of study is reason enough for any director to examine and re-examine his approach to this most vital fundamental of performance. It can be done!

Intonation problems demand constant attention. Most of them can be traced to: 1. Improper listening habits and/or training; 2. Acoustically imperfect instruments (where proper adjustment is impossible); 3. Lack of maturity (i.e., comprehension); 4. Deficient physical characteristics; 5. Faulty training in tone production and control. Students must be taught to listen for the "beat phenomenon," and to recognize intervals and the relevant harmonic structure of music. Listening must be constant and critical. The stroboconn, strobotuner, and tone generator or tuning bar are all mechanical devices that can be used to help instruct students. The strobotuner is considerably less expensive than the stroboconn and can be used as a substitute. The strobotuner gives the student an opportunity to visualize pitch characteristics. Mechanical devices should be used only as an aid in understanding pitch problems. The student must train his ear in proper listening habits through slow practice of scale and interval exercises. The study of major and minor scales with an understanding of the theoretical basis for scales in harmonic, pythagorean and equal temperaments is necessary. The student must have an understanding of what causes the beat phenomenon. He must recognize the quality and characteristic sound of the various intervals. Taping and playback is an excellent device for training the listening processes. The basic principles of proper tone production for each instrument must be maintained for good intonation. Proper breath support, embouchure, and playing position all relate to intonation. Slow practice on unisonal studies is imperative — this gives the student time to listen to himself and others.

It is necessary that the student have a source on which he can rely to guide him in developing a good concept of *tone quality*. Recordings of artists on each instrument (in solo and ensemble) should be available to the student. The practice of recording and playback by tape is helpful. Live performances by guest clinicians or groups and demonstrations by the director should be utilized.

The open throat is most important to the production of a free, resonant tone. There should be no restrictions between the source of the air column in the lungs and its expulsion from the bell of the instrument. This means an open throat, teeth apart (on brasses), and as large an oral cavity as possible.

Mirrors should be utilized to aid in the formation of a correct *embouchure*. A small mirror secured in the lyre of the instrument might prove useful. Direct observation of someone (teacher or student) with a correct embouchure is a common technique. Many method books have excellent pictures of correct embouchure and playing position. Visual aids will be the most helpful in guiding correct embouchure formation.

Strengthening of the embouchure can be achieved through appropriate exercises. Lip slurs, long tones, extended pedal and lip-flexibility exercises help to strengthen the embouchure of brass players, and extended scales, long tones, and arpeggios will aid woodwind players.

The *attack and release* concept is a vital part of any performance and demands attention. Every note has three parts: attack, duration, and release.

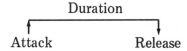

A widely used beginning approach is the legato attack. Four quarter notes would be played as follows:

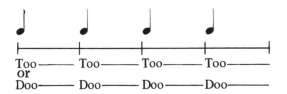

The idea is to "blow through" the note and let the attack of the second note take care of the release of the first note. Spacing between notes could come later, as follows:

Too——— Too——— Too——— Too———

Care should be taken that the tongue doesn't "clip" the release, such as:

Too———t Too———t Too———t Too———t

The release is with the breath and not the tongue. The basic things to keep in mind are: 1. Attack lightly, 2. Blow through the note, and 3. Don't "clip" the release.

The exact placement of the tongue in articulation is a point on which even the experts disagree. The only valid criteria for judging is the result — it must be artistic.

Proper *hand positions and posture* should be ingrained early. Sometimes a problem of hand position or posture will persist to the intermediate or advanced level. If this should occur, a musical solution sometimes works best. Prescribe literature to the student that demands correct hand position. For example, scale and arpeggio studies in sharp keys at progressively faster tempi will tend to "force" correct hand position on the clarinet. Use the metronome to gradually increase the tempo and to provide the student with a definite guide in measuring progress. The metronome can be an invaluable aid in measuring the technical progress of a group on certain warm-up exercises when speed is an objective.

The competition which exists when two or more players perform together should not be overlooked as an opportunity to motivate students in a class setting. Challenges, "play-offs," and contests of various types have appeal to the young musician, provided they are fair and well-planned. Recognition for work well done will many times spur the student to extra effort. The challenge system should always emphasize specific musical values rather than general, somewhat obscure qualities. For example, challenges should emphasize such things as tone quality, articulation, fingering problems, or anything specific, rather than just a piece of music or a particular passage. Challenge systems must spell out in detail what is expected of the students.

It should be pointed out that there is a weakness in any type of voluntary challenge system. After a period of time it becomes apparent that the outgoing, more talented person evolves as the active participant in this type of system. The shy, more timid, less talented person soon becomes content to settle back and sit near the bottom of the section because he knows he can't "beat" the more talented person. As a result he will tend to quit growing musically unless some other means of motivation is used.

Study has shown that there is an alternative to the voluntary challenge system that is much more sound educationally and which will not permit a student to get "lost in the shuffle," so to speak. The alternative is to give well-planned weekly (periodic) assignments to be played by all students individually for a grade. The size of the class and the amount of time available will determine the length of the assignment and the length of time for each student to play. Individual attention may vary from no more than a minute to as much time as is available. The Norman, Oklahoma Try-Out Form illustrates one way that the individual "play-off" may be utilized. Once things are organized, this system can be administered quite rapidly.

Key for Scoring		NORMAN, OKLAHOMA PUBLIC SCHOOLS
I = 1		Band/Orchestra Try-Out Form
I- = 2		
II+ = 3		
II = 4	Audition Material: _____
II- = 5		
III = 6	Recorded in Grade Book by: _____
IV = 7		
V = 8	Name of Section/Band _____ . Date _____ Auditioner _____
(I+ = 0)		

NAME OF STUDENT	Tone	*Scale*	*Chromatic*	*3rds*	*Page 4*	*Counting*	Score	Grade	Chair
1.									
2.									
3.									

This system does not permit a student to withdraw from active individual participation and will help insure continued musical growth by all students. The basic difference in the two systems is that one is voluntary and the other is not. Every student is receiving at least some personal attention under the assignment plan. This individual attention can have the added benefit of giving a feeling of importance to each student, which is necessary to any program.

BASIC ELEMENTS OF INSTRUCTION FOR THE BAND INSTRUMENTS

WOODWINDS. There are certain fundamental aspects of tone production on the woodwind instruments which are relatively common to each. These common elements are:
  a. Position (instrument and mouthpiece).
  b. Embouchure (position of lip, jaw and facial muscles).
  c. Use of the Tongue (position and action).
  d. Breath Support (air column).

FLUTE

a. Position.
  1. It is essential that the blowhole of the flute be centered on the opening formed when the lips are drawn into a small "too" formation.
  2. The instrument is held horizontally, so the line of the lips is parallel with the line of the flute.

b. Embouchure.
  1. The muscles of the face, lips, and jaw must be positioned to control the air stream into the blowhole of the flute.
  2. Approximately 60 percent of the air column enters the flute through the blowhole.
  3. The splitting of the air column causes the tone-producing vibrations.

c. Use of the Tongue.
  Starting a sound on the flute requires the following action: Starting from a position of rest (as low as possible in the mouth), the tongue moves quickly upward so that the tip of the tongue produces a sudden or sharp "too" or "tee," and then allows the air to continue in its directed way with intensity and firmness.

d. Breath Support.
  1. Breath support, air column, and intensity are terms which are used in describing the proper method for blowing a wind instrument. Fundamentally the same for all wind instruments, differences lie in the characteristic amount of resistance to the flow of air offered by the various instruments and in their size.
  2. Breath originates from the lungs and is supported by the diaphragm.
    a. Tension from the diaphragm supports the breath as the instrument is being played.
    b. The air column should be free to flow unrestricted from point of origin.
    c. This freedom requires an open throat, a large oral cavity, and a sound-producing source which vibrates freely.

The resistance of each wind instrument varies characteristically: Flute offers least, and oboe, most. But all require some amount of intensity and concentration of the air column.

OBOE

a. Position.
1. The mouthpiece of the oboe is a double read.
2. The reed should be placed between the lips, with both lips slightly rolled in over the teeth.

b. Embouchure.
1. Embouchure is of extreme importance to type of tone and control of pitch.
2. With the double reed placed between the lips and the lips rolled over the teeth, the lips close around the reed so that no air can escape.
3. The corners of the mouth must be taut and the chin muscles smooth.
4. The pressure of the lips must not pinch the reed.

c. Use of the Tongue.
1. Position of the tongue is much the same as in playing clarinet.
2. The tip of the tongue lightly touches the tip of the reed (the tongue is arched and comes to the reed from above with a very short movement).

d. Breath Support. (See description of breath support in flute section.)
The principles remain the same, but the importance of support is emphasized here because of the characteristic resistance of the oboe and consequent need for more intensity.

BASSOON

a. Position.
1. Like the oboe, the bassoon mouthpiece is a double reed.
2. The reed is positioned straight into the mouth.
3. The lips should be slightly pushed forward, as if pronouncing "pooh."
4. The muscles of the lips close firmly about the reed.

b. Embouchure.
1. Bassoon embouchure differs from that of oboe in that the lips do not roll in over the teeth for bassoon, but are pushed forward and around the reed.
2. There must be no pinching of the reed.
3. The lower teeth should be placed behind the upper teeth (in an overbite position) by allowing the lower jaw to recede.

c. Use of the Tongue.
Tonguing and tongue position are very similar to that for playing the oboe. However, the tongue does not need to be carried as high in the mouth with the different reed angle, and the tonguing is more direct, with short movement and light contact with the reed.

d. Breath Support. (See description of breath support for flute.)

CLARINET

a. Position.
1. The clarinet mouthpiece must enter the mouth at as near a vertical position as possible.
2. The positon of the reed in the mouth must be as near as possible to the point where the reed separates from the lay of the mouthpieaces.
3. The upper teeth will rest only a short distance from the tip of the mouthpiece when the reed is in the correct position.

b. Embouchure.

As with other wind instruments, the embouchure for the clarinet determines the quality of tone produced.

1. With the mouthpiece placed as nearly vertical as possible, the lower lip should be rolled in slightly, with only the red of the lip directly over the lower teeth.
2. The lips should be taut, with tension applied from the corners.
3. The chin muscles should be stretched smoothly down, with pointed chin.
4. Pressure of the lips and teeth must not pinch the reed.

c. Use of the Tongue.

1. The tongue needs to be as low as possible in the mouth when starting a sound on the clarinet.
2. The tip of the tongue should be pointed to touch the reed as near the tip as possible.
3. As the tongue comes into contact with the reed, air pressure is applied.
4. As the tongue is pulled away, the flow of air causes the reed to vibrate properly and produce the sound.

d. Breath Support. (See description of breath support for flute.)

1. Intensity: Clarinet tones are never relaxed and are not pinched but are as "high" as each tone will take.
2. Since the clarinet does not use vibrato, tone quality depends on the concentration and intensity of the air column.
3. Intonation is controlled by voicing in the throat, moving the back part of the tongue to simulate the syllables "ah," "oo," "ee" through low, middle and upper registers.
4. Listen for E natural (fourth space) as a tone which is indicative of how a student is playing. A well-played tone in this register of the clarinet will indicate good embouchure development and good support.

SAXOPHONE

a. Position.

1. Position of the mouthpiece in playing the saxophone is similar, in principle, to that of the clarinet. The main difference lies in the fact that the saxophone mouthpiece enters straight into the mouth.
2. The lower lip should contact the reed at the point where the reed separates from the lay of the mouthpiece, with the upper teeth in contact with the mouthpiece in relation to that position.

b. Embouchure.

1. The embouchure for playing saxophone is similar to that for playing clarinet, except that considerably less tension is needed in lips and face muscles.
2. The lips close firmly around the mouthpiece so air cannot escape.

c. Use of the Tongue.

1. Basically, use the same tonguing styles as clarinet.
2. The tongue is as low as possible in the mouth, and only the tip of the tongue comes in contact with the reed.

d. Breath Support. (See description of breath support for flute.)

1. The tone on saxophone should be "centered" but not overblown, with less intensity

91

required than for the clarinet. No bite or increase in support is necessary on saxophone, since the acoustical construction allows in-tune octaves without these changes.

2. Place the tone by simulating the syllables "ah," "oo," and "ee" through low, middle and upper registers and using good support in all registers.

BRASSES. The basic fundamentals of teaching brass instruments include the following six points relatively common to each instrument:

a. Position.
b. Setting the Embouchure.
c. Use of the Tongue.
d. Breath Support.
e. Voicing (Control of the Air Stream).
f. Special Problems.

CORNET/TRUMPET

a. Position.
   1. Almost the entire weight of the instrument is supported by the left hand.
   2. The left hand third finger is used to operate the third slide tuning ring (unless a first slide trigger is used).
   3. The fingers of the right hand are curved in a natural position and rest with fingertips on the valves . . . *not* extended over the valves. Extending fingers over valves makes fast fingering difficult and sometimes causes pistons to stick.
   4. The valves *must* be pressed straight down.
b. Setting the Embouchure.
   1. The lips are brought together gently, with a slight pucker (say "em"). Turn the lips under very slightly.
      a. Firm the muscles at the corner of the mouth. *Do not* form a tight smile.
      b. The contour of the chin tends to be slightly pointed, with flat and firm cheeks. Watch for puffing cheeks and small air pockets.
   2. Form the embouchure, and blow a steady stream of air through a small opening in the center of the lips. Blow the column of air *through* the mouthpiece, not at it. Have the student produce a buzzing sound without the mouthpiece, then with the mouthpiece.
   3. Place the mouthpiece as near the center of the lips as possible. (The shape and size of the front teeth will cause slight variations.)
      a. Ask the student to play in front of a mirror and check the center position often.
      b. The vertical position will be approximately one-half on the upper lip and one-half on the lower lip. This will vary with individual jaw, lip, and teeth formations.
      c. It is difficult to notice an off-center mouthpiece from the side. (This habit is easy to break at first, extremely difficult later.) Check each student frequently from the front.
   4. The lips in a normal amount of firmness will play a note in the middle register (second line G).
      a. Lips will be brought together more for high notes . . . into a more firm pucker.

    b. Loosen or relax the lips for lower notes.

5. Encourage the student to keep a relaxed jaw and throat while playing. Tension in the throat causes many students to press the mouthpiece rigidly against the lips.

c. Use of the Tongue.

  1. With the lips closed, place the tip of the tongue behind the upper teeth.

    a. The exact placement will vary with the individual size and shape of the tongue.

    b. Avoid placing the tongue between the teeth or touching the lip in any way.

  2. Several syllables may be used for tonguing.

    a. The most common syllable is "too." Sometimes using "thu" will help with placement.

    b. "Doo" will work better for some students. Use "too" for marcato, "doo" for legato.

  3. Action of the tongue.

    a. The air stream is directed at the tongue, which releases it like a valve by pulling slightly away from the teeth. Always begin the action with the air stream — to get the feeling of blowing through the instrument, not at it.

    b. The tongue does not *stop* a tone. (Don't allow "toot.")

  4. Problems to watch for.

    a. Check for jaw movement when tonguing. Jaw movement is not necessary, and indicates poor placement, or tonguing between the teeth.

    b. Check for throat movement while tonguing. This indicates the back of tongue is dropping down for each attack, and affects each tone. (See voicing section.) Only the first inch or so of the tongue is needed.

    c. Try to make the student *aware* of how he tongues. Most think they tongue one way and really do it another.

    d. Have each student check his mirror for problems (a and b).

d. Breath Support.

  1. Have the student relax and take a series of breaths, as if out of breath . . . then set breath against tongue or lip, as in "hup" or "hut." Feel an open throat and a constant pulling up.

  2. Try a "cough" or "blow out a candle" to get the feel of a moving diaphragm.

  3. Have the student stand with back, head, and heels flat against a wall and breathe. (Improper breathing is difficult under these circumstances.)

  4. Avoid movement of shoulders and upper chest when breathing.

  5. Emphasize that proper breathing is relaxed and natural, not something abnormal.

  6. Constantly stress that the breath must flow through the brass instrument, even when articulating. *Keep that support.*

  7. The basic difference in breathing between brasses and woodwinds is that, for high notes, brasses require a much greater speed and volume of wind. (See voicing section.)

e. Voicing.

  1. The back of the tongue is used to form the syllables "ah," "oo," "ee." The action of the tongue when whistling is a good example.

  2. A combination of three actions is necessary to vary a pitch:

    a. First, tightening or loosening of the lips.

    b. Second, action of the tongue — "ah" for low, "oo" for medium, and "ee" for high.

  c. Third, variation of speed and volume of air — increased greatly for high notes, and decreased, with open throat, for low notes.

 3. Keep throat relaxed as much as possible.

f. Special Problems.

 1. Incorrect embouchure.

  a. Turning lips under excessively, or especially, turning lower lip under, leaving upper lip in a normal position.

  b. Puffing out cheeks or developing air pockets around lips. (Watch below as well as above lips.)

  c. Playing with mouthpiece too far to one side, too high or too low on the lips.

 2. Incorrect tonguing.

  a. Bad tongue position, i.e., between teeth or touching lips.

  b. Using too much tongue causes throat to move and affects pitch of each note.

  c. Movement of the jaw for each note, affecting pitch.

 3. Incorrect position.

  a. Holding instrument with right hand (only).

  b. Fingers extending over valves.

  c. Holding instrument pointing down or resting on knee (small students).

 4. Incorrect breathing habits and control.

  a. Relaxing breath support while tonguing, starting breath with each separate note.

  b. Lack of support on high notes, leading to pinched tones and tenseness in the throat and jaw.

 5. Teach the student to press valves down quickly and firmly. When playing a fast passage, "bang" the valves down.

FRENCH HORN

a. Position.

 1. The most accepted method of holding the horn is seated, resting the lower edge of the bell on the right thigh, with the bell pointing so as not to be blocked by any part of the body.

 2. The player should sit forward in the chair so the mouthpipe of the horn will be at least horizontal, preferably sloping down a little, and face the director. (Small children tend to play with horn pointing up, or with the body of the horn held almost vertical.) The body of the horn should be at approximately 45°.

 3. The left hand holds the instrument in position by placing the thumb under the mouthpipe and little finger in the hook. The left hand and wrist should be relaxed so that the fingers can comfortably operate (press) the valves.

 4. Right hand position is extremely important.

  a. The thumb and fingers are held closely together.

  b. The right hand is pressed against the far side of the bell, with the thumb knuckle touching the upper side of the bell.

  c. By leaving the fingers stable and pivoting the palm of the hand to open and close the bell opening, the tone of the instrument and the pitch can be controlled.

        1. As the palm is opened, pitch goes higher.

        2. As the palm is closed or cupped, pitch will drop.

    d. *Never* allow the student to play with the hand resting outside the bell or in any other position than the correct one.

  b. Setting the Embouchure.

    1. Form the lip into a "puckered smile" or say "em." This brings the correct muscles into play for a correct horn embouchure. Do not allow the cheeks or areas around the lip to puff out while playing. Keep chin slightly pointed.

    2. Contracting the muscles of the embouchure (bringing lips together) will enable higher notes to be played. Relaxing the embouchure (dropping jaw away) will help low notes.

    3. Keep a relaxed jaw and throat (open feeling in throat).

    4. Place the mouthpiece near the horizontal center of the lips. Slight variations of the teeth may cause movement to one side. This should not get too pronounced.

    5. Vertical placement is generally 2/3 upper lip and 1/3 lower. This is not difficult for beginners. Check carefully when changing a cornet or trumpet player to horn. *Start out* with the correct placement, and the changeover is not a problem.

    6. The mouthpipe will generally extend horizontally from lips, depending on jaw formation.

  c. Use of the Tongue.

    1. The fundamentals of tonguing are similar to those of other brass instruments. (See cornet/trumpet.)

    2. A softer tonguing attack — "too," but not quite a "thoo" — makes a lighter seal and allows rapid, light tonguing. One authority says that the vowel "oo" works better than "ah" in forming a correct horn embouchure.

    3. Remember to think of the tongue as a valve that interrupts the air stream. Keep the breath going.

  d. Breath Support.

    1. Principles of breath support are similar to other brass instruments. (See cornet/trumpet.)

    2. The horn uses the breathing process as a control device more than other instruments, since the upper partials lie so close together, and the lip cannot make the minute adjustments necessary. Adequate support plus use of the voicing principle will make control of high notes much easier.

    3. Farkas[1] describes three breathing rules:

      a. Deep inhalation . . . diaphragm contraction, abdominal and waist expansion, and rib expansion all working together and done rapidly, as if gasping.

      b. Exhalation with pressure . . . upward pressure and inward pressure of the muscles described above (a).

      c. Resistance . . . arching the back of the tongue to create air pressure.

  e. Voicing.

    1. Back of tongue and throat combine to form syllables to control speed of wind and form resistance to air stream:

      a. Low register, use "ah."

      b. Middle register, use "eh" or "oo."

---

1 Philip Farkas, *The Art of French Horn Playing* (Evanston, Ill.: Summy-Birchard Co., 1956), p. 30.

f. Special Problems.
   1. Incorrect placement of mouthpiece (usually should be in the horizontal center), especially with transfers from cornet or trumpet.
   2. Control problems caused by inadequate support, since many notes are close together and use same fingering.
   3. Incorrect position — especially sitting too far back on the chair and not holding horn up.

TROMBONE

a. Setting the Embouchure.
   1. Bring the lips gently together with a slight pucker.
      a. Be careful that the lower jaw lines up evenly with the upper jaw, so that the mouthpiece will rest comfortably on the lips and the lower lip will not turn under.
   2. Trombone embouchure utilizes more of the lips than that of the cornet/trumpet or horn, and is more "open." The lips should feel as if they are slightly apart when playing.
   3. Place the mouthpiece on or slightly above the vertical center of the mouth. (A student with a thick upper lip may place the mouthpiece a bit higher than one with a thin upper lip.) Watch carefully that the mouthpiece remains near the horizontal center as well. Slight variations may develop, but a student needs to develop equal muscles on both sides.
   4. To play in the high register, the corners of mouth remain firm and the lips tighten by pushing the jaw slightly upward. Avoid mouthpiece pressure — let the lips work against each other, not against the mouthpiece.
   5. Keep the throat open and the sound flowing *through* the instrument.
b. Use of the Tongue.
   1. Trombone tonguing is similar to that of the cornet/trumpet in the position and action of the tongue. The use of the syllable "dah" or "tah" is advisable.
   2. Trombone tonguing requires more flexibility, since many legato slurred passages require the tongue in order to be performed. Legato tongue: Begin on a single tone, usually using syllable "tah"; keep flow of breath going while tongue goes through the motion of saying "tah" or "dah."
   3. Correct tonguing requires no movement of the jaw. If jaw movement is present, it may be caused by incorrect tongue position or more tongue movement than is necessary.
c. Breath Support.
   1. Get into the habit of taking as much air as possible into the lungs. Practice playing until all air is exhausted . . . then take another large breath.
   2. The fundamentals of breathing are similar for all brass instruments. (See breath support, cornet/trumpet.)
d. Voicing.
   1. Fundamentals of voicing are similar for all brass instruments.
   2. Use "ah" for low notes, "ee" for high notes.
e. Special Problems.
   1. Three kinds of slurs for trombone:
      a. Legato slur — to move from one tone to another with the slide moving the same direction.

      1. Use the syllable "dah."

      2. Just as the tongue is starting the "dah," the slide should be diverted to the next position while the "d" is being formed; the slide reaches its destination when "ah" is pronounced, so that the full breath forms the new tone.

    b. Lip slur — to move from one tone to another using the same position (1st pos. F to Bb).

    c. Slide natural slur — possible in instances when the tone moves *one* direction and the slide moves the *other* (1st pos. F to 4th pos. G: slide moves down, tone moves up).

  2. Slide Movement.

    a. Needs to be quick, using wrist and/or arm.

    b. Use alternate positions to move slide as short a distance as possible between notes.

    c. Needs to be carefully coordinated with the tongue.

  3. Embouchure and tonguing problems.

    a. Same things to be watched carefully as on cornet/trumpet.

    b. Use of mirror as self-check.

BARITONE/EUPHONIUM

a. Position.

  1. The baritone/euphonium is held with the left hand grasping the ferrule of the outer tubing or the left arm extending around the outside and resting on or grasping the third valve slide.

  2. The fingers of the right hand are curved in a natural position and rest with fingertips on the valves. Use of the thumb ring is necessary to give the fingers enough leverage to press down the valves (especially for youngsters).

  3. Encourage the students to press the valves *straight* down.

b. Setting the Embouchure.

  1. Basically the same as trombone, except that the baritone/euphonium is a conical bore instrument and requires a more open feeling when blowing.

  2. Because there is relatively little resistance, a great volume of breath will be necessary.

c. Use of the Tongue.

The fundamentals of tonguing are similar to those of the cornet/trumpet or trombone, except that the baritone/euphonium can manipulate slurred passages like the cornet/trumpet and need not use the "trombone legato" tongue idea.

d. Breath Support.

  1. Breath control for the baritone/euphonium requires more volume of air than any other brass instrument except the tuba.

  2. Since the baritone/euphonium does not provide sufficient resistance in itself, the use of the back of the tongue will help to control the air stream. An "open" feeling is necessary to produce the proper tone.

e. Voicing.

Similar to that of other brasses.

f. Special Problems.

Most students do not "fill" the instrument with air and therefore get a small sound. The tone must have resonance and must "sing." Have the student take as large a breath as possible in his practice and exhuast every bit of air, in order to build volume.

TUBA

"Band directors expect very little from their tuba players, and they get it." Until recently, this may have been true. However, at last the "oom-pah" days are about over, and it's high time. The solo tuba is progressing and developing at an amazing rate. Audiences enjoy hearing the tuba. The players have modern horns that are masterpieces in construction and beauty. The range and flexibility is on a par with any brass instrument. The sound, speed, precision and dexterity of the artists astound musicians and laymen alike. An international tuba club has recently been formed. Tubas are indeed "big."

Before outlining the technicalities of playing the instrument, suffice it to say that very few solo tuba players are developed from rejects and failures transferred from other brass sections. The first step is for many band directors and tuba students to upgrade their musical concept of the instrument and realize that a major change has taken place in its position in the family of band instruments.

a. Position.
   1. The student should be shown:
      a. How to sit up straight and hold the horn properly (upright tuba or sousaphone).
      b. How to assemble and adjust the mouthpipe, bits, and mouthpiece.
      c. How to "finger" the valves, i.e., fingertips on the valve buttons, and fingers slightly curved.
      d. How to pick up the instrument and lay it down without damaging the tubing or the bell.
      e. How to open and close doors, and how to get the instrument through doorways and halls without damage.
   2. The upright bass and the sousaphone should rest on their sides.
      a. The upright tuba should never be turned upside down and rested on the bell.
      b. The sousaphone should never be rested on the bell and the curve in the mouthpipe. This will damage both parts.
b. Setting the Embouchure.
   1. Basically the same as baritone/euphonium, except that the tuba requires a more open feeling when blowing.
   2. Since there is very little resistance, a much greater volume of breath will be necessary.
   3. The tendency to puff the cheeks can be checked by tucking in the corners of the mouth.
c. Use of the Tongue.
   The fundamentals of tonguing are similar to those of the baritone/euphonium, except that more tongue must be used, especially in the lower register. Ironically, where cornet and trumpet players often use too much tongue, many tuba players don't use enough.
d. Breath Support.
   1. Due to its size, the tuba obviously requires more volume of air than any other brass instrument and, as well, it offers very little resistance to the air stream.
   2. The back of the tongue will help to control the output of air.

3. Students have to get into the habit of taking as much air as possible into the lungs and developing an adequate air reserve. They should practice each long tone until all air is exhausted—then take another large breath to capacity and sustain the next tone the same length of time.

4. Breathe deeply, even when playing softly, in order to have a well-supported, resonant sound. Most students do not push the air, and as a result, the sound has no resonance — it is soggy, mushy and flat, and furnishes no foundation for the band.

 e. Voicing.

 Similar to that of other brasses, using "ah" for low tones and "ee" for high tones.

 f. Special Problems.

  1. Tuning the tuba:

   a. Tune with a soprano instrument. The beats created by the overtones of the tuba sounding against the tone of the higher instrument are easily discernible.

   b. Tuning with other bass or with baritone players is not recommended, because it requires an exceptionally fine ear and the ability to sustain a perfectly steady pitch for five or six seconds.

   c. Tuba players who play well in tune listen to the instruments playing above them.

  2. The tuba presents a special problem in the mastery of playing short tones with a good, resonant sound. The purpose of the study given below is to make the short notes exactly the same in quality as the long notes at the beginning of the line. Any scale may be used, with each note of the scale being played throughout the entire line. The rests as well as the notes should be counted accurately. The tempo is to be steady and unhurried.

PERCUSSION. The instruments of the percussion section are usually classified into three categories. Some examples of the more common instruments are listed below:

1. Membrane Instruments.
 a. Snare Drum.
 b. Bass Drum.
 c. Tympani (discriminate pitch).
 d. Various Drums.

2. Discriminate Pitch Instruments.
 a. Bells.
 b. Marimba.
 c. Xylophone.
 d. Chimes, etc.

3. Indiscriminate Pitch Instruments.
 a. Cymbals.
 b. Triangle.
 c. Ratchet.
 d. Maracas.
 e. Claves.
 f. Tambourine.
 g. Wood Block, etc.

The plan for teaching percussion must be as detailed and systematic as possible with special emphasis on a musical approach. The drum is not something to "beat on," but is a medium for musical expression which gives emphasis to the pulse of music, and provides support in many ways to the melodic and harmonic structure of music. The student of percussion must understand his role in this perspective if he is to mature as a musician. The student today must be a true percussionist and not just a drummer. Contemporary literature makes more demands on the percussionist than ever before. Teaching techniques must be administered with this in mind.

One problem that seems to persist among young people is the idea that playing the drum is easier than any other instrument. As a result an overflow of students sometimes wants to start on percussion. To counteract this, many school band directors today are starting percussionists on small bell sets. Other schools are emphasizing the importance of previous piano instruction before starting on percussion. Both of these approaches provide the melodic foundation basic to all the mallet instruments and tympani.

The snare drum or a bell set is usually used as a beginning instrument. Since this equipment must be available for regular practice, the student should purchase his own bell set kit, practice pad (or, preferably, a snare drum) and appropriate sticks, etc., as basic equipment. (The care and maintenance of percussion equipment is generally taught by some form of lecture-demonstration. Pamphlets and various forms of visual aids are also recommended.)

The transfer from snare drum or bells to other instruments of the percussion section should be accomplished in a logical, progressive manner, fitting to the demands of the situation. The student should have at least a limited working knowledge about the various percussion instruments by the end of junior high school. Continued development on all percussion instruments is maintained by playing appropriate literature in the band, the percussion class, ensembles, and solo work.

SNARE DRUM

PLAYING POSITIONS. Proper playing position is imperative to the establishment of proper playing techniques. Some general guidelines for snare drum are as follows:

A. The drum should slant to the right side about three to four inches lower than the left (about a 20° angle). The highest edge should be even with the top of the hip bone.

   (Note: A number of teachers are now teaching matched grip for snare drum rather than the conventional grip, since it allows easy adaptation to keyboard instruments and tympani. When using matched grip, the drum should not be slanted.)

B. Teach the Stick Positions One Hand at a Time. (See illustration.)
   1. Left Hand — conventional grip.
      a. Thumb toward ceiling.
      b. Stick held in crotch of thumb.
      c. Wrist straight.
      d. When the stick is resting on the drum, the palm of the hand is *not* toward the ceiling, but toward the right.
   2. Left Hand — matched grip.
      a. Thumb joint straight.
      b. Thumb bone in line with the stick.

    c. All fingers should be touching the stick.

    d. The butt end should be held against the palm of the hand as much as possible while playing.

    e. Back of the hand toward the ceiling.

In matched grip, the right stick is held in the same manner as the left, as noted above.

3. Right Hand.

    a. Thumb joint straight.

    b. Thumb bone in line with the stick—not below the stick.

    c. All fingers should be touching the stick.

    d. The butt end should be held against the palm of the hand as much as possible while playing.

    e. The back of the hand toward the ceiling, the thumb toward the left.

(Note: Do not change the stick position if the student is left-handed.)

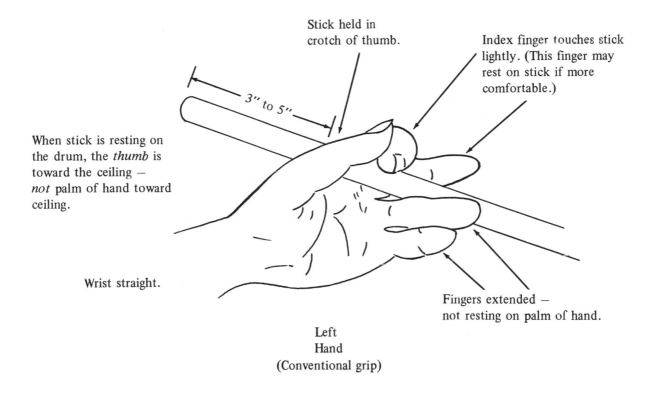

Stick held in crotch of thumb.

Index finger touches stick lightly. (This finger may rest on stick if more comfortable.)

When stick is resting on the drum, the *thumb* is toward the ceiling — *not* palm of hand toward ceiling.

Wrist straight.

Fingers extended — not resting on palm of hand.

Left
Hand
(Conventional grip)

LEFT HAND POSITION. (Explain the left hand first because it seems to be more difficult.)

    a. After the stick and fingers seem to be in the correct position, have the student strike the drumhead (or pad). The movement used should come from a rotation of the forearm and might be compared to the movement used in turning a doorknob or operating an accelerator on a motorcycle. This may also be explained by placing the palm toward the ceiling and rotating the forearm until the palm faces the right. It is often helpful to establish this movement without the stick in the hand.

b. The forearm should be about parallel to the floor. (Have the student assume a position as if he were shaking hands. This will usually place the arm in the correct position.) The elbow should be slightly forward of the rib cage. Do not allow elbows or upper arm to rest on the body.

c. The student should strike the drumhead with the left stick several times using the stick position and forearm rotation as mentioned above. The stick should move rapidly from the highest point (about six to ten inches above the drumhead) to the head and return. Only one clear tap should be heard. Do not allow the stick to rest on the head after the stroke has been made. Check to make sure the forearm does not move up and down.

When the left hand position is understood by the student, start on the right hand position.

When right stick is resting on the drum, the *back* of the hand is toward the ceiling; the thumb is toward the left.

Thumb joint straight — no hump.

Wrist straight.

Pressure here only — stick is held between soft pad of thumb and 1st and 2nd joint of index finger.

1" showing

Index finger and thumb same height on stick.

These three fingers are wrapped lightly around stick.

Right Hand

RIGHT HAND POSITION.

a. One may explain that the right hand position is similar to that of holding a steak knife. All the fingers should be around the stick just as if a tough steak were to be cut.

b. The wrist movement should be up and down, with the palm toward the floor. (Do not allow the forearm to "pump water," i.e., move up and down.)

c. The angle of the stick to the drumhead should be small.

d. After the stick and fingers seem to be in correct positon, have the student strike the drum pad several times. The stick should move rapidly from the highest point (six to ten inches above the drumhead) to the head and return. Only one clear tap should be heard. Do not allow the stick to rest on the head after the stroke has been made. (Check: All the fingers should be around the stick, and the thumb in line with the stick.)

TEACHING METHODS (Snare Drum).

a. The *bounce method* is most widely used. In this method, the sticks are allowed to bounce two or more times for every stroke of the hand. The stick must be free in the hand to bounce.

    1. *Advantage*: Closed rolls may be played after a relatively short period of study. This gives the student a feeling of accomplishment.

    2. *Disadvantage*: The stick position suffers to the point that it becomes incorrect. In the right hand, the ring finger and little finger are not in contact with the stick — an effort to allow the stick freedom to bounce. The index finger of the left hand is usually not held over the top of the stick — an attempt to free the execution with the sticks bouncing. Patterns of rapid single strokes and other intricate patterns will sound sloppy when the bounce roll has been taught. This is due to the fact that a beginning student using a bounce roll will develop a certain stick position which permits the stick to bounce freely without *fine* control of the hand. This technique affects not only the rolls but all playing.

b. The *double tap method*. This method eliminates the point in speeding up a long roll where the sticks begin to bounce. The sticks never bounce; they always sound two taps which are controlled by the hands. (A tap as referred to here is a complete wrist movement of a stick from three to ten inches above the drum to the drumhead and back to the starting point.) The sticks are held firmly rather than loosely.

    1. *Advantage*: Rolls will sound even. A true rudimental sound is possible. Measured rolls, i.e., rolls of a given number of strokes, are more easily understood. A multi-bounce roll will be more easily understood and controlled as a result of studying the rudimental roll. It prevents sloppy and incorrect ending of rolls. Good stick position is easier to maintain.

    2. *Disadvantage*: The average or below average student may become disinterested because learning the roll in this manner is slower. The roll will never sound closed.

In light of the above descriptions, the teacher will have to choose between the two methods. If progress must be rapid, the bounce method will undoubtedly be favored. (Also, most teachers have learned this method themselves and will feel more comfortable teaching it.) It should be kept in mind that this method leads to many bad habits, and the stick position will have to be relearned if the student continues studying percussion. If the bounce method is used, the student should be made aware of the double tap method, and it should be fully explained.

By the end of the second lesson, the stick position should be fixed in the student's mind. The single-stroke roll should be continued and the long roll begun. It should be pointed out repeatedly that speed is unimportant. The student should watch his hands and make corrections as he plays.

OBJECTIVES (Snare Drum).

a. Beginning student, 5th grade:
    1. Knowledge of fundamentals of music.
    2. Ability to read simple whole, half, quarter, and eighth note rhythms.
    3. Knowledge of the first thirteen standard rudiments. This should include long roll, five- and seven-stroke rolls, flam, and flam paradiddle.
b. Advanced student, 6th grade:
    1. Knowledge of fundamentals.
    2. Reading of more difficult notations.
    3. Knowledge of remaining thirteen standard rudiments.
c. Junior high (7th, 8th, and 9th grades):
    1. Use of traps, such as tambourine, triangle, wood block, bells, etc.
    2. Use and care of tympani.
    3. Continued refinement of thirteen standard rudiments, and add the second thirteen rudiments, completing all twenty-six rudiments.
    4. Knowledge of lines and spaces of both treble and bass clef.

VALUE OF SNARE DRUM RUDIMENTS. Many students and teachers question the value of time spent on the standard drum rudiments. The rudiments *are* important because they teach the student control of his sticks, and, at the same time, valuable lessons in the area of band drumming are learned. Control may be learned by other methods (such as the Stone Stick Control Book), however, these exercises do not contribute to the dummer's practical knowledge as well as do the rudiments.

BASS DRUM

Once the student has developed some skill on the snare drum, transfer to the bass drum for ensemble and band purposes should present relatively few problems. Bass drumming problems in the school band are usually an inability of the player to keep the beat steady and an inability to play at the proper volume level with good tone. The bass drummer must be able to *keep his eyes on the conductor*, and to strike the drum so that it can resonate freely. (Striking the drum just off center gives maximum tone quality.) The bass drum should be considered as the backbone of the pulse of the band.

TYMPANI

The major problem involved in transfer to the tympani is usually one of tuning. Tuning should be taught in terms of intervals, i.e., 4th, 5th, 6th, etc. If a snare drummer can match pitches vocally with the piano, generally he will be able to tune tympani with a little extra help.

a. Procedure in Teaching Tuning.
    1. Have student match pitches by singing pitch given from piano or other instrument.
    2. Explain bass clef, names of lines and spaces, and range of tympani. Names of lines and spaces should be an assigned lesson.

3. Explain intervals of a 4th, 5th, 3rd, 6th, and octave. Teach these intervals by using the first two notes of familiar songs.
   a. Examples (singing intervals up from bottom note):
      1. Perfect 4th — "Here Comes the Bride"
      2. Perfect 5th — "Twinkle, Twinkle, Little Star"
      3. Major 3rd — Teach the sound of a major triad; this may be used for the 5th also.
      4. Major 6th — "My Bonnie Lies Over the Ocean"
   b. Examples (singing intervals down from top note):
      1. 5th and minor 3rd — "Star-Spangled Banner"
      2. Major 3rd — "Swing Low, Sweet Chariot"
      3. Major 6th — "Nobody Knows the Trouble I've Seen"
      4. Perfect 4th — "Old McDonald Had a Farm"

4. When the student can sing these intervals, he may start trying to match the pitch he is singing with the pitch of the drumhead. (Strike the drum approximately three inches from the rim.) Depending on the student's vocal range, the pitch may have to be sung one octave higher than actual pitch. Have the student match several pitches given from a piano or pitch pipe. (A pitch pipe is a good source of reference for the student to use to check the drum pitch at the beginning of rehearsals and for difficult tuning problems.)

5. Tuning intervals on one drum.
   a. Tune a pitch as explained in #4 above. (Example: G on the low drum).
   b. Then sing desired interval from pitch tuned in #5a. (Example: If the desired interval is a 4th, the student will sing G, then up to C).
   c. Now the voice is sounding the top note of the interval (C). Strike the head and move the pedal rather quickly, until the pitch of the drum matches the pitch of the voice. (CAUTION: If the interval is small, move the pedal slower. If the interval is large, move faster.) *Strike the head only once.* Repeated striking tends to confuse things. The head will vibrate long enough to find the pitch even when struck softly. The speed of the pedal movement is important.

6. Tuning between high and low drums.
   a. Tuning between drums is somewhat easier because there will always be a reference pitch on the opposite drum. The interval may be checked by playing from the low to the high drum (or vice versa) and listening for the correct interval.
   b. Students have a tendency to restrike the low drum too often when tuning. This should be discouraged once the voice has sung the interval.

b. Stick Position.
   1. Both sticks are held in the same position.
   2. This position is similar to the snare drum right hand.
   3. Palms of hands should be facing the floor.
   4. The sticks should be parallel to the floor when the head of the stick is on the drum.

OTHER PERCUSSION TECHNIQUES

Playing ability and knowledge of the mallet instruments is necessary for the student percussionist today. The bell kits that are available for beginning students provide the necessary equipment for a practical foundation on the mallet instruments. Any method book which provides simple melodies may be used for practice. (Oboe and trumpet method books usually provide good melodic material.)

Among the indiscriminate pitch instruments, the cymbals are most commonly used in school bands. The cymbal chart published by the A. Zildjian Company is quite useful and should be given consideration as an aid in teaching proper cymbal playing techniques.

The remaining miscellaneous percussion instruments that are used from time to time in the band may be taught as the need arises. The major criteria for determining proper playing techniques should be the desired result in performance. Stress, as always, should be on a performance that is artistic and pleasing to the ear. If there is any doubt as to a particular technique, the director should consult a good source book on percussion.

THE CONCERT BAND. Many of the techniques used to obtain results in a small class can be adapted to a large class with very little difficulty. Due to the size of the concert band and the seating arrangement, the problems of blend, balance, intonation, and baton awareness become more prominent. The rehearsal routine should be well planned and should reflect the overall objectives of the band. The band rehearsal must be more than a mere time when students come together to play music. A systematic approach of combining good performance with a full musical education must be incorporated into the rehearsal plan. While this may sound like an impossible task at first, it really need not be — if time is spent in planning a rehearsal routine in keeping with desired objectives.

(The reader should refer at this point to the chapter on innovations for specific examples of a suggested concert band curriculum outline, a suggested rehearsal routine, monthly band quiz items, and assigned record listening for a monthly band quiz. Such examples are representative of how a well-planned, organized program can be implemented to achieve results in keeping with the above-mentioned objectives.)

The seating arrangement that is used for the concert band depends entirely on the circumstances that are inherent to a given situation. The acoustical characteristics of the room, strengths and weaknesses within the band, and the desired results are important factors to consider. The director will obviously need a definite concept of band sound — and this is the *primary* factor in seating. He should not hesitate to experiment with seating if he is not getting the desired results.

Blend and balance are qualities that are closely allied. One factor that affects both blend and balance is the relative dynamic level of different pitches. A chord marked *forte* for the band would not necessarily be played *forte* in all parts. Generally speaking, the lower pitched instruments should play at a stronger dynamic level than the higher pitched instruments in order to achieve a dark sound. The reverse would produce a bright sound. This principle must be kept in mind when the band is playing a crescendo or diminuendo. The degree of crescendo for a tuba would be more than for a cornet, even though both may be marked the same. The degree of diminuendo would be less for a tuba than for a cornet provided both are marked the same. This principle applies to all the instruments of the band according to their characteristic dynamic/pitch levels. This is not to say that the lower frequencies should *always* be louder. This principle is merely pointed out to emphasize its existence. It is up to the director to balance and use this principle to achieve the kind of sound desired.

Students must constantly be reminded to listen "across" the band. They must be taught to recognize the difference between melody and supporting parts. One valid technique is to provide each student with the opportunity of periodically auditing a rehearsal and reporting the results to the band. A tape recorder aids in teaching the qualities of blend and balance by providing the student a means of hearing specific problems as they are pointed out.

The problem of intonation is basically one of critical listening. Practice in vertical chord tuning, using the pyramid theory, will help to solve problems of intonation. Singing parts and simple chord progressions should help to train the ear. Unison studies in the warm-up should be practiced slowly and the pitches matched.

Baton awareness, or the ability to respond to the conductor, can sometimes be a problem. Each student should be given an opportunity to conduct the band. After a student has done this, he will often approach his own playing from a different, more sympathetic viewpoint. The director can deliberately change tempos, forcing more awareness. Above all, the director should conduct in such a manner that reflects sensitivity and musicianship.

SUMMARY. The successful band is a culmination of many things. The band means many things to many people. Students with every conceivable type of background, interest and ability will be in the band. A majority of students will probably start in the band program for any number of reasons other than an intense love of music. The major challenge to the director will be to instill in the student (to as high a degree as possible) an understanding and love for music through the band program. The director should face the fact that there is little chance that anyone will be quite as "wrapped up" in the band as he is. This places a tremendous responsibility on the director to not only "sell" his program, but to follow up with good, solid teaching. There must be discipline, hard work, dedication, sacrifice, responsibility, and loyalty on the part of the student if he is to contribute in any measure to, and benefit from, an outstanding band program. The director must teach in such a manner that will elicit these qualities from the students. This means that he must be a person of high integrity, and dedicated, hard-working, organized, well-prepared, and capable in the skills of his profession. He must teach so that the student can become his own best teacher. The director who can blend these qualities with a good sense of humor and a genuine love of young people cannot help but be successful.

The following article is quoted through the courtesy of the G. LeBlanc Corporation, Kenosha, Wisconsin:

GETTING RESULTS WITH YOUR MUSICAL GROUP

Attitude of Director:

Participate with LOVE in search for BEAUTY and TRUTH. This means there can be no destructive attitude of discouragement or defeat in the face of musical flaws or technical blemish, only pain which seeks healing as an injured child-parent relationship seeks healing. This does not mean there is no conflict, rather that we must accept conflict as necessary tests of our concepts the same way a scientist subjects his theories to experimentation and change. This does not mean an atmosphere of tranquility prevails, on the contrary, we deal with a phenomenon as precious as life itself—we are "Ministers" of music, "Directors" of salvation—and can not and must not tolerate anyone who belittles this responsibility. This means one has a burning sensation which demands consuming energy, intelligence and talent, vitality, enthusiasm, and complete submergence.

Attitude of Student:

As we are able to cultivate in our students the same attitude described for us as directors we achieve an ideal atmosphere. Note, of course, we can not expect the students to seek what we do not.

Practically Speaking This Means:

I. We must be demanding and refuse compromise, for there is no compromise to an ideal. We must work with love and approach all from a postive view; such as, "That is good but let's work to make it better;" "That is fine, excellent, let's challenge ourselves to make it great!"

II. Is tone quality and phrasing important? Then let us reward progress along this line and spend a share of every rehearsal on it.

   A. Do not tolerate poor posture. Students should not use more than the first seven inches of the chair. Psychologists have noted in experiments that children in creative process seem to involve their entire body, that stirring up purely physical energy aids creative stimulation. Be sure trunk is straight and leaning forward. Of course, they must have rest periods.

   B. Do breathing exercises emphasizing use of area directly below the rib cage and not the chest.

   C. Have students "hah, hah" vocally on "f" or "g." If this is feeble their tone will lack core. Student must excite intensity and depth in singing the "hah." Go through scales this way.

   D. Sing first five notes of scale using "hah" then sustain the fifth. Undoubtedly, what you will have to do is make them increase diaphragm intensity ($\Longleftarrow$) as note is held, or the sound will become frail and "drip off the bell on to the floor."

   E. Do not work too long at any one time with the voice. Keep moving from the voice to the instrument. Vocalize the "hah, hah," then transfer to the instrument with "tah, tah." Work with sections, then with individuals.

   F. Concentrate on relationship of attack-body-release. Generally the attack is too hard and the rest of the tone without direction or support. What is necessary is more air *after the attack* and then, for continued vitality, the diaphragm must increase intensity of air as air supply lessens. Ignore the diminuendo for the part and concentrate on intensifying each note. In four counts go from p to f, or f to ff, or pp to ff, etc. Most often it is only a cadence where a real diminuendo is used. Music for the most part is a matter of "ebb and flow." The expansion is what we worry about—the relaxation of intensity takes care of itself as we start the next note.

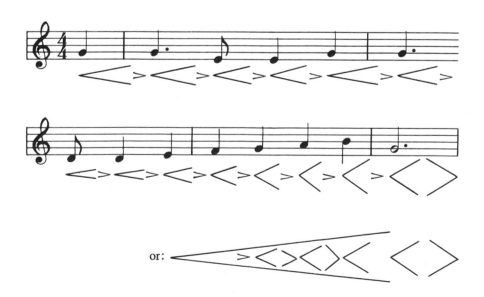

108

G. Be certain to get to every individual at least once a week in rehearsal or as many times as possible, depending on the number of rehearsals and performance obligations. Let your best students serve as examples.

H. If you must accept compromise, accept it with a challenge for the student or group to improve. Then be sure to keep after it a little during every rehearsal so the students know that beauty of individual tones and combinations of tones in a phrase knows no compromise and is ever sought after.

III. Is intonation important? Then spend about 10% of the week's rehearsal time on it.

A. Do not spend the same amount every day. Some days spend five minutes and other days 25 minutes—maybe some days no time at all.

B. Important to generally approach intonation from an intellectual view rather than emotional.

C. Unless student's posture is correct, breath support solid, throat open, and embouchure consistent, no tuning is possible.

D. Instrument must be warmed up before tuning, so play an exciting number or a match to get started.

E. Be sure students play good *mf* or *f* when tuning.

F. Students must be able to produce a steady tone and must *know* their instruments' tuning problems.

G. If at all possible get every student to work with a strobe. It will help them center their pitch as well as understand their instrument.

H. Work with the Johnston Intonation Trainer to develop pitch perception.

I. Reward good tuning.

J. Stress without concession letter "C" above.

IV. Is rhythmic accuracy important? Then do not tolerate ANY degree of sloppiness or carelessness.

A. Spend 5-10% of week's rehearsal time on rhythm. Again it should not be every day but rather without any regularly scheduled pattern. Some days you may spend 20 minutes on it and other days no time at all.

B. In the learning process have the students clap-tap-count-shout (as in the army). Do these things with percussion——All and Anything that will make students feel PHYSICALLY the PRECISE placement of every fraction of every beat.

C. Rhythm is PHYSICAL. Each and every student must feel the pulse—be the pulse—no matter how simple the rhythmic pattern may be.

D. The students must not FOLLOW the conductor, they must be ONE WITH the CONDUCTOR.

E. Rhythm is one of the most tangible of the musical elements and the students love it. Make them *think* and *feel* a good sharp pulse at all times (also *under* very legato playing).

F. Remember there is harmonic and melodic rhythm. Both need unbending attention—separately and together.

V. Is technical accuracy important? Know your students' level and keep expecting and demanding more.

A. Passages involving [musical notation: four eighth notes] or [musical notation: eighth-note triplet marked 3] always suffer. They are not spaced properly within the pulse, or they are not given equal weight. Most often they are too intense at the start and too weak at the end—and squashed together or rushed rhythmically.

B. "Simple" passages of quarter or eighth notes must be carefully spaced and controlled. Metronome is indispensable.

C. Articulation is a major ingredient of technical accuracy. Absolute uniformity is to be sought after.
   1. Attack must have uniform intensity.
   2. The style of legato to staccato must be identified and unified.
   3. Stress and tone duration defined and demanded.

VI. Don't forget dynamics!

VII. Work on balance.
   A. Balance chord in one section.
   B. Balance chord in entire band, adding sections one at a time.
   C. Balance melodic line with bass and harmony.
   D. Take each ingredient separately—polish and add to total texture in proper relationship.

VIII. In the final analysis the music you select determines whether your technical plow is set in good soil or clay. Balance is desirable at all times.
   A. Soul searching music—music of melodic and harmonic beauty—baroque aire or chorale—lovely ballads of any period.
   B. Technically challenging music of classic beauty from baroque—classic—or early romantic period.
   C. Dramatic music—forceful—profound—tearing at the emotions.
   D. Jubilant and exciting music—marches—good Latin numbers—certain contemporary pieces.
   E. Some strictly "fun" music is necessary, but do not overdo. It must be stressed that all is "fun"—that it is a matter of "fun" types, like a good steak is enjoyable in a different way from a candy bar. Avoid cheap jazz (your own integrity of taste must rule here) and unimaginative arrangements of popular music.
   F. In all, strive for representation of the different periods, and/or carefully choose contemporary works which demonstrate quality of the different periods.
   G. Only through this kind of persistance will it ever be possible to force publishers to publish with musical integrity.

IX. Some general remarks.
   A. Stands must be at proper height so within the periphery of vision the music and director can both be seen.
   B. Never more than two on a stand.
   C. Pencils must be in folders at all times. Students must mark everything you stress.
   D. Encourage listening. Ask them to locate the melody—who has the counterline—the harmony—what material is being used in this section—sing the theme—is it major or minor—sing the key note—the root—the scale—the chord.
   E. Insist they get used to watching conductor at all times—even while sight reading.
   F. Have all ingredients herein discussed on your mind at all times. Think quickly, speak clearly and concisely, and keep the pace generally on the bright side so students maintain a sharp edge.
   G. Question your conducting at all times.
      1. Is it clear?
      2. Is it in style?
      3. Does it generate the intensity, the warmth, the dramatic quality you are asking for?
      4. Don't ever take it for granted—work to improve in someway at all times.
   H. There is a fine line between pushing students too hard and not pushing

them enough. It is better to tread this line on the former rather than the latter side.

   I.   Better to eliminate students who are unwilling to give 100%. Only one bad apple is needed to spoil the lot.

   J.   When thinking of my daughter, my concern is that her director be absolutely uncompromising in demand of 100% attention, posture, attitude, etc.—you name it!

   K.   Most parents do not know the difference! WE DO!! A fact which increases our degree of responsibility.

X.   If music is to function as a force to improve mankind, then we must emphasize this relationship constantly.

   A.   To seek and appreciate accuracy in music is to demand truth in life.

   B.   To create and appreciate beauty in music is to become an exponent of goodness—justice—and love in life.

   C.   To become creatively involved in music is to reject passivity and indifference in life.

   D.   To give enthusiasm, optimism, love, honor, dignity, etc. in music is to appreciate and thus possess these ingredients as a human being.

**Frank Bencriscutto, "Getting Results With Your Musical Group."
Kenosha, Wisconsin: Leblanc Publications. Used by permission.**

chapter **8**

Private Instruction

That many of the finest band programs in the nation have made accommodation for private lessons is the result of the perception of directors who recognize the effectiveness of private lessons in developing fine musicianship.

Naturally, a haphazard approach will not produce the desired results. Qualified instructors—persons who are interested in the student and his progress — are important to the success of private lessons. The program should also be established on a continuing basis, with lessons divided into a series, by the semester, or for a school year. Continuity is as essential to progress as daily practice on assignments.

Most successful private teachers write out a lesson plan and suggested practice routine for each lesson and send out periodic progress reports to parents. The most effective teachers identify and work with the problems and weaknesses of each student, and the lesson is more than mere supervised practice for the student — an important reason for having qualified teachers. (It is both interesting and important to note that, whereas it is certainly an asset for a private teacher to excel in performance, mere performance ability will not guarantee a fine teacher — nor should it necessarily be required as a qualification in selecting a private teacher.)

In cases where a large number of students and teachers are involved in the private lesson program, it is desirable for the supervisor to have some control over the program. Factors which need the supervisor's attention would include: 1. the amount charged per lesson; 2. the quality of the instruction; and 3. making certain that all procedures are in agreement with school administrative policies.

A 95% return from a questionnaire sent to selected schools coast-to-coast revealed that every director contacted firmly believed that a private lesson program is a determinant factor in the success of school band programs. (This opinion included many directors who were not able to carry on a program of private instruction in their own schools.) The charge for lessons varied from $2.00 to $5.00, but the majority indicated a charge of $2.50. The percentage of students studying varied from zero to 100%. But in most cases, schools which had lower percentages were either not located close enough to available teachers or were affected by other factors, such as lack of student interest and/or economic factors in the community. Only one school reported a 100% participation: the daily plan of instruction included private lessons for all students during school hours — at no expense to individual students.

In some cases lessons were given by local professional musicians only, in others by staff members only, in some with the help of college instructors, and in many cases by a combination of these. In larger school systems where it is difficult to find enough capable teachers, it is often advantageous to train some of the most advanced students in the high school bands to give lessons (for their own instrument only) to beginners or to younger students. However, the director or supervisor must be very careful to guide the student instructors in what and how they teach. If not handled carefully, this plan can be more detrimental than beneficial. The charge by student instructors should be minimal.

According to the questionnaire, all boards of education sanctioned the private lesson program, and one was noted as encouraging it. All directors made special comments concerning the effectiveness of private instruction. A few samplings are quoted here:

"It is an absolute necessity for a quality program — almost 98% study privately during elementary school years. It is encouraged by our music staff, although not required." *Pennsylvania*

"I attribute a great deal of the excellence of our program to the fact that so many of our students take private lessons. It has become more obvious to me since 1965. Then, 80% of my top band students were studying. Now we are under 30%, and it is much harder to get the same quality. Incidentally, I don't know the reason for the drop." *Ohio*

"To most parents of my band members the cost of private instruction ($3.00) is too high, and the students are not anxious enough to improve themselves." *Oklahoma*

"The private lesson program develops the first chair players and members of the All-State Band and All-State Orchestra." *South Dakota*

"Private instruction has afforded the real strength of our program — usually the students who study privately are the top players in their sections." *Arkansas*

"Students that study privately make more progress and usually sit at the top of the section. I don't feel that private study is for every student, but for those who are willing to put forth the extra effort." *Texas*

"I feel it is the most important factor in a strong program — without question. First chair players in my wind ensemble do some private teaching with our beginners and elementary students ($1.50 for a half hour) and we have been getting some of our best teaching from these students!!" *Michigan*

"This program is very important in providing leadership in each section of the band. A private lesson program has a considerable effect on a band. Even those who do not take private lessons benefit from those who do study, by hearing and imitating proper articulations, tone quality, phrasing and other desirable attributes." *Nebraska*

chapter 9

Marching Band

The high school marching band is a part of the school program offered in music education to qualified students through their participation in performance on wind and percussion instruments. Band as a school subject in the curriculum is primarily aimed at helping each member gain a deeper insight into the art of music, hence broadening his knowledge, skill, understanding, and appreciation of music. The marching band can accomplish some of these ends when planned and directed with care and good taste and guided by proper educational procedures and musical aims. The high school marching band program places emphasis on march music and other varieties of this musical style, which gives the band members an opportunity to correlate his sense of rhythm with his physical coordination. The disciplines of music coupled with those of an efficient marching band afford experiences and require a multiplicity of responses rarely found in the school education program:

1. Patriotism: use of patriotic and seasonal music; proper display and use of the flag; observance of patriotic holidays and events.
2. Band traditions of marching and its music as a supplement not found in concert band.
3. Entertainment at school functions, especially football games.
4. Service to school and community as a mobile musical unit on justified occasions — patriotic, civic, and educational.
5. Enhancement of school and community with color, esprit de corps, pride, identification, and recognition.
6. Disciplines of group uniformity of dress, conduct, teamwork, self-control, precision and citizenship.
7. Performance of well-rehearsed music on the march in a variety of circumstances to large audiences.

The marching phase of the high school band should be balanced and logical, by being subordinate to the teaching and performance of music in the classroom and on the concert stage; it should have perspective, musical purpose, and educational goals; it should have correlation and coordination with the school program and with proper and reasonable community service.

(The above introduction to the marching band is the American School Band Directors Association statement on high school marching bands, written in Dec., 1965 and amended in Aug., 1966. Dating of this material does not destroy its relevancy to band instruction today.)

Following are four brief statements by band directors concerning their personal philosophy of the marching band:

"It is a great motivating factor, helps in sight-reading and discipline. It brings many students into the program." — James W. Nichols, *California*

"The marching band develops physical and mental discipline, and gives the student status among the student body through his participation." — David D. Casto, *Delaware*

"The marching band has relevancy . . . a positive experiential activity." — Jack E. Shelby, *Michigan*

"We are not a precision drill band per se. We have never entered a marching contest. Pageantry has always been our long suit in marching. We have enjoyed much success locally and nationally and we enjoy this type of marching. It is valuable to our program." — Durward B. Howard, *Texas*

These four statements, selected at random with the exception of their geographical representation, are typical of responses and represent majority thinking.

The American School Band Directors Association regards the marching band as one facet of the program to be accomplished in the best possible manner, always keeping in mind that one's first obligation is that of being instrumental music educators, with primary emphasis on concert bands, ensembles, and solo training. ASBDA members responding to a recent survey gave strong emphasis to the following purposes of school marching bands:

1. Provide service to the school and community.
2. Educate for cooperation, teamwork, and discipline.
3. Provide entertainment for school football games.
4. Promote public relations for the school.
5. Promote, support, and develop school spirit, especially at athletic events.
6. Provide a musical experience not found in concert bands.
7. Promote and recognize the school band program.
8. Develop band "esprit de corps."
9. Develop understanding of the element of rhythm for marching band members.

This same survey, in listing the most important of the excellent musical and other advantages that add value to the school marching band, indicates that there appear to be more non-musical advantages to marching band than musical ones. However, the musical advantages cannot be ignored. Both musical and non-musical are listed below in order of emphasis by the number of responses:

Musical Advantages	Other Advantages
1. Rhythmic response.	1. Physical coordination.
2. Production of sound.	2. Discipline.
3. Musical skills.	3. Esprit de corps.
4. Variety of styles.	4. Pride and recognition.
5. Military march music.	5. Teamwork.
6. Memorization.	6. Interest and service.
	7. Large audiences.
	8. Responsibility.

Another item which is of value in the discussion of marching band philosophy is the listing of items and factors which detract from the value of the program (listed in order of emphasis):

115

Musical Problems

1. Lack of attention to musical values.
2. Emphasis on volume.
3. Limited selection and poor quality of music.
4. Lack of effective arrangements.
5. Adverse weather effects on musical performance.
6. Embouchure dissatisfactions.
7. Tempi too fast.

Other Problems

1. Excess time needed and used.
2. Emphasis on girl groups.
3. Tendency to lower standards of music and discipline.
4. Cheapness of showmanship.
5. Wear and tear on music and equipment.
6. Inclusion of non-playing members.
7. Forced adherence to whims of community, school and/or athletic department.

One section of a 1965 survey was devoted to the trends and directions of the school marching band at that time, with the following areas listed in order of emphasis:

1. Better sound; better quality music; better playing; more concert playing.
2. Improved efficiency in playing and marching.
3. More drilling; fewer formations; less pageantry.
4. Tendency toward more show; more entertainment.
5. Emphasis declining, decreasing, lessening.
6. Less drill.
7. Given to dancing girls and drill teams.

One additional summarization from this survey may be of value in determining emphasis which should be placed on the marching band and the formulation of policy concerning the place of the marching band in the contemporary program. Responding to the question, "Do you agree that by nature, by tradition, and historically, bands should march?", 90% replied in the affirmative.

TRAINING. Marching band training is practically non-existent at the elementary level in school programs today. Approximately 50% of programs which include marching band begin the training procedures in junior high school, with the other 50% confining all marching band activities to the senior high level. Among those schools which do begin training in junior high, emphasis is almost completely on basic fundamentals of marching and on music with very limited performance requirements. Among the schools which limit training to the senior high level, one very important addition is made — a pre-school or late summer, one- or two-week training session. The advantages of scheduling this type of session are:

1. No conflict of interest for student time.
2. Balanced scheduling of rehearsals between playing and marching.
3. Rehearsal of music for the complete marching season.
4. Fundamental training of students unfamiliar with marching or with present techniques.
5. Use of competent upperclassmen in fundamental training of beginners and new students.

Training concepts vary widely, according to the background, training and experience of the director, and his philosophy of show format and preparation. However, certain fundamentals are used almost universally, including the following:

Ranks, Files, Interval, Marching Number, Guides, Drum Major, Rank Sergeant, Cadence, Vocal Commands, Whistle Commands, Command of Preparation, and Command of Execution.

Fall In, Attention, Dress Right, Front, At Ease, Parade Rest, Cover Down, and Dismissed — all vocal.

Right Face, Left Face, About Face, Forward March, Mark Time, Halt, Right Flank, Left Flank, Right Turn, Left Turn, Column Right, Column Left, Countermarch, To the Rear, Double to the Rear, Spinning Right Flank, Spinning Left Flank, Forward March Playing, Halt and Continue Playing, Halt and Stop Playing — all vocal and/or whistle.

Posture, Position, Interval, Instrument Position, Mechanics of Step, Length of Step, Precision and Uniformity, Knee Lift, and Guiding.

Some of the methods or systems used in fundamental marching include: Military Marching with Voice Commands; *Patterns of Motion*; Casavant, *Precision Drill*; 8-to-5 drills; Formation procedures; Al G. Wright show band methods, and D. Marcouiller marching methods. (Consult references at conclusion of chapter).

PERSONNEL. The size of the marching unit in any school will be determined by available personnel in the program and the type of show to be produced. The standard size in selected schools recently evaluated was 96, ranging from a low of 40 to a high of 180. The requirement of membership participation in the complete program is almost universal. Very few schools permit students who are not in the concert band program to participate in the marching band, and most schools require that all members of concert band also march.

The drum major plays a very important part in the effectiveness of a school marching band. The drum major becomes the acting band director when the band is on the field, in performance or rehearsal. The band director should be very selective, using leadership ability, musical ability, scholarship, and physical structure as his criteria. An overwhelming majority of school bands require that the drum major be a member of the band. 60% select boys to be the drum major, and 60% also have the drum major use baton and whistle commands while leading the band.

The use of non-musical groups with the performing marching band is a highly controversial subject. Again, personal preference and philosophy will dictate choice in each situation, but importance must be attached to the fact that the marching band is a musical organization and should be the central figure. In the 1965 ASBDA survey, the majority of responses indicated that majorette groups and color guards may be used properly with marching bands, and that drill and dance teams are not to be discouraged. 50% of the directors of recently sampled schools are in favor of using majorette or twirler groups. A majority of these limit the number involved to six or less and use no other non-musical participant.

SYSTEM. All elements involved in marching band are combined eventually in performance. Success in performance is contingent upon the effectiveness of the training system being used. Every process of instruction must be designed to produce a performance which is musical, precise and uniform.

Fundamentals of musicianship, such as fine tone production, precision of attack, rhythmic accuracy, good intonation, and balance must be stressed in the marching band. The music must not be too difficult for the band to play well while marching. Music which is technically easy at the desired tempo but scored well for marching performance will be the most effective. The music should receive adequate rehearsal time off the field in order to "sound" and to be played "musically" for a successful performance. The pre-school rehearsal time is invaluable in this respect, for it is at this time that the music may be rehearsed apart from the marching and the two need only be combined when each area is properly prepared.

Precision of movement depends to a great extent upon the length of step being used. The 8-to-5 system which produces a uniform step of 22.5 inches (8 steps to each 5 yards) permits a great sense of precision. Most band members have no particular problem with a stride of this length and can be uniform in the mechanics of the step: lifting the foot, the toe leaves the ground last and remains pointed down, while the knee lifts to horizontal; forward motion brings the toe down first at 22.5 inches before the heel touches the ground. The uniformity then involves complete appearance and is very effective. A change of pace attitude can be achieved by slowing the tempo and marching 6-to-5 with a 30-inch stride, a greater forward kick, and less knee lift. Length of step must of necessity be a consideration in deciding what cadence is to be used, as must the character of the music being played. 8-to-5 has achieved wide popularity among band directors, but it should be noted that successful shows will demonstrate a variety of step and cadence.

Accuracy of cadence is the responsibility of the percussion section and, quite possibly, one person in that section — the bass drummer. The director can teach the cadence, the drum major can set the cadence in command sequence, and the marching unit can maintain a sense of cadence with varying degrees of accuracy. But the responsibility for consistency and accuracy belongs to the bass drummer. Obviously then, the director should use great care in selection of this leader.

Variety is an important factor in the preparation and the execution of a half-time show. Precision drill holds the interest of many band members and many in the audience, whereas formations and accompanying narration will be of interest to others. Half-time shows which incorporate a combination of these, while using variety in length of step and cadence, basically satisfy the interests of all the members of the band and audience. Planning of any show should be organized along the following lines:

1. Entrance: alignment, fanfare, introduction.
2. Center Drill and Formations
   a. Salute to visiting school.
   b. Drill.
   c. Formation.
   d. School letter and alma mater.
   e. Novelties.
   f. Finale.
3. Exit.

The center drill and formations, involving a major portion of the alloted time, will require careful organization and timing with features to be used limited and varied from performance to performance. The director should plan on spending several hours of his time in the organization of each half-time show because organization at this time provides for successful rehearsal sessions.

REHEARSALS. A guideline of rehearsal techniques will help the band to fully utilize available time.
   A. Preparatory
      1. Squad leaders

      a. Select advanced competent students to be squad leaders.

      b. Teach squad leaders in a special class.

      c. Work out all fundamentals of each show with squad leaders.

   2. Drill field

      a. Be certain that field is lined with 5-yard lines, hash inserts and 1/3 markers.

      b. Mark some sections with the 22.5 length step, and others with 30, for length-of-step drill purposes.

B. On the Field

   1. Squad drills

      a. Mimeograph routine for each squad.

      b. Learn all fundamentals to verbal command.

      c. Practice uniform carriage.

      d. Practice uniform length of step and knee lift.

      e. Develop competition between squads.

      f. Carry on some individual squad drill during each rehearsal.

   2. Full band drills

      a. Maintain squads intact with squad leaders.

      b. Use consistent drum major signals.

      c. Before playing, practice step and style drills with verbal commands and counting, then with drum beat.

      d. Master one drill or formation at a time, first without playing, then with instruments.

      e. Plan percussion cadences which are precise, not too complicated, and interesting.

   3. Band formation

      a. Block band drills.

      b. Company front drills.

      c. Individual responsibility drills based on step 2, 4, etc.

      d. Fundamental facing and movement drills.

The length of time which must be devoted to the preparation of each show will depend partially upon the amount of time which has been devoted to music preparation ahead of the football season. (Reference here is made to the pre-school session which received prior mention in this chapter.) Music preparation can be very thorough during this type of session and reduces the amount of time necessary in preparation of each show. The difficulty of each show will be another time factor, but only of extreme importance if adequate preparation in fundamentals has not been achieved. If the teaching of fundamentals has been sound and the music to be used throughout the season has been adequately rehearsed, each show can be polished for performance in about five hours of rehearsal. The normal length of time actually devoted to preparation of one show varies from five hours to twenty hours.

MARCHING SCHEDULE. Part of the director's planning responsibility lies in the area of schedules. A system that he can follow from year to year is a necessary part of planning. Some considerations in this planning might be:

   1. Check on all football games in schedule and dates of traditional parades.

   2. Contact band directors of visiting schools to determine their wishes.

3. Determine length of each half-time show to be presented.
4. Determine which out-of-town game would be best for a band trip (if this is part of annual scheduling).
5. Contact director of bands in school you wish to visit (for permission).

TRIPS. A large percentage of our marching bands plan one trip per year with their groups and find that this trip can be an important factor in motivation of band members. Students never seem to tire of the bus trip type of activity, no matter how sophisticated they may appear normally. The director who makes plans to have his band appear at the half-time of an away game, in a band-day activity, or perhaps in a district, regional or state contest, will need to plan details of the trip carefully. Time schedules must be precise and published for student and parent information; meal preparations and reservations must be made in advance; chaperones or sponsors must' be arranged for ahead of time and must be responsible persons; and finances must be managed. Few directors find it necessary to seek outside finance when a trip is part of the yearly plan, since this expense must be included in the school district budget. Those who must raise extra money do it in the same way as in other fund drives: magazine or candy sales, concert ticket sales, work projects by students (with those who do not raise enough money through the project making up the difference with out-of-the-pocket donations), assignment of activity funds, and the use of athletic department funds.

UNIFORMS. Uniforms for marching band and concert band are discussed at length in two other chapters of this Course of Study. Inventory is discussed in the chapter devoted to Organization of the Band Program, and uniform specifications are discussed in the chapter devoted to Factors Involved in Buying Band Uniforms. Comment here will be restricted to disciplines concerned with the wearing of the uniform by marching band members and related grooming as expressed by ASBDA members in the 1965 survey. The disciplines:

Uniforms

1. Always worn complete.
2. Clean and pressed.
3. Shoes shined.
4. Proper fit, especially length.
5. Cap on properly.
6. Buttons always buttoned.
7. Exact uniformity.
8. Worn with pride, respect and military bearing.
9. Unadorned with excessive accessories.
10. Inspections required.
11. Uniform style in good taste.
12. Proper and conservative use of medals and other adornments.

Personal Grooming

1. Hair styles conservative, fitting and neat.
2. Body cleanliness.
3. Personal neatness.
4. No jewelry.
5. Conservative make-up.
6. Clean shaven.
7. Inspections required.

MATERIALS. Publishers have produced a wealth of material which should be considered for use by the high school marching band director. Vast improvement has been made in arrangements, variety of music, printing, and instrumentation for the marching band in the past few years. Music which is designed specifically for special occasion shows, for formation shows, for low bleacher shows, for precision drill, and for every conceivable combination of sounds and tempi is now available. Most band directors are able to purchase commercial arrangements of all needed music for a marching season. There are many directors who still prefer to arrange music for their groups to take advantage of peculiarities or strong points in their instrumentation, but available materials have negated this as a necessity.

Many materials are available today which can be of assistance in training the marching band and in show preparation. Many of our major universities have marching publications which are of value to the high school director: University of Michigan, University of Minnesota, Purdue University and the University of Florida are four which are frequently mentioned.

The position of the marching band is perhaps best summarized by the following quotations:

> In answer to the question "What do you feel is the value of your marching band activities to your complete band program?": "Many hours are spent on articulation, spacing, balance and proper breath support — all of this carries over. It builds tremendous spirit and unity among band members. It creates great enthusiasm from, and rapport with, the community."
>
> — Jerry Hoover, *Jefferson City, Missouri*

> Responding to the question, "Of what value are your marching band activities in achieving your band program objectives?": "I feel that the marching band can take care of the social objectives which I think are very important in the way one shapes his life. Cooperative feeling — realizing the dependence of individuals. Pride not only in one's self, but in the organization. Responsibility, promptness, obedience, which are essential if one is to have success, no matter what line of work is done. Readiness to adapt oneself to a group. Pleasant relationships and friendships. Self-respect and confidence. Response to natural and legitimate desires to stand well in the opinion of others. Desire to serve others." — Hector Espinosa, *Tucson, Arizona*

REFERENCE MATERIALS

Casavant, A. R. *Precision Drill.* 14 Vols. San Antonio: Southern Music Co., 1957.

Dale, Carroll R. *Fundamentals of Drill.* Chicago: Gamble Hinged Music Co., 1942.

Dvorak, Raymond. *The Band on Parade.* New York: Carl Fischer, Inc., 1937.

Hindsley, Mark. *Band At—ten—tion.* Chicago: Gamble Hinged Music Co., 1932.

Johnston, Lawrence. *Parade Technique.* Rockville Center, N.Y.: Belwin, Inc., 1944.

Lee, Jack. *Modern Marching Band Technique.* Winona, Minn.: Hal Leonard, 1955.

Marcouiller, D. *Marching for Marching Bands.* Dubuque, Ia.: Wm. C. Brown, 1958.

Moffit, Bill. *Patterns of Motion.* Winona, Minn.: Hal Leonard, 1964.

Wright, Al G. "The Show Band," *The Instrumentalist* (Evanston, Ill.), 1957.

chapter 10

Stage Band

In preparing an adequate music program the administrator should give considerable thought to a program that includes more than just band, orchestra and chorus. The program should include the formation of music theory classes. It would then behoove those in charge of the course of study to include in the presentation a portion covering the origin and development of jazz. A further consideration should be given to the relevant happenings surrounding the students and to their music. Do existing school music groups contribute adequately to the musical, spiritual and social betterment of the community? Would a stage band have a place in the curriculum? Many educators think not . . . and, unfortunately, if the opportunity were afforded them, many music educators would not be ready or qualified to teach the techniques of stage band, either because of their own attitudes or because of their own lack of knowledge.

Some of the most frequently quoted reasons for placing the stage band in the music curriculum are:

1. It provides another avenue of experience not usually found in the concert band.
2. It is a medium for self-expression.
3. It is a truly American contribution to music.
4. It provides a mobile musical unit for school and community service.
5. It provides an opportunity for individual development according to each participant's interest and ability.

Schools with reputable music programs maintain an active stage band. If the music director properly prepares the student for a desirable experience, he will have little problem in recruitment; and after this initial recruitment, he will find an environment more conducive to good teaching. It must be immediately understood that this same organization can have a highly negative effect if improperly manipulated. To "blast at will" causes the general effect to be extremely "recreational," meaning that unlimited liberties are taken in performing the music.

The amount of time and effort given to this activity by the school and its musicians presents the most responsive answer to the question of the position of the stage band in the average community. It has been found that most organizations of this nature rehearse on the average of only once a week, and usually outside the regular school day. Many educators adhere to the "outside time" policy in order to disenchant the students.

Recent statistics have provided musicians and educators with enlightening commentaries as to why stage bands may be in the process of being downgraded by many school authorities. Research indicates that of an approximate 14,000 college and university music graduates in 1970 only a small percentage was exposed to jazz. We should acknowledge that a complete instrumental music program includes the element of jazz, and it can be best supplied by a stage band program. Those planning to teach instrumental music should prepare themselves in this area. College graduates who find themselves deficient in jazz exposure would benefit greatly by consulting with a private tutor and/or by examining available teaching materials. Two often-quoted treatises on this subject are "A Guide to Improvisation" by John La Porta and "Improvising Jazz" by Jerry Coker. (Other course books are listed at the conclusion of this chapter.)

STRUCTURE. Once the music teacher has acquainted himself with jazz and has prepared himself for presenting this phase of music education to his students, he need only ask, and he undoubtedly will be surrounded by more students than he can reasonably serve. Fortunately, the criterion for stage band size now seems to be established on the merits of the "big band" sound. The structure of such an organization is normally five saxophones (two altos, two tenors, one baritone), four trumpets, four trombones, and four rhythm. This figure may be enlarged or decreased at the instructor's discretion — his considerations being compatible with the selected musical arrangement. Most commercial "charts" are prepared for this basic instrumentation. Like instruments are placed in choir arrangement, with the lead musician being situated in the center of each choir.

Because of the nature of the instrumentation and the arrangements, only the strongest, most proficient musicians should be considered for membership in the stage band. It is reasonable to assume that a large percentage of high school students finds the music of the stage band appealing and, for this factor alone, students desire to participate in such an organization. Some basic factors in the selection of musicians are:

1. Does the student have the proper instrument?
2. Does the student have the desire?
3. Does the student have the ability?
4. Is the student reliable?

If these qualifications are met, then the final selection should be based on the required instrumentation and the individual ability of the student (determined by the director by means of an audition system).

The need for doubling instrumental parts in stage band arrangements is a frequent cause for concern. To the uninitiated, doubling might at times give cause to frustration. However, the examination of a considerable number of "charts" used in performance provides the information that doubling, though not essential, is helpful. Typical doubling: saxophone/clarinet, oboe, flute, bassoon; trombone/horn; bass trombone/tuba.

IMPROVISATION. Leading authorities of the stage band, lab band, or jazz group concur that the element of improvisation is one of the strongest reasons for having this type of organization available to the students. Don Verne Joseph, an outstanding adjudicator of stage bands, has indicated that there are five factors responsible for the outcome of jazz improvisation. The first of these is *intuition* — which controls the amount of and use of originality; second, *intellect* — which governs the technical problems and the form the melody is to take; third, *emotion* — which determines the mood; fourth, *sense of pitch* — which transfers the heard or imagined pitches into letter names and fingerings; and last, *habits* — which enable the fingers to find established pitch patterns immediately.

A variety of techniques requiring very little formal training may be employed in learning the art of improvisation: "Relax on the printed solo;" "Experiment with the melody;" "Teach blues patterns;" "Written notes must precede improvisation;" and "Write out solos, and then begin the breakaway."

"*Relax on the printed solo.*" An example of this would be to embellish the given melodic line or chordal structure by ornamentation or variation. The ability to break away from the printed material is a definite requirement for jazz performance. Relaxation does not mean losing sight of tone, pitch, rhythm or any other musical factor, but rather, the ability to diminish or augment the melodic line, to vary it by the addition of "extra" notes such as passing tones, neighboring tones, blues notes, etc. When this occurs, a style begins to emerge. No matter how inadequate and immature this style appears, it must be nurtured until fully developed.

The element of relaxation moves in sympathy with "*Experiment with the melody.*" It is not unmusical to change the mode to fit one's personality. A liberty of this nature is part of the creative ability of the performer that the instrumental instructor must expect and desire in this form of musical organization.

"*Teach blues patterns.*" This prompts the response that a knowledge of harmony is essential. Although the chord patterns found in some "ad lib" sections appear difficult, the simple knowledge derived from the study of traditional blues chords is fruitful. A twelve-measure blues-chord sequence follows:

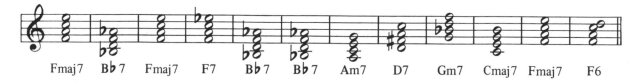

Fmaj7   B♭7   Fmaj7   F7   B♭7   B♭7   Am7   D7   Gm7   Cmaj7   Fmaj7   F6

". . . there is, in the blues, more frequent harmonization with seventh chords of the dominant type, especially with those on the flat or subdominant sides of the key . . ."[1]

Frequent experimentation in improvisation is of extreme importance to the young musician. There are numerous reports of schools experiencing more than average success by "allowing" jam sessions either before or following the normal school day. Care must be taken that these do not become noise sessions and thus obliterate other teaching and learning experiences to which the student has previously been exposed.

This leads directly to "*Written notes must precede improvisation.*" One of the prime requisites of every instrumental instructor should be to advocate accuracy in the matter of note reading. This includes the elements of quality, pitch, duration, intensity, and all the myriad factors that influence a proper and concise reproduction of the printed page. It is only after this note reading ability has been mastered that the student should be allowed to deviate from the printed page and enter into improvisation. It is strongly urged that the first "ad lib" solo be "written out" by the performer until he is confident in his own endeavor.

In order to facilitate the features of improvisation, a few comments on the preparation and reading of chord charts will prove advantageous to the serious jazz student. The following rules are those most frequently used in the preparation of "commercial" as well as "special" charts:

1. The capitalized letter is the "root" name of the chord.
2. Major chords use capital letters.
3. Minor chords use small letters.
4. Scale degrees may be added to any chord, i.e., D♭6.
5. Slanted lines indicate the beats within the bar of music.

---

[1] Willi Apel, *Harvard Dictionary of Music* (Cambridge: Harvard University Press, 1950), p. 375.

PERFORMANCE. There seems to be no national criteria available in either the area of stage band rehearsal or performance. The great majority of instructors agrees that the stage band has a vital part in the contemporary curriculum. There is a concensus asserting that the stage band must not be "the tail that wags the dog." The music program that schedules the stage band rehearsal in the school day enjoys greater success than where rehearsals are outside the school. If a program is to have any support from the students, the stage band should have at least one scheduled rehearsal a week and approximately six performances for the school year. This would insure adequate rehearsal time plus a sound stimulus for participation.

The type of performance for which a stage band may be engaged is guided by the type of school. Those schools that promote the vocational aspects of education naturally tend to produce a stage unit that is trained in the commercial/professional vein. These bands perform for more "dance" activities than do those which come from schools that are college-preparatory oriented. No matter what the school situation, a variety of performance outlets is quite possible as one considers school assemblies, basketball/football games, school socials, community shows, service and civic club programs, television and radio presentations, as well as the aforementioned dances. The stage band has the potential of being one of the schools most potent public relations organizations because of its flexibility, versatility of program, and perhaps most important, the enthusiasm of the student performers.

REHEARSAL TECHNIQUES. Return for a moment to the consideration of improvisation. A very normal process can be logically presented for the teaching of techniques in this area:

1. Short rhythmic or melodic phrases may be presented by the instructor and "imitated" by the student.
2. Short rhythmic or melodic phrases may be presented by the instructor and "answered" by the student.
3. The student may prepare and present his own ideas in a purely creative attitude.

It follows that an avenue for composition and arranging is provided through the stage band. Such opportunities for self-expression greatly enhance the previously mentioned reasons for participation. Also, because of the nature of the music, a greater variation in style and phrasing may be presented through this organization than in larger groups, i.e., "swing," "ballad," "latin," "Dixieland," "progressive," and "rock."

A further technique is presented through the opportunity of working on "balance." In all playing there must be an awareness for the proper amount of "lead." All members of the section must play as loudly as the lead, but never overpowering that part. In modulations, that part containing modulatory notes must be heard, but not to the extent of destroying the lead.

Another consideration in teaching balance is the use of vibrato. The style, quality and quantity of the vibrato must be matched within the section and must blend with that produced by the lead. Because of the size of each section, it is possible to achieve similar vibrato and tone production. In larger ensembles a faulty tonal concept may be covered by the mass. However, the individuality of the stage band makes each musician aware of his differences, and thus, tonal balance becomes imperative to a good sound.

Finally, a technique that is used more frequently with the stage band than perhaps with any other organization is that of "listening." There are reasons which may account for this. First, the normal size of the stage band corresponds to bands which have been publically acclaimed as leaders; and second, many music instructors associate closely with the recording artists. Stage bands have at their listening disposal the recording artistry of such bands as Count Basie, Les Brown, Buddy Rich, Woody Herman, and many others. Most schools require their students to spend considerable time listening to and analyzing the music of these artists, not necessarily for imitative purposes, but for acceptance of and exposure to their various styles.

INDIVIDUAL TECHNIQUES. While the brass and woodwind sections have the facility to change style and character with each composition, for the percussionist certain factors remain constant and thus provide ample opportunity for this performer to study his technique diligently.

Clem de Rosa in an article, "Stage Band Drumming Plus Musicianship," states that there are four primary functions of the stage band drummer: time, taste, tone, and technique.

Time must be steady and solid, for this is the backbone of the band. The percussionist should develop his right hand to such a degree as to play any cymbal beat comfortably at any tempo. Too often the cymbal part is an indefinite amount of noise which destroys the rhythmic concept produced by the other members of the band.

For the development of *taste*, four sounds are used:

1. Short sounds (rim shots, choked cymbal, sharp blow of the snare).
2. Long sounds (roll and crash cymbal).
3. High-pitched sounds (snare drum and cup of cymbal).
4. Low-pitched sounds (bass drum and tom-tom).

The relationship of these four sounds to the rest of the band is that the trumpets are considered "high" while the trombones and saxophones are "low."

Tone is controlled by the choice of cymbals plus the tension of the drums. In selecting a high-hat cymbal, the 13 or 14 inch sizes are the most practical. The bottom cymbal should be medium-heavy in weight and pitch, and the top cymbal lighter in weight and pitch. The ride cymbal should be of the 18 to 20 inch variety. Much enhancement of sound may be accomplished by using the sizzle cymbal. A word of caution — *too thin or low pitched cymbals are inadequate.* The heads of the snare should be tightened so as to produce a crisp sound. The bass drum and tom-tom heads should be loosened to eliminate the "ping" sound.

The fourth function, *technique*, may be summarized simply: the percussionist must have a *more than adequate* ability.

A uniqueness in stage band techniques is found in playing eighth notes, accents, syncopation, smooth attack, short-light attack, and long-heavy attack. The performance of the various techniques of articulation has been summarized in a chart prepared by Matt Betton and found at the conclusion of this chapter.

FINANCES. When programs are augmented by additional organizations, an increased strain is placed upon the budget. No set rules may be offered as to raising the amount necessary to support the stage band. Since most stage band members must first be members of the concert band, marching band, or orchestra, the "parent" group frequently provides the necessary revenue. A budget for a stage band may be as small as $200 to $250 for music, but it would not provide for the purchase of equipment such as drum sets, guitar outfits, amplifying equipment, stands, lights, and uniforms. Instructors may increase the purchasing power of their organization by using the token remunerations given for their presentations. Some stage bands even become self-sufficient by using the monies received from dance engagements.

In conclusion we recall once more the original question: "What is the role of the stage band in the music curriculum of the schools?" It is part of the American heritage and its music belongs to the American public. Therefore, it must be studied, taught, and presented to students. There exists in stage band music and in its performance by students a close proximity to musical creators of our American culture. To deprive the young scholars of the opportunity for exploration along these lines would be like removing the vitamins that promote wholesome, healthy bodies. Provisions must be made for the positioning of the stage band in the structure of the school music program.

REFERENCE MATERIALS

Coker, Jerry. *Improvising Jazz*. Englewood Cliffs: Prentice-Hall, Inc., 1964.

Dedrick/Polhamus. *How the Dance Band Swings*. Kendor Music, 1958.

Flanagan. *How to Build a Dance Band*. Southern Music Co., 1955.

Jazz in the Classroom, Vol. 1-6, records and scores: Berklee Press.

La Porta. *Dance Band Warm-ups*.

Risso. *Theory Method and Workshop*. National Band Camp, Inc., 1962.

Sanders. *Training the School Dance Band*. Chappell and Co., 1956.

Seibert. *Swing Now, Pay Later*.

Wiskirschen, Rev. *Developmental Techniques for the School Dance Band Musician*. C.S.C. Berlee Press, 1961.

STAGE BAND ARTICULATION[2]

HEAVY ACCENT: hold full value	THE SHAKE: a variation of the tone upwards (much like a trill)
HEAVY ACCENT: hold less than full value	LIP TRILL: similar to shake but slower and with more lip control
HEAVY ACCENT: short as possible	WIDE LIP TRILL: same as above, except slower, with wide interval
STACCATO: short (not heavy)	DU: false or muffled tone
LEGATO TONGUE: hold full value	WAH: full tone (not muffled)

[2] M. E. Hall, *Teacher's Guide to the High School Stage Band* (Elkhart: H. & A. Selmer, 1961).

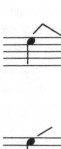 **THE FLIP:** sound note, raise pitch, then drop into following note (done with lip on brass instruments)

 THE SMEAR: slide into note from below and reach correct pitch just before next note (do not rob preceding note)

 SHORT GLISS UP: slide into note from below (usually one to three steps); no individual notes are heard

 LONG GLISS UP: same as above except longer entrance

 SHORT GLISS DOWN: the reverse of short gliss up

 LONG GLISS DOWN: same as above, except longer exit

 SHORT LIFT or RIP: enter note via chromatic or diatonic scale, beginning about a third below

 LONG LIFT or RIP: same as above, except longer entrance

 SHORT SPILL or FALL-OFF: rapid chromatic or diatonic drop; the reverse of short lift

 LONG SPILL or FALL-OFF: the reverse of the long lift

 THE PLOP: rapid slide down harmonic or diatonic scale before sounding note

 INDEFINITE SOUND: deadened tone; indefinite pitch

 THE DOIT: sound note, gliss upwards from one to five steps

chapter **11**

Innovations in Teaching

The survey of the selected schools in this study has brought to light few "new" and innovative procedures which might be regarded as significant. It seems obvious that those band programs which are widely regarded for superior teaching remain deeply rooted in their traditional approach to teaching.

While no programs represent a totally new approach, many do have some significant aspects in their course of study which are innovative. One of the selected schools in this study, Brooklyn Center High School, Minneapolis, Minnesota (Richard E. Papke, Director), can be recognized for its imagination and extremely methodical approach to designing curriculum. Most of the procedural activities listed by Mr. Papke are not singularly "innovative," but the total effect is a band curriculum which rises above the traditional and certainly deserves mention in this chapter. The following is the "Concert Band Curriculum Outline" used at the Brooklyn Center High School:

SUGGESTED CONCERT BAND CURRICULUM OUTLINE
by
Richard E. Papke
Brooklyn Center High School
Minneapolis, Minnesota

I. Organizations
   A. Concert Band, Varsity Band, Marching Band, Pep Band, Stage Band, _____ .
   B. Rehearsal schedules and grade level of participants.
   C. Use of rehearsal time for "music education" in addition to preparation for performance. (See rehearsal outline.)

II. Lectures
   A. Grade 10 — Music theory, terms, history, ear training.
   B. Grade 11 — Music theory, terms, history, harmony, ear training, form, arranging, composition.
   C. Grade 12 — Monthly "Senior Seminar" for discussions of aesthetics, philosophy, conducting, review of lectures.

III. Lessons — Private or group, as can be scheduled.

IV. Ensembles — Use one-half of one band rehearsal weekly for ensemble practice and recital by one ensemble.

V. Sectional — Scheduled by section leaders, as necessary.

VI. Quizzes — Use one-half of one band rehearsal monthly.

VII. Term Paper — Required; no length requirement; any approved music topic; no grade given.

VIII. Field Trip — One or more field trips yearly to Minnesota Orchestra or similar organization.

IX. Conducting — Required of all seniors in Concert Band.

X. Composition — Encouraged of all band members.

XI. Band Council — Meets monthly.

XII. Homecoming Football Show — Planned by seniors in band.

XIII. Grading — Monthly quizzes, weekly solo-soli, lessons.

XIV. Critiques — Submitted for any musical event attended; extra credit.

XV. Philosophy Question — One question required from each member yearly.

X-VI. Responsibility — Often delegated; section leaders schedule sectionals, audition all new members, teach some lessons.

XVII. Miscellaneous — Yearly instrument switch and exchange teaching; outside reading encouraged for seniors planning on music careers; transposition; improvisation; filmstrips; MUSIC 100 series; Blueprint score series; score analysis; composers.

"Obstacles are those frightful things you see
      when you take your eyes off the goal." —Hannah More

"Everything yields to diligence." —Aristophanes

SUGGESTED REHEARSAL ROUTINE:

DAILY	—	1.	Posture and breathing exercises; tone holding 30 to 60 seconds.
DAILY	—	2.	Warm-up and stress: tone, intonation, balance, blend, attacks, releases, conducting techniques to obtain eyes, pianissimos (Treasury of Scales, etc.).
MONDAYS	—	3.	Solo-soli method; hear each individual in band on two to four measures of assigned exercises.
TUESDAYS	—	3.	Key recitation.
WEDNESDAYS	—	3.	Solfege exercises.
THURSDAYS	—	3.	Scale and chord exercises; scales—major, minor, harmonic minor, melodic minor, chromatic; arpeggios—major, minor, diminished, augmented; ask members to play any scale or arpeggio and another identify; jazz chord sequence.
FRIDAYS	—	3.	All twelve major scales.
DAILY	—	4.	Sing and tune; chord singing.
DAILY	—	5.	Sight read and incorporate lecture materials of style, theory, harmony, history, form, etc.
DAILY	—	6.	Rehearse concert number and incorporate lecture materials. (Put composer's name on blackboard first, then title.)
DAILY	—	7.	Same as number 6. (Again emphasize composer's name.)
DAILY	—	8.	Same as number 6. (Again emphasize composer's name.)
DAILY	—	9.	Remind brass to do "range" exercises.

Rehearsal Recapitulation:

A. Daily incorporate all "music education" materials into rehearsal.

B. One-half rehearsal weekly for ensembles and chamber group recital.

C. One-half rehearsal monthly for quiz.

D. One rehearsal monthly for MUSIC 100 series of slides, records, worksheets.

"Teach so that the student becomes his own best teacher."

"Behold the turtle. He makes progress only when he sticks his neck out." —James B. Conant

ASSIGNED RECORD LISTENING FOR MONTHLY BAND QUIZ 1968-69
(*indicates score available to use while listening)

Music History Period	Records and Scores
SEPT.: Baroque (about 1600-1750)	*1. Blueprint Series: *Brandenburg Concerto No. 4* — Bach
	*2. *Brandenburg Concerto No. 2* — Bach
	3. "Tocatta and Fugue in D minor" — Bach
	4. Band: "The Southerner March" — Alexander
OCT.: Baroque	*1. Blueprint Series: *Royal Fireworks* — Handel
	*2. *Brandenburg Concerto No. 1* — Bach
	*3. *The Water Music* — Handel
	*4. Band: "Chorale and Alleluia" — Howard Hanson
NOV.: Classical (about 1750-1827)	*1. Blueprint Series: *The Magic Flute* — Mozart
	*2. *Symphony No. 40 in G minor* — Mozart
	*3. *Symphony No. 100, "Military"* — Haydn
	*4. Band: *First Suite in Eb* — Holst
DEC.: Classical	*1. Blueprint Series: "Egmont Overture" — Beethoven
	*2. *Symphony No. 29* — Mozart
	*3. *Symphony No. 94, "Surprise"* — Haydn
	*4. Band: "Roman Carnival Overture" — Berlioz
JAN.: Romantic (about 1820-1900)	*1. Blueprint Series: *Symphony No. 4*, "Italian" — Mendelssohn
	*2. *Symphony No. 3*, "Eroica" — Beethoven
	*3. *Symphony No. 3*, Brahms
	*4. Band: "Suite of Old American Dances" — R. R. Bennett
FEB.: Romantic	*1. Blueprint Series: *Symphony No. 9*, "New World"— Dvorak
	*2. *Symphony No. 5* — Beethoven
	*3. *Symphony No. 6, "Pathétique"* — Tschaikovsky
	*4. Band: "Trittico" — Nelhybel
MARCH: Contemporary (from about 1900)	*1. Blueprint Series: "Lincoln Portrait" — Copland
	*2. *Firebird Suite* — Stravinsky
	*3. *Rodeo* — Copland
	*4. Band: "Psalm for Band" — Persichetti
APRIL: Contemporary	*1. Blueprint Series: "An American in Paris" —Gershwin
	*2. *Le Sacre du Printemps* (The Rite of Spring) — Stravinsky

131

MAY: Miscellaneous

    *3. *Symphony No. 5* — Shostakovich
    *4. Band : "La Fiesta Mexicana" — H. Owen Reed
    1. "The Unanswered Question" — Charles Ives
    2. Electronic Music — Cage
    3. "West Side Story" — Leonard Bernstein
    4. Band: "The Bartered Bride Overture" — Smetana
    5. Band: "Incantation and Dance" — John Chance
    6. Band: "Festive Overture" — Shostakovich

(See also Play-Along and Music Minus One records, History of Music in Sound — Volumes 1-10, and all records in the band library — records with solos, jazz, stage band, etc.)

> "Knowledge is not an end in itself, it is a means to an end.
> The end is life enlighted, life ennobled, life empowered.
> The end is not knowledge, but wisdom, not scientific method, but Truth."

> "Without brains, you are a fiasco.
> Without means, you are an amateur.
> Without heart, you are a machine.
> It has its dangers, this occupation."
>
> — Vladimir Horowitz

CONCERT BAND QUIZ ITEMS (Monthly)

  I. Musical Terms — Usually three items.
  II. Music History — Usually three items.
     MUSIC 100 — Usually one item.
     History of Instrument — Usually one item.
 III. Music Theory, Harmony, Melodic and Rhythmic Dictation — Usually eight or nine items.
 IV. Record Recognition — Usually four items.
  V. Rhythm — Usually one item.
 VI. Composers — Usually one item.
VII. Musicianship — Usually one item.
VIII. Aesthetics-Philosophy — Usually one item.
 IX. Percussion — Usually one item.

Note:

Seniors in the band are to answer all quiz items to the best of their ability.

Juniors in the band answer only those quiz items marked for juniors (about three-fourths) and may attempt the senior items for bonus points.

Sophomores in the band answer only those quiz items marked for sophomores (about one-half) and may attempt junior and senior items for bonus points.

> "You will have to practice long and faithfully before you realize that you cannot play."
>
> — Beethoven

BREATH IMPULSE

Another instructional technique found in the selected schools of this study was the "Breath Rhythmic Impulse Method," originated in the Norman, Oklahoma public schools. This is a system of teaching students greater feeling for rhythmic pulse through what is essentially a diaphragm vibrato. Developed in the 1950's by Norman instructors William C. Robinson and James A. Middleton, B.R.I.M. teaching was found in 10% of the selected schools in this study, representing a wide geographic area.

A comprehensive explanation of B.R.I.M. teaching and an objective measurement of its effectiveness can be found in a dissertation by James Middleton, "A Study of the Effectiveness of the Breath Impulse Technique in the Instruction of Wind Instrument Performers," University of Oklahoma, 1967. (Available through University Microfilms, Ann Arbor, Michigan.)

A school band program which has in past years received wide acclaim for its innovative teaching is the McMinnville, Oregon school band. The present director Donald C. Scott does not now classify his program as "innovative" but does cite two curriculum practices which can be used as examples in the category of innovations:

1. Creative projects are required of all junior and senior (band) members. Sophomores often do this too. Examples are electronic music, band or ensemble compositions or arrangements, rock and/or stage band compositions.

2. A program of individual lessons (each student in Jr.-Sr. High is given an individual lesson every two weeks).

WEEKLY PRIVATE LESSONS

The Morgan School in Clinton, Connecticut has developed a program of weekly private lessons which is above the traditional concept of school band instruction. William Gagnon describes his program as follows:

"The Board of Education employs five part-time teachers who give every band member (92) a private lesson each week. This is during school time and the teachers are professional artist musicians who hold bachelor and masters degrees in music. The school also employs an adult accompanist for the chorus and a part-time voice teacher who offers private voice class two days per week. These seven part-time teachers are in addition to Mr. Gagnon who conducts all band and chorus classes."

DIAL ACCESS

A school-wide innovation reported by several schools and having implications especially for music teaching is the "Dial Access Information Retrieval System" (DAIRS). Dial access systems consist essentially of a means of remote control which permits any number of individual students to achieve separate access to any number of continually available audio and video programs—usually recorded on magnetic tape. The means of remote control may be any device capable of connecting the student via a switching mechanism to the selected program. It has become increasingly common over the past few years for students to study at their own pace at individual locations, and to have access from these locations to many sources of audio or visual information such as slides, filmstrips, audio tapes, records, etc.

A dial access system is essentially no more than the coordination of what was previously a multitude of separate, uncoördinated, audio-visual components. Dial access systems (as distinct from language lab equipment) have been in use for only a few years, but there are already approximately 250 installations at all educational levels in the United States. The vast majority of these installations are being used as foreign language laboratories, even though most of them can be, and expect to be, adapted to other instructional uses at some future date.

As language labs, these installations provide access to audio information only. But as the use of dial access systems spreads to other disciplines and the cost of video components is reduced, more and more installations will accomodate both audio and video program material.

Terms which are used to describe the various systems include "Dial Select," "Random Access," "Remote Access," and other similar phrases. Different terms sometimes denote real differences in the techniques used, but the basic elements of the various systems are similar. It is becoming customary to refer to all of them as dial access systems. Use of such system is reported by Earl C. Benson, band director at Hubert Olson Junior High School, Bloomington, Minnesota:

"The Dial Access System located in the Learning Resources Center contains from three to six program sources in music every week. These include a history appreciation lesson, a theory lesson, and an appreciation lesson in contemporary music. Tapes on advanced musicianship — including harmonic, rhythmic and melodic dictation — are also placed on the system. Worksheets are available in band, choir or orchestra classes to supplement these recorded lessons. The dial system may be used by all students and works much like a telephone dial with headsets. The tapes and worksheets were developed in the music department and have been used extensively for the past two years. Examples of the worksheets are as follows:

WORKSHEET No. 1: Primitive Music — Greek Music

Question:

1. What do we mean by primitive man?
2. When, in relation to the birth of Christ, did primitive man exist?
3. What was life like during primitive times?

In this lesson listen for a general description of primitive music and the name of one civilization which made major contributions to music and art.

4. Describe the very earliest type of music made by primitive man.
5. Name one purpose for the use of music by primitive man.
6. What was one of primitive man's major advances in music?
7. What civilization made important advances in musical systems and musical instruments?
8. Name the four sections of the contemporary orchestra.
9. Did Greek art influence other civilizations?
10. The type of music which developed 2,000 years ago and developed from earlier civilizations was called_____.
11. The language used was_____.
12. The official language of the Roman Church was_____.
13. The earliest type of harmony, with more than one melody sung or played at the same time, was called_____.

14. What kind of music is associated with the worship of the early church? _____

15. In England, the roving musicians who roamed the countryside were called _____.

16. In Germany these singers were called _____.

17. In France roving musicians were called _____ .

18. The instrument of the wandering musicians in Europe was the _____ .

19. The keyboard instrument which was introduced in 1450 was the _____.

20. About fifty years after the development of the clavichord, a later keyboard instrument was introduced. It was the _____ .

21. Music which is made up of several melodies sounding together is called _____ music.

22. The composer of the "Pope Marcellus Mass" was _____ . What nationality was he? _____

WORKSHEET No. 3: The Classical Period in Music

Questions:

1. The "Father of the Symphony" was _____ .

2. Franz Joseph Haydn was born in the same year as one of our presidents. What president had the same birth date? _____

3. Haydn added another form to the symphony. This dance form was the _____ . Its meter is _____ (4/4, 3/4, 6/8, 2/4?).

4. The composer of the Classical period who brought opera to its highest development was

   _____ .

5. What was Mozart's nationality? _____

6. What instrument did Mozart introduce into the orchestra? _____

Ludwig Van Beethoven was a revolutionary composer of the classical age. He is considered by many to be the greatest of all composers. Beethoven's compositions were filled with originality and power, emotion and strength. His compositions bridge the gap between the Classical emphasis on form and restraint, and the Romantic emphasis on freedom and emotion in music. His works include: 32 piano sonatas, 9 symphonies, concertos, chamber music, one opera, choral works, and hundreds of smaller compositions.

7. What was Beethoven's nationality? _____

8. What instrument plays the bridge between the fourth and fifth movements of the *Pastorale Symphony?* _____

The three significant contributions made to music during the Classical Period were:
1. Establishment of opera as we know it today.
2. Development of symphonic form.
3. Introduction of the clarinet as an orchestral instrument.

WORKSHEET No. 5: Music of the Romantic Period

1. When did the Romantic Period start? _____

2. The music of the Romantic period was written by Paganini to _____ .

3. Does the solo violin stand out from the rest of the orchestra? _____

4. A solo selection written for voice is called an _____ .

5. What musical form is especially associated with the name Rossini?_____

6. What voice sings the solo in the example? _____
   (Ex.: alto, tenor, soprano, bass)

7. Which is more prominent in the Rossini opera, the orchestra or the soloist?_____

8. The "Waltz King" of Austria was _____ .

9. What is a typical quality of Strauss rhythms?_____

10. Who was the first composer of popular songs in the United States? _____

11. The trumpet player of "Old New Orleans" who did much for the "blues" was_____ .

12. What was the earliest type of jazz in the United States? _____

13. What instrument played the solo in the "Beale Street Blues"? _____

14. Music written with a theme which reflects on the music and traditions of a particular country is called nationalistic music. A composer who writes music which reflects these feelings is called a _____ composer.

15. What was Brahms' nationality? _____

16. Did Tchaikovsky consider himself a nationalistic composer? _____

17. The listening example written by Modeste Mussorgsky was entitled _____ .

Georges Bizet was born in Paris, France in 1838. *Carmen*, one of the most successful operas of all time, received its first performance three months before Bizet's untimely death.

18. In what country is the setting for the opera *Carmen*? _____

19. What voice signs the "Habanera" from *Carmen*? _____

Ruggerio Leoncavallo was born in Naples, Italy in 1858. He is known strictly as a composer of operas; his opera *Pagliacci* was his most successful work.

20. What was Pagliacci's profession?_____

21. Is Leoncavallo famous for any other compositions?_____

Edvard Grieg was born in Bergen, Norway in 1843. He was considered the voice of Norway for the way his compositions reflected the rich heritage of his beloved homeland. Grieg's nationalistic spirit is especially evident in his short lyric forms and in the "Peer Gynt Suite." His *Piano Concerto in A Minor* is one of the most popular piano concertos in the concert field.

22. The champion of nationalistic music in Norway was _____ .

23. What is the name of Grieg's best-known work?_____

24. The symphony composed by Antonin Dvorak as he observed the new land of America was _____ .

25. What was the nationality of Dvorak? _____

WORKSHEET No. 7: Music of the Twentieth Century

Maurice Ravel was born in Ciboure, France in 1875. Ravel, composer, conductor, and pianist, showed a profound attraction to strong rhythms, brilliant orchestrations, and novel sounds in his music. Ravel's music indicates his great interest in ancient instruments and music, as well as in American jazz.

Composers of the 19th century were looking for new ways of expressing themselves through music. NEW SOUNDS!

1. What is the name of one of Ravel's most famous compositions? _____
2. What percussion instrument plays the typical bolero rhythm? _____
3. The best-known work of Claude Debussy is _____ .
4. What do we call the kinds of music similiar to "Clair de lune"? _____
5. What was Debussy's nationality? _____

Manuel de Falla of Spain was a nationalistic composer. His harmonies, rhythms, and melodic combinations in the "Ritual Fire Dance" could only have been created in the 20th century.

6. Did De Falla use any Spanish rhythms in his music? _____
7. Music without a key feeling is called _____ .
8. Short bits of melody repeated over and over again is called _____ .
9. Clashing harmonies are called _____ .
10. The twelve-tone system as developed by Schönberg used twelve chromatic notes in what ways?
   _____
11. Why is music written in the twelve-tone system called *atonal*? _____
12. Did you find twelve-tone music shocking? Why? _____
13. Menotti used the twelve-tone system in his opera _____ .

George Gershwin was born in Brooklyn, New York in 1898. Gershwin chose jazz as his particular medium in music composition. From "Tin Pan Alley" to the concert hall, Gershwin has made a major contribution to the music of our American heritage. His representative works include: *Rhapsody in Blue*, *Concerto for Piano and Orchestra*, *An American in Paris*, and *Porgy and Bess*.

14. Gershwin's great folk opera was _____ .
15. What was one of the main ingredients in Gershwin's music? _____
16. What voice sings "Summertime"? _____

Dmitri Shostakovich was born in Petrograd, Russia in 1906. Shostakovich, contemporary composer of the Soviet Union, has been both praised and criticized for his political and musical views. His music generally reflects the moderate stand taken by Soviet composers in regard to contemporary music. Shostakovich has composed in most of the traditional forms, including symphony, concerto, opera, chamber music, and music for films."

Mr. Benson also reports the following as innovative features of the music program at his school:

1. Resource Room for Music

   In addition to large and small group rehearsals in band, students are encouraged to use a special room set up for them in the Instructional Resource Center. This room is equipped with phonographs and headsets for individual listening. A large record collection is available, featuring the finest in choral, orchestral and wind band listening. Musical scores are also available for those students who want to analyze the music while listening. This is also a place for quiet musical reading and composition. Supervision is student directed.

2. Music-Minus-One Series

   Music students have at their disposal a nearly complete set of music-minus-one albums. These may be used at school in practice rooms or may be checked out for use at home. A percussion room with a complete drum set is also available.

ORGANIZING AND HEARING ASSIGNMENTS

Several schools list as innovative their plans for organizing and hearing assignments. Two examples of this idea are the band programs in Hutchinson, Kansas (Leroy Esau, Director) and Jefferson City, Missouri (Jerry Hoover, Director). The essential concept is that of assigning specific work (scales, exercises, etudes, excerpts from the music which is being performed, listening, reading, theory, etc.) to students in band, much in the manner that individual assignments would be made in academic areas. For example, students in English write themes, students in math work problems, students in band play scales. In the Jefferson City band program, every student is heard (individually on his assignment by a band director) for a grade and a chair each week. Mr. Hoover gives the following chart as an example of how his procedure is used:

JEFFERSON CITY, MISSOURI BANDS

TRYOUT AUDITION FORM

T—Technique   P—Pitch
A—Articulation   H—Hand Position
R—Rhythm   D—Dynamics

Instrument/Class _____ Date _____ Auditioner _____

Name	Tone	Scoring	Total Errors	Seating	Grade

Mr. Hoover stresses that an important aspect of making his plan work is the efficiency of the instructor in "moving" the audition. Students are asked to play quickly with a minimum amount of talking or time-wasting.

AUDIO-VISUAL RHYTHM READING

Christian Brothers High School, Memphis, Tennessee (Ralph Hale, Director) has developed an audio-visual system for aiding the reading of rhythms. Mr. Hale describes this procedures as follows:

"It is our theory that rhythm patterns are the musicians' vocabulary and should be read and recognized as groups the same as reading words. With this in mind, we made slides to use in a carousel slide projector. The first set of twenty-five slides has only the patterns introduced in the Band Builder Book I in 4/4 time. The second set of twenty-five slides has only the patterns introduced in Book II of the Band Builder series in 4/4 time. The third set contains patterns in 2/4, 3/4, and 6/8. The fourth set has more advanced patterns in all times. Our system of counting is related to the foot pat and is always done to a metronome. (Metronomes are mounted on the wall in each practice room.) By setting the metronomes on 60, the slides can be used in succession as one 25-measure exercise. The slides are rearranged and a new exercise is available.

"We also use a tachistoscope with the projector. With this setup we can show the slide at one second or 1/50 of a second duration and have the student play what he saw. This teaches the student to read patterns instead of notes. It is a form of speed reading for musicians. This can be done in groups or by individuals."

TEAM TEACHING

Team teaching is another innovative device noted by several of the selected schools in this study. Two of the strongest advocates of this approach are the Clovis, New Mexico band program (Norvil Howell, Director) and the Greensboro, North Carolina Band at Grimsley High School (Herbert Hazelman, Director). Mr. Hazelman describes the value of team teaching in his school as follows:

"If I had to pick the one facet of our program which contributes most to its success, it would be the fact that the six full-time band teachers assigned to our school work as a team. All six are involved with the senior high school band as directors, assistants, and semi-private teachers. All six also work in the two junior high schools — five at Kiser and two at Lindley (obviously one man works in both schools). Four of the six also do elementary school work. We are fortunate to have one ex-band director who is principal of one of our elementary schools, and he does the band teaching in his school. Our staff operates without friction and each member complements the others. Each man teaches to his strengths, i.e., the two best jazz musicians handle the stage bands, our gung-ho marching men do the marching band, woodwind specialists are not asked to teach brass players and vice versa. All in all we have a very happy situation — one which makes working together a profitable and pleasurable experience."

SUMMARY

One respondent stated that his "innovations" were hard work and an open mind for new ideas. In light of the fact that this study has shown that most schools continue to be performance oriented, and that, by and large, the innovations are not major nor radical in nature, perhaps this comment might be taken more seriously and regarded as giving some insight into the real mainstream of thought in improving school band instruction in the United States.

chapter 12

Teaching in Disadvantaged Areas

Before accepting a position in one of the schools in a disadvantaged area, the band director considering such a move would do well to employ every means possible to acquaint himself thoroughly with the conditions under which he will be required to work. Regardless of previous experience or training, there is no substitute for the latest local information regarding the school and the area.

The racial, ethnic and socio-economic problems of these areas have been well documented by the mass media of the country. The seriousness of these problems will be felt very keenly in the classroom. Should the new director lack the initiative, drive, genuine interest and determination to follow through on the needs of his students, the realization of his mistake in accepting the position will become evident very soon. In a hard-core trouble spot, a hasty transfer may be the only alternative.

Although the director can do little toward changing the local conditions that breed the difficulties under which the students must live, he can at least make a sincere effort to understand them. The following are a few of the causes for the circumstances under which the school must function:

1. A lack of self-respect (or self-image) by a large number of its students.
2. A shortage of stable homes, and therefore low family concepts.
3. A serious lack of interest by many parents in either the student or the school.
4. Lack of money by everybody, including the school district.
5. The presence of interracial and intra-class hostilities.
6. A general low achievement level in educational basics.
7. A low threshold of tolerance for discipline or rule of authority by many students.
8. Language difficulties.
9. Cultural differences.

The positive factors may not appear to be many, but they are significant:

1. There are youngsters who are good citizens, good students, hard workers, loyal and are the backbone of the band program.
2. Music is a very important part of the culture.

The type and style of some of the music may not be the same as the music heard in other communities, nevertheless, the interest in music and music-making are strong points for the program. It has been mentioned earlier that the director must meet the musical needs and desires of his students if he is to survive on the job. These needs may require a major shake-up in his traditional approach to the school band program. A typical school concert band may not be at all possible. By making special musical arrangements, and balancing the instrumentation that is available, there may be possibilities for organizing a good sounding wind ensemble. The group could be an all-brass band of perhaps only 12 or 14 members. For the students who have no interest in this organization there could be other outlets for their musical endeavors such as stage band, jazz band, rock band, "soul" shows, folk music ensembles of various combinations, pep band, drum corps, etc. Because personnel will naturally change from year to year, annual adjustments will have to take place every fall. Sometimes the personnel resources are very slim, other times they may be fairly plentiful. There may be occasional use of guest players who can sit in to fill instrumentation vacancies. Some schools or areas may frown upon outside players participating in the school musical organizations. Experience has shown that this is no problem. Quite the contrary. The administration and the students of the band are more than pleased to have these additions in order to fulfill their commitments to the school and to the community.

3. There is a very real desire on the part of the students and the community for the youngsters to perform and entertain as often as possible, and in as many ways as possible.

There is far more local musical activity than is generally known. There are many lodge parades, conventions, trips and ceremonies. There are frequent church music festivals, sporting events that are not part of the school athletic program, folk music festivals, dedications, talent shows, jazz, rock and "soul" shows, benefit concerts, etc. All of these affairs have music, and the members of the school music program enjoy taking part. The performers may be any one of the organizations listed previously. If the occasion is long enough and on a large enough scale, there is a good possibility that all of them will appear on the program at one time or another.

4. Due to various government sponsored anti-poverty programs, the opportunities of employment for youth have improved.

When spelling out the "success factors" employed by the directors teaching in these circumstances, it soon becomes evident that basically these factors are no different than the approaches and attitudes that are so essential in achieving results in any school, regardless of the locale. Even if the band were in a privileged community, these factors would still hold true. The main difference is in the degree of application and hard work. Another difference is the need for more flexibility in making adjustments to fit the available instrumentation.

The first and most important approach to success is a whole-hearted desire to meet the musical needs of the band members, and to relate, identify and communicate with them in every way possible to establish a wholesome working relationship. Communication and identity with students throughout the entire school are essential. This includes getting involved in all the school activities that concern the improvement of the spirit and efficiency of the students. Regardless of how pressed for time the director may be, he should make a special effort to attend and support PTA drives, performances put on by other school departments, special meetings and assemblies.

The director should set a reasonable objective as soon as possible. He should be optimistic and show confidence that he believes sincerely that success is entirely possible. There could be a public performance for a civic affair, a school assembly, a PTA concert, a concert tour of the schools in the neighborhood, or a parade or trip out of town. Praise and recognition for a job well done should be given to everyone concerned immediately after the event. There should be no delay.

There should be a well-established policy of behavior. There should be a daily routine of instruction. None of these procedures are novel, but in many cases the teachers simply give up. Perhaps the reader has noted how repeatedly it has been pointed out that the director must be genuinely interested in the program and determined to follow through. Herein lies the crux of the whole problem with some teachers who accept positions in such schools. Rarely is failure the result of lack of technical knowledge. Almost any well-trained band director in the country could do the job. It simply resolves to the question of whether he has the desire to do the job.

Ironically, the director, if he has the wisdom to accept it, will discover that even failure to accomplish all or even part of his objectives can result in a different reward of the highest order. This is the inner confidence that he has done the best be could for the students. He knows he has set a good example for them to follow in solving their own problems and accomplishing their own goals. The interaction relationship between the band director and the students on a day-to-day basis can also be very rewarding. In a few short years he will be pleased to discover that he has played a far more significant part in the lives of his students than he realized.

chapter 13

Facilities

Once the experiences are selected for the band program, with objectives of musical competence identified and defined, specific plans may be drawn to accomplish the task. The *sequence of experiences* which are intended to lead to the desired level of accomplishment are established by careful consideration of the objectives, course offerings, time allotments, with provisions for individual differences. Defining the obejctives of the band program establishes the types of facility, material, equipment and procedure that will be needed to accomplish them.

The band department requires certain special facilities in order to operate effectively. The location of the rehearsal room is important both for efficiency in moving equipment and personnel and for minimizing disturbance to other classes. Band classes are often three to five times the size of an average academic class of thirty students, which thus necessitates sufficient space consideration. Because many instruments and other special equipment items are used, facilities for storage and security are required. Because the volume of a band is great, careful attention must be given to acoustics. Proper illumination also presents special problems. Ventilation, heating, and humidity control are important factors in that they help maintain proper intonation and protect expensive instruments.

In determining both the present and future needs of the music program, judgments should be based on the local educational philosophy and objectives, projected enrollment statistics, immediate number of students to be served, and relative amount of funds available. A planning committee should be appointed to facilitate the task. The committee should include school administrators, music teachers, competent architects and acoustical engineers, heating, ventilation, and lighting experts, state education department personnel, college and school faculty members, pupils, parents, and other interested community leaders. Visits to new school buildings and conferences with others who are engaged in planning a music suite or who have recently gone through the planning and construction process may prove to be very helpful.

MUSIC ROOMS

Ideally, the music suite would be best located in a separate building conveniently situated between the school auditorium and the athletic field. Practically, however, such a plan—besides being costly in construction, heating, and maintenance—might present other disadvantages, and might not be in keeping with overall school construction plans.

A good, practical location for the music suite is in a wing or portion of the main building, with direct access to the stage and auditorium. It should have a direct outside entrance to permit community and evening use as a separate unit, and to make it easier for the marching band to assemble out-of-doors for practice, athletic events, and parades.

The transmission of sound to other areas of the school building is a factor which should be given careful consideration. Physical isolation should be sought. If it cannot be fully achieved, it is possible to reduce the transmission of sound to other areas by means of the acoustical treatment of rooms, insulation, and the use of mechanical air-conditioning systems. A separate ventilation system should be planned in order to eliminate transmission of rehearsal sounds throughout the building.

The various rooms of the music suite should form as compact a unit as possible in order to facilitate proper supervision and convenient storage of instruments, equipment, music, and other materials.

A few cautions regarding location of rooms within the music suite may be in order. In some schools the doors of the small practice rooms open directly into a large rehearsal room. In spite of acoustical treatment, sound is transmitted between the rooms, making it impractical to use all rooms simultaneously. In planning the suite, it is better to design the practice rooms so that the doors open into a hallway or separate corridor. Practice rooms may be separated acoustically from the rehearsal rooms by placing storage rooms or "dead air" walls between them. Glass windows should always be provided in practice room doors.

The use of the auditorium for regular rehearsals has some advantages, particularly in adjusting the seating and becoming accustomed to the acoustics of the auditorium prior to a concert. As a general rule, however, problems arising out of scheduling conflicts with the drama and other departments make it desirable to have a separate room for conducting regular rehearsals of performing organizations.

TYPES AND SIZES OF MUSIC ROOMS.

Factors to be considered in planning types and sizes of music rooms are:

1. School and community population.
2. Trends in school and community population.
3. Music offerings and projected needs.
4. Cultural traditions of school and community.
5. Number of music teachers.
6. Other possible uses for music rooms.

The music departments of most schools have shown a marked increase in pupil participation beyond that which might be attributed to a normal increase in school population. Academic credit is now allowed for participation in music performing groups as well as for formal courses in music. The supply of music teachers has increased, and the quality of music instruction has improved.

Area, county, district and state music festivals have helped to spur pupil interest in music activities. Clinics, conferences, and conventions sponsored by the American School Band Directors Association, State Music Educators Associations, and the Music Educators National Conference have contributed to the increased effectiveness of the music education program in schools throughout the country.

INSTRUMENTAL REHEARSAL ROOM. In estimating the appropriate size of the instrumental room, allow approximately 30 sq. ft. of floor space for each person.

Instrumental directors are not in complete agreement regarding the desirability of having built-in risers for the instrumental rehearsal room. Of course, players in the back rows can see the conductor better when they are seated on risers. On the other hand, there is a tendency for the percussion and large brass instruments to overbalance the group from their elevated position.

Some school music directors prefer to have raised platforms for their instrumental groups. By installing semi-permanent risers or commercially constructed portable risers, it is possible to move them into the auditorium for concert performances.

Risers for the instrumental rehearsal room should be at least 48 inches deep in order to accommodate instruments, stands, chairs and pupils. The highest riser should be at least 72 in. deep in order to accommodate unusually large instruments, such as string basses, tympani, and other large percussion instruments. The elevation of each level should be from 6 to 10 in., depending on the height of the ceiling.

High ceilings are very important in helping to achieve optimum acoustical treatment. Music produced by a large instrumental organization is at times intensely loud and can be deafening to the ears, unless there is ample space to facilitate sound dissipation and absorption.

Walls which are broken into segments and have angles of varying degrees are recommended by acoustical engineers as an aid in the deflection of sound. This helps to prevent the formation of "standing waves" at certain frequencies and permits a more evenly distributed balance of sound throughout the room. This becomes increasingly important if the room is to be used for recording or broadcasting purposes. Many modern band rehearsal rooms have installed deep-pile floor carpeting and drapes on traverse rods to control the acoustical properties of the room. More will be said about this in the section on acoustics.

Furnishings of the instrumental music room should include folding chairs with retractable tablet arms, designed to encourage good playing posture. These chairs are especially functional as more and more conductors include the teaching of theory and music appreciation in their rehearsal periods. Occasionally students are expected to take notes and write examinations.

Modern instrumental rooms provide storage space for all instruments around the back of the room or as near as possible to their playing position. In addition to improving efficiency and ease of handling, this arrangement helps to prevent accidents and possible damage to the instruments.

Large schools have a need for separate rooms for the band and orchestra. Essentially the size and arrangement of the two rooms should be similar. But because of the greater volume of sound produced by a band, the band room should have a higher ceiling or provide more absorption by additional acoustical treatment of the ceiling, floor and walls.

RECORDING AND BROADCAST CONTROL BOOTH. Recent developments in closed- and open-circuit television, improvements in recording and broadcasting equipment, and increased use of school facilities by adult community organizations have made it advisable to include a broadcasting and recording control booth adjacent to the instrumental rehearsal room. Such a control booth should be well insulated against sound transmission and should have double glass, soundproof windows for direct viewing of performing groups.

GENERAL MUSIC, THEORY, APPRECIATION CLASSROOM. A regular academic classroom accommodating 30 to 40 pupils may be used for classes in general music, theory, and appreciation. Acoustical treatment and sound insulation is quite essential. Space should be provided for one or two pianos, radio-phonograph, television, tape recorder, teacher's desk, and filing cabinets in the front of the room. The front wall should be equipped with a chalkboard with some permanently painted music staffs. Part of the walls should be equipped with a bulletin board for displaying music materials. A film screen and electrical outlets should also be provided. The rear wall should be equipped with electrical outlets for film projectors, opaque projectors and overhead projectors. A closet should be provided for storing music stands, extra chairs, music books, recordings, and other teaching materials. The room should be located near the other music rooms to facilitate the moving and sharing of materials.

INSTRUMENT CLASS, ENSEMBLE, AND SECTIONAL REHEARSAL ROOM. This classroom for individualized instruction (including sectionals and small ensembles) may be slightly smaller than a regular classroom. It should be acoustically treated and should be located near the other music rooms. Where the school offers class instruction in piano as well as in band and orchestra instruments, such a room should be large enough to hold a number of studio upright pianos or small electronic pianos. Electrical outlets should be provided every 4 to 5 ft. around the baseboard of the room.

LISTENING ROOM. Modern schools throughout the country have added a new type of room to the music suite—the listening room. It has proved to be a most popular and valuable addition. It is equipped with several high-fidelity turntables, each having multiple sets of earphones. In some schools, this room is a part of the music suite, in others it is located in or near the library, or is part of a student lounge. The record library should be near the listening room so that pupils may conveniently select recordings for leisure or for assigned listening.

PRACTICE ROOMS. Practice rooms for individual use are quite essential to the development of a superior school music program. Local policy regarding individual and small ensemble practice before, during, and after school will determine the necessary number and size of practice rooms. Some may be just large enough for one person, his instrument and a music stand (6 x 8 ft.). Others will be large enough for an upright studio piano and one or two instrumentalists with chairs and music stands (8 x 10 ft.). A few should be large enough for two pianos (8 x 12 ft.); and others should be large enough for trios, quartets, and other small ensembles (10 x 12 ft.). Acoustical engineers suggest that rooms having nonparallel walls (slightly trapezoid in shape) are superior acoustically.

In planning the location of practice rooms, special attention should be given to the means of supervision and to the minimizing of sound transmission into other areas. By arranging the practice rooms in a series along a corridor and equipping them with soundproof, double glass windows and an intercommunication system, they may be supervised easily from a central point. Proper acoustical treatment and insulation will help to absorb the sound and prevent its transmission to other areas.

STORAGE ROOMS.

Instruments. For convenience and safety, provision should be made to store all band and orchestra instruments at the rear or sides of the rehearsal room. Individual compartments of sizes appropriate for each instrument should be provided. Steel lockers equipped with locks and ventilated doors are most serviceable and give the best protection. A felt cloth lining helps to prevent scratching and reduces clatter. Compartments constructed of wood or plywood are also practical but do not provide adequate security unless equipped with doors and locks. Ventilation, heating, and humidity must be carefully controlled.

Designs for cabinet lockers for individual instrument storage follow:

1. Material*
   a. Sides and all vertical pieces made of 3/4 in. hardwood surface-bonded plywood.
   b. Shelving to be laminated 1/2 in. masonite or hardwood plywood.
   c. All exposed surfaces to be natural finish with a plastic varnish.
   d. Hinges—substanial cabinet type, chrome plated.
   e. Locks to be attached and mortised from back surface into door. All locks keyed —2 keys for each lock. All locks master keyed.

2. Construction
   a. All shelving mortised and glued into vertical dividers.
   b. Cabinets to be backed with 3/8 in. plywood, natural finish on inside only.
   c. No handles on cabinet doors.
   d. Approximate dimensions shown on drawings.
   e. Cabinets are to be built in individual units for maneuverability.

   *Other materials such as steel may be used. Similar cabinets are available from commercial manufactures—however, at a greater cost.

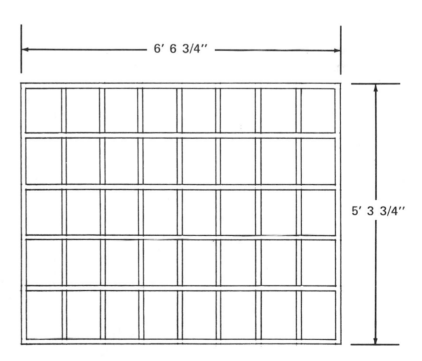

"A" Cabinet/Lockers:

Clarinets, Flutes and Oboes

6' 6 3/4"

5' 3 3/4"

40 Cabinets — 9" x 12" x 28" inside
(May be constructed in two units.)
Scale: 1/2" = 1'

6′ 9 3/4″

5′ 3 3/4″

"B" Cabinet/Lockers:

Alto Saxophones, Cornets and Trumpets

24 Cabinets — 12″ x 15″ x 28″ inside
(May be constructed in two units.)
Scale: 1/2″ = 1′

6′ 10 1/2″

5′ 3 3/4″

"C" Cabinet/Lockers:

Bassoons, Tenor Saxophones and Trumpets

15 Cabinets — 15″ x 20″ x 38″ inside
(May be constructed in two units.)
Scale: 1/2″ = 1′

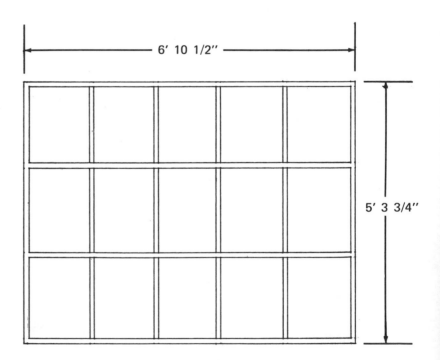

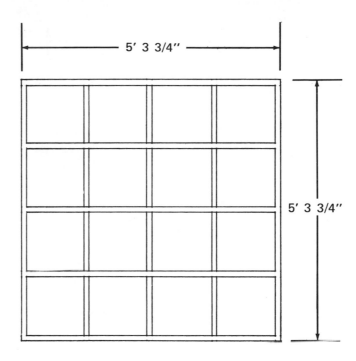

"D" Cabinet/Lockers:
Bass Clarinets and Trombones

16 Cabinets — 15" x 15" x 38" inside
(May be constructed in two units.)
Scale: 1/2" = 1'

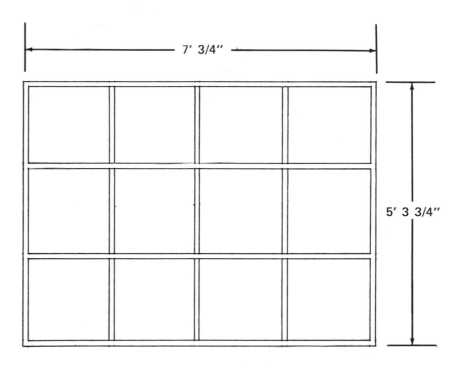

"E" Cabinet/Lockers:
French Horns and Baritones

12 Cabinets — 20" x 20" x 38" inside
(May be constructed in two units.)
Scale: 1/2" = 1'

149

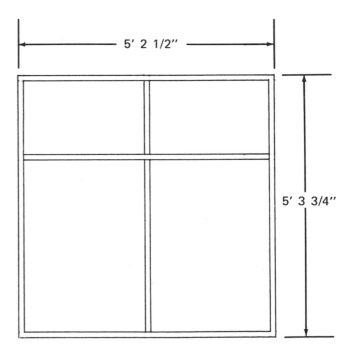

"F" Cabinet/Lockers:

Bass Drums and Tympani

4 Cabinets — 36" x 36" x 38" inside
(May be constructed in two units.)
Scale: 1/2" = 1'

"G" Cabinet/Lockers:

Small cabinets — Snare Drums
Large cabinets — Sousaphones or Tubas

2 Cabinets — 18" x 42" x 38" inside (double doors)
2 Cabinets — 30" x 42" x 38" inside (double doors)

(May be constructed in two units.)
Scale: 1/2" = 1'

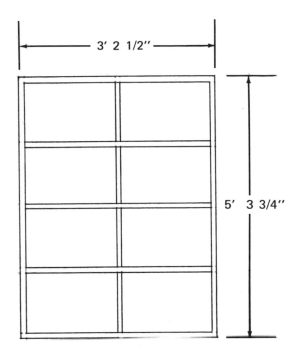

"H" Cabinet/Lockers:
Snare Drums and other percussion equipment

8 Cabinets — 18" x 18" x 38" inside
Scale: 1/2" = 1'

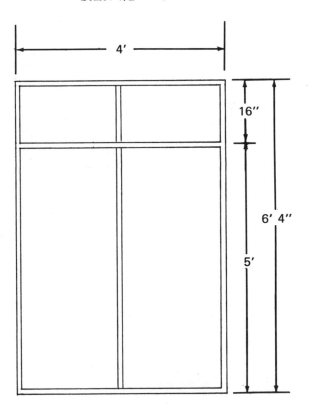

"I" Cabinet/Lockers:
Violas and Cellos

2 Cabinets — 24" x 15" x 38"
2 Cabinets — 24" x 60" x 38"
Scale: 1/2" = 1'

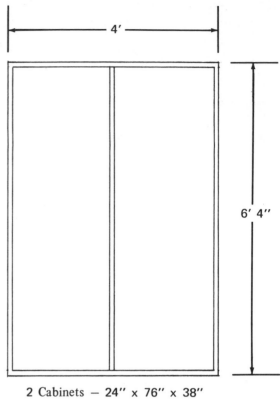

"J" Cabinet/Lockers:
String Basses

4'

6' 4"

2 Cabinets — 24" x 76" x 38"
Scale: 1/2" = 1'

Uniforms. Band uniforms and other school-owned attire represent a sizeable investment and must be protected against moths, dust and theft. They should be kept free from wrinkles and systematically arranged for efficient distribution and return. A separate room with Dutch doors is usually provided for dispensing and receiving garments. The space should be high enough that uniforms or robes will not touch the floor when hanging on racks. Notches and labels help to keep the uniforms at equal intervals and facilitate identification. Separate compartments should be provided for caps, belts and other accessories.

Music Library. The size and arrangement of the music library room will depend somewhat on the type of filing system used for instrumental music. For band compositions legal size steel cabinets are most commonly used. To make use of the space above the filing cabinets, wooden compartments with sliding doors may be constructed for the storage of less frequently used materials.

Space should be provided for work tables, a desk, chairs, and some type of music sorting rack. Music sorting racks and filing cabinets may be purchased or constructed of wood or masonite.

Repair Shop. An instrument cleaning and repair area should be provided near the instrumental rehearsal room. A small separate room which can be securely locked is necessary. It should contain a work bench, a rack for tools, and a cabinet for storing extra parts. It should have electrical and gas outlets as well as a sink with hot and cold running water.

OFFICES. Office space for music personnel depends on the size of the school and the magnitude of the music program. It is essential that comfortable, attractive, efficient office space be provided for the director of music and for each member of the music staff. A desk, two or three chairs, files, cabinets, shelves for books, and space for other special materials and equipment should be provided. A double glazed window should view the large rehearsal area. Acoustical insulation of the office is essential for efficient operation.

ACOUSTICS[2]

The term "acoustics" may be defined simply as the science of sound. Like any other science or engineering specialty, it involves principles, laws, formulas, mathematical calculations, and a vast store of technical data. This discussion will be limited to those elements of architectural acoustics which should be of major concern to any person involved in the planning of a music suite. When these elements are taken into consideration before the rooms are constructed, favorable sound treatment can be obtained with little, if any, additional cost.

Two general purposes are served by architectural acoustics. First, to provide a satisfactory acoustical or sound environment, and second, to provide good conditions for hearing and learning.

The acoustical environment of a given space is determined by the intensity and character of all sounds existing in that space and by the way in which sounds are prolonged and spread within the space. A satisfactory environment for a given space can be specified only in terms of the functions which that space is to serve. Rooms must be insulated from one another and from other building noises.

Satisfactory hearing conditions in an enclosed space require: 1. sufficiently low level of background noise, 2. adequate separation of successive sounds (reverberation control), 3. proper distribution of sound, and 4. sufficient loudness of the sounds which are to be heard.

SPECIAL PROBLEMS RELATING TO ACOUSTICS.

BACKGROUND NOISE. The location of the music suite and the rooms within the suite largely determines the extent of the background noise. Playground or shop noises can be a disturbance to an organization in rehearsal. On the other hand, sounds from the music suite become noise factors to other classrooms, library, and offices. If separation cannot solve the acoustical problem of background noise, it is possible to find other solutions, namely, insulation, placing barriers in the path of the sound, or using materials that dissipate or absorb sound energy.

REVERBERATION. Reverberation is defined as the time in seconds for sound to die away to one millionth of its initial intensity. Rooms serving different purposes require different reverberation times. Large rooms tolerate longer reverberation than small ones. The reverberation time of any room or auditorium should lie within certain acceptable limits: Too long a reverberation time makes hearing difficult and the acoustical environment uncomfortable, while too short a time makes the room sound dead, and music seems to lose its natural tone and resonance.

The reverberation time of any room may be controlled by the use of certain construction materials which have known coefficients of absorption. An acoustical engineer should be

[2] *Acoustics and Educational Facilities,* a report prepared by the research staff, Center for Architectural Research, Rensselaer Polytechnic Institute, New York State Department of Education (1966).

consulted during the early stages of planning a music suite so that the reverberation time will be as satisfactory as possible for each different room. Occasionally, because of personal preferences, the reverberation time of a finished room may require modification by the addition or subtraction of small areas of acoustical materials.

DISTRIBUTION OF SOUND. Sound should be equally distributed throughout the entire area of the room, and there should neither be dead spots nor excessively live spots. The shape of the room determines to a marked degree the manner in which sound is distributed within it. The shape plus the angles of the walls determine the direction in which reflected sound will travel. Sometimes flutter echoes—multiple reflections of sound back and forth between hard parallel surfaces, noticed especially when clapping the hands—are a serious problem. They may be eliminated by using nonparallel wall construction or by adding segments of acoustical tile in appropriate places on opposite walls. Standing waves, observed as unusually loud resonance at certain low frequencies, are sometimes a problem in small rooms. This may also be corrected by using nonparallel wall construction and by the proper placement of acoustical tile on portions of the wall. Adjustable double-fold drapes provide excellent control of acoustics. Carpeted floors add much to beauty and sound absorption.

AMPLIFICATION WITH ACOUSTICAL REFLECTORS. A common problem faced by music directors is the great loss of sound from the stage to the audience in the school auditorium. This is particularly true of choruses and orchestras when the sounds produced are relatively soft, but it also applies to the concert band. The loss of sound is due to dissipation of sound in the high open space above the stage and absorption into the stage curtains and drapes. A solution is to purchase or construct suitable acoustical reflectors which are placed behind and above the performers. Reflectors made of hard materials with smooth, painted surfaces make it not only possible for the audience to hear the performers more satisfactorily, but they also help the players and singers to hear each other, thus improving the intonation, balance, blend, and general quality of the performance. Several manufacturers have designed portable acoustical reflectors which may be adapted to choral or instrumental risers. These reflectors have demonstrated their great value beyond a shadow of a doubt. Electronic amplifiers are also helpful, but they are generally avoided by music directors and performers, because they tend to distort quality and balance, especially when more than one performer is involved.

For a more detailed discussion of acoustics and other important factors involved in planning the music suite, see:

Instrumental Music Room Designs, Construction and Equipment. Report prepared by the research committee, American School Band Directors Association, 1959.

Acoustics and Educational Facilities. Report prepared by the research staff, Center for Architectual Research, Rensselaer Polytechnic Institute. Troy, New York, 1966.

Music Buildings, Rooms, Equipment. Music Education Research Council Bulletin No. 17. Music Educators National Conference, Washington, D.C.

ILLUMINATION

Careful attention to illumination is necessary in planning music rooms because of the special nature of the work that they serve. Printed or manuscript music is usually very fine in size, and the smallest details are extremely important. Musicians are expected to read accurately and rapidly from a page in the vertical position, and the distance from the eye to the page varies with the kind of instrument played. Irregular seating arrangements complicate the problem of glare, especially since the music rooms are used day and night throughout the year.

The minimum foot-candle requirements for music rooms should be the same as for sewing rooms, drafting rooms, art rooms, and other rooms where fine detail work is to be done, i.e., 70 to 100 foot-candles of illumination should be maintained on the surface of the music stands. Visual comfort depends not only upon ample light (foot-candles), but on a reasonably low brightness difference between various surfaces within the visual field. A high contrast between the printed music and the page on which it is printed is desirable. On the other hand, high brightness differences within the remainder of the visual field — particularly between the page of music and the walls or ceiling — should be limited.

The color and finish of the walls, floors, ceilings, furniture, and equipment should provide a pleasing and stimulating environment with low brightness differences and freedom from glare.

A special bulletin entitled *School Lighting Standards*, including the Regulations of the New York Commissioner of Education (Section 165), may be secured free of charge by writing to the Division of School Buildings and Grounds, State Education Department, Albany, New York 12201.

HEATING, VENTILATION, and HUMIDITY CONTROL

Since temperature and humidity have a marked effect on the pitch and maintenance of musical instruments, it is important that uniform temperature and humidity be maintained in the rooms of the music suite. Sudden changes in temperature are likely to cause serious damage to certain instruments, especially strings and woodwinds, as well as to some instruments in the percussion family.

A temperature of 68°-70° Fahrenheit is recommended for all music rooms. If possible, separate thermostatic controls should be provided for each room of the music suite.

Proper ventilation is exceptionally important in all music rooms. Pupils singing or playing wind instruments use the oxygen content of air more rapidly than do pupils in regular classroom activity. Mechanical ventilation is the best way to supply healthful, invigorating conditions within music rooms. It has the further advantage of making it possible to close windows, or to have no windows at all, in order to keep the sound from disturbing other areas. Most modern music facilities are being constructed without windows.

If air ducts are used to ventilate other rooms or sections of the building, it is imperative that special precautions be taken to prevent sound transmission. Ducts must be lined with fireproof sound-absorbing material and should contain baffles to prevent sound from being transmitted.

Mechanical air conditioning of all space in the music suite provides the best year-round control of temperature, ventilation and humidity. This would permit the maintenance of relative humidity within the desirable range of from 50 to 60 percent. If complete air conditoning is not possible, the installation of a humidifier for use in the winter months should be carefully considered. Some schools have found that the cost of the humidifier may be saved in the expense of tuning pianos alone, to say nothing of the savings in damages to string, woodwind and certain percussion instruments.

chapter 14

Buying Band Uniforms

The average band director will be faced with the responsibility of the selection and purchase of a set of new uniforms for his band about once in ten years. When this occurs he and his school administration will have many questions to answer and decisions to make.

Uniforms vary greatly because of the infinite variations available in design, decoration and material. It is safe to state that the estimated cost of an individual uniform may range from $30 for a jacket to $150 for a complete uniform with attractive and exciting accessories.

The ASBDA Uniform Research Committee, Walter Lake, St. Paul, Minnesota, chairman in 1966-1967, enlisted the cooperation of Mr. W. E. Stanbury and his uniform manufacturing company to put together a set of definitions of terms, explanations of manufacturing procedures, and suggestions for proceeding to make an intelligent selection and purchase of a set of uniforms. The guidelines following are taken from Mr. W. E. Stanbury's report.[1]

Purchasing band uniforms is indeed a science. To make the best purchase—one that will give you the set of uniforms you contemplate, made in the style and quality you select, and shipped to you on schedule—requires some knowledge of the particular requirements of uniform manufacturing. It is not anything you can go into "off the cuff" without risk of disappointment.

The purpose of this chapter is to help draw up a set of values and a procedure of choice to assist in obtaining the best possible uniform value when you are faced with this responsibility. Technical information acquired only from uniform salesmen may be incomplete, since sometimes the salesmen themselves are not too well informed. These pages cover a number of points you may never have thought of, as well as the basic information every band director should have.

The information following is in answer to the questions often raised by school people faced with the problems of purchasing band uniforms. Their question, put briefly, is: "How can we tell which uniform offer represents the best value, since all salesmen claim, 'My uniform is the best'?" "When we purchase by bid under public specifications, why shouldn't we take the lowest bid?"

The answer is that all uniforms are NOT alike: different manufacturers, following the same specifications, will turn out vastly different uniforms in accordance with their abilities—and you probably have not considered their experience in providing valuable extra features. One must also consider the manufacturer's reputation for standing back of his product, his experience and plant equipment.

When buying uniforms on bid, the Armed Services first inspect the plant of successful bidders and then place resident inspectors who check every operation during the course of manufacture, rejecting all uniforms that fail to meet specifications. Obviously this procedure is impractical for the average school buyer. His best protection is in knowing the manufacturer with whom he plans to do business.

---

1 This is only one of many such guidelines furnished by various uniform manufacturers.

WHAT IS THE BEST VALUE? It is one that gives the most for the dollar you spend — not necessarily the lowest bid, but one that will provide the uniform and service you anticipate. It will be manufactured by a responsible firm with a reputation for service both on the original order and during the years the uniforms will be worn. It will be serviced by a competent representative whose primary interest is in assisting you to a better uniform.

WHAT IS A GOOD UNIFORM? First and most important is style, because without style you will have nothing. It must be well tailored from good materials so that its "good looks" will hold up during the expected years of service. It should fit well, be comfortable to wear, not bulky or heavy. Its size should be clearly identified for easy refitting to new students each year, with built-in allowances for a normal year's growth. There will be ample material for necessary alterations. It will carry features that will make the uniform more serviceable, give added years of wear, and reduce the cost of maintenance. It will be shipped on the date specified and be packaged for easy distribution, negating the necessity of cleaning or repressing before wearing.

HOW TO SELECT A STYLE. Use the information received from the uniform manufacturers you've written to and start assembling ideas on styles, trims, accessories and color combinations. Don't worry about minor details, since these can be decided upon later.

Ask the manufacturers for a conference with a qualified representative (one at a time, when it is convenient for you) and explore in depth exactly what each firm can do for you. (Nothing is to be gained from a joint session of competing representatives, no matter how fine their products . . . and much can be lost.) Find out from each man the qualifications of his company and try to determine whether they can actually produce the kind of uniforms you want and need. Talk with him about style suggestions—which of course should be distinctive from those worn by neighboring schools and ask him to submit wash drawings of appealing styles in your school colors. This is one of many services provided without charge by the better houses, along with knowledgeable suggestions as to the best fabrics, trims and accessories. Outfitting your band to the best advantage in style, comfort and durability can be a most important point in some climates.

OUTER FABRICS. The most popular and the most practical material for a band uniform is whipcord, preferred because of its excellent color, wearing and tailoring qualities. Whipcord is available in all wool (14 to 16 oz.), and a blend of 45% wool and 55% dacron (12 to 14 oz.). Both qualities are available from several mills in a wide range of standard colors. These fabrics are to be examined, preshrunk and mothproofed before cutting. In certain climates showerproofing is desirable. It is important that you select the best fabric and weight for *your* particular purpose, and here a well-informed sales representative will be helpful.

LINING. A heavy duty, close weave, high quality men's wear all-rayon lining is the best. It is any reputable company's experience that the darker shades of standard men's wear coat lining give the best service—they wear better and are stain resistant. Linings are preshrunk before cutting.

INTERLININGS. The foundation of any coat is the material that lies between the outer fabric and the lining of the front. This material must be:

a. Wrinkle- and crease-free.
b. Firm but flexible.
c. Resistant to change by all dry cleaning methods.
d. Properly cut to style, sex and size.
e. Well made and reinforced.

Interlinings should be made from preshrunk, heavy duty hymo canvas with hair chest reinforcement, all properly padded and quilted. Low priced uniforms may have coat fronts that are full of sizing and reinforced with synthetic hair cloth. These soon break down, and the coat will lose its shape.

PATTERNS. The uniforms should be cut from patterns designed to fit growing girls and boys—patterns so designed that the finished uniform will look good on the original band and can be passed on each year to new students without loss of style or fit. Such patterns require talent plus a lot of experience.

But, good materials and proper patterns are of little value unless backed by good workmanship. The well-tailored uniform is light in weight, comfortable to wear, and will retain its original good looks through years of service. For your guidance, we list below a rundown on tailoring grades and desirable features.

TAILORING GRADES. Men's tailoring is graded according to the amount of handwork and tailoring details involved. For all practical purposes, Grade 4 represents the best and Grade "X" the lowest. The bulk of men's popular priced clothing is tailored in Grade 2, a happy combination of hand and machine work. This grade of tailoring produces a comfortable hard wearing uniform available at reasonable cost. Some manufacturers tailor uniforms in Grade "X," a low-cost all machine-sewn uniform that may look good when new and freshly pressed, but soon loses its shape and style.

The careful buyer will examine sample garments before making any decision. A clue to the quality of tailoring used will be found in the armhole construction. Examine how the sleeve lining is attached to the body lining. Grade 2 tailoring has hand-tailored armholes — the sleeve lining is hand felled by many small stitches to the body of the coat. Grade "X" tailoring has a 100% machine-sewn lining. This is one difference that you can see. Many differences are covered by the lining, and thus, hidden to the eye.

The argument for the machine-made coat is: "It will wear longer." The fallacy of this claim is proved by examining men's clothing at your local clothiers: What you might save on the purchase price between the two grades of tailoring is not worth the loss in appearance, comfort, and service. It is an undeniable fact that the Army Quartermaster requires a hand-tailored armhole in all woolen uniforms where hard wear is the rule.

OUTLETS. Generous outlets should be left in the body of the coat and the pant waist as well as sleeve and and trouser hems. Trousers may be made with an adjustable waist. Do not be misled by extravagant outlets sometimes shown by inexperienced manufacturers . . . these are only selling "gimmicks" and of no value to you.

IDENTIFICATION. Since uniforms are passed on to new students each fall, it is important that they be properly identified. Each garment should be identified with a large permanent number, plus sex, height, weight and body descriptions, and accompanied by a permanent record to make future distribution easier.

TAILORING TIPS. Features that contribute to a good uniform:
a. Each uniform is individually cut by hand, not mass cut with other orders.
b. Generous outlets in all seams.
c. High quality linings, canvas and other trimmings.
d. Front of the coats should be shaped under pressure on contour presses. It is very important that this operation be done while the garments are in process. If done properly, the coat will always hold its shape.
e. Converters or overlays should be as carefully tailored as the uniform. The standing collar

should be tailored in the same manner as described below in par. "h." The front of the converter should have a preshrunk hymo interliner, and the body of the converter should be contour-tailored so as to fit natural body lines and, when worn, look a part of the coat. Poorly cut and tailored converters often have the effect of a "sandwich board."

f. All braid trimming should be hard-wearing, fast-color braid.

g. Collars are hand-shaped and sewn to the coat by hand. A properly made collar will always "hug" the neck.

h. Standing military collars should be semi-adjustable and not of the old style "choker" type. These collars will have a removable liner, not only to protect the collar from wear and tear, but for sanitary reasons.

i. Lapels, edges and front must be shaped and trimmed by hand. A common violation of good tailoring practices is often found in these spots.

j. Armhole construction is always by hand and never by machine. Check your clothing stores, and you will find that good quality suits always have the armhole seam sewn to the coat by hand and not by machine.

k. Buttonholes. There are two ways to make buttonholes: the "cut first" or "cut after" process. When metal buttons are used, the "cut after" buttonholes provide the best wear.

l. Extra value coats will have an inside right-breast pocket or a lefthand music folio, perspiration shields made from wool, and generous outlets. The coat should be fully lined for longer service. The lining should fit the coat properly. There should be an opening at the center back so that ornamental buttons can be removed whenever necessary, and a pleat in the back and bottom hem to prevent strain.

m. Trousers. Boys and girls trousers should be cut alike, i.e., with zipper fly. This permits interchange of garments. Trouser waists may be made adjustable — this permits instant change of waist size and permits girls to wear boy's trousers, and vice versa.

PREPARING SPECIFICATIONS. A good set of specifications will describe exactly the style of uniform you wish to buy, the materials from which it is to be made, the quality of workmanship you demand, and the date of completion.

Most manufacturers will be glad to help you by supplying their own standard specifications, along with recommendations to suit your special requirements. You can study these and combine the best of each into your own "spec sheet." A word of warning: there are some uniform makers who pay little if any regard to specifications, so that it is up to you to be certain that the bids you receive are based on garments made to your quality specifications. On your listing, be sure to describe in detail the style you want without using a manufacturer's model number. Use the mill number of the fabric you select, rather than a number or name assigned to it by any one manufacturer. List in detail the tailoring features and the quality of trims and accessories you want in the finished garment. State (and get confirmation of) the required date of shipment.

PROCUREMENT TIME. Plan early. Do not delay planning or purchasing until "the last moment," because the manufacturer needs time to develop an outstanding style which will be particularly appropriate for your school. You'll need time, too, to prepare specifications, call for bids and place your order. Depending upon the season of the year, the manufacturer will need an additional three to five months' time to complete your order. (In winter or early spring, a "pilot" uniform and the entire order of finished outfits may be completed within 90 to 100 days, but more time must be allowed at other times of the year to avoid disappointment.)

The following pages include the various forms that may be used as guides in the purchase of uniforms.

INVITATION TO BID ON THE
CONSTRUCTION AND SALE OF BAND UNIFORMS

SECTION I

GENERAL REQUIREMENTS

SAMPLES. Your bid, to be considered, must be accompanied by samples of exact materials you propose to furnish, together with a finished sample uniform to show general styling and quality of workmanship. This sample need not be made to exact detail, materials or color combinations — it is to show styling, fit and workmanship. Any stock sample will suffice.

The school reserves the right to inspect the workmanship of the sample, and in particular its inner construction, and for this purpose will open the lining if necessary.

APPROVAL SAMPLE. The successful bidder will, when notified of award of the contract, make up and submit for final approval one complete sample uniform in the exact style, material, color and trim combination decided upon. This sample will be promptly examined by the school and you will be immediately notified of:

a. Its acceptability.

b. Changes required.

After this final approval, and not before, you, the manufacturer, are to proceed with the main order. This sample may be retained by the school, and, with specifications, becomes a basis for judging the quality and material of the main order. Failure of the order to meet specifications or to prove not equal quality as the sample shall release the Board of Education from any or all obligations to contract manufacturer, his agent, or his dealers, and shall enable the Board of Education to place the order with whom they please, without obligation or restriction as to the manner of purchasing.

QUALITY OF WORK. To avoid any controversy regarding a standard for the quality of work and manufacturing procedure, the Board of Education has adopted Army Quartermaster specifications. Any uniform supplied under this bid must meet U.S. Army Quartermaster specification No. Mil-C-13990 in the coat and No. Mil-T-13982 in the trousers. With the exceptions noted below, this applies to general construction, type of stitching, sewing threads, findings, etc. These exceptions are:

Coat may be made in a No. 2 grade quality of tailoring rather than No. 4, eliminating handmade top collars, hand-felled shoulder seams and the sleeve hem. But the following operations must be included:

1. Collar: hand-shaped top and bottom, interlined with bias collar canvas blind-felled to under collar; 8 rows of felling under collar; machine-felled outer edge and under collar to body of coat.

2. Lapels, Edges and Fronts: hand shaped and trimmed; lapel and bridle felled with 6 to 8 rows of blind stitching; canvas trimmed, and tape

blind-stitched on inner edge; edges pressed open, basted, and stitched.

3. Facing: edge must be blind stitched to the canvas (not held by buttons).

4. Armhole: must be open construction, i.e. shoulder and sleeve head pad, together with body lining and canvas, all basted by hand or machine to armhole of coat. After this operation, the sleeve lining is to be hand-felled (with close, silk stitches) to the armhole, with proper distribution of fullness.

CUTTING. Each uniform shall be cut by hand to fit the measurements of the student for whom it is intended. Cutting must be done by patterns, especially designed for the style, sex and size of the student. Generous outlets shall be left in the back, side and sleeve inseam together with pant waist, crotch seam and hem.

MEASUREMENTS. Measurements shall be taken by the manufacturer's representative. Uniforms shall be designed so there is due allowance for normal growth. Shoulders shall fit correctly, even if the boy or girl shall make a reasonable amount of growth.

IDENTIFICATION. Each part of the uniform (cap, coat, trousers, belt, etc.) shall be identified by a large (1"x2") permanently displayed number and a size record. The number is to be placed on the inside of the cap, inside the lower left coat front, and in the trouser waistband. All numbers and size records shall wear and be permanent for the life of the garment. The size record shall contain information as to sex, height and weight of the individual, as well as specific measurements.

PERMANENT SIZE RECORD BOOK. The manufacturer shall furnish the band director a record book containing a complete size history of each uniform together with its identifying number. This record shall be bound, of a permanent nature, and have space for remarks and additional sizing information.

PACKING. Uniforms shall be packed in wardrobe containers, with each uniform on a separate metal hanger in such a way that they will be ready for immediate use, i.e., no pressing or cleaning necessary on the school's part before the uniforms are used.

SECTION II

SPECIFIC STYLING INFORMATION

Note: You, the purchaser, must supply necessary data to inform each bidder as to the exact uniform style you wish to purchase, its component parts (with accessories), together with the quality and colors of material. It is important that your specifications be complete and clear. If you have difficulty in describing the style of your choice, feel free to refer to the style number from any catalog, listing the name of the catalog and the style number. This applies to accessory items as well as the actual uniform.

If you wish assistance, feel free to call upon any of the salesmen or write direct to the office of the manufacturer. (Note: The Stanbury Company or any reputable uniform manufacturer will be pleased to write up your Specific Styling Specifications as an assistance to you and/or your committee.)

MATERIAL. Describe the type of material favored, such as whipcord, gabardine, etc., weight of material and finish desired (showerproof—mothproof).

SHAKO, CAP OR OTHER HEADWEAR. Describe style, color of top and band, type of ornament and front cord, and advise whether a white or black visor is wanted.

CAP PLUME. Describe style, height and colors.

COAT. Describe style, color or colors, as well as location of all trimmings. It is important that you describe the trimming you desire, especially if these vary from the catalog illustration of the style selected. Mention if the coat is to be fully lined; also if it is to have pockets (either inside or outside).

TROUSERS. State style, colors, details of leg stripes, waist adjustment, and any other feature you wish to add.

CONVERTER OR OVERLAY. Describe style and material of basic converter, front and back. Indicate the details of the trim on the front, back, and collar of the converter. Indicate if converter will be secured at waist by a belt or side fasteners.

CITATION CORD. Describe style, colors and number per uniform.

SHOULDER EMBLEM. Describe briefly details of style, color, size and location (usually one on each sleeve).

BELT. If belt is wanted, state style, quality and color.

SPATS. Describe material, color and type of closure (snaps, buttons or zipper).

TIES. Indicate style and material.

DICKEYS. Indicate color, material, and color of buttons.

GLOVES. Give color and material.

SUSPENDERS. Indicate color.

CUMMERBUNDS. Describe style (imitation, full, or sash), material and color.

REMARKS. Include under remarks any additional information you think pertinent to your own program. If you wish to examine samples and interview sales representatives, set a time and date for such showings. Allow ample time for salesmen so that you can fully examine each offering.

SECTION III

DETAILED MANUFACTURING SPECIFICATIONS

MATERIALS. The basic uniform material to be fine wale whipcord, mill weight not less than _____oz., equal to Lot _____. Material to be London shrunk and meet all U.S. shrinking specifications. Before cutting, cloth shall be mothproofed by an accepted and approved moth resistant finish and carry a five-year written guarantee by the laboratory providing this protection. The material shall be of standard quality and color that may be duplicated later.

LININGS. Coats to be full lined throughout body and sleeves with a 120 count perspiration-proof men's quality rayon lining guaranteed for the life of the uniform. Sleeve lining to be of same high quality.

POCKETS. Outer pockets to be as specified under General Specifications. Inner pockets shall consist of one upper right breast properly piped and made from cotton silesia.

INNER CONSTRUCTION. Coat shall have fronts innerlined with a fine quality hymo coat front reinforced and properly padded by approved methods. These fronts shall be tailored to fit the individual coat in style, sex and size.

QUALITY OF CONSTRUCTION. All workmanship must be in a grade designated as No. 2. In general, this grade shall meet the specifications as to general construction, sewing threads, stitches per inch, and trimmings, together with general sewing procedure, as laid down by the Army Quartermaster for the manufacture of men's clothing. No substitute for the above will be considered as the committee is not interested in cheaply made machine-constructed armholes, sleeve linings, etc. If you cannot bid on a *Grade 2 quality* coat, you are asked not to submit a quotation.

BRAIDS. All braiding, unless otherwise specified, shall be Rice quality.

BUTTONS. Buttons on coat to be of Waterbury or equal quality, dome shaped (or flat) with lyre design, in gilt (or nickel) finish. All utility buttons must be hand-sewn and secured to an anchor button on the inside of the lining. Ornamental buttons to be countersunk and secured inside with toggle.

BUTTONHOLES. Buttonholes to be constructed on a Reece or Singer buttonhole machine, by the *cut first* or *cut after process* (purchaser must specify). Ends of buttonholes must be securely bartacked and sealed against raveling.

SWEAT SHIELDS. Sweat shields to be of wool cloth, rayon piped, and securely fastened by hand or machine to the inside position of the armhole.

COLLAR CONSTRUCTION.

a. Open collar. To be made in accordance with Army Quartermaster specifications. This includes blind stitching of canvas to under collar with a minimum of 6 rows of stitching, hand shaping and notching of both under and top collars to insure proper fullness, and blind stitching of collar edge to insure a thin elastic seam so coat will hug to wearer's neck. Under collar must be closely felled to body of coat.

b. Standing collar. Must be of the semi-adjustable type made of heavy woven buckram, all properly reinforced; collar must be lined with preshrunk Cramerton Army twill for long wear and finished in front with heavy metal hooks anchored with heavy tape — removable, snap-in, washable liner must be included.

COAT SLEEVES. Coat sleeves shall be of design specified by the Army Quartermaster for the construction of officer's clothing. Patterns must provide an easy-action armhole, giving complete freedom of arm movement without causing the coat to pull or bind and permitting a smooth fit along the back and shoulder at all times. Sleeves shall have at least 2" turn up at bottom of cuff, with like amount in the lining.

PRESSING. Coats must be carefully underpressed as work progresses, and the fronts shaped under pressure on contour forms. Upon completion of each garment, it must be carefully off-pressed and inspected for any defects.

TROUSERS.

a. Regular band style. Made with 2 pockets and trimmed down the leg as specified.

b. High waisted. To be worn with waist length coat; 1 fob pocket only; suspender buttons; no belt loops. Trimmed down the leg as specified.

c. Waist band curtain. To be of durable cotton "Iron Cloth" for maximum wear and innerlined with woven buckram.

d. Belt loops. 7 standard belt loops, bartacked at top and bottom for added strength.

e. Suspender buttons. 6 suspender buttons blind-stitched so the thread will not show on the outside of the pant; buttons to be composition "ivory."

f. Fly closing. To be of talon solid brass zipper or equal quality; safety lock slide; blind button fastener at top.

g. Outlets. There will be generous outlets in the back of the waist, the seat, the crotch inseam and bottom.

h. Bottoms. To be plain with a minimum 3" turn up.

i. Heel guards. Securely fastened but easy to move when trouser length is altered.

j. Leg stripe. To be style and quality described, running full length of the pants, including turn up at bottom, so that trousers may be lengthened or shortened without patching.

k. Adjustable waist band. Waist band should be made adjustable on each side with a Prentiss-quality solid-brass zipper. This zipper is to be attached to the pant so that alterations may be easily made.

SHAKO CONSTRUCTION. Shako is to be built around a one-piece molded plastic body, guaranteed not to break or crack. Sides of shako to be covered with_____material, permanently cemented to body. Side bands and top to be of plastic material. Side bands to be sewn to the body to assure proper bonding. Sweat band is to be constructed from stretch plastic material and made adjustable for 3 sizes. The sweat band will be sewn to the body of the shako so that there will be no stitches to cut into the forehead. Visor to be of heat-molded, crack-proof solid plastic.

CAP CONSTRUCTION (military style). Cap is to be of the patented "Kant-Krush" construction. The cap is to be constructed around a spring steel frame. A spring steel band will support the cap band, which will be secured to the frame. Lining and cap fabric will be held to the frame at band by at least four rows of machine stitching. There shall be a spring steel crown support and plume holder fastened to the band support. The crown support shall be 1" wide. Attached to the top of the crown support shall be a ¼" spring steel band which will hold the crown of the cap in shape. In addition, there shall be a steel band permanently sewn into the crown's outside diameter. The sweat band shall be of leather, machine turned, so that no stitches will cut into the forehead. A waterproof liner shall cover the inside of the crown. The visor shall be of heat-molded, break- and crack-proof plastic. (Note: Shako and cap specifications apply only to basic headgear. In addition to this plumes and plume holders, front ornaments, front cords or straps, finish of visor, etc. must be considered.)

GUARANTEE. The manufacturer shall guarantee all uniforms delivered under the contract to meet all specifications, to fit correctly, and to be made from the material described.

INVITATION

Date _____

The _____ School will purchase _____ uniforms of the style, material and color specified and invites your written bid.

Bids will be received up to _____ P.M., _____ , 19___ .

The school reserves the right to accept any bid meeting specifications, regardless of price. The school also reserves the right to accept any portion of the bid, waive irregularities in bidding and to proceed in any manner considered in its best interest.

In submitting your bid please specify the number of days required to supply a sample uniform and the time required for delivery of the complete order after we have approved the sample.

In setting forth these specifications it is the intention of the school to offer equal opportunity to all bidders. Styles referred to by number and company name are for descriptive purposes only and are not restrictive. The school feels that standard styles, materials, linings and sundry items are equally available to all reputable manufacturers. Any bidder desiring to use a material contrary to the specifications must specify this substitution in his bid and submit satisfactory proof of its quality.

Bidder must furnish itemized quotations showing the cost of each item, the total price per uniform and the total price of the entire order. Any allowance or cash discount for payment within a certain period after delivery shall be indicated on the bid, otherwise it will be presumed that payment is to be made on the basis of net 30 days.

School _____

Purchasing Agent _____

Mail sealed bid to: _____

Mail samples to: _____

BID FORM

Attention: _____

Gentlemen:

The bidder certifies he has familiarized himself with your specifications, and has carefully read Sections I, II and III and understands their contents. Any uniforms furnished by us will be in the style and quality requested.

Quanity	*Item	Unit Price	Extended Price
_____	Shakos (caps)	_____	_____
_____	Plumes	_____	_____
_____	Coats	_____	_____
_____	Trousers	_____	_____
_____	Converters or Plaques	_____	_____
_____	Citation Cords	_____	_____
_____	Belts	_____	_____
_____	Spats	_____	_____
_____	Ties	_____	_____
_____	Dickeys	_____	_____
_____	Gloves	_____	_____
_____	Suspenders	_____	_____
_____	Cummerbunds	_____	_____
_____	_____	_____	_____

Terms: _____

If awarded the contract, the undersigned agrees to ship a sample uniform within _____ days and to ship the entire work within _____ calendar days after approval of sample and receipt of necessary details and measurements.

Signed _____ Title _____

Company _____ Bus. Tel. _____

Address _____ Date _____

*Select only those items listed which are incorporated into your uniform. Accessory uniforms (Majorettes, Drum Major, Director, Color Guard, etc.) are included in the total order. List them separately.

A GUIDE TO THE COMPETENT EVALUATION OF BAND UNIFORMS

The specialization trend which has entered into all phases of our existence has made its appearance to a great degree within our educational institutions. A comparatively recent development in this area has been the increasing number of occasions when school administrators call upon the department of Home Economics to evaluate the various sample uniforms received in conjunction with bids submitted on the local institution's purchase of band uniforms. The administrators concerned, in most instances, have had little or no experience in evaluating the various garments, other than in a very cursory fashion. As a result the department of Home Economics finds itself charged with the responsibility of reviewing the samples and of making intelligent recommendations.

The purpose of this discussion is to present a series of guidelines which the department can use in carrying out this responsibility. The first consideration is to recognize the fact that band uniforms utilize men's tailoring exclusively. There are sound reasons for this. Band uniforms are expected to be worn for many years and during these years will be worn by many different students. The uniforms are made from fabrics of greater density and firmness than those used in the manufacture of women's wear. As a result there are tailoring techniques used which are peculiar to men's wear, and the finished uniform must be compared with the quality of tailoring found in the better grades of men's tailoring. Practically all of women's wear is made from a soft, "drapery" material and in most instances is of machine-made construction. The designs are for current style only and not for long wear.

It is obvious that there are certain guidelines which can be defined, and it is important to remind oneself of the differences in tailoring and the purpose for which the particular garment is intended. The following salient points should be considered as a band uniform is evaluated. These points, when considered as a whole, will give the Home Economics department a sound frame of reference for intelligent evaluation:

1. Style. The criterion for evaluating the style is how the uniform will look on the band in both marching formation and on the concert stage. Therefore, observe the style at a distance rather than close by. The uniform should appear its best a short distance away from the examiner.

2. Fit. Band uniforms are worn by different students from year to year. They must fit—not only the student for whom they were originally tailored, but they must also fit succeeding individuals —without a loss of style. Determine if the manufacturer provides a scale system for fitting the uniforms to new personnel from year to year. If it is provided, and it should be, is it simple to operate and reasonably accurate?

3. Outlets. Does the garment have sufficient outlets, each in its proper place? Are there heel guards at the bottom of the cuff of the trousers, and can these be changed when the legs are lengthened or shortened without disturbing the clean appearance of the cuff? If the coat has a standing collar, will it automatically adjust itself to the neck size of the wearer? Are the coats trim and well fitting without appearing to be bulky? Trousers to be used with regular length coats should have adjustable waist attachments. This is not necessary for high-waisted trousers, since they are supported by suspenders, and, in addition, the side adjustments detract from the appearance of the high waist effect.

4. Material. The preferred material for band uniforms is whipcord. It is manufactured in various qualities and in fourteen-ounce and sixteen-ounce weights of all wool, as well as a dacron-wool blend of fourteen-ounce weight.

    a. Select the quality and weight which best serves the purpose for which it is intended. It is the

167

opinion of the writer, based on many years experience, that the all-wool fabric is the most satisfactory. It tailors more readily, has better color and is easier to care for over the years. The finest cloths are double dyed with chrome bottom dyes. This treatment provides a richness of color which is unequalled and a color which will retain its "bloom" through the years. These materials cost more but they are more than worth the additional expense.

b. In evaluating the cloth, look for firmness and crispness. Uniforms made from such fabrics are more resistant to wear and require less pressing. To test for firmness and crispness, squeeze a swatch of the cloth tightly in your hand. Hold it tightly for a moment or two and then release your grasp quickly. A fine quality cloth will "spring back," wrinkle free. Beware of cloth with a "soft" texture as it will not retain its body over the years and it is much more liable to wrinkle. Determine whether or not the cloth has been preshrunk and mothproofed, and by what process. The old fashioned cold water method of shrinking is still recognized as the best and most dependable. The most widely accepted mothproofing process is the non-toxic and odor-free type which is guaranteed for a minimum of five years.

5. Tailoring. The better band uniforms are tailored in the same manner as better men's clothing. The construction is a combination of hand work and machine work, each in its proper place.

a. The collars will be set and felled by hand.

b. The sleeves will be set by hand in separate operations. The sleeve lining will be hand felled into the armhole, using close stitches of nylon thread. This is the most comfortable and durable type of armhole construction possible.

c. The lining of the body of the coat, the canvas, and the padding will all be attached to the outer shell by long basting threads.

d. The coat collar, lapel, and edges should be hand-shaped for proper symmetry. The inside of the collar and the lapels will be padded with close-blind stitches.

e. The edge of the canvas will be trimmed away from the front edge of the coat. The edging tape should be blind stitched along the inner edge. Check the edges of the coat. Are they thin and flat, or is there a raised bead along the edges? Reject the coat with the thick edge, since it will lose its shape and soon wear out.

f. The inside of the facings should be blind stitched to the canvas so that the coat will not separate when stress is applied. To test this stitching, grasp the inner edge of the facing in one hand and the coat front and canvas in the other hand, then try to pull the garment apart. If separation does occur, reject the coat, since the construction is inferior.

6. Buttons and buttonholes. Better clothing will have the buttons sewn on by hand, using waxed linen thread. All of the cheaper garments will have buttons attached by machine. Machine stitching is loose and flimsy. If the lock stitch should break, the button will come off at once.

Buttonholes are made in two ways: the "cut first" or the "cut after" process. The "cut first" process has the best appearance when new, but the "cut after" process will maintain a pleasing appearance over the years.

7. Linings. Band coats should be full lined with a fine-quality all-rayon lining material, preferably in a dark color to avoid soiling.

   a. Linings should be pleated down the center of the back as well as across the bottom.

   b. Coats having removable buttons should have an opening in the center of the back seam to allow the cleaners to remove the toggles which hold the buttons in place.

   c. Innerlinings should be a good quality, preshrunk hymo, all properly reinforced and padded.

8. Sweatshields. Sweatshields which have been treated against perspiration are a basic requirement for a top quality garment.

9. Trousers.

   a. Inspect the trim on the trousers. This will usually be in the form of a stripe on each trouser leg. Be sure each is straight and has been properly sewn to the garment. The stripe should not end with the bottom of the trousers but should continue to the end of the material on the turn-up at the end of each leg.

   b. Turn the trousers inside out and observe carefully that the waistband lining and the pocketing material is the type which will wear for the life of the garment. In this instance, a material such as rayon should be avoided. Be certain that the waistband adjustment has a good method for keeping the flap tight and snug to the waist. The crotch should be reinforced with a durable lining. There should be ample outlets in the center seam of the back as well as down the inside of each leg. The bottoms should have a generous turn-up, and there should be a protective heel guard on the inside of the bottom of the leg.

10. Headgear. The popular headpiece today is the West Point style shako. It is constructed around a molded plastic body.

   a. Test the firmness of the shako body. If it seems to be soft, do not accept it.

   b. Be sure the side bands are sewn on and not glued on. They must be sewn to guarantee that the covering will not slip.

   c. The liners of the better shakos have a soft, air-cushioned construction, free from rough stitching, and permit easy adjustment. Such shakos seem to "float" on the head, and at the same time they are not easily dislodged while the band is marching.

   d. The less expensive shakos have the linings attached with a zig-zag stitch which leaves imprints on the wearer's forehead. Often times these shakos have a heavy lap of lining at the back which causes discomfort to the youngster. Seldom do these shakos adjust readily, and in most instances they wobble a great deal during the maneuvers of the band.

   e. The better caps are constructed over a steel support to insure longer life. The front support is made of steel with a plume socket built into the support.

   f. The cap should have an air-cushioned sweatband, and the inside of the top should be protected with a large plastic liner.

   g. The shape of the sweatband should be oval to conform more readily to the head of the wearer.

   h. The visors of both the shakos and the caps should be of plastic and must be firmly stitched to the frame.

11. Danger signals. Listed below are five simple points to remember as you approach the responsibility of evaluating and making recommendations regarding the band uniforms. Many of your colleagues have found them to be most helpful:

   a. There are uniforms which simply do not have a good appearance, but there is no obvious reason. In practically all cases, this would be a uniform which is overstyled. It has so much trim that the effect is lost when viewed from a distance. Remember to inspect the quality of material and workmanship at close range, but evaluate style from a distance. There are certain gimmicks you will come to know, such as "hinged sleeves," etc. These are the mark of poor tailoring. It merely indicates a manufacturer has tried to replace the more costly tailoring with a less expensive process — at the sacrifice of style and comfort.

b. Beware of fabrics which are soft to the touch. Insist on proper shrinking and mothproofing. Avoid material having dull colors. Do not be influenced by the "famous name brands." Usually the quality has no relation to the reputation of the original name.

c. Avoid high color women's wear lining. They are pleasing to the eye when new, but they soon soil and do not give the expected service.

d. Completely machine-made garments. Many arguments will be given, but basically the only purpose behind complete machine manufacturing is to lower the cost of construction. One can never expect a machine-made garment to have the attractive appearance, the outstanding style, and the comfortable fit that is characteristic of the tailored uniform. If the reverse were true, the bulk of fine men's suits would be manufactured by this procedure.

e. Low bids do not necessarily mean the best value. Therefore, first compare the quality of the materials and workmanship. Only after you have done this should you compare the prices. An unusually low bid indicates an inferior uniform, either in material or workmanship, or both.

In conclusion, you are reminded that uniforms are purchased primarily to enhance the appearance of your band. They must be attractive on the original wearers and be inter-changeable over the years. They should give years of outstanding service without excessive maintenance costs. They should be provided with a method of size identification whereby the band director can systematically fit the bandsmen from year to year. The uniforms should be shipped to you clean and ready to wear. No pressing or other expense should be required. The more reputable manufacturers will ship the uniforms in wardrobe containers.

The best value in a uniform is the one which will give you not only what is wanted but also what is needed.

ADDITIONAL SUGGESTIONS. Your purchase has now been made, and the pilot sample received. Try it on a student of the correct size and examine it from all angles. Remember that the public will see your band's uniforms from some distance, so also check how it looks from a distance of 25 feet or more. Also, to check its comfort, ask your model how the uniform feels. Be sure to inspect each part of the uniform on the inside as well as the outside, to be sure of quality workmanship. If you decide on some minor changes in style, these usually can be made at little if any change in the cost of the finished uniform.

Each part of each complete uniform should be identified by a code number keyed to sex, height and weight. The better manufacturers will supply you with a record book which identifies each part of every uniform and provides adequate space for keeping a complete "history" of each uniform part as it is reassigned year after year.

It is strongly recommended that all uniforms be stored at the school and removed from storage for each wearing, in order to prevent loss and to avoid having uniforms that are not fresh. If school space is not available, then periodic inspections should be made to be sure that all uniforms are complete, clean and free of wrinkles.

ABOUT CLEANING. Uniforms get hard wear, and like any other valuable clothing, they should be given reasonable care in order to give maximum wear. Dry cleaning and pressing are essential once a year, and twice a year or even more often is advisable if they are exposed to a good deal of perspiration or soiling. White garments must be cleaned only by a cleaner experienced in handling white garments, and should never be cleaned along with colored fabrics, or color damage may ensue.

Hats or shakos should never be dry cleaned. They can be safely hand washed, with reasonable care; even synthetic fur shakos can be washed in soapy, lukewarm water, and then rinsed. High-color feather plumes should not be dry cleaned; also, they may run if they become wet, so they must be protected from snow and rain. Metallic fabrics and braids can be safely dry cleaned, but should never be pressed with a hot iron.

New uniforms may spot if caught in the rain. Such spotting is removed, however, with the first dry cleaning and pressing. In the event that uniforms become soaking wet, either from perspiration or from rain, they should be hung up on proper hangers in a cool room, with plenty of space around each one to allow ventilation. It is recommended that they be cleaned and pressed after drying to avoid shrinkage.

OVER-THE-SUMMER CARE. Recall all uniforms at the end of each school year and examine them for any damage such as lost buttons, tears, etc., and have them repaired. Then have them dry cleaned and pressed, and hang them on wooden hangers, protected with opague coverings, in a storage room free of excess light. The finest of colors may fade if exposed to sunlight through the summer months. Care should be taken not to crowd the hangers together or uniforms will become wrinkled during storage and need pressing again when it's time to put them on.

Shakos should be stored with visors down (never on their sides or tops) in suitable dust-proof containers. To keep plumes in proper shape, return them to the tubes in which they were received. Belts, spats and other accessories can be stored in suitable containers and should also be cleaned before storing them for the summer.

Keep your uniform record book up-to-date, checking each garment as it is turned in before vacation. Then in the fall you will be able to fit each boy or girl with ease in a uniform of the proper size, maintaining good band appearance without unnecessary and expensive alterations. Indeed, alterations should be avoided if possible, since they tend to destroy the styling and shorten the life of the uniforms.

When your band becomes larger, so that you need additional uniforms, you'll have additional reason to be grateful that you selected a quality manufacturer. Reputable companies keep complete files on each order and use the most colorfast materials, so that you may order additional uniforms with confidence that they'll be just alike in color and style.

Finally, the ultimate life and wearing satisfaction you will receive from your new uniforms will depend largely on the care you give them: keep uniforms in repair, dry clean regularly, and store properly on concave wooden hangers when not in use.

chapter 15

Equipping the Band Program

Modern musical instruments, electrical teaching devices and other mechanical aids available to music instruction are often almost miracle apparatus. Such inventions require regular care and maintenance or repair of worn and broken parts. Equipment of any nature is no better than its maintenance. An expensive automobile may be made inoperable for the want of a small, inexpensive piece of electric cable. In our modern push-button society, maintenance is of prime importance.

Musical instrument manufacturing companies generally supply instruction booklets for the care of their particular products. The band director should include instruction in the proper care and maintenance of instruments in his teaching program. Insistence and emphasis on these points will pay handsome dividends in respect to maintaining the instruments in good playing condition.

The equipment of a music department is extensive, complex, delicate, and in need of regular care and maintenance. All school-owned instruments need to be inventoried. The inventory record of equipment should identify the item, serial number, value or purchase cost, date of purchase, and condition. If the item is to be checked out to students, a checkout system is an absolute necessity.

The music director should develop a program for regular inspection and maintenance of all school-owned equipment. A written evaluation of the condition of each item, the approximate cost of repair, and the expected life of the equipment—with or without maintenance, is necessary. It is helpful to recommend sources of maintenance service to the administration. The inclusion of such information is likely to encourage the securing of the service. Many school systems have forms for requesting maintenance or repair work. If such forms do not exist, a conference with the supervisor or administrator might provide the opportunity for designing such a form. A plan for handling emergency repair is absolutely essential.

Because nearly all of the instruments and equipment of the band may be very expensive, easily damaged, lost or stolen, each school district should establish a group insurance plan. Group insurance may be secured from a number of insurance companies for a small fee per hundred dollar evaluation of the instruments, and protects against damage, fire loss or theft.

Requests for new equipment should be based on a stated need as related to the educational objectives and justification in the band program. The request should include estimated cost, life expectancy, and detailed specifications for quality equipment.

Care must be taken when spending public funds to secure the greatest quality and service from each dollar. Likewise, it is the band director's responsibility to be able to advise parents and students as to quality merchandise when considering the purchase of an instrument.

AUDIO-VISUAL EQUIPMENT.

1. *Tape Recorders.* When selecting a tape recorder for use in reproducing music for evaluation and teaching purposes, care must be taken to investigate the manufacturer's claims. There are a number of salient factors concerning a tape recorder that should be checked and compared with other machines.

   Criteria for evaluation of tape recorders should include:

   a. Frequency response range — the wider the spread in cycles and the fewer the decibels stated, the better. For example: a frequency response of "50-14,000 HZ $\pm$10db at 7 1/2 ips" is not nearly as high quality reproduction as a frequency response of "50-14,000 HZ $\pm$3db at 7 1/2 ips." The lower the decibel level, the better the quality. Generally, the frequency response for a quality band recording needs to be in the "40-18,000 HZ $\pm$3db at 7 1/2 ips" range.

   b. Wow and flutter specifications indicate the extent to which recorded tones are distorted by variations in tape speed. They are expressed in percentages. The lower the percentage figure, the better. Less than 0.3% would be an excellent range.

   c. Signal-to-noise ratio specifications indicate the extent of audible background noise by comparing the loudness of the program (signal) to the loudness of the background noise. It is expressed in decibels. The larger the db figure, the better and clearer a recorder is likely to reproduce the sound. A signal-to-noise ratio of around 50 will be considered good.

   d. Power output specifications should be indicated by a specific method. The Electronic Industries Association has issued a widely accepted standard for power output: "3.6 watts EIA, 3 watts continued at less than 5% harmonic distortion."

   e. Other considerations:

      1. Can the heads be easily reached for cleaning?
      2. Projected use should indicate whether the machine should be monaural or stereo.
      3. Is there provision for recording *and* playback?
      4. Are speed (ips) choices sufficient to allow flexible use?
      5. Are the kinds and number of input and output connections adequate for multiple use?
      6. Are controls simple to operate?

   There are many variables in selecting a tape recorder. Define your recording objective and seek the best help and advice available before purchasing.

2. *Microphones.* It is doubtful that many of the tape recorders found in the schools today will be equipped with an adequate microphone. The recorder can only put on tape those sounds that the microphone picks up. If a quality tape recorder is to function as designed, the importance of the microphone should not be underestimated. There are two ways of acquiring microphones: just record with any mike supplied with the tape recorder, or follow the plan of the professional who selects different mikes for different recording situations and is always looking for a better mike. The fact is, most good tape recorders are capable of producing better sound than is fed to them by the inferior mikes often furnished with the machines.[1]

---

[1] Arnold Berndt and Ray Brandon, *American School Band Directors Association Research Report* (August, 1967), p. 16.

There are many different types of microphones. The following is a list of some of them, with brief comments about each:

a. Carbon Microphones — the cheapest of all microphones. These mikes have a very limited frequency response, are quite noisy, and are not suited for high fidelity use.

b. Crystal and Ceramic Microphones — omni-directional. These mikes seem to be susceptible to hum pickup, unless a relatively short, shielded cable is used. There are two types of crystal mikes: the "bimorphic" type — inexpensive, and produces a response up to 7000 HZ only, and the "sound-cell" — more expensive than the "bimorphic," and has a response up to 10,000 HZ. Ceramic mikes are quite similar to crystal mikes in performance and price, but are not quite as susceptible to heat and humidity changes.

c. Dynamic Microphones — quite satisfactory if not too cheap. The pick-up pattern is normally omni-directional but can be made directional through special design. One of the more important features of the better dynamic mike is its low output impedance. This requires the use of a special step-up transformer such as those built into some recorders. When used with a recorder having only a high impedance mike input, a transformer must be inserted in the mike cable near the mike input.

d. Condenser (capacitor) Microphones — approach the ideal in frequency response, directionality and dynamic range characteristics. They have the disadvantage of requiring more attention and have more cable to handle in a recording session. As a result, the possibility exists that more things can go wrong than with the simple cable-to-amplifier hookup of a dynamic mike. Condenser mikes are generally slightly less expensive than dynamic microphones of similar quality, but are still expensive.

e. Ribbon Microphones — generally flat in frequency response, but low in distortion. In the better models, frequency response ranges from 20 to 20,000 HZ. The pickup pattern is bi-directional, which has the advantage of being able to eliminate or minimize unwanted sounds in the mike in a different direction. The ribbon mike is quite fragile and is strongly affected by wind.

f. Uni-directional Microphones — more important than the bi-directional mike pattern from the standpoint of eliminating unwanted sounds.

When selecting a microphone there are four important characteristics to keep in mind:

a. Impedance. A low impedance mike will not give satisfactory results with a recorder having a high impedance input; and likewise, a high impedance mike will not work on a low impedance recorder. When used with more than 25 feet of cable, a high impedance mike may develop a hum, and with 100 feet of cable, may sustain a high frequency loss of as much as 16db at 10,000 HZ. Therefore, a high impedance mike should not be used if 20 or more feet of connecting cable is required.

b. Pickup Pattern. The pickup pattern of the mike to be selected is more or less determined by the conditions under which it is used:

1. Omni-directional mikes are best when the program material (signal) is located where extraneous noises can be controlled. The omni-directional mike is often more desirable for monaural recording of concerts. It not only picks up the direct sounds, but also the reverberation of the auditorium — which adds life to the recording. This

type of mike may be used with home recorders when pickup from all directions is desirable (news conferences, interviews, etc.).

2. Bi-directional mikes give results very similar to those achieved with an omni-directional mike, but have the advantage of no side pickup. Thus, through proper placement, some unwanted sounds can be eliminated.

3. Cardioid or uni-directional mikes are preferred when there is a high level of unwanted sounds. A good mike of this type has a ratio of about 10 to 1 in pickup from the front to back. This type of mike is desirable for stereo recording, where directional effect is needed.

It would seem that the desirable mike would be one with a variable pickup pattern. Such a mike is rather expensive. It would be cheaper to have both omni- or bi-directional and uni-directional mikes.

c. Frequency Response. The frequency response of mikes used for band recording should be very broad. But it must be remembered that unless recording conditions are ideal, many unwanted sounds in the low frequency range will be picked up from such interferences as air conditioning, traffic noise, etc.

Mikes with ideal frequency response, while fine under certain conditions, are perhaps not the best for recording in the average band room or school auditorium. A mike with a response falloff at about 50 HZ will many times prove more satisfactory for school recording than a mike with a frequency response flat down to 30 HZ.

d. Sensitivity. The sensitivity of a mike is rather low, and the rated sensitivity is given in db below 1 volt, such as 70 db or 50 db. The smaller the number, the more sensitive the mike. A high-fidelity mike usually has an output of about 60 db and presents no problem; but some super-fidelity mikes will have less output, which then requires more pre-amplification and can cause amplifier noise problems.

It can be seen from these facts, that, in selecting a mike, many things must be considered. No one characterisitic alone should determine which mike should be selected. Always keep in mind where and how it is to be used and the equipment with which it is to be used.

3. *Record Players*. Available in a wide variety of sizes and designed for many uses. The selection should be based on the intended use. In preparing to make a selection, the director needs to consider the following points:

a. Portability. Is the machine to be moved about?

b. Is it light, compact and attractive in design?

c. Is the instrument case sturdy, easy to handle and free from vibration?

d. Will it give good service with a minimum of maintenance?

e. Does the machine provide the quality of reproduction and power necessary for its particular use?

f. Is needle changing easy and convenient?

g. Are the electronic circuits transistorized or vacuum tube?

h. Are there input and output connections for microphone and external speakers?

i. How does the cost compare with various makes and models of like quality?

If the equipment is to be a permanent installation, then other considerations will enter into the selection. In considering a high fidelity record player for installation in the band or music room, the director should first identify and define the technical and service requirements. Once he has completed such a task, he can present the justification for a quality instrument. The evaluation or specifications should include: ease of operation, dependability, frequency response, quality of performance, reputation of manufacturer, availability of service, and comparative costs.

4. *Public Address Systems.* In selecting a public address system, the same basic questions need to be asked as in selecting either a tape recorder or record player. The first step in selection is to identify and define the needs. Then study and selection can proceed on some knowledgeable basis. Do not hesitate to ask recognized experts in the field of electronics or public address systems for help and advice.

5. *Portable Public Address Systems.* A number of hand-carried voice-amplified speakers are available. The same steps of identifying and defining need, performance requirements, portability, service ability, and cost should enter into the selection of the equipment.

6. *Projectors and Screens.* Movie, 16mm or 8mm film and slide projectors, opaque and overhead projectors are modern teaching aids. The selection and purchase of such equipment again should be based on the established criteria of identifying and defining the needs, performance requirements, service ability, dependability and comparative cost. The use of any of these projectors necessarily requires a screen. Such a screen should be attached to the wall for convenience and ease of viewing. Selection should be based on the requirements of use, viewing, life expectancy, convenience and cost.

7. *Video Tape Recorders.* The advent of the television record-and-play-back system has provided many new approaches to teaching and the evaluation of learning experiences, not only in academic areas, but in the music program. The development of teaching techniques in using this new device has only begun. However, those who have used it claim that the potential is great.

For example, a student may perform a musical excerpt with which he is having problems. The video tape is ready for instant replay. The student may discover the solution to his problem on his own, or, with the instructor, establish a procedure for practicing and overcoming the problem.

The portable video tape recorder has also been successfully used for improving marching band performance. Since the recorded performance can be replayed immediately, the instructor and students can discuss and plan solutions to performance problems.

The purchase of a video tape recorder for school use is not an easy financial decision, particularly considering the initial cost. Portable TV systems currently on the market cost between $3,000 and $18,000, plus associated sound and camera equipment. The extent of proposed use within the district must justify the expense of the purchase. Cost of recording and playback may run from $10.00 to $30.00 per hour, depending on the type and size of machine.

Legal problems frequently surround the use of video tape. For instance, consider if there could be a conflict when recording from the programs released from regular commercial stations for replay in the schools. What will be the rights and compensations of the institution, teacher, and crew involved? Many more such questions may need to be considered.

A most compelling reason to consider the acquisition of a portable video tape recorder would be to bring expensive material from remote sources into the school system. As well, the many uses of studio equipment, the storage of recorded material, and student and teacher educational growth can justify the initial cost of video tape systems.

In the period between 1964 and 1970 great advances were made in the growth and perfection of television systems. This discussion has only presented the subject. Much study and objective writing of a video tape program needs to be done before launching into such a program. Some reference sources follow:

Clarke, R. Walton, *1966 Schoolman's Guide to ETV Communications*. Philadelphia: Jerrold Electronics Corporation, 1966.

Costello, Lawrence F. and Gordon, George N., *Teach with Television*, 2nd ed. New York: Hastings House, 1965.

Diamond, Robert M., ed., *A Guide to Instructional Television*. New York: McGraw-Hill, 1964.

Educational Facilities Laboratories, *Design for ETV (Planning for Schools with Television)*, prepared by Dave Chapman, Inc., Industrial Design. New York: Educational Facilities Laboratories, 1960.

Educational Policies Commission, *Education and the Spirit of Science*. Washington, D.C.: The National Education Association, 1966.

Erickson, Carlton W.H., *Fundamentals of Teaching with Audiovisual Technology*. New York: Macmillan, 1968.

————. *Administering Instructional Media Programs*. New York: Macmillan, 1968.

Griffith, Barton L. and MacLennan, Donald W., *Improvement of Teaching by Television*. Columbia, Mo: University of Missouri Press, 1964.

8. *Sound Generators and Electronic Sound Devices.* There are several electronic devices available and essential to the band program:

   a. The Lektrotuner — an electronic device which sings out an accurate and continuous tone pitched at A-440 or the B♭ a half step higher. It is audible to an entire musical organization as a tuning note reference. The cost is around $70.00 (1971 list price).

   b. The Strobotuner — an electronic device which will measure the sharpness or flatness of a pitch being played into its microphone. The visual indication provides the student with an eye-mind concept of the pitch. The instrument will measure (by a selector) each of the twelve half-step tones in an octave. The cost of this item is about $225.00 (1971 list price).

   c. The Stroboconn — electronically measures any of the twelve half-step tones in an octave. The difference between the Strobotuner and the Stroboconn is that the latter will measure any tone — without a selector. The cost of this instrument is about $775.00 (1971 list price).

d. The Dynalevel — an electronic innovation which measures visually the loudness or softness of sound. It costs approximately $297.00 (1971 list price).

FURNITURE AND MISCELLANEOUS EQUIPMENT.

1. *Posture Correct Chairs*. Band rehearsal chairs should be sturdy, comfortable and conducive to good playing posture. The wooden or steel frame straight chair with the flat wooden seat and curved back is the most commonly used. The chair should have an eighteen-inch seat height for high school students. Many folding chairs should be avoided, for they are frequently not conducive to good playing posture.

2. *Stools*. Six to ten thirty-inch high stools of either adjustable, swivel or fixed type are needed in the rehearsal room for string bass players, percussion players, and the conductor.

3. *Music Stands*. About two-thirds as many music stands as players are required for the average band. An additional one or two music stands will be needed for each practice room. The most satisfactory model has no screw adjustment at all, but is raised, lowered or tipped by hand pressure. A high quality music stand may be purchased for about $12 to $18 each. Such stands have a life expectancy of about ten years.

4. *Instrument Stands*. A number of band instruments (such as tubas, baritone saxophones, and percussion instruments) require some kind of supporting stand so the student can play with ease, comfort, and reasonably good posture. Several music instrument manufacturers supply instrument stands of good quality. The director should check the accessory catalogue at his local music dealer for guidance in securing the proper stand.

5. *Instrument Storage Cabinets*. Experience has shown that when the music department provides individual lockers for the safekeeping of student- and school-owned instruments there is far less breakage and repair work. It is true that individual lockers are somewhat expensive. However, when the value of the instruments is considered, the added cost of this "insurance" is rather low. The average value of a music instrument may be around $200. If there are 100 members in the band, the total investment is near $20,000. A set of band lockers will cost at most about $5,000. A number of companies manufacture attractive and durable sets of instrument cabinets at reasonable cost.

6. *File Cabinets*. Steel file cabinets are essential to the proper cataloguing and maintenance of the band music library. Since the cost of music is very high, the only safe way to care for the music is in steel file cabinets. (The cost of score and parts for one work for concert band may be as high as $75 to $100.) Open shelf storage simply does not offer the protection needed for music. Legal-size and letter-size, four- or five-drawer cabinets are usually used. File cabinets are also needed for storage of records and other pertinent material.

7. *Music Sorting Rack*. In the operation of a comprehensive band program, a large number of copies of individual instrumental parts are handled. A special set of shelving, so arranged to conveniently hold several copies of music for each of some forty or more different parts, aids in the efficient and accurate distribution and sorting of music.

8. *Folio Cabinets*. Due to the large number of students generally active in an on-going band program, the storage and availability of the daily rehearsal music presents a problem. A cabinet of shelving, spaced to accommodate each music folio, makes it convenient for the student to pick up his daily rehearsal music and to return it to the cabinet at the close of the rehearsal.

Several types of cabinets are available from school furniture companies and are available in two folio sizes: concert and march size.

9. *Office Equipment.* All band programs need an office furnished with an adequate desk, chairs, file cabinets, typewriter with table, and a telephone. A telephone is essential to the band program — for the safety of the large number of students in the band program in case of accident, for the convenience of the band on returning from an out-of-town trip, and for the director, who often needs to coordinate various programs and activities in more than one school and in the community.

10. *Duplicating Machines.* A spirit duplicating machine is essential to the operation of a good band program. Almost daily, band directors need to distribute bulletins for students and parents, marching charts, calendars of events and instructions for a variety of activities.

11. *Repair and Maintenance.* Some type of facility is necessary for students to clean and oil their instruments. Many band programs find it economical and efficient to have a small room adjacent to the band room for instrument maintenance and repair. Such a room needs a sink with hot and cold water, a work bench, storage cabinets for spare parts and repair equipment. A minimum repair kit should contain the following items:

1 tool box; 1 box cork grease; 1 bottle valve oil; 1 bottle slide oil; 1 bottle key oil; 1 bottle lacquer conditioner; French horn valve strings; 3 cornet top valve springs; 3 cornet bottom valve springs; 1 sax mouthpiece screw (brass); 1 sax mouthpiece screw (silver); ½ doz. assorted flute pads; 2 Sousaphone bell screws (brass); 3 pieces assorted cork; 1 doz. small waterkey corks; ½ doz. large waterkey corks; 1 set clarinet pads; 1 doz. small clarinet screws; 2 lyre screws; 1 doz. assorted flat spring screws; 1 doz. assorted valve felts; 2 doz. assorted needle springs; ½ doz. soft saxophone pads; 2 sheets sandpaper; 2 saxophone mouthpipe corks; 4 assorted valve corks; 1 piece fine emery paper; 1 piece stick shellac; 1 tube pad/cork cement; 3 waterkey springs; 1 box tuning slide grease; 1 doz. flat springs; 1 piece leather for sax key bumpers; 1 oboe swab; 1 Utica pliers; 1 No. 4 knife; 1 spring hook 14″ rat-tail file; 14″ black mill file; 1 buckskin mallet; 1 long screwdriver; 1 medium screwdriver; 1 clarinet lock screwdriver; 1 piece hardwood for straightening sax keys; 1 piece hardwood for removing valve caps.

12. *Full-length, Wall-mounted Mirror*, size 36″ x 72″. Experience has proven that when an individual sees himself in a full-length mirror, he immediately evaluates his appearance, posture, and attitude. He will most often improve his appearance by standing taller, lifting his head, and checking his clothing. Many times a sober face will change to a smile. The cost of a good mirror is less than a hundred dollars, and it pays for itself many times each day.

chapter 16

Budget and Finance

The band director in any school system is expected to display leadership in all the activities that contribute to the success and well-being of his department and school. The music program needs to be supported with sufficient funds to assure the achievement desired by the community. The director must be able to assure those who provide the funds that every dollar is well spent for goods and services and that they are receiving full value.[1]

This chapter will discuss the nature of budgets, patterns of budgetary operation, sources of financial support, elements of budget building, and administration, in terms of building a band program.

A budget is a plan estimating costs and the proposed expenditure of funds in support of a program. Planning is the basis for making a budget. The plan of a band program budget is based on the objectives of the program and includes identifying and describing all the elements necessary to achieve the objectives of the program.

The purposes of the budget, as defined by Mort and Reusser[2], identify five areas served by the school budget. Although these purposes refer to the financing of the total educational plan, it will be seen that portions of the total budgeting process apply to the band program:

1. Projection of school program into future.

   As an educational plan is laid for the future (at least one year), the budget represents the underwriting of the plan accepted by the Board of Education and community.

2. Estimation of expected revenues.

   The budget anticipates and estimates the amount of money to be obtained from various sources.

3. Estimation of expenditures.

   After the educational plan has been identified and described, the cost may be estimated and allocations made in support of the various programs.

4. Determination of amount to be raised.

   After the school income and expenditures are estimated, the budget will show what money must be raised by other means, or which programs must be cut back. A well-described and documented program is least often cut back.

5. Aid to the operation.

   The budget accepted by the Board of Education and community reflects the emphasis they wish placed on the various programs of the educational plan. The popularity shown a particular program by the community will be directly reflected in the overall plan.

---

[1] Keith D. Snyder, *School Music Supervision* (Boston: Allyn and Bacon, 1959).

[2] Paul R. Mort and Walter C. Reusser, *Public School Finance,* 2nd ed., (New York: McGraw-Hill Book Company, 1951), pp. 161-162.

BUDGETARY PROCEDURES.[3] The financial support of a music program may be considered under four different budget plans. Each has its strengths and weaknesses.

1. Departmental Budgets.

   The music director is responsible for estimating needs of the music department, presenting the plan and documentation of the proposed expenditures to the superintendent of the schools or his designated officer of budgets. In such a plan, the program of the music department is conceived as a unit. It cuts across school lines, and all music activities come under the planned budget. The advantage of this plan is that the total music program operates as a unit.

2. The Autonomous School Budget.

   Each school is allocated a portion of the funds to support its educational program. The danger of such a plan is that it may cause the system-wide music program to be unequal and uncoordinated. Although theoretically it would fit individual schools, programs that need close coordination often suffer.

3. Split Music Budget.

   The split music budget provides a separate financial allotment for the band, the orchestra, and the vocal programs. Each phase of the music curriculum receives an allocation to be expended independently of the others. It is obvious that such a plan has little unity. All schools should have a total music program.

4. The fourth budget plan is no plan at all.

   The music director presents his expenditure request to the principal or the superintendent for allocation of whatever funds are available. It is obvious that this system holds little opportunity for building a sound music program.

The band director in any school must have a clear understanding as to the source and amount of financial support available for the operation of his program. Generally there are three sources of funds to support the band or music program:

1. Taxation.

   Public funds are the result of the philosophy that education is the responsibility of the state and local community, and to some extent, the federal government.

2. Special Funds.

   Special funds from income other than taxes are often available to various educational programs in the schools. These funds come from ticket admissions for concerts, selling of various products for profit, and many other schemes devised by educational programs that do not receive adequate financial support. It is difficult to defend the necessity of music departments having to expend untold amounts of energy to raise funds to support the activity or program. However, public financing is often inadequate to support the music program.

   Sometimes the band is given an allocation from athletic gate receipts for its part in entertaining the audience. Since there is considerable expense in supplying music and entertainment for the various athletic events, it is only reasonable that the band program receive some financial support from the athletic department.

---

[3] Snyder, *op. cit.*, pp. 231-232.

If the school music program *is* a part of the overall educational program, it should be funded in the same manner as all other educational programs. But since public funds are not always adequate for total support, the imaginative band or music director must often find other means of financial support.

3. Gifts.

Local clubs, organizations and/or individuals often present gifts of varying amounts for specified or general use. Gifts "for general use" prove most advantageous because they may be used where needed.

Preparing a budget for the operation of a band program involves several sequential steps. One plan is as follows:

1. The objectives of the program must be defined in such a way as to be a part of the overall educational plan. Each item eventually must be converted into a cost factor.
2. The planning phase of the budget outlines the sequence of musical events and when they are to take place. Each event involves materials, equipment, space, process and personnel. Each item eventually must be converted into a cost factor.
3. Organizing the items of the budget based upon the stated objectives will provide a justification for the items and amounts requested.
4. The budget request should contain supporting information for all requests. The following items should be included:[4]
   a. Cover letter.
   b. A budget summary.
   c. Proposed program revenue.
   d. Proposed program expenditures, with explanation for each item.
   e. Proposed monitoring and evaluation scheme.

After a budget is adopted and funded by the Board of Education, it is the responsibility of the Superintendent of Schools to supervise the expenditure of the funds. The superintendent normally delegates the program responsibility to the music director. The music director then becomes responsible for administering, implementing and supervising the expenditure of funds. He should know at all times the status of his budget in achieving the program. Periodic reports should be made to the superintendent or the designated officer. If an objective evaluation scheme (as described in Chapter Two) is tied to the budget, valid and concrete information will be available for future budget decision-making.

The responsibilities of the music director in administering the departmental budget include the following items:

1. The music director continually needs to apprise the school and community of the status of the programs for which public support was provided.
2. Complete and up-to-date inventories of all materials, equipment and supplies must be maintained. Systems for checking out equipment and cataloging music must be accurate and continuous.
3. A regular plan of budget accounting is necessary. All staff members in the music department must be involved in the budget operation. All planned budget expenditures must be held within projected amounts.

---

[4] Snyder, *op, cit.,* p. 241

4. The budget and finance process is a continuum. There are a number of deadlines which must be met. For example, at the end of each month the music staff should evaluate the status and adequacy of the operational budget. Planning and supporting information should be gathered monthly, with the month of February or March set as the time for the first draft of the next year's budget. The proposed budget should cover such items as:

a. Staff.
b. Space.
c. Music.
d. Supplies.
e. Maintenance.
f. Repair and replacement of equipment.
g. New equipment.
h. New programs.
i. Performance group travel.
j. Rental of auditorium, if required.
k. Piano tuning.
l. Professional travel.
m. Professional library.
n. In-service workshops.

The music educator—band or otherwise—has an important responsibility in the financial and moral support of the school administration, the Board of Education, the students and the community, as well as providing information in regard to the objectives of the program and its achievements. The band director must be a competent musician and have administrative ability. He must have expertise in curriculum development—its planning, organizing and implementing. He must be versed in guidance and counseling, and have compassion for people, young and old. Above all, he must have warmth as a human being, inviting the confidence of all with whom he comes into contact.

Budget is so directly related to the success of a music program, that to illustrate its importance, an actual budget proposal is included here for reference and guidance. (Although this budget does not necessarily follow all the detailed criteria of the preceding presentation, the variations are of minor significance.)

PROPOSED DEPARTMENT OF MUSIC BUDGET

Spencer, Iowa Community Schools
1970-1971 School year

Submitted by

_____

PREFACE

The proposed budget for the school year 1970-1971 was prepared after the following steps had been taken:

1. A meeting of all staff members was held on Monday, January 19, 1970 for the purpose of holding an in-depth discussion of departmental needs for the 1970-71 school year.
2. I scheduled personal conferences with each member of the music staff concerning the exact needs for his area of instruction.
3. A survey of all school-owned music equipment (including pianos) was made to determine condition, estimated cost of repair or overhaul, and replacement value of items no longer usable.
4. Mr. John Clifford, our school piano service man, was consulted concerning piano repairs, adjustments, tuning, and replacement.

In view of the inflationary factors in the national economy, it would seem reasonable to request that a financial cushion be provided somewhere in the school budget to absorb the probable increase in costs.

Department of Music

(For economy of space, detailed lists of items in the Spencer, Iowa budget are not included here. However, the headings can suggest format and be useful as a guide.)

INFORMATION CONCERNING THE LIFE EXPECTANCY OF SCHOOL-OWNED BAND INSTRUMENTS AND BAND UNIFORMS

1. SCHOOL-OWNED BAND INSTRUMENTS: The National Association of Band Instrument Manufacturers conducted a three-year study of the life-expectancy of school-owned band instruments and found that the average school-owned instrument has a life-expectancy of 10.1 years. As our records will show, Spencer's school-owned instruments last from two to three times this long, which proves that we take care of our equipment.

2. BAND UNIFORMS: The National Association of Uniform Manufacturers conducted a comprehensive survey in 1962-63 and found that the average life of school band uniforms is 7.3 years. We used our last set at least this long, because we take care of this equipment.

   In the past four years the Spencer Band Boosters Association has spent in excess of $19,000 for uniform equipment for the senior band. This year the Band Boosters are spending an additional $3,445.00 for new blazers for the junior bands.

Chairman of Music Dept.

I. REPAIRS OF INSTRUMENTS

    Elementary Schools (itemized)

    Junior High Schools (itemized)

    Senior High Schools (itemized)

    Total repair budget for the year 19 $ _____

    New band instrument cases $ _____

                 TOTAL FOR SECTION I $ _____

II. REPLACEMENT OF EQUIPMENT

    Elementary Schools (itemized) $ _____

    Junior High Schools (Itemized) $ _____

    Senior High Schools (itemized) $ _____

    Band books; Teaching guides; Manuscript paper;
    Method books; Reference material; Sheet music, etc. $ _____

    Miscellaneous items, such as drum heads, mutes,
    etc. $ _____

                 TOTAL FOR SECTION II $ _____

III. NEW EQUIPMENT NEEDED

    Elementary Schools (itemized) $ _____

    Junior High Schools (itemized) $ _____

    Senior High Schools (itemized) $ _____

                 TOTAL FOR SECTION III $ _____

IV. LIBRARY NEEDS

    Educational Recordings and Tapes $ _____

    Ensemble music; Sheet music; March books;
    Library reference materials; Library filing
    material; Manuscript paper; March folios;
    Concert band folios, etc. $ _____

                 TOTAL FOR SECTION IV $ _____

V. MUSIC

BAND MUSIC—Elementary Schools $_____

BAND MUSIC—Junior High Schools $_____

BAND MUSIC—Senior High Schools $_____

STAGE BAND MUSIC—Junior High Schools $_____

STAGE BAND MUSIC—Senior High Schools $_____

REPLACEMENT MUSIC—All schools $_____
(to supply missing or needed parts)

TOTAL FOR SECTION V $_____

VI. PROPOSED BUDGET FOR SMALL, MISCELLANEOUS REPLACEMENT ITEMS:

(Percussion accessories; Phonograph styli; Valve and slide oil; Reeds for staff members; Tapes; Batons; Repair equipment for woodwind instruments, etc.)

Elementary Schools $_____

Junior High Schools $_____

Senior High Schools $_____

TOTAL FOR SECTION VI $_____

VII. MAINTENANCE OF ELECTRONIC EQUIPMENT

(Maintenance of recording machines, microphones, record players, Stroboconns, etc.)

TOTAL FOR SECTION VII $_____

Totals:

SECTION I $_____

SECTION II $_____

SECTION III $_____

SECTION IV $_____

SECTION V $_____

SECTION VI $_____

SECTION VII $_____

GRAND TOTAL 19_____ BUDGET $_____

Note: This budget is up $ _____ / down $ _____ compared to last year for the following reasons:

PROPOSED BUDGET FOR THE CLOVIS, NEW MEXICO MUNICIPAL SCHOOLS

Band Music Program

BAND ORGANIZATIONS IN THE CLOVIS SCHOOLS

ELEMENTARY SCHOOL BAND PROGRAM

Sixth grade bands meet daily at the following Clovis Elementary Schools:

SCHOOL	DIRECTOR
Bella Vista	N. Howell
Highland	N. Howell
Guadalupe	T. Mayfield
Eugene Field	T. Mayfield
La Casita	T. Mayfield
Lincoln-Jackson	T. Mayfield
Parkview	P. Wilson
Zia	P. Wilson
Sandia	D. Echols
James Bickley	D. Echols

There are 172 sixth-grade band students in the total program. With the exception of thirty-two students (National Defense Education Act), they are participating on individually-owned instruments ranging in price from $100.00 to $350.00. Elementary band music is provided by the Clovis Schools. Each of the above bands meets daily from 30 to 45 minutes depending on the individual school schedule. Private instruction is available to elementary band students through qualified instructors from Eastern New Mexico University. At the present time we are using six instructors from Eastern. Private instruction is not required, but available for interested students. Some private students will enter solo competition in the District Festival. Clovis band directors feel the private program is an important factor in the success of the total program.

CLOVIS ALL-STAR ELEMENTARY BAND

The All-Star Elementary Band is made up of outstanding sixth grade band students and represents each of the Clovis Elementary Schools. The Band rehearses at 8:00 a.m. Saturday mornings in the High School Band Building. Membership in this organization is determined by audition.

NATIONAL DEFENSE EDUCATION ACT

Thirty-two students from Eugene Field, La Casita, Lincoln-Jackson, and Our Lady of Guadalupe Elementary Schools are participating in band with instruments made available through the National Defense Education Act. Without this help it would have been impossible for these students to participate in the band program. At this point Mr. Mayfield, the Director, feels the program has been most successful, and the students are doing acceptable work. Ten of the NDEA students are participating in the All-Star Elementary Band.

PROPOSAL:

Clovis Band Directors would like to present an All-Elementary Band Night Concert, featuring a combined band made up of all band students from each of the Clovis elementary schools. This band of some 172 students would perform as a single unit and not as individual schools. There would be *no* competition between schools. It would provide an opportunity for band members to perform in a large group one day a year. It would be their big night. . . a chance to perform for mom and dad.

The concert would be held on a Saturday night. *No* school time would be needed in presenting this program. *No* school buses would be needed to transport students.

The band directors urge approval of this proposal.

JUNIOR HIGH SCHOOL BAND PROGRAM
MARSHALL JUNIOR HIGH SCHOOL

Cadet Band — seventh grade students.

Marching Band and Concert Band — eighth and ninth grade students.

Small Ensembles — These groups do not meet during the school day, but after school and at night.

Sections — These groups are made up of sections of like instruments (clarinets, cornets, etc.) and meet daily after school and on Saturdays.

GATTIS JUNIOR HIGH SCHOOL

Cadet Band — seventh grade students.

Marching Band and Concert Band — eighth and ninth grade students.

Beginning Band — seventh, eighth, and ninth grade students.

Small Ensembles — These groups do not meet during the school day, but after school and at night.

Sections — These groups are made up of sections of like instruments (clarinets, cornets, etc.) and meet daily after school and on Saturdays.

SENIOR HIGH SCHOOL BAND PROGRAM

Wildcat Marching Band — grades 10, 11 and 12.

Concert Band — grades 10, 11 and 12 (same personnel as Wildcat Marching Band).

Swing Band — "The Keynotes"; this group meets after school and at night, plays for civic clubs, basketball games, etc.

PROPOSAL: It is recommended the Swing Band be scheduled during the school day. It is difficult to perfect jazz arrangements without adequate rehearsal time.

Small Ensembles — These groups meet after school and on Saturdays. Small ensembles also meet at night.

Sections — These groups are made up of sections of like instruments (clarinets, cornets, etc.) and meet daily after school and on Saturdays.

ENROLLMENT

TOTAL ENROLLMENT 1966-67

Marshall Junior High School band program .... 140 students

Gattis Junior High School band program .... 100 students

Clovis Senior High School band program .... 100 students

Clovis Elementary band program .... 172 students

Total: 512

ANTICIPATED ENROLLMENT 1967-68

Marshall Junior High School band program .... 140 students

Gattis Junior High School band program .... 130 students

Clovis Senior High School band program .... 110 students

Clovis Elementary band program .... 200 students

Total: 580

BAND TRAVEL 1967-68

MARSHALL JUNIOR HIGH SCHOOL

ENMU Homecoming Parade

Portales, New Mexico

(Three buses — not overnight; University hosts Band for noon meal)

189

District Marching Contest
Hobbs, New Mexico
(Three buses — not overnight; students pay own meals)

Southeastern District Solo and Ensemble Festival
Portales, New Mexico (ENMU)
(Two buses — not overnight; students pay own meals)

Southeastern District Junior High School Instrumental Music
Festival
Artesia, New Mexico
(Three buses — not overnight; students pay own meals)

GATTIS JUNIOR HIGH SCHOOL

Eastern New Mexico Fair Parade
Roswell, New Mexico
(Three buses — not overnight; parade committee hosts noon
meal)

ENMU Homecoming Parade
Portales, New Mexico
(Three buses — not overnight; Univeristy hosts Band for noon
meal)

District Marching Contest
Hobbs, New Mexico
(Three buses — not overnight; students pay own meals)

Southeastern District Solo and Ensemble Festival
Portales, New Mexico (ENMU)
(Two buses — not overnight; students pay own meals)

Southeastern District Junior High School Instrumental Music
Festival
Roswell, New Mexico
(Three buses — not overnight; students pay own meals)

SENIOR HIGH SCHOOL

Manzano Football Game
Albuquerque, New Mexico
(Three buses — not overnight; students pay for own meals)

Portales Football Game
Portales, New Mexico
(Three buses — not overnight; students pay for own meals)

Artesia Football Game
Artesia, New Mexico
(Three buses — not overnight; students pay for own meals)

ENMU Homecoming Parade
Portales, New Mexico
(Three buses — not overnight; University hosts Band for noon meal)

Southeastern District Marching Band Contest
Hobbs, New Mexico
(Three buses — not overnight; students pay for own meals)

All-State Band Auditions
Roswell, New Mexico
(Two buses — not overnight; students pay for own meals)

New Mexico All-State Band Clinic
Albuquerque, New Mexico
(One bus — Band Boosters pay housing; meals paid by students)

Lamesa Invitational Band Contest
Lamesa, Texas (held on a Saturday)
(Three buses — not overnight; students pay for own meals)

Southeastern District Solo and Ensemble Festival
Portales, New Mexico
(Three buses — not overnight; students pay for own meals)

Southeastern District Instrumental Music Festival
Clovis, New Mexico

Tri-State Music Festival
Enid, Oklahoma
(Three buses — Band Boosters pay housing; meals paid by students)

BAND MUSIC BUDGET REQUESTS

The annual amount budgeted for each band to purchase new music is inadequate. In the past, band directors have had to purchase additional music from their activity funds in order to have enough.

GATTIS JUNIOR HIGH SCHOOL

Marching Band music	$100.00
Concert Band music	$450.00
Cadet Band music	$150.00

Total: $700.00 (Received last year: $300.00)

MARSHALL JUNIOR HIGH SCHOOL

Marching Band music	$100.00
Concert Band music	$450.00
Cadet Band music	$150.00

Total: $700.00 (Received last year: $300.00)

CLOVIS SENIOR HIGH SCHOOL

Marching Band music	$300.00
Swing Band music	$200.00
Concert Band music	$500.00

Total: $1,000.00 (Received last year: $500.00)

Special arrangements for the Wildcat Marching Band cost $25.00 per arrangement. Special arrangements of music are needed when a particular selection is not published.

AVERAGE COST FOR ONE ARRANGEMENT OF BAND MUSIC

	Junior High	High School	Elem.
Marching Band	$ 9.00	$10.00	
Concert Band	$15.00	$20.00	$12.50
Cadet Band	$12.50		
Solo and Ensemble	$ 5.00	$10.00	$ 4.50
Swing Band		$10.00	

High school music will cost more per arrangement because of length and difficulty of number. *One* arrangement purchased this past year=$99.00.

PRESENT USE OF BAND MUSIC IN CLOVIS SCHOOLS

	Jr. High School	Sr. High School
Marching arrangements	15	25-30
Concert arrangements	25	25-35
Cadet Band arrangements	10-20	
Swing Band arrangements		35-40
Solos	10-15	20-30
Ensembles	20-30	30-50

1. Various ensembles (brass groups, clarinet choirs, etc.) play for civic clubs, festivals, concerts, etc., which requires a large amount of ensemble music for these activities.
2. Most students are interested in individual advancement through solo performance. Solos are used for All-State Band auditions, contest, and concert performance.

3. High School swing Band plays for home basketball games, civic clubs, and concerts.

4. Marching Bands perform for football games, pep rallys, parades, and other activities. All of these performances call for a great amount of music.

5. Sometimes it is difficult to judge the possibilities of a piece of music without actually performing it.

6. Because of the size of the bands, it may require two or even three arrangements of one peice of music in order to have adequate parts. Even then students may have to share one piece of music.

7. Some band music is needed for reading and training purposes (not necessarily for performance).

TOTAL BAND BUDGET REQUEST
1967-68

EXPENDITURES:

Equipment	$ 6,130.00
Clovis High School Band Travel	1,000.00
Marshall Junior High School Band Travel	200.00
Gattis Junior High School Band Travel	200.00
Band Instrument Repair	2,500.00
Band Music (Clovis Senior High School)	1,000.00
Band Music (Gattis Junior High School)	700.00
Band Music (Marshall Junior High School)	700.00
	Total: $12,430.00

NOTE: Since 1962, all gasoline, oil, and driver expenses incurred by junior and senior high school band travel has been paid by the Clovis Municipal Schools and not from band activity funds.

ADDENDUM

PROPOSED INCREASE IN BAND DIRECTORS' SALARY INCREMENTS:

At the present time Band Directors receive the following salary increments:

Elementary Band Director — none
Junior High School Band Director — $300.00
High School Band Director — $600.00

The following increases are recommended:

Elementary Band Director — $600.00
Junior High School Band Director — $600.00
High School Band Director — $600.00

This is a reasonable request, and our Band Directors are deserving of serious consideration.

* * * * * * * * * * *

BAND BOOSTERS BUDGET —Clovis High School Band (for information): Listed below are band expenses to be paid by the Band Boosters during the 1967-68 school year:

1. Contest entry fees..$ 600.00
   Includes entry fees for the following band events:
   All-State Music Clinic
   District Marching Contest
   Lamesa Invitational Contest
   District Concert Contest
   Six-Flags Band Contest
2. New Mexico All-State Clinic (motel) expenses.......   300.00
3. Band Clinician fees 300.00
4. Six-Flags trip.. 1,000.00
   This fee represents housing in the Six-Flags area and possibly some meals. Students will need to pay for majority of meals themselves.
5. Formal band pictures..   25.00
6. Marching Band sound and color film 125.00
7. Band Camp scholarships 300.00

   Total: $2,650.00

chapter 17

The "Successful" Band

Effective teaching is based upon adequate background and training, interest and effort in performing to the peak of capability, and on a well-formulated, valid philosophy. An insight into what makes a contemporary band and its program "successful" might be gained from the study of philosophies expressed by directors of schools in which effective teaching is carried on. To acknowledge, at this point, that band directors are concerned with student development and that their teaching is educationally sound is a matter of importance. To recognize that these same directors do have basic philosophies — varied as they may be — is the purpose in concluding with the following statements:

"My attitude toward my work has always been: Start from where you are and go as far as you can go. If possible, try to do something new and different each year that will add impetus, strength and excitement to the program. Look forward to every new year and every new day as an exciting challenge that holds much promise for self-development and the development of those you teach. To be enthusiastic and excited about your work is an immediate challenge to your students, and this optimistic approach is a stimulus which is contagious among the students.

"Continual professional growth is a must for the successful teacher. Reading, professional contacts, counseling with many others, and personal involvements in related activities give strength to one's preparation and ability. A constant quest for betterment of self and students will add a needed professional touch to the overall program.

"One's first duty is to the administration, the faculty, the department and the total school. One cannot be a loner — for himself or for his department. The most successful teacher is the one who works with and for the school through his department.

"A successful program usually stems from a proper attitude on the part of the majority of students and good leadership from officers, with the understanding that things must happen. The director must be behind the scenes to guide and direct the action — but it works. Students like responsibility and, with proper leadership and direction, are capable of doing the job. Next to this the director must be a tireless worker who knows how to plan and inspire young people to do or work at the top of their ability. If these are done, discipline will usually be a small item.

"The successful director must know the community and be willing to work for its growth and development, for civic pride must be felt and desired by the students. The music staff must be a compatible group, since nothing creates problems like dissension. Staff members must be professional in all relationships with each other, the administration, and with colleagues in the region and state. All should have a constant desire for personal improvement and the growth of their program. Staff members should work and plan together. Our staff does this and it works effectively. Ideas and plans are shared for the good of all. Our planning is done as a complete staff project. Our members are not afraid to experiment.

"At times my home life is subjugated by the demands of my work, but I try to make up for it at other times. I like to do things at home and do find time to do many improvement projects. With two daughters at home and in junior high school, we have close contacts with school life, and all work in church: Sunday School, choir, young people's activities, and the Board of Stewards. We have been here twenty years and have seen the community and school system grow tremendously. There is a lot of civic pride evident, and we are proud to be a part of such a wonderful experience."

—J. Raymond Brandon, *North Little Rock Senior High School, North Little Rock, Arkansas*

"Any degree of personal success in the band field might come from the initial good beginning I had on my major instrument and the preparation I received in college. I have spent a great deal of time acquainting myself with the literature of the band, and I have always been keenly interested in the techniques of teaching the various instruments of the band. I have tried to place emphasis on the individual in the band, making sure he knows how to perform well on his instrument.

"I believe that band experience should be a pleasant one for students, and I try to use only as much discipline from the podium as is necessary for the rehearsal. I believe the real success of a high school band program begins with the success of the grade school experiences of band members, and I work hard to make the young students have a good beginning with much attention to fundamentals of playing. We are most fortunate in Hutchinson to have a fine teaching staff that is dedicated in their work with young people, and this greatly helps our success at the high school level."

—Don Corbett, *Hutchinson High School, Hutchinson, Kansas*

"One is inclined to hedge a little or exaggerate a great deal when he tries to assess his own liabilities or strengths. I think that the overriding factors at the center of every successful program with which I've been familiar would have to be enthusiasm and organization—and in that order.

"The successful band director must first be a teacher, then a musician. Hopefully these two are so closely related that he is a teacher/musician, but the kind of example he sets for students—in moral and ethical character—is uppermost in my mind as *the* trait that characterizes the ideal. I think also that there must be a candid—honest—relationship with students. A relationship that reflects, in its flexibility and individuality, a warm, affectionate, giving and receiving experience.

"Discipline of a highly autocratic nature has no place in a school situation. Discipline that is the result of the student's recognition of its need, an intrinsic self-discpline, is the only reasonable approach to making music within the educational context. I think that our rehearsal discipline here is quite loose, yet it is one of intense musical involvement because of the necessity of aural awareness. There is a control that is a two-way experience. We all want to make music—whatever discipline is necessary to reach that end is there.

"The relationship of our staff to the community is almost wholly dependent on the nature of performance obligations. Our four junior highs are neighborhood junior highs, and the teachers in those schools, and their feeders, relate to that portion or segment of the community as one arm of the school curriculum. The high school teachers have a good deal more community interaction. The staff relates to the high school with indifference or enthusiasm, depending on how they use the examples of the high school groups. The younger staff tend to identify readily, the older staff are somewhat more isolated (by their own choice) and prefer to do their "own thing." One of the keys to our success is the flexibility this kind of autonomy produces. Each man is free to set up his own goals, to reassess and evaluate their effectiveness in relationship to the other work in the city, and feel a sense of independence and self-satisfaction. As a result, we have a staff that has been together throughout the building program here. In terms of tenure, the band staff's years of service here are as follows: 16-14-14-12-2-2.

"I think my professional obligations and enthusiasm have kept me from my family more than was good for any of us. By the same token, the kids, my kids, have had ample evidence that their dad is "putting his money where his mouth is!" They know how important my work is and share with me the fun of making music and involvement with these ideals that reaffirm values. I do try to spend my "spare" time with the family and, as a result, find personal hobbies secondary to the kids' interests. I think also that a band man's wife must be a soul of incalculable patience and understanding; for, if she is married to both an ambitious and devoted band man, she must expect to do many things alone! It is the old problem of joining rather than fighting!

"I look back on nearly two decades of working with kids, staying in one place long enough to have established some ideals, traditions and heritages, contributing something to my community, my church, my family, and myself, and wonder if one man's life was meant to be so rich and satisfying. Truly, I feel that this is the Good Life, and I'm thrilled to have been able to be a part of it and look forward to more of the same with my alloted years."

—Jim Croft, *Oshkosh High School, Oshkosh, Wisconsin*

"We are extremely demanding of the students and right with our discipline, yet the kids know when we can have fun together. They know also that we love them. So, when we are hard on them, they bounce back for more.

"I operate rehearsals on a tension-release philosophy. You can grind hard if you know when to let up or have a good laugh. You can verbally knock a child down if you pick him up and show concern and affection.

"Basically, a good band program is dependent upon three things:

1. Student-teacher relationship — which I discussed above.
2. Sound approach to your teaching (techniques, consistency, etc.).
3. A good organizer who is willing to work as hard as possible.

"The success of my program often demands my time from the family. But as the commercial says, you must learn to grab for the gusto of life — it only goes by once.

"Consequently, my three sons, my wife and I really know how to make the most of our time together."

—Jerry Hoover, *Jefferson City Public Schools, Jefferson City, Missouri*

"It is difficult to determine what is meant altogether when we speak of success. However, my situation here has its own particular problems, especially in the last two years, wherein many of my better performers were zoned to other schools. We received very little in return from these other schools! This school is predominantly black, and therefore one must deal with those problems that are brought on by generations of discrimination and neglect. This situation breeds a particular type of individual, but if you help this individual to see the worth of any educational opportunity, the problem of distrust of authority is replaced by love, or at least, cooperation.

"We, therefore, work on the whole child. His music, his outlook, his ambition or lack of it. Hard work is the answer both on the part of the director and the students. Pride in accomplishment is the outcome. Better yourself is our hope and aim. Do whatever there is to be done in band, in English, in mathematics, do it right — make it perfect. We feel that the results are well worth the effort. We win a few, lose a few, but we try; for the ghetto is a state of mind, not a particular area of housing! As far as a band director's family is concerned, my wife and daughter (who is in the band) understand the extra hours and effort put forth by me — and live with it!

"Thank you for choosing our program to be part of your research effort."

— Emery L. Fears, Jr., *I. C. Norcom High School, Portsmouth, Virginia*

"I believe music offers a tremendous medium for communication and expression to its individual participants. But this will come forth only in a properly conditioned atmosphere. Students must be made to feel important and find identity within the group and with the teacher. Personal contact is kept up with the student by having an individual play-off for each student each week. A sense of humor is vital. I joke and kid students on their individual bases. By the teaching of correct fundamentals, the holding up of the challenge for each student to do and be his best, along with enthusiasm for work, the atmosphere is set for success. A willingness to work hard and a dedication to serve the students and the community results in confidence and a warm relationship in the community. High quality performance tends to build morale and helps in achieving a sense of pride both for the students and the community."

—Dean George, *Liberty Junior High School, Hutchinson, Kansas*

"Statement of characteristics of a successful school band director — best summed up by an intense love of students and love of music. Approach to student relations — be as fair as possible and honest at all times; admit your errors, be human, be patient.

"I use lots of psychology and work hard to see that each student is identified, not only by me, but by the entire concert band. I tease a lot and work on the quiet band members to try and bring out their identity.

"I am always very interested in all of the band members and strive to make sure that each one knows this. I continually display this interest in each one and make sure I am always available to help them with all problems — musical, personal, etc. I give a lot of reponsibility to the seniors each year, and leadership develops greatly as a result.

"Discipline — I am not a dictator-type band director. Our rehearsals are not absolute silence, for we all react after a number, and I use lots of humor and music education in the rehearsal, plus much variety of method and repertoire.

"Relationship to staff — I work hard to maintain an excellent working relationship and friendly status with the entire staff . . . especially coaches and custodians.

"Professional position effect on family — drastic for the first five to eight years; only now am I able to gradually give some time to my wife and two boys. I am finally spending fewer nights and weekends at the high school, and this allows for family gatherings.

"No short cuts, just lots of hard work and lots of time doing this work."

—Ralph McCartney, *Brooklyn Center High School, Minneapolis, Minnesota*

"I suppose that having been selected as a participating member of this ASBDA survey should be reason enough to be considered successful. I suppose that on the basis of the performance of the groups for which I am directly responsible in relation to other schools, we could qualify under the term "successful."

"If performance is a valid criterion, and it certainly can and must be one of them, I would admit to being successful. However, when I think in terms of areas which are being neglected, then I cannot consider myself or my department an unqualified success.

"We are severly hampered in time allocations, the rigid structure of the traditional schedule, and above all, the rigidity imposed on students who are, because of the economic status of our community, college bound. It has been impossible to even consider a separate theory course in our school. I think the recent North Central Evaluation Team pointed this up.

"However, on the basis that our performing groups are rated as successful, I offer the following statements:

1. I have found it easy to be a "friend" of the student as well as a taskmaster. This requires walking the tightrope, and on occasion this has caused some minor problems. But the problems have been so few in relationship to the good that has come out of this mode of operation, that I would not change my methods.

2. My relationship with staff, both within the department and with those in other areas, have been very pleasant. Within the music staff, I would have to say that they have been outstanding. The entire staff supports one another from the bottom to the top and vice versa. One and all are proud of the net product of our efforts.

   In respect to other staff members, I must say that they too have been pleasant. About the only thing that one could possibly say of a negative nature can be stemmed from some jealously of others in respect to the prestige of the music department in relation to others.

3. Relationships with the community have been excellent and the resulting support has made things possible for the music department. Within reason, we have been quick to respond to the musical demands of our community and school.

4. As to my relationship with my family, I am afraid that I must say that I do spend more time with my work than I should. But again, I must say that of my free time, all is spent with my family. I must say that my relationship with my family is above my fondest expectations.

5. Last but not least (and this is alluded to in section 4), I think the biggest single reason for success has been my willingness to work beyond what is demanded of me from a contractual standpoint. I am more than willing to do this as my contribution to the students and what they in turn can do for future generations as long as health and vigor are a blessing with me.

—Edwin J. Melichar, *Edina Schools, Edina, Minnesota*

P.S. I almost omitted a most essential ingredient: a great staff that is dedicated beyond the normal call of duty. Without them, all efforts would be in vain. With the exception of one part-time person who is attending the university in pursuit of the M.A. degree, all are people with an M.A. in Music Education."

appendix

appendix

FORMS AND PRINTED MATERIALS

AUDITION SHEET for CONCERT BAND
Brooklyn Center High School — Minneapolis, Minnesota
(Concert Band section leaders do auditions)

_____ Name of student

_____ seconds   1. Demonstrate how long you can hold a tone.

(circle one)

Good	Fair	Poor	2.	Tone quality in number 1.
Good	Fair	Poor	3.	Posture in number 1.
Good	Fair	Poor	4.	Embouchure in number 1.
Good	Fair	Poor	5.	Demonstrate proper breathing.
Good	Fair	Poor	6.	Play the scale and arpeggio exercise in B-flat concert. (Drums perform on bells or xylophone.) Scales: major, rel. minor, harmonic minor, melodic minor, chromatic. Arpeggios: major, minor, diminished, augmented, and 7th.
Good	Fair	Poor	7.	Play the E-flat concert scale and arpeggio exercise.
Good	Fair	Poor	8.	Play the following major scales: (concert) A♭, F, C.
Good	Fair	Poor	9.	Play the following major scales: (concert) D♭, G♭, G, D, A, E, B.
Good	Fair	Poor	10.	Drums only: Perform the 26 rudiments and demonstrate the following instruments: bass drum, cymbals, tympani (include tuning), xylophone, traps.
Good	Fair	Poor	11.	Demonstrate holding the instrument properly.
Good	Fair	Poor	12.	Explain transposition (concert pitch).
Good	Fair	Poor	13.	Tuning— What to do if sharp? Flat?
Good	Fair	Poor	14.	Explain time signatures.
Good	Fair	Poor	15.	Explain key signatures; name all flats and all sharps in order. (Ask key signatures of C, F, G, etc.)
Good	Fair	Poor	16.	Music terms: Allegro, Andante, D.S., D.C., cresc., rit., accel., f, pp, dim., etc.
Good	Fair	Poor	17.	Count some rhythms in concert band folder.
Good	Fair	Poor	18.	Demonstrate tonguing.
Good	Fair	Poor	19.	Solfege— Sing a simple exercise at sight.
Good	Fair	Poor	20.	Sight read from the concert band folder.
Good	Fair	Poor	21.	Play the "Star Spangled Banner."
Good	Fair	Poor	22.	Play the school song.
Good	Fair	Poor	23.	Play a tone from pp to ff and back to pp.
Good	Fair	Poor	24.	Demonstrate good attack (starting a tone).
Good	Fair	Poor	25.	Demonstrate good release (ending a tone).
Good	Fair	Poor	26.	Explain balance, phrase, expression.
Good	Fair	Poor	27.	Explain use of eyes, ears, heart in band playing.
Good	Fair	Poor	28.	Range— How high and low on the instrument?
Good	Fair	Poor	29.	Play with the metronome at 60, 120, and 132.
			30.	Pledge good attendance, practice, discipline in all band activities, including rehearsals, sectionals, lessons, lectures and appearances, and work toward a full music education in band.

**Read aloud to person being auditioned: MEMBERSHIP IN THE BAND REQUIRES SELF-DISCIPLINE, HARD WORK, SACRIFICE, LOYALTY, DEDICATION, RESPONSIBILITY, AND ABOVE ALL, INTEREST AND DESIRE. Individual musical growth can come through your desire and interest and personal effort by means of purposeful practice on your instrument. Brooklyn Center High School Bands have a fine tradition involving good performance combined with a full musical education. This demands interest and involvement on your part. Be proud of your band and make the band proud of you as a member. Good luck.

AUDITION SHEET
LaSalle-Peru Township High School Band
LaSalle-Peru, Illinois

Student's Name	Inst.	Scales	Prepared Material	Sight Reading	Final Grade

BAND GRADE CHART
Sapulpa, Oklahoma

NAME	ASSIGNMENT	MEMORY	ATTACKS	SCALES / RUDIMENTS	WARM-UP DRILLS	TONE	RHYTHM	STYLE	FIELD GRADE	
1.										
2.										
3.										
4.										
5.										
6.										
7.										
8.										
9.										
10.										

BAND AUDITION FORM
Temple High School — Temple, Texas

Comments

Prepared Selection _____

Scales _____

Sight Reading _____

_____ Marching Band Workshop   _____ Varsity Band

_____ Stage Band   _____ Concert Band

_____ Sectional   _____ Wind Ensemble

Parent's Name _____

Address _____   Telephone _____

Grade Next Year _____ Instrument _____

Teacher _____

CONTEST MUSIC CHECK INFORMATION
Temple, Texas

Circle below the period or periods when you can have your contest music checked. If you do not have a Study Hall, music will have to be checked after school. (Highlighters may use 6th period; all percussion will be checked together at night.)

PERIODS: 3   4   6   7· After School   Evening (Percussion only)

Section: _____   Name: _____
    (2nd cornet, 3rd clarinet, etc.)

CHALLENGE-JUDGE REMINDER
Temple High School — Temple, Texas

Name _____ Date _____

This is a reminder that you are scheduled to judge Challenges on _____
morning this week. Please report to Practice Room No. 5 at 7:30 a.m.

_____
Band Secretary

JUDGE'S RECORD FOR CHALLENGES
Temple High School — Temple, Texas

5 — Excellent
4 — Good
3 — Average

2 — Poor
1 — Weak
0 — Unacceptable

PLAYER	0 — 5 Rhythm and Tempo	0 — 5 Intonation, Accuracy, Tone, etc.	0 — 5 Phrasing, Expression, Tonguing, Slurring, etc.	0 — 15 TOTAL POINTS

CHALLENGE SHEET
LaSalle — Peru, Illinois

Anyone may challenge any member of his section by posting the Challenge on this sheet and arranging a time with the director for the Challenge to be played. Challenger must allow one full week from the time Challenge is posted before Challenge is played.

It is the responsibility of the two people involved in a Challenge to report to the director on the day of the Challenge. If one does not show up, the other is declared the winner.

Music for Challenges will be taken from the following: 127 Book, Lazarus Book, any music in the folder, and sight reading.

PERSON CHALLENGED	CHALLENGER	DATE AND TIME OF CHALLENGE

EIGHTH GRADE AUDITION
Spencer, Iowa

Name: _____
(Last)   (First)

Instrument: _____

Your Father's Name: _____

Your Address: _____ Telephone: _____

* * * * * * * * * * *

(Note: Each category will be rated A, B, C, D, or F. "A" will represent the best possible rating, etc.)

PART 1: Scales

 A. Chromatic scale _____ D. C major scale _____

 B. F major scale _____   E. G major scale _____

 C. B♭ major scale _____

PART 2: Selections from First Division Band Method, Part IV

 A. Technical accuracy _____

 B. Dynamics _____

PART 3: Band Selection

 A. Technical accuracy _____

 B. Dynamics _____

PART 4: Tone _____

Recommended for Senior Band _____ Not recommended for Senior Band _____

EIGHTH GRADE AUDITION FORM
Spencer, Iowa

Name: _____
          (Last)   (First)

Instrument: _____

Your Father's Name: _____

Your Address: _____ Your Telephone No.: _____

EXAMINATION

1. Chromatic Scale: _____ (possible 5 points)   4. E♭ Major Scale: _____ (possible 3 points)

2. D Major Scale: _____ (possible 3 points)   5. Band Selection: _____ (possible 10 points)

3. F Major Scale: _____ (possible 3 points)   6. Tone: _____ (possible 10 points)

General Comments: _____

Recommended: _____ Not Recommended: _____

BRASS INSTRUMENTAL LESSON ASSIGNMENT
Lenoir High School Band
Lenoir, North Carolina

Name _____ Grade _____ Instrument _____

Method Book _____

Pages	Exercise	Lesson Dates	Grades

Concert Repertoire
1. _____
2. _____
3. _____

PERCUSSION LESSON ASSIGNMENT
Lenoir High School Band — Lenoir, North Carolina

Name _____ Instrument _____ Grade _____ Period _____

DATE	WARM-UP ROUTINE	RUDIMENTS	METHOD BOOK	CONCERT REPERTOIRE

MARCHING AUDITION FORM
Jefferson City Senior High Marching Band
Jefferson City, Missouri

+ = Good   0 = Average   — = Poor

Name	Tardies	Absences	Attitude	Swagger	Knee Lift	In-Step	Rare Back	Turns

GRADING SYSTEM FOR PARTS CHECK
Temple High School — Temple, Texas

CONCERT MUSIC
For grading concert music

HALFTIME MUSIC
For grading march (halftime) music

For every stop, one letter grade lower.

Music may be played over, but *that* grade will be considered final — good or bad.

	Concert	Halftime		
50				
49				
48		4		
47	A	4		
46	A⁻	3.9		
45	B⁺	3.7	3.8	
44	B	3.4	3.5	3.6
43	B⁻	3.1	3.2	3.3
42	C⁺	2.9		
41	C	2.7	2.8	
40	C⁻	2.4	2.5	2.6
39	C⁻	2.1	2.2	2.3
38	D⁺	1.9		
37	D	1.7	1.8	
36	D	1.4	1.5	1.6
35	D⁻	1.1	1.2	1.3
34	F	0		

A 4 points (0-1 mistake per song)
B 3 points (2-3 mistakes per song)
B⁻ 2.5 points (4 mistakes)
C 2 points (5-6 mistakes per song)
C⁻ 1.5 points (7-8 mistakes per song)
D 1 point (Over 8 mistakes per song)
F 0 points (Totally unacceptable)

213

PERCUSSION LESSON CHART: Harr Bk. I

Lenoir High School — Lenoir, North Carolina

Name _____ Grade _____ Period _____

SECTIONS	PAGES	COMMENTS	GRADES
Single Sticking	13 14 15 16 17 18 19 20 21 22 23 24 25 26 27 28 29 30		
Triplets	42		
Dotted Notes	45		
Syncopation	57 58		
5-Stroke Roll	32 33		
7- and 9-	34		
13- and 17-	35 36 37		
2/2 Meter	38 39 40 41		
Flam Accents	45		
4-Stk. Ruffs	46 47		
6/8 Meter	48 49 51 52 53		
Ruff	54		
3/4 Meter	55		

PERCUSSION LESSON CHART: Harr Bk. II
Lenoir High School – Lenoir, North Carolina

Name _____ Grade _____ Period _____

SECTIONS	PAGES	COMMENTS	GRADES
5-Stroke Roll	74		
7-Stroke Roll	75		
Flam	76		
Accents–Ruffs	77		
9-Stroke Roll	86-87		
13- and 17-	91		
Flam Tap	92		
Paradiddle	93-94		
Flam Paradiddle	78		
Flamacue	79-80		
Ruff–Drag	81		
Double Drag	82		
Double Paradiddle	83		
Ratamacue	84		
Triple Ratamacue	85		
Drag Paradiddle 1.	95		
Drag Paradiddle 2.	96		
Flam Paradiddle-Diddle Lesson 25	97		
Double Ratamacue	98		
Compound Strokes	99		
3/4 Meter	102 103 104 105		
6/8 Meter	108 109 110 106		
2/2 Meter	111 112 113 114		
Solos	90 115 116 117 118 119 120 121 122 123 124 125 126		

BAND AUDITION AND SEMESTER EXAM
Springfield, Oregon

Student _____ Instrument _____

Rate performance and technical skills: 10 points for superior to 1 point for poor.

ETUDE No. _____ points _____

ETUDE No. _____ points _____

ETUDE No. _____ points _____

Other _____ points _____

General rating of performance on above assigned and selected materials:

____ SUPERIOR ____EXCELLENT__ ABOVE AVERAGE _ AVERAGE ___ POOR

TONE (Is it characteristic? Is it even throughout range?
     Is it pleasing?)   points _____

RHYTHM   points _____

ARTICULATION (Accurate? Well-played?)   points _____

DYNAMICS (Observed? Contrast?)   points _____

PHRASING (Unplanned? Musical?)   points _____

ACCURACY OF PERFORMANCE   points _____

RANGE FACILITY AND CONTROL   points _____

TOTAL POINTS   _____

Comments: _____

Rating of Musicianship:

____ SUPERIOR ____EXCELLENT__ ABOVE AVERAGE _ AVERAGE ___ POOR

Preparation for Exam-Audition:

____ WELL PREPARED__PREPARED ___ SHOWS WORK __ MORE WORK NEEDED __ UNPREPARED

Work Needed in Following Areas: _____

Ready for Symphonic Band? _____ Which Band? _____

SIGNED _____

WATKINS-FARNUM PERFORMANCE SCALE
Sample School Averages
Hutchinson, Kansas

The first number indicates the average; the second number indicates the number of students that took the test.

School	1st test 5th grade 1 year	2nd test 5th grade 1½ years	1st test 6th grade 2 years	2nd test 6th grade 2½ years
ALLEN	31-14	34-14	51-16	51-18
AVENUE A	15-4	22-4	27-7	31-7
FARIS	38-23	44-26	50-21	54-22
GRABER	33-38	42-34	48-25	49-22
GRANDVIEW	40-7	45-7	30-2	47-1
LAKEVIEW	33-13	37-12	42-10	42-9
LINCOLN	28-8	26-8	26-8	31-8
McCANDLESS	31-18	35-12	42-16	46-16
MORGAN	40-43	41-37	49-25	52-25
ROOSEVELT	33-20	33-17	43-20	43-19
WILEY	38-17	39-16	62-17	58-17
WINANS	37-9	39-9	35-11	39-11
ALL SCHOOLS (69-70)	33-212	37-206	42-178	45-175
ALL SCHOOLS (68-69)	26-176	34-177	37-162	45-159
ALL SCHOOLS (67-68)	24-171	35-176	36-140	45-126
ALL SCHOOLS (66-67)	21-138	34-134	30-98	40-93

WATKINS-FARNUM PERFORMANCE SCALE
FORM B
Score Sheet For B♭ Cornet, Clarinets, Baritone 𝄞

Name _____Date _____

Instrument _____Years Studied ___

School _____Grade ____Age ___

PROGRESS CHART

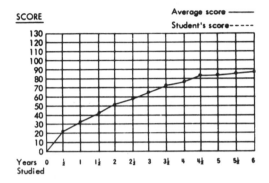

SCORE

Average score ———

Student's score-----

Years Studied: 0 ½ 1 1½ 2 2½ 3 3½ 4 4½ 5 5½ 6

SCORING SUMMARY

(Student's score is "possible score" less errors)

Ex.	Possible score		13	Errors		Score
1.						
2.	"	"	10	"		"
3.	"	"	10	"		"
4.	"	"	10	"		"
5.	"	"	10	"		"
6.	"	"	10	"		"
7.	"	"	10	"		"
8.	"	"	10	"		"
9.	"	"	10	"		"
10.	"	"	10	"		"
11.	"	"	10	"		"
12.	"	"	14	"		"
13.	"	"	10	"		"
14.	"	"	10	"		"

GRADE ☐   TOTAL SCORE ☐

Remarks _____

_____

GRADING CHART

GRADES FOR CORNET CLARINET BARITONE

Years	½	1	1½	2	2½	3	3½	4	4½	5	5½	6
A	35	50	62	70	77	83	88	90	92	94	96	98
B	25	40	48	55	61	66	70	74	78	82	84	86
C	15	30	35	40	45	50	54	58	62	65	67	69
D	5	15	25	30	35	40	44	47	50	52	54	56

Sample—At the end of one year if the score of a clarinet player is 50 or higher the grade will be A. At the end of one year a score of between 30 and 39 will earn a horn player a B.

Errors may be indicated in two ways:
1. Draw a cross through the incorrect measure.
2. Indicate the type of error by using the symbols on pages 6, 7 and 8.

Pitch	P	Change of tempo	T
Time	R	Expression	E
Slur	S	Holds or pauses	R
Rest	R	Repeats	𝄇

Test begins here: Check only one error per measure.

Note: In order to keep the number of score sheets to a minimum two groups of instruments are combined on this sheet. The example below is for Clarinet. Other instruments will obviously play the lower octave on certain passages as written in the test book.

WATKINS-FARNUM PERFORMANCE SCALE EXERCISES

HALL OF FAME

Award of Merit

THIS CERTIFICATE
IS PRESENTED TO

IN RECOGNITION OF A DIVISION _____ RATING IN THE
JUNIOR HIGH SCHOOL MUSIC COMPETITION FESTIVAL.

Dated _____ , 19 ____

Signed _____

Music Award
Tucson Public Schools

This is to certify that

....

from...*School*

has completed the course in..

and is eligible for..

....*Teacher*

....*Principal*

NAME _____

BAND MANUAL

for

CONCERT BAND MEMBERS AND PARENTS

– A Complete Digest of Band Policies and Regulations –

Brooklyn Center High School
Minneapolis, Minnesota

Richard E. Papke, ASBDA
Director of Bands

TABLE OF CONTENTS

"Music exerts a power than no one can comprehend. This power rises to such a height that the understanding fails to reach it."

—Goethe

PREFACE

This band manual has been written for the Brooklyn Center High School Concert Band members and their parents with the hope of giving information regarding the various phases and activities of the instrumental music program at Brooklyn Center High School. The manual also contains the policies and regulations of the band.

All band members and parents are urged to read the entire manual carefully at the beginning of each school year to avoid conflicts with the policies and rules stated herein.

I. THE BAND BEATITUDES

Blessed are they who play with spirit,
    for theirs will be a band with style.

Blessed are they that listen,
    for they shall have good intonation.

Blessed are they who follow the conductor,
    for they shall obtain precision.

Blessed are they of pure tone,
    for they shall be a credit to their band.

Blessed are the sincere players,
    for they shall be called artists.

Blessed are they which practice righteously,
    for they shall achieve perfection.

Blessed are they which do hunger and thirst for good music,
    for they shall be satisfied.

Blessed are ye who play with good posture and deep breath,
    for your instruments shall be filled.

Blessed are the fine bands,
    for they inherit a glorious tradition!

"There must be individual achievement if there is to be achievement in our music ensembles. The progress of each student will reflect in the performances of the bands in which he plays, and they in turn will act as his benefactors in providing him with an outlet for his expressive talent and a basis for the furtherance of his appreciation." —*Mark Hindsley*

II. ACHIEVING MUSICIANSHIP

A. The Importance of Attitude.

The greatest single factor that will determine the success of any individual is *attitude*. Students should use these two words— "I WILL." It takes intense dedication to reach goals. Students should learn to discipline themselves to daily practice on long tones, interval study and scales, in concentrated and routine practice. Again, the "right attitude" must be there, with *sincerity, concentration,* and *dedication* as the basic foundation.

"Everything depends on the attitude of the artist toward his subject. It is the one great essential."(R. Henri) *Music only becomes alive when it is made to live*—its colors are the colors that are given it; and thus it lives or dies. The serious young musician will warm up carefully in the middle register of his instrument, playing scales and long tones, and concentrating on intonation and correct tone production. Such an attitude makes an artistic performance inevitable and is the factor which makes the difference between a musical organizaiton and a group of people holding musical instruments.

Approach each new band piece the same way: What can I make out of this? What is this musical phrase trying to say? Am I giving every last effort to make my part contribute to the whole sound of the band? This is the attitude of the true musician.

The director is trying to lead you in this experience at every rehearsal. Some of you will not get the message, but the ones who do will make the whole worthwhile for all. Music *is* an academic discipline, but it is not something that only the few especially gifted can appreciate. Music is not something that is mysterious and difficult to understand, though it is a complicated science. It is demanding, and only by great effort and study can you really be rewarded as a performer. By acknowledging these disciplines, we can challenge the boundaries of our limited perception and really appreciate the beauty of life.

Analyze your own attitude and try to develop more receptivity. You who are in the band are a favored few. The band can do much for you. *Make the most of it in every rehearsal and every performance. Make each rehearsal like a concert.*

B. The Importance of Discipline.

Because of the nature of the organization, band discipline must, of necessity, be strict. Band students and parents must be willing to accept the ideals, principles and rules of the organization.

Because the band members are constantly on display, each must always be aware of the importance of good behavior. The student should remember that he represents his organization, school, and community whenever he performs or appears publicly. Any misconduct casts a direct reflection on our school and community and may well undo the good work of hundreds of loyal students.

A good band is built on discipline: but let us agree on the definition of discipline. Discipline is order. It is also many other things, but primarily, discipline is order. There is order in all things physical or material, as well as in all things spiritual or intellectual. With orderliness comes attainment of things worthwhile.

> "Order is Heaven's First Law; it applies especially to Band practice."
> "A Place for Everything and Everything in its Place."
> "A Quiet Person is Welcome Anywhere."
> "Music is a Picture Painted on a Background of Silence."

To implant these ideals of order and discipline in the minds of band members is to lay the foundation both for good musicianship and good citizenship. (See Part V: "The Band's Ten Commandments.")

III. A STATEMENT OF BAND POLICY

In order to help band members and parents understand their areas of responsiblity, a statement of band policy is herein set forth. Becoming familiar with this policy will help each band member make the most of his fine opportunity to become a better person through his association with music.

We firmly believe that the child should improve through daily progress. In the instrumental music program we feel that when the child has lost the will to improve himself in order to make a better contribution to his fellow man, he is perhaps wasting the time of the school, his fellow students, and the community by continuing in this program. We are firmly convinced that the happiest child is the one that is improving himself through regular habits of practice and daily progress. He must not only know right from wrong, but must be able to stand for his principles. He must develop a high sense of purpose toward which he is willing to work.

We intend to conduct the instrumental music program in a manner that will encourage all students to achieve these goals.

A. The Band Member's Responsibility to the Instrumental Music Program.

1. Be regular in attendance and to account for all absences.
2. Make a real effort to learn and improve daily.
3. Become responsible for and expect to assume the consequences of his actions.
4. Be personally clean, neat, and to dress appropriately.
5. Have the proper respect for those in authority.
6. Follow all classroom rules, school regulations, and all travel instructions issued for trips.
7. Be honest and fair with others concerning equipment, music, and school life in general.
8. Cooperate with fellow band members and to share with them the responsibilities and privileges that are a part of the band program.
9. Contribute positively to his music education and that of others by the best use of his talents.
10. Read and play music with insight and expression.

11. Improve his knowledge and understanding of music theory, harmony, and history, as well as develop good listening habits.

B. The Responsibilities of the Instrumental Music Department.

1. Provide the band members with the proper kind of rehearsal room, ventilation, lighting, seating, music stands, instrument storage space and such other equipment as is considered necessary to aid in developing the student's music ability and to help him form good citizenship habits.
2. Plan each day's assignments and encourage daily progress of the entire band.
3. Provide the band with a full musical education through rehearsal, performance, teaching, testing, and listening.
4. Suspend any uncooperative member from the band program until a conference is held with the member, parents, and administration, in order to work out a plan for the member. It is the responsibility of the department to see that all members conform to the school and department policies.
5. Dismiss members that are not adding to the band program due to poor attitude and/or lack of improvement. It has been found that this sort of person adds little to any program of music education.
6. Supervise the students in class or on school-sponsored band trips. Each student will receive written information about the plans for a trip, the type of dress, and the complete schedule.
7. Grade the progress of each member on his instrument and his music education. A "poor progress letter" is to be sent to inform parents of problems.

IV. THE BROOKLYN CENTER BAND CODE (A System of Guiding Principles)

A. Integrity.
1. "Friends, if we be honest with ourselves, we shall be honest with each other." — George MacDonald
2. To what extent can others rely on my integrity?

B. Respect.
1. "Men are respectable only as they respect." — Ralph Waldo Emerson
2. How often do I respect the other person's opinion, even though it may differ from mine?
3. How does my respect effect the moral beliefs of my associates?

C. Responsibility.
1. "Responsibility is like a string of which we can see only the middle. Both ends are out of sight." — William McFee
2. To what ends do I strive to carry out a promise?
3. What responsibilities have I to my school, church, and country?

D. Friendliness.
1. "The only way to have a friend is to be one." — Ralph Waldo Emerson
2. What is my attitude toward the newcomer?
3. By what standards do I judge my friends?

State High School League Music Rules

The music by-laws for Brooklyn Center High School will be the same as those stated in the official handbook for the Minnesota State High School League, which, briefly stated, are as follows:

Article I: Eligibility — Section 1.

Use of Alcohol, Tobacco, and Drugs.

1. Alcohol. A student shall not use or have possession of a beverage containing alcohol during the school year or during the season of rehearsals, regardless of the quantity. Students violating this rule shall be suspended from participation in all forthcoming school and public musical performances for eighteen (18) school weeks, from the time of the infraction, for the

first violation and shall also be declared ineligible for any musical awards for the school year. A second violation will be cause for dismissal from all musical organizations. The student will be re-programmed accordingly.

2. Tobacco. A student shall not use tobacco during the school year or during the season of music rehearsals or participation in any music activity sponsored by the League. Students who violate this rule shall be suspended from participation in all forthcoming school and public musical performances for three (3) weeks for the first violation and shall also be declared ineligible for any musical awards for the school year. A second violation will be cause for dismissal from all musical organizations. The student will be re-programmed accordingly.

3. Drugs. A student shall not consume, have in possession, buy, sell, or give away any drug defined by law as a drug to be dispensed by a doctor's prescription (unless specifically prescribed by his own doctor) during the school year or during the season of music rehearsals. Students violating this rule shall be suspended from participation in all forthcoming school and public musical performances for one (1) calendar year from the date of the violation and shall also be declared ineligible for any musical awards for the school year. A second violation will be cause for dismissal from all musical organizations. The student will be re-programmed accordingly.

In addition:

a. Reporting violations. The word of any reliable adult who saw the violation will be used when reported to the music director(s) or administration.

b. If a violation of the rules is reported, a conference will be held with the following in attendance: the student allegedly violating the rule, the student's parents, the director(s) of the musical organization(s) of which the student is a member, and the adult who reported the violation. These people shall discuss the infraction and all penalties to be administered.

V. THE BAND'S TEN COMMANDMENTS

1. Thou shalt warm up thine instrument silently and tune softly before each rehearsal.
2. Thou shalt constantly assume the position and attitude of attention during each rehearsal and performance, and at any other time the conductor's podium is occupied; thou shalt not use the back of thy chair when playing thine instrument.
3. Thou shalt use thine eyes to see the music and the conductor, thine ears to hear the music and the teaching, and thy mouth *only* to play thine instrument; thou shalt make all necessary movements unobtrusive.
4. Thou shalt not play thine instrument any place in the school building or on the school grounds outside the music rooms, unless under specific direction.
5. Thou shalt fill the air with music at least thirty minutes daily by practicing on thine instrument; blessed is he who maketh the heavens resound much longer.
6. Thou shalt not be late to nor absent from any rehearsal or performance of thine organization.
7. Thou shalt care for thine instrument, music, uniform, and all other properties which are entrusted to thy use; they shall be kept in good condition and stored properly; nothing shall be lost, misplaced or missing when needed.
8. Thou shalt be loyal, honest, courteous and sportsmanlike in all thy dealings with thine organization and its members.
9. Thou shalt conduct thyself to show pride in and reflect credit to thy school and thine organization.
10. Thou shalt love thine instrument and thy music and thine organization as thyself.

From SCHOOL BAND AND ORCHESTRA ADMINISTRATION by Mark Hindsley. Copyright 1940 by Boosey and Hawkes, Inc. Renewed 1967. Reprinted by permission.

VI. BANDS AND BAND MUSIC IN AMERICA

It must have occurred to all observers of musical progress that high school and college bands of America are gradually assuming a position of commanding importance as musical and educational organizations. Educational institutions— secondary and collegiate— increasingly recognize the place of distinction, respect and dignity that the band is earning for itself.

The band has become a highly functional musical institution in these United States. Its versatility, popularity and utilitarian appeal are noteworthy and recognized. These attributes have been evidenced by the band's democratization of music for American audiences of extremely mixed tastes. It gives delight to the musically unsophisticated and has a tremendous place in popular affection.

It is a splendid form of community organization because it reaches great numbers of people in an immediate way. It is closely linked with our American Way of Life, since it is democratic in tradition and function... a God-given art intended for all mankind.

A Brief History of the Brooklyn Center High School Band

The band was started in the summer of 1961 with twenty-one members, with Mr. Richard E. Papke as the director. Summer instruction was held on the Earle Brown Elementary School gymnasium stage since the high school was still under construction. The band played for home football games, played at other fields, and finally obtained use of the band room in January as the school neared completion. The first concert was performed with the choir in December, 1961 on the stage of the Earle Brown Elementary School. The band also performed in the District Music Contest (receiving a B-plus), gave their First Annual "Pop" Concert in Hawaii, and performed at the school's dedication and first graduation.

In the summer of 1962, the band marched in its first parade, the Aquatennial, and was awarded third place. The second year band grew in number to thirty-five and displayed new uniforms at their First Winter Band Concert in January, 1963. The band was chosen as "Pep Band of the Week" on WCCO's "Prep Parade" and was then voted "Basketball Band of the Year" honors at the end of the season. Another District Contest (B-plus) and Second "Pop" Concert in Spain concluded the second year for the band.

The third year membership grew to sixty and the band presented its Second Winter Band Concert in January, 1964. This year's District Contest awarded the band its first "A" rating for a stirring performance of "Titus Overture" by Mozart and "First Suite in E-Flat" by Holst. The band went on to the State Contest and received "A" ratings from all three adjudicators. This time the band journeyed (musically) to France for its Third "Pop" Concert. The summer of 1964 brought the band a second place in the Aquatennial Parade and a fourth place in the international Lions Club Parade in Port Arthur-Fort William, Canada.

The fourth year proved to be musically very taxing. The band, now seventy-five members strong, performed "Finale from Symphony No. 4" by Tschaikowsky at the Third Winter Band Concert, "Italian in Algiers Overture" by Rossini at the District Contest (receiving three A-starred ratings), and "Finale from the New World Symphony" by Dvorak at their Fourth "Pop" Concert in Japan. The District Contest of 1965 also proved to be quite a success in solos and ensembles: sixteen A-starred ratings out of eighteen entries. The band also won a fifth place in the Lions Parade in Moorhead, Minnesota.

The fifth year displayed another "A" rating at the District Contest for Mozart's "Marriage of Figaro Overture" and a second place trophy and two-hundred dollars in the Lions Parade in Winona, Minnesota.

The sixth year brought another "A" in the District Contest for the band for a performance of the "Roman Carnival Overture" by Berlioz. The First Brooklyn Center Invitational Band Clinic was held in December with Columbia Heights and Burnsville bands performing. The band traveled to Winnipeg, Canada and won a fourth place in the Lions Parade.

February clinicians obtained each year were: Mr. George Regis, 1962; Mr. Herb Streitz, 1963; Dr. Frank Bencriscutto, 1964; Mr. Butler Eitel, 1965; Mr. Reuben Haugen, 1966, and Mr. Miles Johnson, 1967.

VII. THE SEVEN CARDINAL PRINCIPLES OF EDUCATION

The National Association of Educators outlined for themselves and all teachers a set of criteria for determining the fitness of subjects to be taught in schools. They arrived at a set of factors which they entitled, "The Seven Cardinal Principles of Education." These seven are:

1. Health.
2. Mastery of Fundamental Processes (which means, the development of bodily coordination—sight, hearing, muscular control, etc.).
3. Vocation.
4. Avocation.
5. Citizenship.
6. Family life.
7. Social adjustment.

In other words, in order to be worthy of being placed in a public school curriculum, a subject would have to be identified with one or more of these principles. For example, athletics, the purpose of which is to develop the body, is identified with principle number two, Mastery of Fundamental Processes.

Of all school subjects evaluated, however, music was the *only* one which could be identified with all seven of these cardinal principles:

1. In music, good posture is taught constantly; it is necessary for proper playing, and essential for good health.
2. The study of a musical instrument develops a mastery of fundamental processes (bodily coordination) to a great degree.
3. Music is universally recognized as a noble vocation.
4. As an avocation or hobby, music is almost number one in popularity and satisfaction.
5. Citizenship, reduced to its fundamentals, is merely the exercise of a cooperative attitude. Band training encourages such an attitude by virtue of its demands for playing together.
6. The value of music within the family speaks for itself. Music has that cohesive element which tends to clamp and cement together the family relationship.
7. The importance of adequate social adjustment is underlined by a recent fact revealed by the United States Department of Labor and Commerce: More workers lose their jobs through lack of ability to get along with fellow workers than for any other reason. They are socially maladjusted. Individuals who develop a talent for playing music quickly overcome shyness and become well-balanced persons, able to adjust themselves quickly to changing situations.

Music is the only subject that can be identified with all seven of the cardinal principles of education:

1. MUSIC makes for good health.
2. MUSIC develops bodily coordination.
3. MUSIC is an excellent vocation.
4. MUSIC as a hobby brings great pleasure.
5. MUSIC builds good citizens.
6. MUSIC cements the family relationship.
7. MUSIC develops socially mature persons.

VIII. BROOKLYN CENTER BAND OBJECTIVES

The Brooklyn Center Bands form an integral part of life at Brooklyn Center High School and are recognized as an all-school activity. It is one of the largest and most colorful voluntary student organizations, and its members form an active, cosmopolitan group.

The Brooklyn Center High School Concert Band has four primary objectives:

1. Cultural: To contunue the development of music appreciation and understanding through the study and performance of the best in music.
2. Educational: To develop interested and discriminating listeners and provide a well-rounded musical background.

3. Service: To lend color and atmosphere to certain athletic and community affairs, while promoting and enhancing the dignity and reputation of Brooklyn Center at all concert appearances.

4. Recreational: To provide all students at Brooklyn Center with an opportunity for worthy use of leisure time, an emotional outlet, and good social experiences.

The director is concerned that each band member receive a full musical education, which includes the teaching and learning of musical knowledge, in addition to attaining a superior performance of a wide variety of music. The director is also interested in developing the personality and citizenship of each member of the band.

IX. BAND ORGANIZATION

A. Board of Education.

B. Administration: Superintendent; Principal; Assistant Principal; Elementary Principal.

C. Instrumental Music Department: Director of Bands and Music Department Chairman.

D. Band Officers (Elected) and Duties.

1. President.
   a. Student representative of the band.
   b. Conducts all Band Council meetings.
   c. Sees that council meetings are held periodically.
   d. Appoints committees for social events, ticket sales, publicity, etc.
   e. Promotes band activities — social, educational, etc.
   f. Coordinates all student officers of the band.
   g. Reports to the director any problems or suggestions that may improve the band program.

2. Vice-President.
   a. Assumes all duties of the band president when necessary.
   b. Assists band president wherever possible.

3. Secretary.
   a. Handles all band correspondence and letters for director.
   b. Types band reports and letters.
   c. Keeps band scrapbook: records band activities and history.
   d. Takes daily attendance.

4. Senior Representative — represents seniors of the band at all Council meetings.

5. Junior Representative — represents juniors of the band at all Council meetings.

6. Sophomore Representative — represents sophomores of the band at all Council meetings.

E. Band Staff (Appointed) and Duties.

1. Librarian.
   a. Responsible for library and all music — filing and cataloging.

2. Uniform Manager.
   a. Responsible for uniform cabinets and all uniforms and accessories.
   b. Inspects uniforms and cabinets monthly for cleanliness and neatness.

3. Equipment Manager.
   a. Responsible for the arranging of the chairs and stands for each rehearsal and for each public appearance. Also checks to be sure that all necessary equipment is available.

4. Business Manager.
   a. Handles all financial matters.
   b. Assist in trip arrangements.

5. Publicity Manager.
   a. Directs and devises all publicity for the many activities of the Brooklyn Center Band.
   b. Contacts radio, TV, newspapers; school P.A. announcements, posters, etc.
   c. Responsible for printing of programs and tickets for concerts.

6. Student Conductor.
  a. Takes over rehearsal if necessary.
  b. Assists in rehearsal set-up.
  c. Conducts at events as assigned by band director.
  d. Displays student leadership.

7. Drum Major.
  a. Takes complete charge of the band in all marching formations.
  b. Assists the director in marching band drills.
  c. Inspects the rank lieutenants.

8. Rank Lieutenants.
  a. Inspect ranks for proper uniform, music preparedness, cleanliness of instruments, and proper marching technics.

9. Head Color Guard.
  a. Inspects and drills the Color Guard for all marching appearances.

10. Twirler.
  a. Prepares routines for all marching appearances.

11. Instrument Manager.
  a. Has charge of all school-owned instruments. Students desiring the use of such property contact the Instrument Manager and are issued a contract.

12. Student Announcer.
  a. Responsible for writing scripts for and delivering all public announcements.

F. Band Council and Duties.
  1. Council is comprised of the band officers and class representatives.
  2. Meets monthly to discuss band projects and/or problems.
  3. Responsible for maintaining band esprit de corps.

G. Section Leaders and Duties.
  1. Responsible for weekly sectionals to drill music and fundamentals.
  2. Prepare section for music to be performed.
  3. Make monthly inspections of their section's music folders and instruments.

X. BAND CALENDAR

The band calendar is set in the fall each year. A copy of the entire year's appearances is posted in the director's office. A copy of each month's appearances is posted on the band bulletin board monthly.

A list of all outside rehearsals and appearances is mimeographed and placed in each music folder, and copies are available for parents upon request. Attendance is required at all rehearsals and appearances unless a "Request for Excuse" card is filled out and then *approved* by the director. *Correlate band with school and outside work!* Most band appearances are listed on the calendar, but occasionally special performances may be necessary during the school year. Any band member can, by careful planning, arrange his schedule and necessary outside work so as not to be affected in the least by band participation. Few exceptions are made in the policy of requiring members to make all appearances. By skillfully budgeting one's time, there will be time for a genuine musical experience and real pleasure, providing the bandsman considers his band work as a major part of his school activities.

Rehearsals:
  1. Concert Band: Daily— Monday through Friday, during 4th hour of school day.
  2. Junior Band: Daily— Monday through Friday, 7:30 A.M. to 8:10 A.M.
  3. Marching Band: During 4th hour as needed and all Monday evenings in the month of May from 7-8 P.M.
  4. Stage Band: One period a week (to be arranged).
  5. Grade 6 Band: Twice weekly, after school, on Tuesday and Thursday.

6. Grade 5 Band: Twice weekly, after school, on Monday and Wednesday.

When the musical or marching performance of the band is in jeopardy, extra (full or sectional) rehearsals will be called.

List of Appearances:
1. Four home football games; Homecoming half-time show (Sept.-Oct.).
2. High School Band Day at University (Sept.).
3. Homecoming Queen Coronation (Oct.).
4. High School Assembly Concert (Oct.).
5. American Education Week Concert (Nov.).
6. Concert at Band Boosters-Lions Dinner (Nov.).
7. Basketball games (Nov.-Dec.-Jan.-Feb.). — Pep Band/Stage Band.
8. Two Hockey games (Dec.-Jan.).
9. Invitational Clinic (Dec.).
10. Winter Band Concert (Jan.).
11. Guest Clinician Clinic (Feb.).
12. Local Solos/Ensembles Recital/Contest (Feb. or Mar.).
13. Exchange rehearsals with neighbor bands (Feb.-Mar.).
14. District Music Contest (Mar.).
15. Evening "Pop" Concert rehearsals (Apr.).
16. "Pop" Concert (Apr.).
17. Marching Band rehearsals — all Monday evenings, 7-8 P.M. (May).
18. Graduation (June).

In addition, solos and ensembles from the Brooklyn Center High School Concert Band perform for community groups. Students are encouraged to organize small ensembles and to be of service wherever possible.

Students are also encouraged to organize their own dance bands (combos, etc.). Each such group should appoint one person as director to be responsible for the actions of the group. The following rules will serve as a guide for the student leaders of such combos:

1. Any organization wanting a school dance band (combo type) for after-dances, class parties, etc., should submit a requisition to the school band director, stating the name of the group desired. The requisition should be signed by a faculty member and give details of date, time, place, and cost.

2. The student leader of the combo will contact the faculty member to arrange details of the dance.

3. Following satisfactory performance at the dance, the faculty member should fill out a Request for Payment form making the check payable to the student leader of the combo.

4. The maximum paid combos shall be $10.00 per member.

5. The student combos should be made up entirely of Brooklyn Center High School Band students.

Organizations desiring professional bands should see the band director.

XI. BAND EQUIPMENT

A. Instruments: The school owns many instruments, including piccolos, oboes, bassons, alto and bass clarinets, contrabass clarinet, tenor and baritone saxophones, French horns, English horn, baritones, basses, percussion, etc. These instruments are issued by the band director or Instrument Manager. At the time of issue, the bandsman will be asked to sign an Instrument Contract Rental Form. Students and parents will be held responsible for the care of the assigned instruments.

An instrument Rental Fee is charged and due by the end of October.

B. Uniforms: The school owns seventy-five (75) band uniforms which are issued to Brooklyn Center Concert Band members. Uniforms are issued by the Uniform Manager and at the time of issue the bandsman will be asked to sign a Uniform Rental Contract Form. Students and parents will be held responsible for the care of the assigned uniform and all accessories.

A Uniform Rental Fee is charged and due by the end of October.

Band members will be issued a coat, pair of trousers, hat, belt and buckle, dickey, pair of braids, plastic cover bag, and a hanger. Plumes will be distributed at marching band appearances by the Uniform Manager and Rank Lieutenants. No extra items are to be placed in the plastic uniform bags, as they tear easily. Each band member must supply his own pair of *white shoes, white socks, and white gloves* for all marching band appearances. Each band member will need to supply his own *black shoes, black socks,* and *black bow tie* for all concert band appearances. Place your name on all personal items. Keep shoes in your school locker. The uniform is to be worn at all times as prescribed by Brooklyn Center Band regulations. Any loss of any uniform item should be reported to the Uniform Manager at once. Each student will be held responsible for any loses or damage occuring to the uniform while issued to him.

Uniforms are to be treated as the beautiful and valuable item they are. They are to be hung neatly and properly at all times.

There is only one right way to wear the uniform: all buttons buttoned and belt buckled.

C. Music and Folders: Show respect and care for all music issued to you. The large, black Concert Band folders are not to go home; the music may be removed for home practice, but must be at every rehearsal.

Concert Band music is to be kept in alphabetical order in the folders, with march-size music and warm-up or instruction books in the left pocket, and all Concert-size music in the right pocket.

During the marching season, individual marching music folders will be issued, and each individual is responsible for the folder and all music issued. Music lost will be charged to the individual and, at times, may have to be hand-copied by the individual responsible for losing the music. *Keep a pencil in the folder at all times.* Make use of the warm-up materials and instruction books in the folder to make daily musical progress.

D. Miscellaneous (Books and Records): All music books, theory books, instrumental methods, solos, ensembles, and records may be *signed out* for use by band members for a limited time.

E. Care of Equipment: It is every band member's responsibility to show the utmost of care for all band equipment, instruments, music, uniforms, folders, band rooms, etc. Percussion players are especially urged to take care of all traps and keep them neat in the percussion cabinet. The band rooms and instrument storage rooms are not to be used for personal storage or for waste materials. Use the wastebaskets for items to be thrown away, and use your student locker for storing personal items.

F. Monthly Inspection: Section leaders will conduct monthly inspections of the music folders and instruments in their sections. The Uniform Manager will also inspect the uniform cabinets and all uniform bags monthly.

It is the responsibility of every band member to clean his own or school-owned instrument monthly or as often as needed. A band instrument is very fragile, complicated, and built as precisely as a fine watch. Careful handling and cleanliness is very important.

Brass instruments should be rinsed out with lukewarm water frequently, for the chemicals in the moisture of the breath will attack and eventually destroy the brass. Oil the valves and place cork grease or vaseline on the slides. Clean the mouthpiece also. Woodwinds should be kept clean by swabbing. Wash the mouthpiece monthly in lukewarm, soapy water.

G. Repair: All school-owned instrument repairs must go through the band office. Students are urged to use only professional repairmen to work on their instruments and are not to attempt repairs on their own.

H. Mouthpieces: All Concert Band members must have an approved mouthpiece with their instrument, i.e., Sumner No. 3 for reeds, Bach (special number for each instrument) for brass.

I. Insurance: Instrument insurance is available for privately-owned instruments.

XII. MUSIC ROOMS

A. Band Room: Band members are to keep the band room clean and neat. Keep the chairs and music stands in place and use the wastebasket for items to be thrown away.

B. Practice Rooms: To be used for practice or study only. Keep the practice rooms clean and neat.

C. Instrument Storage Rooms: To be used for instrument storage only. All other items are to be kept in the student's school locker. Keep the storage rooms clean and neat. Instruments are to be put in their cases and the cases closed while in the storage rooms. *No instruments are to be in the storage rooms over weekends!*

D. Listening Room: This room is reserved for required monthly listening assignments or for other records checked out from the band library. Personal records are to be cleared with the band director before being used in the listening room. Earphones and scores are provided. Band members are reminded to use extreme care in handling records, using the phonograph, and the earphones. Recommended reading material is also available in the listening room.

Keep this room clean and neat also.

E. Director's Office and Library: The director's office is *private,* and it used for private lessons. The library is also private and to be used only by the band librarians. Any item leaving the director's office or library is to be checked out and signed out with the band director's permission.

Band members may receive a permanent pass from study hall to the band room, but they must practice one-half of the period and then study or listen the other half of the period. No tardiness will be tolerated. Only study, practice, or required listening will be allowed.

XIII. MEMBERSHIP REQUIREMENTS AND REGISTRATION

MEMBERSHIP REQUIREMENTS

A. Beginners' Band
1. Any interested student with no previous band experience is eligible.
2. Normally started in fifth grade.
3. Continues on as sixth grade band.
4. Rehearsals held twice weekly; private lessons.

B. Junior Band
1. Open to students with limited previous experience (usually those who have had fifth and sixth grade band) or to sutdents who have not completed Cadet Band requirements.
2. Daily classes before schools; private lessons and ensembles— as they can be scheduled.

C. Cadet Band
1. Open to students who have completed the band test on their instrument and whose sections in Concert Band are complete.
2. Daily classes.

D. Concert Band
1. Admission by passing audition and satisfactory completion of band test.
2. Daily classes; weekly lectures; weekly sectionals conducted by section leaders; private lessons and ensembles as they can be scheduled; monthly quizzes; required monthly listening; monthly inspections of music folders, instruments, uniforms; term paper. Composition/arranging encouraged, but not required.

E. Marching Bands
1. Combined Cadet and Concert Band— as number of uniforms allows.

REGISTRATION

Before admission to the Brooklyn Center High School Concert Band, students shall have completed:

1. The written test covering the fundamentals of marching, musicianship, and musical knowledge.
2. A playing audition with the band director.

A. Written Band Test
1. Posture, Breathing, Embouchure: List the fundamentals necessary for the practice of proper musical fingering, posture, breathing, and embouchure.
2. Transposition: Be able to transpose for your particular instrument from a piano score. Students will be asked to write a quartet arrangement of some simple song for their instrument.
3. Tuning and Tone Production: Describe the method of tuning your particular instrument and the fundamentals necessary for proper tone production.
4. Rhythm, Counting, Time Values: Be able to write and count rhythmic equivalents for the more common rhythmic patterns.
5. Vocabulary: Know the meanings of the common musical terms.
6. Scales: Be able to write major and minor scales (transposed correctly) for your particular instrument.
7. Arpeggios, Chords, etc.: Write the major scales and the three major chords (I, IV, V) in each key.
8. Fingerings: Know the common alternate fingerings, positions, resonant fingerings, trill keys, etc. on your particular instrument.
9. Conducting: Be able to recognize and interpret the conductor's actions while in rehearsal, and be able to assume leadership of the band in the absence of the conductor.
10. Articulations: Recognize, define and be able to demonstrate the markings used for the common forms of articulation.
11. Intervals: Using a major scale, write five common intervals.
12. Solo Performance: Perform an approved solo at some authorized function.
13. Listening: Demonstrate development of good listening habits and ability to read full orchestral score while listening to a recording. Be able to recognize recordings from suggested listening list.
14. Sight reading: Be able to identify the habits and skills necessary for good sight reading.
15. Ensembles: Perform approved music at some authorized function.
16. Marching Fundamentals: Know fundamentals of football marching band and street parade work.
17. Instrument Care, Music and Folder Care, and Uniform Care: Students should know the proper manner of caring for instruments, music, folders, and uniforms. Various methods of making emergency repairs and adjustments on their instruments will be discussed.

B. Audition
1. Demonstrate proper posture.
2. Demonstrate proper embouchure.

3. Demonstrate proper and characteristic tone.
4. Demonstrate proper breathing.
5. Demonstrate counting of various rhythmic patterns.
6. Pass a satisfactory amount in an approved method book.
7. Play all twelve major scales, chromatics, and arpeggios.
8. Percussion— Rudiments 1 through 26; demonstrate correct use of cymbals, bass drum, timpani (and tuning of timpani); xylophone melodic exercises.
9. Pass satisfactory number of lessons in Rubank Advanced, Book I (Drums— Harr: Stick Control, Podemski, Goodman Tympani, Modern Xylophone).
10. Demonstrate proper position.
11. Play scale and chord exercise in concert keys of B-flat and E-flat: Major scale, minor scale, harmonic minor, melodic minor, chromatic; Major chord, minor chord, diminished chord, augmented chord, seventh chord.
12. Solfege and play exercises as directed: sing 1-3-5-3-1, 1-4-1, 1-5-1, 1-6-4 , 1-7, 1-6-2-4-1, 1-3-5-7, 1-7-3-5-1.
13. Demonstrate correct tonguing. (Double and triple also— as directed.)
14. Demonstrate correct tuning.
15. Score well in band tests (written).
16. Form habits of looking at key, time, tempo, dynamics, repeats, etc.
17. Pledge good attendance at all rehearsals, sectionals, lessons, performances.
18. Demonstrate knowledge of Concert Pitch.
19. Demonstrate good habits of care for instrument, case, music, folder, uniform.
20. Reed players demonstrate knowledge of selecting good reeds, and have six good reeds in case at all times (to rotate). Double-reed players demonstrate knowledge of reed-making and adjusting.
21. Demonstrate sight reading skill from music selected by director.
22. Play the "Star Spangled Banner" and School Song from memory.
23. Demonstrate dynamics by playing *pp* up to *ff*, with good tonal quality at both ends.
24. Demonstrate ability to play with metronome at 48, 60, 120, 132, 152.
25. Demonstrate proper attacks, releases, balance, phrases, precision, breath support, style, taste, expression, feeling, concentration, etc.

XIV. PRACTICE: All instruments must either be taken home daily for ½ hour practice or student must sign in during study hall and do ½ hour practice, or else be dropped from band program for one year.

1. Practice daily for progress and results.
2. Assemble instrument carefully and lubricate regularly or as necessary.
3. Warm up the instrument.
4. Condition the embouchure by playing l-o-n-g t-o-n-e-s. Start each tone pianissimo, then, in one breath, crescendo to fortissimo, decrescendo to pianissimo. Listen and play in tune with good tone quality at all dynamic levels. Do not overblow on the fortissimo or allow the tone to go flat.
5. Limber the fingers by playing scales and exercises— slowly at first, increasing the speed only if the patterns can be played evenly.
6. Practice the assigned lesson or music parts. When unable to play a particular phrase or group of notes, STOP. Make an exercise out of the difficult part. Practice it slowly at first, then gradually build up to proper speed.
7. Practice for results— not just for some specific length of time. It's more fun to play if you can play well, and practice makes this possible.
8. After a practice session is over, dry the inside of woodwinds and drain moisture from brass instruments. Then wipe off the outside of the instrument. Carefully return the instrument to its case. Avoid damage: do not keep stands, mutes, music or other objects in the case unless a place is provided for them.
9. See Appendix for "How to Practice at Home Hints," "Check List for Points to Watch in Home Practice," and "Daily Practice— How."

Practice for good tone.
Practice softly too, even at pianissimo.
Practice with expression.
Practice at a regular time each day.
Parents should supervise practice whenever possible.
Use only the front one-fourth of the chair when sitting, and use good posture.
Practice standing sometimes.
Practice difficult measures over slowly at least twenty times, then increase speed.
Good tone is the most important musical tool!

XV. TIPS FOR TOP PERFORMANCE

A. Always keep your instrument in good playing position so that these points may be achieved successfully.
B. Assume correct playing position and posture for your instrument.
C. Breathe deeply, using proper diaphragm control.
D. Assume and keep correct embouchure.
E. Check music for time and key signatures before starting to play.
F. Watch the director carefully for tempo and interpretation.
G. Think and look ahead so that you will be ready for any course the music may take.
H. Always be in tune with the band.
I. Think and produce the best tone of which you are capable.
J. Practice difficult passages slowly for accuracy.
K. No gum, pop, popcorn, etc. before or while playing.
L. Concert Band Daily Check List:

Proper Warm-Up	Phrases
Posture and Position	Attacks and Releases
Tone and Embouchure	Rhythm
Proper Breathing	Style
Eyes — Watch the conductor!	Dynamics
Ears — Listen for intonation!	Precision
Heart — Feeling and expression!	Breath Control
Enthusiasm — Life, spark	Solfeggio
Concentration	Beauty of Sound
Balance	Practice

XVI. BAND CURRICULUM IN BRIEF

A. Rehearsals: Daily, with emphasis on developing top musicianship through drill in musical style and interpretation, technics and skill, and the best performance possible. Use of musical knowledge gained from lectures in theory, harmony, listening, and history. Only two members per music stand.
B. Sectionals: Once weekly with section leader.
C. Lectures: One thirty-minute lecture weekly with band director. All band members will need a music staff notebook.
D. Private Lessons: *All* band members receive one private lesson weekly, on tone, scale and chord exercises, Rubank Advanced, Harr Advanced, Supplementary Books, Solos. One line of exercises in Rubank Advanced should be covered each week.
E. Required Listening: Three records are required monthly, plus use of scores.
F. Ensembles: All senior band members must be in one ensemble: schedules to be arranged.
G. Solos: All band members are encouraged to prepare solos.
H. Pep Band: Appointed (plus volunteers), performs at athletic events.
I. Stage Band: Rehearsals as can be scheduled.
J. Monthly Quizzes: To include material covered in lectures, required listening, and rehearsals, plus questions on musicianship, aesthetics and philosophy.

K. Monthly Inspection: Instruments and music folders (alphabetical order) inspected by section leaders; uniforms inspected by Uniform Manager.

L. Term Paper: Formal style— typed and double spaced. Due end of second quarter. Any approved musical topic. No grade and no required length, to be written for educational value.

M. Composition/Arranging: Encouraged, but not required.

N. Miscellaneous: Written paragraph critique of any musical events attended; outside reading encouraged, especially music majors.

O. Homecoming Show: All seniors in Concert Band help plan.

Concert Band gives the advanced instrumental student a wide musical background and a love of good instrumental music to carry over into adulthood. Emphasis is placed on developing technique, form and style in good music. Opportunities for solo and ensemble performances are also included. There are daily drills and lectures on proper breathing, solfeggio, tonguing, tone, rhythm, scales, intonation, basic rudiments, musical terms, technical developments; studies in music history, music theory, and harmony; and required record listening and score-reading for appreciation and understanding. Outside reading is also encouraged for a deeper understanding of these topics. A term paper is required and a composition or arrangement is encouraged, but not required. All of this helps the student develop the broadest and highest possible level of musicianship. There are many appearances and performances of the group from September to the end of July.

Rehearsal Procedure.

1. Promptness: Be on time.
2. Self-discipline: No talking when the director is on the podium.
3. Respect and Courtesy: No talking when the director is talking.
4. Rehearsal Schedule: Arrange music immediately in proper order as indicated on the blackboard.
5. Tuning: Section leaders' duty (daily). Listen carefully at all times during rehearsal, and tune to the band.
6. Be Neat: Keep all band rooms clean and neat.
7. NO BAND IS BETTER THAN ITS REHEARSALS! Rehearse as if it were a concert.
8. Read the band bulletin board daily for announcements.

Important Guidelines for Band Members.

1. Self-discipline.
2. Punctuality, dependability, attendance, daily practice.
3. Cooperation.
4. Tone quality and intonation.
5. Care of instrument, music, uniform.
6. Ability to count rhythms and understand rhythm patterns.
7. Musicianship, and record listening habits.
8. Knowledge of theory, harmony, history.
9. Keep school grades up.

Rehearsal Hints For a Better and Happier Band

1. Always *listen* while playing; learn to "sing" through the instrument, so that the tone will be beautiful in quality, and well in tune.
2. Always be courteous and polite to the director and fellow bandsmen. Try to understand the other fellow's point of view— learn to live the golden rule.
3. Take proper care of all instruments—keep them immaculately clean. Brass players should keep valves and slides properly oiled; woodwinds should keep a supply of good reeds on hand at all times.

4. Never talk when the band is playing— not during rehearsals nor during a concert. Never talk while the band director is giving instruction or is on the podium.

5. Always work out individual parts in private practice sessions.

6. Ensemble playing should be devoted entirely to acquiring musicianship and artistry. Be sure that your playing is a help to the band and your fellow players— not a hindrance. Practice to be perfect.

7. Learn the correct fingerings— study the fingering charts carefully and accurately. Learn the special fingerings for trills and fast passages, but use them only when absolutely necessary. Learn to play in all keys. Become familiar with all key and time signatures.

8. Learn good posture: breath is the very "soul" of tone, and only with the body erect can we breathe deeply and correctly. Sit with the feet flat on the floor— crossed legs look out of place, and they hamper correct breathing.

9. Learn an accurate, definite system of counting time. Only by such a system can "time patterns" and articulations be played correctly. Counting time is the foundation of accurate, rapid sight reading.

10. Never beat time in any manner at a concert. Never beat time at a rehearsal, unless specifically requested by the director.

XVII. ATTENDANCE

The attendance system must apply with equal force to all band members.

Membership in the Brooklyn Center High School Band Automatically Includes Attendance at all Rehearsals, Sectionals, Lectures, Lessons, and Performances.

Absence due to illness or accident will, of course, be honored. However, the director must be notified before a performance.

"Request for Excuse" card: This card is to be used for all requests for excuse from any band activity. Members are reminded to then check with the director to see if the "request" is approved.

Specific arrangements must be made with the director in the event of conflicts with other school activities. Except in the case of accident, excuses must be checked in advance.

Band members who are on the varsity squad in an athletic event will be excused at the director's discretion.

Band members are discouraged from becoming members of the athletic backup crews, such as cheerleaders, managers, etc., and should make a choice between band and that activity.

Unexcused Absence: An unexcused absence from any special rehearsal or a performance is grounds for a grade of "F", loss of credit, and a summary dismissal from the band.

Seating Arrangement: The seating in large sections has a definite pattern which is set by the director for the proper balance of band parts. Daily "Solo-Soli" exercises will provide opportunity for moving up or down in the section. Challenges are also available for the chance to move up, but no challenges are allowed two weeks prior to a major performance.

XVIII. BAND GRADES

Grade of "D" Not recognized as a passing grade in the Brooklyn Center Band; used only to point up a definite need which must be corrected during a probationary period.

Grade of "C" 1. Minimum required attendance at band performances.

2. No apparent individual effort to improve through practice.

3. Minimum contribution to band activities; reluctant to assume responsibility.

4. Rehearsal conduct erratic and uncertain; lacking in self-discipline.

5. Poor scores on monthly quizzes.

Grade of "B" 1. Prompt, attentive and alert at all rehearsals and performances.

2. Assumes musical responsibility in band; consistent practice to insure satisfactory performance.

3. A positive contribution to band activities; definite self-improvement through private lessons and/or individual practice.

4. Exercises good self-control, self-discipline and good, cooperative spirit in band group activities.
5. Fair scores on monthly quizzes.

Grade of "A" 1. Shows positive leadership and interest in his particular section; shows independence and resourcefulness in assisting rehearsal procedures.
2. Outstanding progress in self-improvement through consistent individual practice and solo and ensemble participation.
3. Strong, positive contributions to the band and music department as a whole through participation in Pep Band, Stage Band, Ensembles, Council activities, etc.
4. Personal integrity and character best exemplifies the principles of the Brooklyn Center Band code of conduct and the Brooklyn Center High School code of ethics.
5. Good scores on monthly quizzes.

Better use of practice time will help a band member's grade.

Parents are encouraged to consult the director at any time in regard to the band grade and their child's progress in the band. A close contact of parents and director will indicate a strong interest in the band program and can thus aid both parties in understanding and solving any problems.

XIX. BAND TRIPS

A. A complete schedule and rules for the specific trip will be issued to each band member.
B. Be on time.
C. An adult chaperone will be on each bus and *no* changes in buses will be allowed.
D. Buses are to be treated with care and all refuse is to be placed in the box placed on the bus for that purpose. Keep the bus clean!
E. Special care should be taken to see that all personal and school property is properly cared for:
1. Pack and pad instruments for travel.
2. Hang uniforms neatly when not in use.
3. Place identification and band decal on all school and personal items.
F. No one is to leave the group formation for any reason whatsoever until properly dismissed by the director.
G. Students will be given as much free time as is consistent with the educational intent of the trip. Students must return at the appointed time.
H. Parents should arrange to meet the students at the assembly points upon the students' return.
I. No smoking or drinking of alcoholic beverages will be tolerated at any time at any band function. Violators will be dismissed from the band.
J. Only exemplary conduct will be accepted from members of the Brooklyn Center Band. Members must be on their best behavior at all times, especially on the buses, in a hotel, and at all group appearances.
K. There is only one right way to wear the Brooklyn Center Band uniform.
L. Private cars will not be used. All members are expected to use the buses provided.

XX. AWARDS, HONORS AND SCHOLARSHIPS

A. Award Eligibility:

Awards are given for loyalty, dependability and outstanding contributions to the Brooklyn Center High School Band program. Participating in the District Music Contest and receiving an "A" rating also deserves award mention. Students should not expect to receive special rewards or recognition for minimum service and average participation.

B. Awards may be given for:
1. Outstanding service as a member of the Band Staff.
2. Active participation in solo and ensemble sork.
3. Participating in and receiving an "A" rating at the District Music Contest.

4. Positive leadership in sectional rehearsals, band activities, and other areas of the music department, i.e., Stage Band, Pep Band, Student Conductor, Drum Major, etc.
5. Obvious, consistent and thorough preparation of concert material.
6. Faithful attendance at special and sectional rehearsals.

C. Awards are not given when reprimands, disciplinary action or unsatisfactory conduct jeopardize the award eligibility.

D. "John Philip Sousa Award" for Outstanding Senior Bandsman
  1. Must be a senior in the band.
  2. Voted on by the Concert Band membership.

E. Band Booster Camp Scholarship
  1. Must be in grades nine through eleven.
  2. The Boosters will pay half of the camp costs for each sholarship recipient.
  3. The Boosters will increase the number of scholarships given each year by one.
  4. The scholarship essays will be judged by the administration of the high school.
  5. The purpose of the scholarship is to stimulate and encourage the study and performance of music by Brooklyn Center High School band members and to foster a wider knowledge, understanding, and appreciation of good music by providing financial assistance for the advanced study of music by worthy students of the Brooklyn Center High School Band.

XXI. BROOKLYN CENTER BAND BOOSTERS CLUB

The parents and friends of the band members at Brooklyn Center, which includes beginners' bands at Earle Brown Elementary School, Junior Band, and the High School Concert Bands, have for many years maintained the Band Boosters Club. The Boosters have consistently supported the music groups of the instrumental music department and have rendered invaluable financial aid and parental backing to all the instrumental organizations. The success of the Instrumental Music Department is due, in large part, to the active participation of the Band Boosters.

Some of the objectives of the Boosters are:
1. To arouse, stimulate and maintain an enthusiastic interest in all phases of the instrumental music department at both grade and high school levels in the public schools of Brooklyn Center.
2. To cooperate with those in charge of the instrumental music department and the School Board to the end that this department be brought to and kept at the highest possible degree of efficiency.
3. To develop a closer relationship betwen parents and the school, fostering the musical interests and education of the children, and stimulating the knowledge, performance and appreciation of finer music.
4. To assist in the purchase of uniforms, instruments, and other equipment not regularly provided for in the school budget.
5. To augment or encourage educational trips, exchange programs, or concerts that are approved or sanctioned by the school.
6. To aid in chaperoning on band trips.

Membership: Membership of the Brooklyn Center Band Boosters Club shall consist of all parents and friends of the band members enrolled in the various instrumental music organizations in the Music Department of Brooklyn Center Public Schools.

XXII. HOW PARENTS CAN HELP
A. At Home
  1. Show an interest in the music sutdy of your child.
  2. Arrange a regular *time* for him to practice.
  3. Find a quiet *place* where he can practice without interruption.
  4. Help him with his practice as much as possible by counting, studying music texts, etc.

5. Help the student keep a daily record of his practicing.
6. Give him a safe place in which to keep his instrument.
7. Keep the instrument in good repair with reeds, etc. in the case.
8. Be very careful of school-owned instruments. The cost of repairs is very high.
9. Teach him to be on time at rehearsals and lessons, etc.
10. Make faithful attendance at all activities important.
11. Encourage him to play for others when opportunity arises, in the home, at school, church, and in the community.

B. At School

1. Keep a record of the student's various music activities.
2. Notify the teacher if he is to be absent or tardy at lessons, rehearsals, etc., and explain why.
3. See that he takes his instrument and his music when needed at school.
4. Teach him to be punctual at lessons and rehearsals, etc.
5. See that he keeps up with classroom studies and makes up work he has missed.
6. Visit rehearsals and lessons occasionally.
7. Discuss with music teacher anything that will help him to understand your child.
8. Attend concerts and parents meeting whenever possible.
9. Attend Band Booster Club meetings. (Two meetings yearly.)
10. Help with parent activities.

SO YOUR CHILD WON'T PRACTICE?

The last round of applause could still be heard in the small concert hall where three boys were putting away their instruments. "Gosh, we did alright," said Stan, the thirteen-year-old, to his brothers. "Fun, too," said Gale, a year younger, as he tossed his music in a folder. "And now for something to eat," said Roy, snapping his instrument case shut.

The program for the local Sunday Evening Club was over. My husband and I were being surrounded. The gentlemen nearest my husband beamed. "I bet you never have to make those boys practice," he said. "Indeed we do," replied my husband. The pleasure on the man's face changed to surprise and curiosity. "But the way they play, I thought—'" "They're regular boys and practicing doesn't come any more natural to them than washing their ears," answered my husband, "but both are part of their daily schedule."

Others crowded in, congratulating us on our three sons' performance as if it had been something spectacular. I couldn't understand. Was our family concert so unusual—playing music together and in solo? This could have happened in our living room most any evening. "How do you get your boys to practice?" The question seemed to come from several people. I looked up at them, wondering how to answer, when my husband spoke. "We teach them to practice. Our children are no exception." "But they play as if they enjoy it," said the woman at my left. "They do. After all, it's a form of self-expression. And playing for others gives them an added sense of achievement. But that doesn't mean they like to practice. It's our job to see that they do practice. We help them." "How? came the blunt question. I thought of how hard it would be for a child to read and write by himself. Only through daily help and practice does it become easy and natural for him. Music is no different. But there are ways to motivate his daily practice. So—

"First of all," I said, "we establish a regulation: one-half hour of practice each day, to be finished before 7:30 P.M. I feel that if children know what is expected of them, what they may or may not do, they have something to hold to. It gives them a feeling of security, which is essential to their happiness. Each of our boys has different hours of working best. With Gale, the one who played piano for you, it's early morning. As soon as his breakfast is finished, he practices until school time, getting most of it done then. He doesn't like to practice, but good music grades bring reward. This year it will be some special fishing tackle.

"With Roy, ten-years-old, a half-hour practice session is too long. Two fifteen-minute periods for him. We sometimes have to help him, and each week of good practicing brings an extra privilege, a new ball, a movie or an afternoon picnic.

244

"Stan, thirteen-years-old, has many after-school sports. He practices best after dinner. Radio and television are his to see only after his practice is finished. A solo or number mastered merits a Saturday movie, hamburger for the gang, or a new baseball bat..."

"Do they watch the clock while they practice?" came the question. "We have no clock in the living room. They check the time when they start, and after fifteen or twenty minutes, they call out, 'What time is it, Mom?' If they waste time, I simply add an extra five minutes and tell them it has been added. After the first few weeks, it seldom happens."

"But I thought children should never be forced to practice. It might kill their love for music," said a feminine voice in the group. "Let us look at it this way. Children are not mature in their judgment. We, as parents, must enforce what is right for them. If you review the early life of Haydn, Mozart, Beethoven and many others, you will find their training was part of their daily schedule, and not because they chose it to be. Free choice, in most things, is not for children. We know our boys are not genius material. They're normal, mischievous youngsters full of energy and curiosity. And we want to give them preparation for experiences ahead by taking them by the hand and leading them. And one of those doors leads to the enjoyment of music.

"Music, a language of the feelings, goes beyond the printed or spoken word. It holds no barrier of race, creed or nationality. One of the finest forms of self-expression for all ages, music is relaxing, uplifting, and alway teaches children that it requires patience and daily supervision. The latter is our job, as parents—just as it is our job to enforce a reasonable bedtime, whether they approve or not. Yet, many parents indulge in the belief that it is wrong to hold a child to a daily practice period. If he wants music, he must do his practicing on his own. Is it because they, as parents, are content to take the path of least resistance?"

"Let's look at it objectively. In a recent survey of our penal institutions, it was found that only a scattered few among the thousands of criminals had ever received any regular musical instruction or participated in a band, orchestra or chorus during their childhood. Music and delinquency seldom mix."

"To make the daily practice period more enjoyable and worthwhile to both pupils and parents, here are some suggestions we hope you will find helpful:

FIVE KEYS THAT WILL OPEN THE DOOR TO MUSIC

1. Assist your child with his practicing.
2. Be generous with your interest and praise.
3. Credit each achievement with some form of recognition.
4. Help him develop the habit of daily practice.
5. Encourage note-reading rather than playing by ear.

It may take all five keys to unlock your practice problem, but try them all before giving up. MUSIC IS ONE THING YOUR CHILD WILL NEVER THANK YOU FOR NOT GIVING HIM!

XXIII.   SUMMER BAND PROGRAM

The type of summer band program offered will vary according to the number of students interested and how vacations and work conflict with the summer band scheduling. Each spring information will be given to band members concerning the summer band program.

All band members are urged to continue their lessons and practice. Continued individual improvement is still a must for the good of the band. Band members are also encouraged to attend band camps, take private lessons outside of school, and make progress in any possible way.

Sectionals should be scheduled by section leaders with their new sections for the coming school year.

XXIV.   BAND IS GREAT FOR TRAINING THE MIND

Band is the best mind trainer on the list. Band teaches orderly thinking! Not only does the musician have to think in orderly manner, and make correct, instantaneous responses to hundreds of printed symbols, but he must also fit his playing into that of the group. So band teaches cooperation as well.

Consider the problem from this standpoint. Our senior band is playing a simple march. We have 80 players, each of whom must correctly perform approximately 500 notes, which makes a total of 40,000 notes to play. Any one of those notes could be played too long or too short, too early or too late, too loud or too soft. In addition the notes must all be played in tune, in relationship with the other notes of an individual instrument as well as in relationship with all the other instruments.

Add to this the fact that a simple printed quarter note can mean any one of five different pitches: natural, sharp, flat, double sharp and double flat, and the player must remember the key signature at all times and quickly adjust to the accidentals.

Add still further the fact that a simple quarter note may be counted in so many different ways. It gets one beat in 4/4 time, two beats in 3/8 time, 1/3 of a beat in fast 6/4, 2/3's of a beat in fast 6/8 and half a beat in ala breve or cut time.

To further compound the problems, rests of all sizes and shapes must be properly counted. Players must know all the notes on their instruments and how to finger them. Clarinets and bassoons have a range of about 40 half- steps, flutes 37, brass instruments at least 31, and saxophones the same.

On top of all this we must add the feeling and expression of the music. We must know how to handle the six levels of dynamic change and when they mean what they say and when they don't. How to change gradually or suddenly to a different volume level. (All this while remaining in tune.)

All these things are pointed out to show how many chances for mistakes there are. They run into the millions, but only one way to play right! It is really a wonder the students can do it at all. You can see now why it takes so many years for a person to learn to play well. There is so much to learn.

Also consider this: It is impossible to play well seated next to a person who is playing badly. In a geometry test a person getting all the answers wrong will not affect the person in the next chair. This is not so in the band. No amount of good notes will cover up one bad one.

You can easily see that music is great for training the mind and for learning cooperation, and, by the way, it is really fun to play in the band.

XXV. I AM MUSIC

I AM MUSIC, most ancient of the arts. I am more than ancient; I am eternal. Even before life commenced upon this earth, I was here — in the winds and the waves. When the first trees and flowers and grasses appeared, I was among them. And when Man came, I was at once the most delicate, most subtle, and most powerful medium for the expression of Man's emotions. When men were little better than beasts, I influenced them for their good. In all ages, I have inspired men with hope, kindled their love, given a voice to their joys, cheered them on to valorous deeds, and soothed them in times of despair. I have played a great part in the drama of Life, whose end and purpose is the complete perfection of Man's nature. Through my influence human nature has been uplifted, sweetened and refined. With the aid of men, I have become a Fine Art. From Tubalcain to Thomas Edison a long line of the brightest minds have devoted themselves to the perfection of instruments through which men may utlize my powers and enjoy my charms. I have myriads of voices and instruments. I am in the hearts of all men and on their tongues, in all lands and among all peoples; the ignorant and unlettered know me, not less than the rich and learned. For I speak to all men in a language that all understand. Even the deaf hear me, if they but listen to the voices of their own souls. I am the food of love. I have taught men gentleness and peace; and I have led them onward to heroic deeds. I comfort the lonely, and I harmonize the discord of crowds. I am a necessary luxury to all men.
I am MUSIC.

— Allan C. Inman.

APPENDIX

SPECIAL BAND RULES AND REGULATIONS

1. If the band has an engagement and you cannot be present, don't say anything.
2. Don't wear your uniform unless you desire it; your own clothes will make the audience think you are a soloist.
3. Always wear your cap on the side or back of your head.
4. Remember a little decoration improves the uniform, such as a flower stuck in the cap or a few medals on the coat.
5. In a parade, just walk along any old way; this will cause the bystanders to think you were engaged for what you know, not for what you do.
6. Remember the ladies on the sidewalk like to have you holler at them; this will show the other fellow that you stand out.
7. If you hear another band playing, don't fail to say, "Oh, that is simply rotten," and say it so strangers may hear it.
8. Have a good time on any engagement; remember it is your picnic, and you were invited to enjoy yourself.
9. Always wait until the band is about to play and then ask, "What cher goin' to play?" No matter what it is, don't fail to remark, "What, that bum thing?"
10. Always play as loud as you can to show the people that you are the whole band.
11. Start to grumble about playing too often as soon as the parade starts. Inform those around you that if it wasn't for crippling the band you'd go home.
12. If you see a lady friend of one of the band members, yell out, "Say, Jack, there's Jennie." Jack will feel grateful for this.
13. If you are playing at a banquet let your first question be, "When do we eat?"
14. If you go along quietly in a parade the people will think you are only a good musician; to avoid this, keep up a conversation with members on the opposite side of the band.
15. When anyone asks you where you were taught music, just say, "Oh, I picked it up." Never give the director any credit.
16. Develop the artistic temperament. Criticize the leader, and buck all tempos. You have studied and you KNOW.
17. Don't attend rehearsal if you can find anything else to do; the other fellows are the only ones who need to rehearse. If you do attend, be sure to come late.
18. When the band is on parade and halt is called, sit down on the curb, this will show that you are a concert performer and that it makes you tired to walk.
19. Never polish your instrument. This is an amateur's trick, and you want to appear as a professional.
20. Allow your tuning slide to get stuck so you cannot move it. Then the band will have to tune to you.
21. Always play middle C at the end of a strain an octave higher; this will be a strain on both you and the audience.
22. If you are asked to play a second or third part, pack up and go home. Let your slogan be "solo or nothing."
23. When the leader steps on the podium for order, begin to improvise. If everyone does this, the ensemble will be beautiful, and it makes the leader good-natured.

MUSICAL INSTRUMENT INSURANCE APPLICATION
Brooklyn Center High School — Brooklyn Center, Minneapolis, Minn.

Name _____ Date _____

Address _____

Instrument _____

    Serial No. _____ Amt. of Ins. $ _____

    When Purchased _____ Cost $ _____ New _____Used _____

    Accessories _____ Amt. of Ins. $ _____

    When Purchased _____ Cost $ _____ New _____ Used _____

Condition of Instrument (to be filled out by band instructor)
    List Major Defects.

Signed _____
                    Instructor

Cost to pupil — $1.00 per $100.00 of value (minimum premium, $1.00)

Signed _____
                    Owner

(To be added to Musical Instrument Floater Policy carried by the school Covers fire, theft, accidental damage, vandalism, vehicle damage and other risks with a few minor exceptions.)

MONTHLY FOLDER and INSTRUMENT INSPECTION
by Section Leaders

I. FOLDERS

1. Only concert music (alphabetized) in Concert Folders.
2. Large size concert music on right side.
3. Octavo and march size music on left side with Sign-Out Card.
4. Only Warm-Up Books, etc., in the Warm-Up Folders (large on right, etc.)
5. Pep Folios in place.
6. REMINDER: Use only old folders to take out music.
   Black Folders do not go out!
7. CAUTION: Do not be careless about music!
   Always turn book covers back to normal and be careful of sheet music so as not to tear it.

   Note: Lost music results in a charge for the music and HAND COPYING a new part.

II. INSTRUMENTS

1. Pull all slides all the way out — use vaseline or cork grease where necessary.
2. Check that valves and slides are oiled.
3. Check mouthpiece for cleanliness.
4. Check if instrument is cleaned and polished.
5. Check for 3 reeds in each case.
6. Check case for cleanliness.
7. Check drums: snares, heads, oil screws, clean chrome, etc.
8. Check for bad dents which affect intonation.
9. Tighten lyre screws.

III. UNIFORMS: Check if clean and neat.

CHECK LIST FOR GOOD SIGHT READING

I. TIME SIGNATURES:	Complete understanding of the top and bottom numbers.
II. COUNTING TIME:	Note and rest values, rhythm patterns, baton beats, foot beats.
III. KEY SIGNATURES:	Knowledge of major and minor scales, names of notes, intervals, arpeggios and chords with correct fingerings (regular and alternate).
IV. ARTICULATION:	Tonguing, slurring, tie, legato, staccato, accent, fingering.
V. PHRASING:	Breathing, style, melodic motion, singing tone, listening.
VI. EXPRESSION:	Crescendo, diminuendo, climax, terms of expression, imagination.
VII. TEMPI:	Meaning of M.M., tempo indications (Andante, Allegro, accelerando, ritard, rubato, etc.).
VIII. VOLUME:	Dynamic markings, balance, solo and accompaniment.
IX. MISCELLANEOUS:	Repeat signs and endings, measure repeats, Da Capo (D.C.), Dal Segno (D.S.), Coda, Fine, fermata, pick-up notes, attack and release.

CHECK LIST FOR GOOD EXPRESSION IN MUSIC

A. Dynamics (degree of loudness and softness); Six important levels:

1. *pp* = pianissimo
2. *p* = piano
3. *mp* = mezzo-piano
4. *mf* = mezzo-forte
5. *f* = forte
6. *ff* = fortissimo

Crescendo — gradually louder; Diminuendo — gradually softer. (Anyone can play loud. It takes a good musician to play soft.)

249

B. Balance: Melody — must be predominant; Harmony — must be subordinate to the melody; Counter melody — next in volume to the melody; Rhythm — should be felt. (Learn to listen "across" the band.)

C. Articulation: Legato tones — played smoothly and connected; Staccato tones — separated and played lightly; Marcato tones — separated and played with emphasis; Attack and release — starting and stopping of the tone; Accent — emphasis given any particular note (more air, not more tongue!).

D. Tempi: Metronome indication (M.M.) — number of beats per minute; Terms: Andante, Allegro, ritard, etc.; the mood of the expression, the swing or general spirit; individual judgment; tradition.

E. Phrasing: A phrase is a sentence of music - movement from one note to another through a series of musically related notes. To bring about this movement, most phrases gradually crescendo to the climax (usually the highest tone) and then diminuendo from this point to the end of the phrase.

F. Accent: All notes in a passage marked *ff* or *pp* are not always played in the same volume: Long tones are stronger tones, short tones are lighter tones; after beats are played ligher than down beats; accented tones are separated tones; syncopated tones are separated and "pushed"; dotted notes should be played with approximately three times the power or accent that is given to the following short note. Breath control is important.

G. Expression: Musical expression is an art. Encourage the student to use his imagination. All music must possess the quality of movement. Each note, regardless of its duration, must convey the feeling of movement. It's not what you play, but the way you play it! Encourage the student to desire to do something besides "get all the notes."

CHECK LIST OF PLAYING PROBLEMS AND THEIR CURES

FLUTE & PICCOLO:
Sharp — Check tuning cork in head joint; blow down slightly into the tone hole.
Flat — Check tuning cork in head joint; blow slightly across tone hole.
Airy Tone — Hole in lips too large; compress the air more; blow more gently.
Poor Technic — Daily practice of scales and arpeggios.

OBOE & BASSOON:
Sharp — Play closer to the tip of the reed; use less pressure (bite) on the reed.
Flat — Use a firm embouchure and more lift by the right thumb; cut a little off the cork end of the tube.
Poor Technic — Practice scales daily.
Reed — Should "crow" freely; use feather for cleaning. If hard-blowing, soften the tip by gently pressing it together several times between the forefinger and the thumb after it is well soaked. If low tones are difficult, scrape the ends slightly; if too soft, trim the tip.

CLARINET & SAXOPHONE:
Flat — Reed too soft; inferior mouthpiece. Use a firm embouchure and more lift by the right thumb. There should be a feeling of wedging the mouthpiece in between the lower lip and upper teeth. Keep chin pointed down. Use more breath support. Try blowing the mouthpiece alone; the tone should sound approximately "concert C."
Pinched Tone — Try more mouthpiece in the mouth.
Squeaks — Try less mouthpiece in the mouth. Check reed for warping and uneven strength. Check mouthpiece for nicks, mars, cracks and warpage.
Sluggish Tonguing — Due to faulty jaw and tongue movement: Use the tip of the tongue with a minimum movement and firm embouchure.
Poor Technic — Practice scales daily. Try silent fingering; count aloud, and place thumb-1-2-3-4-5-6, then reverse.
Nasal Tone — Faulty reed and embouchure.

CORNET, ALTO HORN & BARITONE:	High Tone Trouble — Mouthpiece cup may be too deep; lack of breath support. Try syllable "Tee."

CORNET, ALTO
HORN &
  BARITONE:

High Tone Trouble — Mouthpiece cup may be too deep; lack of breath support. Try syllable "Tee."

Low Tone Trouble — Mouthpiece cup may be too shallow; lack of breath support. Try syllable "Tah."

Pinched Tone — Teeth too close together; tongue too high; throat too tight.

Airy Tones — Too much pressure. Check mouthpiece.

Fuzzy Tones — Leaky valves; leaky water key; lack of a "centered tone."

Cracking Tone — Try "doo" tonguing in place of "too."

Scooped Notes — Usually caused by articulation "Too-ee" instead of "doo" or "too."

FRENCH HORN:

Missing Pitch — Practice intervals of a 2nd slowly, without using the tongue (say "whoo"); then 3rds, then 4ths, 5ths, etc.

Intonation — Right hand position raises or lowers tone.

Dark Tone — Use less hand in bell.

Light Tone — Use more hand in bell. Other problems are similar to those of the cornet.

TROMBONE:

Legato Slur — Correct coordination of the tongue and slide. Use "doo" or "loo." Other problems are similar to those of cornet.

TUBA:

Muddy Tonguing — Due to over-tonguing through the lips; too much tongue pressing against the attacking surface.

Pinched Tone — Teeth too close together. Try tilting the head slightly upward. Other problems similar to those of cornet.

BASS DRUM:

Excessive Ring — Incorrect use of the left hand, the right hand or the right knee in dampening.

SNARE DRUM:

Uneven Rolls — Use the practice pad more. Check sticks for equal balance. Tune drums correctly.

TIMPANI:

Uneven Rolls — Due to tendency of one hand to strike harder than the other. Be sure to use only single stroke rolls for timpani. *Never* double stroke rolls. Stand in front of a mirror; then, using a pillow as a timpani, start roll slowly. Use straight up and down motion of arms and sticks.

Uneven Sound — Moisten the head to within one inch of the edge. As the head becomes slack, the handles should be tightened the same number of turns until a 3/8" collar forms on the rim. Then wipe off the excess moisture and let dry slowly.

CHECK LIST FOR SOLUTION OF CLARINET PROBLEMS

I. Assembling: Use great care. Left hand on upper joint; right hand on lower. Make sure the connecting links clear each other and "line up" properly.

II. Warming-up: Place all fingers down on instrument (low E) and blow warm air through the instrument. If very cold, it is best to warm the tuning barrel on the outside with hands first before warming inside. Move all keys in case they have dry pads stuck to hole, leaving a slight leak. Moisten reed twice.

III. Embouchure: All players use slightly different angles from their body depending upon the teeth, but *remember to blow over the reed*, not between the reed and the mouthpiece. Lower lip firm; do not move mouthpiece in the mouth. Breathe through sides of mouth; pointed chin; head up; good posture; arms relaxed at the side of the body; a little of lower lip rolled over teeth, but not too much (use a mirror now and then to check on yourself — you should be able to see some red of the lower lip); experiment with amount of "bite" on mouthpiece — too much will bring squeaks easily, and too little will give a small tone. Upper teeth should rest *lightly* on mouthpiece.

IV. Finger Position: Firm pressure, but not a tight grasp; curve fingers without overlapping holes; each finger should move like a little hammer, without withdrawing too far from the hole; right thumb carries weight of the instrument. Cover hole with ball of the finger. Remember to finger the note before you blow.

V. Posture, Breathing: Good posture is very important. Practice standing — often; back straight, head up, feet flat — one ahead of the other (do not cross legs). Learn to breathe deeply and quickly — think of the air going to the bottom of the lungs. When you exhale you should feel the pressure of the diaphragm pushing back into position.

VI. Tone: Air is important for a big full tone. Five minutes per day on sustained tones will do wonders for tone quality if you listen to your tone and try to improve it. (Practice with the eyes closed.) Start with fairly full tone — a strong forte. Later, try crescendo-decrescendo (***ppp*** up to ***ff*** and back to ***ppp***). The decrescendo will always be harder to control. Be careful your tone does not go sharp when playing softly in the low register. Remember that the best quality is obtained when the tone is at its sharpest (not "out-of-tune sharp," that is); so keep the lower lip firm. Smooth, legato scale passages will assist in developing tone too, along with legato arpeggio figures of 8ths, 10ths, and 12ths.

VII. Mouthpiece: A medium open lay is best for general use. Make sure the lay is level and the tip is not chipped. Clean regularly with a soft cloth — *not* a cleaner on a wire rod. Place the reed just slightly below the tip and put the ligature on evenly. Always dry reed carefully after putting it in place. Use great care in taking off and replacing the mouthpiece cap — many mouthpieces and reeds have been ruined by careless handling of the cap!

HINTS ON HOW TO PRACTICE AT HOME

I. The Warm-up (The most important part of your daily practice).

A. Warm-up with the utmost care: do not abuse lips, embouchure, etc., during this part of your daily practice nor at any other time.

B. Warm-up Hints for Brasses:

1. Start warm-up by buzzing lips gently (merely blow air through lips formed for playing) and allow lips to start buzzing freely without using a harsh tongue to start the buzz.

2. Next, take your mouthpiece, using only the thumb and index finger to hold it lightly, and start buzzing on it. Buzz long tones until your lips feel ready to respond with agility and flexibility.

3. Next put the mouthpiece into the horn. Start the warm-up on the horn very gradually with long tones, concentrating mainly on the lips and breath. Take deep breaths, and use the least possible amount of pressure on the lips.

4. Each brass player's lips are different and therefore the time required to warm-up properly will also vary. Daily practice will on the average require about 10 to 15 minutes of good, proper, relaxed warm-up.

a. Play long tones in the middle register at about mezzo-forte.

1. DON'T play high, low, loud, or soft.

b. Play long tones in half steps, going from 2nd line G to 1st space F♯ back to G — all slurred (brass clef instruments: 1st space below the staff (F) to E back to F; etc.); then, F♯ to F♮ to F♯; then, F♮ to E to F, etc. ALWAYS SLUR! (Take horn away from lips after each group of three notes.)

c. Or: Play long tones from G to F♯, to G to F♮, to G to E, to G to E♭, etc., all slurred. (Bass clef: F to E, to F to E♭, to F to D, etc.) Play these slurred as long whole notes. Take the horn away from the lips often.

d. Other warm-up possibilities:

1. Lip slurs.

2. Scales: major and minor, using various articulations.

3. Tonguing exercises: single, double, triple tongue, etc.

4. Intervals.

5. Use plenty of short rest periods between parts of your warm-up. (Do finger exercises during these rest periods to strengthen your finger dexterity and coordination.)

C. Warm-up Hints for Reeds.

1. Be sure reed is placed properly and that all the "ruffles" have been taken out (flatten reed against the flat surface of the mouthpiece before placing it on the mouthpiece). Be sure to moisten the reed well in mouth.

2. Warm-up on long tones in your middle register, listening very intently for good intonation on the "throat" tones (these are often very flat).

3. Practice going across the "break" evenly without any change in tone, being sure all fingers move evenly together. "Pop" them down in place to be sure they cover properly.

4. Concentrate on getting a very good tone in all registers of the instrument.

5. Work on chromatic scales for proper alternate fingerings, good finger dexterity, coordination, and intonation. Once again — LISTEN!

6. Practice the "hi-tone" exercise for proper high note fingerings and good tone in the upper register.

CHECK LIST FOR POINTS TO WATCH IN HOME PRACTICE

1. Use good posture at all times; practice sitting part of the time and then standing.
2. Practice in front of a mirror. Watch lip formation, embouchure, etc., and watch for any movement of lips, jaw or chin.
3. Be sure (especially reeds) that your chin is pointed down.
4. Reeds, watch your embouchure in the mirror. Be sure the lower lip is not too far in. You should see some red of the lip showing, chin pointed down and the corners firm.
5. Always use a proper warm-up every day. This is very important because you are developing your playing habits.
6. Start each practice with long tones. Watch to correct any bad habits of lip formation, embouchure, lip or jaw or chin movement, etc. Listen for good tone!
7. Count each exercise before you practice it. Be sure you can count it properly or else you won't practice it correctly.
8. Practice the exercises your director has assigned until perfect, then go on to the tunes. Don't just practice the tunes!
9. Practice hard parts very slow at first, then gradually faster until they are perfect.
10. Work on range daily. Work range both directions for ease of obtaining a good tone on the outer ranges of your instrument and also the ability to attack the tone cleanly on the first attempt.
11. Always listen to yourself and strive for a better tone each day.
12. Don't allow any careless mistakes in your practicing. Be fussy and try to be perfect in all of your practice sessions and at all times.
13. Have a system of regular daily practice periods (2 or more per day, etc.) — before supper, after supper, or in the morning, etc., and have rest periods during each practice session. Practice several ten minute periods each day. The rest period during a practice session or between practice sessions is very important and necessary. Organize your practice sessions so they are regular and worthwhile.
14. Listen to good records of your instrument and try to imitate the tone, etc.
15. We all have weaknesses, so work daily to eliminate them. Work to improve:
    1. Breathing.
    2. Tonguing.
    3. Lip technic (lip slurs for brasses).
    4. Finger technic.
    5. Tone.
    6. Expression.
    7. Sight reading.
    8. Range.

DAILY PRACTICE "HOW'S" FOR BEGINNERS

A. Find a definite *place* to practice daily.
B. Find a definite *time* to practice daily. Set aside two special fifteen-minute times each day' for practice, and use these times regularly!
C. Practice thirty minutes or more daily six days a week.
D. The Big "4" Correct Habits to watch daily:
   1. Correct embouchure — use mirror.
   2. Correct position.
   3. Correct posture.
   4. Pleasing sound.
E. Use the following routine *twice* daily for your practice:
   1. 1 minute daily on breathing exercises: 1. Hand on stomach while filling up for 4 to 8 counts; then hold 4 to 8 counts, hiss out all air, using stomach pressure. Repeat 3 times! 2. Hands behind head exercise — take quick breath ("hup"), hold, think and aim; let air out in form of embouchure. Repeat 3 times, using more air each time. 3. Walking exercise — 6 steps in, 6 holding, 6 out, 6 not breathing. Repeat 3 times and increase steps. Put hand on stomach often to check breathing.

      Think of stomach pressure as "grunting." Think of filling stomach as if it were a balloon, etc. Swimming under water also helps to build breath control.

   2. ½ minute daily on mouthpiece and mirror exercises. Use mirror often to watch for correct embouchure. Use steady stream of air and try for your best, pleasing sound. (Brass: buzz lips first, then buzz mouthpiece.)
   3. ½ minute daily on correct assembly. Be very careful.
   4. ½ minute daily to check correct position (hands, fingers, elbows, lips, cheeks, chin, etc.). (Reeds: check reed placement on mouthpiece.)
   5. ½ minute daily to check correct posture. Sit up, feet on floor, left foot slightly forward, sit tall.
   6. ½ minute daily asking yourself these questions *before* each exercise:
      a. What are the note names? (Name each note.)
      b. What are the fingerings? (Name each fingering and put fingers down.)
      c. Can I sing the exercise? (Sing the exercise.)
      d. How many counts in each measure? (Go through and count aloud and tap feet.)
      e. Play exercise several times — each time faster, but always good sound, not just speed.
   7. 10 minutes daily on assigned exercises. Practice slowly — for perfection.
   8. ½ minute daily asking yourself these questions *after* each exercise:
      a. Is my embouchure correct?
      b. Am I holding my instrument properly?
      c. Is my posture correct?
      d. Is my tone pleasing?
      e. Do the notes really sound right?
      f. Are my fingerings correct?
      g. Is my counting steady and even?
      h. Am I playing evenly?
      i. Am I breathing correctly?
   9. ½ minute daily always rest in between exercises and ask yourself the questions in No. 6 before exercises and No. 8 after exercises.
   10. ½ minute — using a red pencil, mark in counting for assigned exercise.

Total: 15 minutes (Do twice daily.)

UNISON SCALES FOR BAND

DIRECTIONS:

1. Find the name of the scale (concert pitch) in column 1.
2. Follow that line to the right until you come to the column for your instrument; this is your *transposed key.*
3. Find that note back in the first column and play the notes of the scale from left to right to go up the scale, and from right to left to go down the scale.
4. Chromatic scales beginning on C, E♭, F, A♭ or B♭ may be played by finding the starting notes as in steps 1 and 2, then play from the top to the bottom of the column to go down the chromatic scale one octave, or from the bottom to the top to go up the chromatic scale one octave.

C and Bass Clef Instruments	B♭ Instr.			F Instr.	E♭ Instr.	D♭ Instr.	Key Signatures
Scale Step 1	2	3	4	5	6	7	8
B♭	C	D	E♭	F	G	A	B♭ 2♭'s
A	B	C♯	D	E	F♯	G♯	A 3♯'s
A♭	B♭	C	D♭	E♭	F	G	A♭ 4♭'s
G	A	B	C	D	E	F♯	G 1♯
G♭	A♭	B♭	C♭	D♭	E♭	F	G♭ 6♭'s
F	G	A	B♭	C	D	E	F 1♭
E	F♯	G♯	A	B	C♯	D♯	E 4♯'s
E♭	F	G	A♭	B♭	C	D	E♭ 3♭'s
D	E	F♯	G	A	B	C♯	D 2♯'s
D♭	E♭	F	G♭	A♭	B♭	C	D♭ 5♭'s
C	D	E	F	G	A	B	C 0♭'s or ♯'s
B	C♯	D♯	E	F♯	G♯	A♯	B 5♯'s
B♭	C	D	E♭	F	G	A	B♭ 2♭'s

255

GOOD SIGHT READING HABITS

1. Music is passed out. Band members place it face down on the music stand.
2. Conductor studies score for a few minutes.
3. Signal is given for players to turn the music over and examine it (sight read).
4. Conductor takes a few minutes to explain the music to the players.
5. The band plays the new music "at sight" (it has been "sight read" in No. 3).

Suggestions:

1. Players must not talk to one another while reading. Each player must be trained to "stand on his own feet."
2. Note all the markings and tempo indications.
3. Think about the style of the music.
4. Discuss tonality, rhythm, etc.
5. Rehearse each new piece of music this way.

Good Readers do two things:
1. They read ahead.
2. They memorize the patterns of sound they have just read.

Practical requirements for developing good "sight reading" ability:
1. Recognize and understand key signatures.
2. Recognize and understand meter or time signatures.
3. Recognize the sound of notes by their position in relation to the staff. Be able to hear intervals accurately, and know the fingerings for all notes.
4. Recognize and understand note values, and be able to relate these to note groupings and rhythmic patterns.
5. Recognize and understand the rhythmic implication in articulations, staccatos, slurred groupings, and so on.
6. Recognize and understand the words and symbols by which tempo and dynamics are given.
7. Recognize and understand the words by which expression is indicated.
8. Have an understanding of the basic theory of music.

Physical requirements for developing good "sight reading" ability:
1. The ability to play in tune and with good tone quality over the entire range of the instrument.
2. The ability to count time accurately and incisively, and to beat time correctly.
3. The ability to control the tone and play with expression.
4. The ability to control breathing and make phrasing intelligible.
5. The ability to control tonguing and master the basic articulations.
6. A thorough knowledge of fingerings and alternate fingerings.
7. The ability to maintain adequate speed.

Practice to retain pitches:
1. Sing or play a single tone, talk for a short while, then ask band to sing the tone.
   a. At first use a three-minute talk, and with a little practice, try to stretch the elapsed time to an hour, then two hours, and even a full day! Practice listening!

DAILY WARM-UP TIPS & TECHNICS

I. Warm-up.
   This part of your daily playing is the *most important* part, therefore, use it with great care.
   Big "4" Don'ts for Proper Warm-up:
   1. Don't play high.
   2. Don't play low.
   3. Don't play loud.
   4. Don't play soft.

Play in your middle register, mezzo-forte, and gradually extend the register and dynamic level as your lips and embouchure begin to respond with agility and flexibility.

II. Techniques.

Strive to master all phases of your instrument, not just one part. Work for progress and results.
Big "4" Techniques to Cover Daily:

1. Breath.
2. Tongue.
3. Lip.
4. Fingers.

Each day: attempt to strengthen your breathing technique and gain better control; attempt to strengthen your tonguing muscles to gain control, evenness, and speed (in this order — never speed first); attempt to strengthen your lip muscles to gain endurance in your playing (long tones are good); attempt to strengthen your finger muscles for better dexterity and control.

III. Other Phases to Cover as Needed.

1. Range — brasses especially.
2. Hi-Tone Exercise (clarinets).
3. Scales.
4. Intervals.
5. Lip slurs.
6. Chords (broken arpeggios).
7. Triple tonguing.
8. Double tonguing.
9. Single tonguing.
10. Flexibility exercises.
11. Long tones.

NOTES TO CONTEST SOLOISTS AND ENSEMBLES

1. Get your piano accompanist early and practice together often.
2. Time your solo (3½ to 4 minutes, no more).
3. Practice (How you practice the solo is very important):
   a. Practice standing — (except French horns, bass clarinets, bassoons, etc.). Trumpets especially — stand up and hold horns up. (Elbows out slightly.)
   b. First work out the passages that prove difficult for you. Go over these passages until they can be played ten times perfectly.
   c. Always breathe in the same places. Mark them in pencil.
   d. After you have worked out all the hard spots in your solo, play the entire solo from the beginning *once* with no stops.
   e. Now put the solo away for the day, but remember the places you had trouble with, and practice these spots the next day.
4. Know your solo inside and out: Work out all technical difficulties in advance of the contest.
5. Memorize your solo: You'll play much better if you don't depend on music.
6. Tone: Constantly work for a better tone. Watch your intonation at all times. Strive for good tone and for better quality at all times.
7. Phrases: Be sure your solo is played with good musical phrasing. You will need good breath control for this.
8. Interpretation: Give the solo some meaning for yourself as well as for the listener. Watch the tempo, rhythm, and overall expression of the solo. Let the listener be able to say, "That soloist said something to me with his music."
9. Music, not notes: Be sure you do not present a solo of notes, but rather a *musical* composition. Say something musically. Practice your solo for its music, not just the notes.
10. Technique: Work on accuracy, good phrasing, and on all the special instrumental techniques of your solo.
11. Ten Times Through Perfectly: then it is ready for the contest or public.
12. Tune-up: Do this slowly; take lots of time. Flutes tune-up to B♭ concert and C concert; clarinets and all others to B♭ and F concert.

13. Have confidence in yourself and your solo. Play with authority.
14. Appearance: Stand tall, erect; have confidence; relax and play to the best of your ability. Hold your instrument properly.
15. Announce your solo (title and composer). This will aid in relaxing you.
16. Nervous? Try biting your tongue lightly, and take big, deep breaths.
17. Musicianship: This comes from experience and years, but think about it at all times.
18. Ratings: Remember, not everyone will get a "A" rating. Go into the contest with the thought of obtaining a musical experience, some constructive criticism, and valuable information in furthering your musical education.

GOOD LUCK!!

SOME MUSICAL TERMS AND SYMBOLS

1. *f* (forte) — loud
2. *p* (piano) — soft
3. *mf* (mezzo-forte) — medium loud
4. *ff* (fortissimo) — very loud
5. *pp* (pianissimo) — very soft
6. *fp* (forte-piano) — start loud, then get soft immediately
7. *fz* (forzando) — forcefully accented
8. Moderato — moderate tempo, moderately
9. Andante — moderately slow, smooth flowing, in a walking tempo
10. Allegretto — moderately fast (faster than Andante, but slower than Allegro)
11. Allegro — lively, brisk, rapid
12. Presto — very fast
13. Maestoso — majestically; with dignity
14. Largo — very slow; slow and solemn; broad
15. Lento — very slow (between Andante and Largo)
16. ♩ stacc. (staccato) — separated; disconnected; short note, but tone must still be present
17. rit. (ritard.) — gradually slower
18. accel. (accelerando) — gradually faster
19. D.C. al Fine (Da Capo) — from the beginning, to the Fine
20. D.S. al Fine (Dal Segno) — from the sign (𝄋), to the Fine
21. ♩♩♩♩ (tenuto) — sustain notes full value; broad
22. March tempo — in the tempo of a march
23. tutti — for all; for all the instruments
24. a tempo — resume original speed (as after rit. or accel.)
25. ✕. — repeat the preceding measure
26. // — pause
27. M.M. — Maelzel's Metronome; indicates the number of beats per minute (Ex. ♩ =120)
28. cresc. (crescendo) — gradually louder
29. decresc. (descrescendo) — gradually softer
30. dim. (diminuendo) — gradually softer
31. morendo — dying away
32. allarg. (allargando) — gradually slower and broader
33. rall. (rallentando) — gradually slower
34. rall. e dim. — gradually slower and softer
35. più mosso — more motion, faster
36. meno mosso — less motion, slower
37. marc. (marcato) — marked with emphasis; accented
38. dolce — sweetly; song-like
39. molto — very; much
40. subito — immediately; instantly; suddenly
41. simile — the same; continue in like manner
42. poco a poco — little by little
43. sempre — always; continually
44. divisi — divided; performers on each part
45. tacet — silent
46. ◁ (crescendo) — gradually louder
47. ▷ (decrescendo) — gradually softer
48. > — accent mark; accent, or stress the tone
49. ⌢ — fermata, hold or pause; watch director
50. ♩♩♩ — legato; smooth and connected; no break between tones

259

YOUR MUSICIANSHIP

A Manual for Junior High School Instrumentalists

Hubert Olson Junior High School
Bloomington, Minnesota

In order to be adequately prepared to perform the finest in instrumental literature, it is essential that each member of an instrumental organization know and understand the basics of musicianship. It is for this reason that this brief booklet has been prepared. Herein you will find a list of commonly used terms. It is your task to learn and to implement them in your playing.

A fine instrumental organization is made up of fine musicians. In order to secure the confidence and rewards that come with fine musicianship, you, as an instrumentalist, must strive to do your very best and to always put out 100%. Your directors will meet you halfway.

If you have any questions concerning these materials, your directors will be most happy to explain in detail those items which may puzzle you.

You are expected to *know* the facts and suggestions contained in this booklet. We will go on *from this point* in daily rehearsals.

YOUR MUSICIANSHIP

Your musicianship can develop only through unrelenting effort. No doubt you have heard the axiom "Practice Makes Perfect." That says a lot, and in very simple terms; but it has quite an important loophole. You see, practice makes perfect only when the practice itself is perfect. Repetition means progress only if it is a repetition of the correct principles. For example, you might sow a thousand grass seeds, but you won't grow one blade of grass unless the seeds have been sown properly. It is for this reason that we need to know how, what, and why to practice. Careful study of this outline should give you a clear picture of how to develop your musicianship.

HOW TO PRACTICE

Select a time of day that will be as free as possible from interruptions, and try to use this same time every day — "rain or shine."

Choose a place where you will be as free as possible from distractions that may be caused by improper temperatures, poor light, or noises.

Have your objectives well in mind. (Just what do you hope to accomplish during the practice period?)

Criticize yourself more severely than others would dare to criticize you! The criticism should be based on the objectives listed below.

Make sure your posture is correct. Unless your instrument makes it impossible, stand up often to practice. Play in front of a mirror occasionally.

Isolate troublesome passages and work on them. Reduce the tempo until all elements have been mastered; then gradually increase the speed, keeping all elements under control, until you have reached the desired excellence of performance.

Above all, be patient.

Objectives:

1. Correct breathing.
2. Tone.
3. Intonation.
4. Reading ability and technique.
5. Articulation.
6. Rhythm.
7. Phrasing.

ANALYSIS OF OBJECTIVES

1. Correct Breathing. To breathe properly while playing an instrument, only the diaphragm area should move — not the chest or the shoulders. The air must come directly from the diaphragm, through the mouth, and into the mouthpiece. The throat must not stop or start any tone, but rather, must remain open. Blow as if you were blowing out a candle or singing the syllable "ah."

Ration your air supply; make the least amount of air produce the biggest possible tone. Do not use up all air on the attack — you will need an ample amount for a proper release. Think of breath support like a pitcher filled with water: As long as there is sufficient water behind the escaping water, you have a healthy stream. Thus, as long as there is sufficient air behind the escaping air, you have a healthy tone.

2. Tone. Fine tone quality may be achieved through the diligent practice of sustained tones. There is a great deal of beauty in a single tone. Sing it out softly as well as loudly; don't ever hold it at one stagnant dynamic level.

In order to be able to concentrate on the sound you produce, it is better not to use music, but rather, to invent your own tone exercises. For example, play each note on your instrument as a separate tone study, or slur scales as slowly as possible within one breath in an attempt to achieve evenness of quality throughout the range of the instrument. Other possibilities include sustained octave jumps or other interval skips and playing slow melodic passages while listening carefully.

The more you can perceive in the expression of one tone, the more musically mature you are. Think of every tone as consisting of "Attack — Body — Release." Attack and release are the consonants; they define the tone. The body is the vowel — the life of the tone. This is where you project yourself. Remember, there is no tone without life-giving energy.

3. Intonation. There are two general pitch problem-areas.
   a. Attacking the note in tune.
   b. Maintaining the correct pitch while the note is sounding.

Overcoming the first problem may require work with the Strobotuner to learn the particular pitch problems of the instrument. The ability to make the necessary fingering and/or lip adjustments and proper breath support are also important in correcting faulty intonation.

The second problem may be remedied by sustaining notes in the following manner:

concentrating to keep the pitch level constant. A common fault is the tendency to be sharp while playing softly and flat while playing loudly. An exception to this is the flute which is very easily sharped by overblowing, especially in the upper register.

Unfortunately, there is no simple solution to the pitch problem, especially when considering temperature and fatigue as factors. The ear is the final judge. You must always listen carefully to yourself and everyone around you, and work relentlessly to develop naturalness, consistency, and correctness of embouchure (facial muscles, lips, and tongue).

Factors Important to Tone and Intonation

Each student must learn to rely upon his own ears and not those of the director. He must become "tone-and-intonation-conscious."
   – Correct posture, hand position, and head position have a decided and direct effect upon tone and intonation. An alert body is directly associated with an alert mind and a vital sound.
   – It is impossible to accomplish anything on brass instruments unless the instruments are held properly.

– Carelessness is the biggest single impediment to the development of musicianship. You *must* learn to be the strongest critic of your own playing.

– In general, students should learn to play with full, healthy tone quality before attempting to play pianissimo; but, of course, one should never confuse full and round with loud and rough.

4. Reading Ability and Technique. Being able to read easily through a large variety of music is a very important aspect of your musical growth. To develop this phase of musicianship, use a portion of your daily practice session to just read through technical and soloistic passages, introducing new materials to yourself every few days.

Whereas reading ability is developed by constantly playing new material without necessarily mastering it, technique is developed by persistently practicing difficult passages and exercises (such as scales and arpeggios) until they *are* mastered.

Becoming an excellent technician with very little reading ability is a serious problem of too many young musicians. Technique and reading ability must develop hand in hand. A solo and ensemble festival defeats its purpose for an individual if he works on his solo or ensemble to the complete exclusion of all other material. Unfortunately, this is too often the case, when it would be so simple to avoid by continuing to spend a little time reading through new marterial during each practice session.

5. Articulation. Articulation concerns the use of the tongue. There are two basic tonguing styles — legato and staccato. The legato tongue employs a very smooth attack which allows no space between succeeding tones, whereas the staccato attack is short and necessitates space between succeeding tones. Of course there are countless degrees in between.

Several syllables which can be used to achieve a legato attack are "tu", "du", "lu", and "la." With these syllables the tongue remains suspended after the attack so the tone may "sing." Syllables used to achieve a staccato attack are "taht" or "toot." With these syllables the consonant "t" is used to start and stop the tone instantly, as the word staccato phonetically suggests. Woodwind instruments should learn staccato first with diaphragm "spurts," without stopping the tone with the tongue (leave "t" off end of syllable), then later, develop the tongue-stopped tone. Both are needed. Brasses, however, should almost never stop the tone with the tongue. Theirs should always be a diaphragm release.

Two ways to practice tonguing are: 1. Repetition of a single note; 2. Coordination of the tongue and fingers on scale passages and different exercises. Use different degrees of both legato and staccato styles of tonguing in your practice. Work for clarity. Strive for pitch defintion — not just a percussive attack. Work for uniformity of attack in volume, pitch, and duration.

6. Rhythm. One of the biggest problems in sight reading is rhythmic accuracy. A simple way to improve this is to write out a rhythmic pattern and use it on every note of a scale. (Change scale and pattern weekly.) Consultation with your director is especially desirable here, and, of course, necessary to further any of the objectives. An example follows:

Simultaneously clap the given rhythm and recite the necessary subdivided counts, while tapping the foot in the basic meter.

Play the pattern on the same or different note of a scale in a variety of ways: *mf* — staccato; *mf* — legato; *pp* — staccato, etc.

(A metronome is very valuable, especially for individual home practice.)

262

7. Phrasing. Technically, a phrase is a division of a melody or line, generally four to eight measures in length and often indicated by a long, curved line over it. Phrasing, however, has the added meaning of expressing your particular melody or part in context with the character of the composition and the mood and spirit which it reveals.

A phrase must grow in warmth, intensity, and beauty just as a flower blooms. One must always be conscious of direction: Are you moving toward the top of the arch or away from it? Do not forget there are many smaller arches within the larger one.

Is the composer trying to set a joyous or a sad mood, a vigorous or a solemn mood? Is the melody or accompaniment to be tender or cruel, light or heavy, flowing or rhythmic? Just like a sentence it has its downward and upward, its forward and backward flow. It has its antecedents and its consequents, its questions and its answers. Everything is there for the imaginative mind of a musician to discover. This is the part of music that requires the surrender of the heart and the soul. This is the part of music that allows us to enter into another world — the world of musical expression. Remember, the notes on the printed page mean absolutely nothing until someone brings them to life through performance. As Mr. Machlis, Professor of Music, Queens College, New York, stated, "The more complete our surrender to the work of art, the more deeply we penetrate to its essence — and the greater our gain."

GENERAL COMMENT

If you are not sure you are tonguing correctly or working correctly on any other objective, do not hesitate to consult your director.

Every effort you put forth to raise your standard of musical achievement should make you personally proud. With sincere and meaningful effort on your part you will find music to be a field of limitless rewards, a path into a way of life, and the epitome of all that is good. It was Plato, one of history's greatest philosophers, who said, "Music is a moral law. It gives soul to the universe; wings to the mind; flight to the imagination; a charm to sadness; gaiety and life to everything else. It is the essence of order and leads to all that is good, just, and beautiful — of which it is the invisible, yet dazzling, passionate and external form."

The main task before you as young musicians is to understand the described objectives and challenge yourself to develop and think about them, both singularly and as a unified whole representing your musicianship.

MUSICAL TERMS

accelerando (accel.) — gradually faster
Adagietto — slow, but not as slow as Adagio
Adagio — very slow
agitato — agitated; rapid
al Fine — to the finish
alla — in the style of
allargando (allarg.) — gradually slower and broader
Allegretto — light and moderately quick, but not as fast as Allegro
Allegro — rapid; lively
Andante — moderately slow, but moving
Andantino — a little faster than Andante
animato — spirited
appassionato — intensely; passionately; with deep feeling
arioso — in vocal style (see also Cantabile)
assai — very
a tempo — in time; generally implies a return to original rate of speed

263

ben — well (such as ben marcato - well marked)
brillante — brilliantly
calando — gradually slower and softer
Cantabile — in a singing style
chromatic — by semi-tones
coda — the final added measures of a musical composition
con amore — with tenderness
con anima — with animation
con brio — with spirit
con fuoco — with energy
con grazia — with grace
con spirito — with spirit
crescendo — gradually louder
Da Capo — from the beginning
Dal Segno (D.S.) — from the sign
diminuendo (dim.) — gradually softer
dolce — sweetly
energico — energetically
etude — a study
fermata — a hold or pause
forte (f) — loud
fortissimo (ff) — very loud
forza — force
forzando — forcefully accented
furioso — furiously
giocoso — joyfully
grandioso — grand or noble style
Grave — very slow and solemn
Grazioso — gracefully
Larghetto — slow, but not as slow as Largo
Larghissimo — very slow; slower than Largo
Largo — very slow
legato — smooth and connected
leggiero — lightly
Lento — very slow
L'istesso — the same
Maestoso — majestically
marcato — marked; with emphasis
marcia — march style
marziale — martial
meno — less
mezzo — medium; half
Moderato — moderately
molto — very
morendo — dying away
mosso — motion; movement
moto — motion; movement
non troppo — not too much
opus — a musical work or composition
ottava ($8va$) — an octave
pesante — heavily; with emphasis
pianissimo (pp) — very softly
piano (p) — softly
più — more
poco — little

poco a poco — little by little
Prestissimo — very fast; faster than Presto
Presto — very fast
Primo — first
rallentando (rall.) — gradually slower
religioso — in solemn style
ritardando (rit.) — gradually slower
ritenuto — gradually slower
rubato — lengthening of certain beats at expense of others
Scherzo — playfully; usually in rapid tempo, with rhythmic and dynamic contrasts
Scherzando — in light, playful style
segno — the sign
sempre — always; continually
senza — without
sforzando (*sfz*) — forced; with emphasis
simile — the same
smorzando — dying away
soli — a group of solo performers
solo — a composition or passage for one performer
sordino — mute
sostenuto — sustained
staccato — separated, detached
stringendo — gradually faster
subito — suddenly
tacet — silent
tempo — time, speed
Tempo di Valse — waltz time
tenuto (ten.) — sustain full value
un poco — gradually
valse — waltz
Veloce — very fast
Vivace — vivacious; lively
vivo — lively; brisk

TEMPO MARKINGS

Generally very slow to slow	**Generally medium**	**Generally fast to very fast**
Larghissimo	Andante	Allegretto
Largo	Andantino	Allegro
Larghetto	Moderato	Vivace
Grave		Veloce
Lento		Presto
Adagio		Prestissimo
Adagietto		

BAND INSTRUMENT TRANSPOSITIONS

Concert Pitch		C	F	G	B♭	D	E♭	A	A♭	E	D♭	B	C♯
C Instr.	Written Pitch	C	F	G	B♭	D	E♭	A	A♭	E	D♭	B	C♯
B♭ Instr.		D	G	A	C	E	F	B	B♭	F♯	E♭	C♯	D♯
F Instr.		G	C	D	F	A	B♭	E	E♭	B	A♭	F♯	G♯
E♭ Instr.		A♭	D	E	G	B	C	F♯	F	C♯	B♭	G♯	A♯

BROOKLYN CENTER HIGH SCHOOL – Minneapolis, Minnesota
CONCERT BAND QUIZ No. 1
(Seniors—all questions; Juniors –just *; Sophs.–just #;
Bonus points for answering questions correctly outside your class)

I. MUSICAL TERMS:
   #*1. Allegro – _____
   *2. Andante – _____
   3. articulation – _____

II. MUSIC HISTORY:
   #*4. What are the approximate dates for the Baroque period? _____
   *5. Name two major composers of the Baroque period: _____
   6. Describe the style of the music of the Baroque period: _____

III. MUSIC THEORY, HARMONY, MELODIC & RHYTHMIC DICTATION:
   #*7. Fill in the proper answer: Treble or ____clef; Bass or ____clef.
   *8. Another type of clef, movable, is the ____clef.
   9. The combination of treble and bass clefs, as in piano music, is the _____
   #*10. A dot after a note indicates what? _____
   #*11. Explain the numbers in a time signature: _____
   #*12. Music is an art whose chief property is (volume, sound, melody). (Underline 1)
   *13. One definition of music is that it is the art of expression in _____
   *14. Four elements of music are melody, harmony, _____ , and _____
   15. Another word for tone color is (intonation, embouchure, timbre). (Underline 1)
   *16. What is musical notation? _____
   *17. The study of musical notation can help develop the ability to hear in our minds what we see on the music staff. This study is called music (theory, harmony, composition). (Underline 1)
   #*18. Melodic dictation:

   #*19. Rhythmic dictation:

IV. RECORD RECOGNITION: title   composer   period
   #*20. _____   _____   _____
   #*21. _____   _____   _____
   #*22. _____   _____   _____
   #*23. (Unknown) _____   _____   _____

V. RHYTHM:
   #*24. Write in the counting:

266

VI. COMPOSERS:

#*25. Name the composer of "Suite in Minor Mode": _____

#*26. He originally wrote this piece for the _____

#*27. Explain the main words of the title — suite, minor and mode: _____

_____

#*28. Explain the difference between a transcription and an arrangement: _____

_____

VII. MUSICIANSHIP:

#*29. Describe the style of a march: _____

VIII. AESTHETICS-PHILOSOPHY:

#*30. Why does an arrangement of a pop tune sound different and often inferior to the original?

_____

DRUMS: Write out the following rudiments: 5—stroke roll _____ Flam _____

CONCERT BAND QUIZ NO. 2
(Seniors—all questions; Jrs.—just *; Sophs.—just #;
Bonus points for answering questions correctly outside your class)

I. MUSICAL TERMS:

#*1. cantabile — _____

*2. D.C. — _____

3. con brio — _____

II. MUSIC HISTORY:

#*4. The concerto grosso was a major form of composition in what period? _____

*5. In the concerto grosso, what is the group of soloists called? _____

6. In the concerto grosso, what is the accompanying group called? _____

#*7. Briefly explain the form studied so far in the Music 300 series: _____

_____

III. MUSIC THEORY, HARMONY, MELODIC & RHYTHMIC DICTATION:

#*8. The highness or lowness of a sound refers to the _____ of a sound.

#*9. The loudness or softness of a sound is known as _____ .

#*10. The quality of sound is known as _____ .

#*11. Explain the following sound terms: fundamental; partials; overtones; natural harmonic series:

_____

*12. The four basic elements of music are: _____ , _____ , _____ , _____ .

*13. Rhythm has three factors — meter, duration, and tempo. Explain meter: _____

_____

*14. Explain duration as applied to rhythm: _____

*15. Explain tempo: _____

*16. Explain metronomic markings: _____

*17. Explain simple and compound meter: _____

*18. Explain duple and triple meter: _____

*19. 6/8 meter is: (simple duple, compound duple, simple triple, compound triple) meter. (Underline one)

#*20. Melodic dictation:

267

#*21. Rhythmic dictation:

$\frac{6}{8}$ | ———————————————————————————— ||

IV. RECORD RECOGNITION: title   composer   period

#*22. _____   _____   _____

#*23. _____   _____   _____

#*24. _____   _____   _____

#*25. (Unknown-pick period & composer)   _____

V. RHYTHM:

#*26. Write in the counting:

VI. COMPOSERS:

#*27. Name the composer of the "Water Music": _____

#*28. What form is this piece of music? _____

#*29. What event and/or person caused the composition to be written? _____

_____

#*30. Name another famous Bach family composer in addition to Johann Sebastian: _____

VII. MUSICIANSHIP:

#*31. Explain polyphonic, homophonic, and monophonic: _____

VIII. AESTHETICS-PHILOSOPHY:

#*32. What are the advantages and disadvantages of arranging a "pop" tune for the band?_____

_____

DRUMS ONLY: Write out these rolls: 7-stroke _____ 9-stroke _____

CONCERT BAND QUIZ NO. 3
(Seniors—all questions; Jrs.—just *; Sophs.—just #;
Bonus points for answering questions correctly outside your class)

I. MUSICAL TERMS:

#*1. dolce — _____

*2. fermata — _____

3. giusto — _____

II. MUSIC HISTORY:

#*4. What period features the following: terrace dynamics; ornamental, driving rhythms; figured bass; concerto grosso?_____

*5. From what period is *Marriage of Figaro* by Mozart? _____

6. Describe the style of the music of the Classical period: _____

_____

III. MUSIC THEORY, HARMONY, MELODIC & RHYTHMIC DICTATION:

#*7. The four basic elements of music are: _____ , _____ , _____ , _____ .

*8. Meter is another name for _____ signature.

9. The active tones of a scale are numbers _____

10. The movement from an active tone to a rest tone is called _____ .

#*11. The lowest partial is called the _____ .

#*12. Most sounds, instead of being a single tone, are composed of many pitches called _____ .

#*13. Overtones are _____

#*14. The natural harmonic series is _____ .

#*15. Timbre is the result of the number and intensity of _____ .

#*16. The four properties of sound are _____ , _____ , _____ , _____ .

*17. Meter is divided into two categories: _____ and _____ .

*18. Give an example of compound duple meter: _____

#*19. Melodic dictation:

#*20. Rhythmic dictation:

IV. RECORD RECOGNITION:

	title	composer	period
#*21.			
#*22.			
#*23.			

#*24. (Unknown-pick period & composer) _____

#*25. Which record (heard this month) is your favorite and why? _____

#*26. Which composition rehearsed this month did you like best and why? _____

V. RHYTHM:

#*27. Write in the counting: _____

VI. COMPOSERS:

#*28. Name the composer of "Clair de Lune". _____

VII. MUSICIANSHIP:

#*29. Define musicianship: _____

VIII. AESTHETICS-PHILOSOPHY:

#*30. Briefly describe your musical learnings during each year in concert band, grades 9 through 12: _____

_____

_____

DRUMS ONLY: What stroke is used exclusively on the timpani? _____

CONCERT BAND QUIZ NO. 4
(Seniors—all questions; Jrs.—just *; Sophs.—just #;
Bonus points for answering questions correctly outside your class)

I. MUSICAL TERMS:
#*1. legato — _____

*2. L'istesso — _____

3. marcato — _____

II. MUSIC HISTORY:
#*4. What period features these qualities?: delicate, light, precise, beauty, proportion? _____
_____

*5. From what period is the "Water Music Suite"? _____

6. Describe the style of the Baroque period: _____
_____

III. MUSIC THEORY, HARMONY, MELODIC & RHYTHMIC DICTATION:
#*7. An _____ is the distance between two notes.

*8. If a major interval is flatted it becomes a _____ interval; when the upper tone of a perfect interval is flatted it becomes _____, and sharping the upper tone of a perfect interval makes it_____ .

9. Consonance is _____ and dissonance is _____,_____.

#*10. Identify the following intervals using the full interval name:

*11. What kind of note is ◻ ? _____

*12. The tonic is the _____ and the dominant is the _____ note of a scale.

#*13. 9/8 is a _____ meter.

#*14. ¢ is called cut time or _____ and is the same as (2/4, 2/2).

*15. Circle the primary and secondary beats or accents:

#*16. The _____ is the smallest interval in the tonal system of most music in the U.S.

#*17. Musical tones occurring in a stepwise sequence, unaffected by accidentals, can also be called (polyphony, diatonic). _____

#*18. The tone E to the closest F is an interval of _____ ; A to B is a _____; B to C is a _____ .

#*19. The half steps in major scales are _____ and _____ .

#*20. The signs ♯, ♭, ♮, 𝄪, ♭♭ as a group are called _____ .

*21. Two notes which look different, have different names, but sound the same are _____ .

#*22. Melodic dictation:

#*23. Rhythmic dictation:

IV. RECORD RECOGNITION: title   composer   period

#*24. _____ _____ _____
#*25. _____ _____ _____
#*26. _____ _____ _____
#*27. (Unknown-pick period & composer) _____
#*28. Which record heard this month is your favorite & why?_____
#*29. Which composition rehearsed this month did you like best & why?_____
_____

V. RHYTHM:

#*30. Write in the counting:

VI. COMPOSERS:

#*31. Name the composers: "Water Music" — _____ ; *Marriage of Figaro* — _____

VII. MUSICIANSHIP:

#*32. What trait stands out in "good" musicians? _____

VIII. AESTHETICS-PHILOSOPHY:

#*33. Briefly explain why it is possible or impossible to be a good musician without being a per-
former: _____
_____

DRUMS ONLY: Of what value are mallet instruments to the band?

CONCERT BAND QUIZ NO. 5
(Srs.—all questions; Jrs.—just *; Sophs.—just #;
Bonus points for answering questions correctly outside your class)

I. MUSICAL TERMS:

#*1. rit. — _____
*2. sostenuto — _____
3. poco più mosso — _____

II. MUSIC HISTORY:

#*4. What problems will a band encounter in performing an orchestral transcription from the
Classical period? _____
_____

III. MUSIC THEORY, HARMONY, MELODIC & RHYTHMIC DICTATION:

#*5. Pitch, intensity (dynamics), timbre, duration are properties of _____ .

#*6. M.M. stands for _____ .

*7. Explain ♩ = 96 _____

*8. Three different tones form a _____ .

*9. Four different tones form a _____ .

*10. The lowest note of a triad is called its _____ .

11. The chords built on the first and fifth tones of a scale are called the _____ and respectively.

#*12. Melodic dictation:

#*13. Rhythmic dictation:

#*14. Explain sonata-allegro form: _____
_____

IV. RECORD RECOGNITION: title   composer   period

#*15. _____ _____ _____

#*16. _____ _____ _____

#*17. _____ _____ _____

#*18. (Unknown) _____ _____

#*19. Which record heard this month is your favorite & why? _____
_____

#*20. Which composition rehearsed this month was your favorite & why? _____
_____

V. RHYTHM:

#*21. Write in the counting:

VI. COMPOSERS:

#*22. Name the composer of the "Water Music Suite": _____

VII. MUSICIANSHIP:

#*23. What type of music seems to bring out your musicianship the most? _____

VIII. AESTHETICS-PHILOSOPHY:

#*24. How do you maintain enthusiasm for a piece of music when you know the goal of perfection is impossible? _____
_____
_____
_____

DRUMS ONLY: How do you solve a rushing or dragging problem? _____

CONCERT BAND QUIZ NO. 6

(Srs.—all questions; Jrs.—*only; Sophs. — # only; Bonus points if you do more)

I. MUSICAL TERMS:
  #*1. marcato — _____
   *2. Scherzo — _____
    3. Vivace — _____

II. MUSIC HISTORY:
  #*4. Briefly explain the style of the Baroque period: _____
  _____

   *5. Briefly explain the style of the Classical period: _____
  _____

    6. Name two composers of the Romantic period: _____
  _____

  #*7. What composer bridged the Classical & Romantic periods?: _____
  #*8. Briefly explain the development of your instrument during the 18th century: _____
  _____

III. MUSIC THEORY, HARMONY, & MELODIC-RHYTHMIC DICTATION:
  #*9. The triad built on the first note of a scale is called _____ .
  *10. The lowest note of a triad is called its _____ .
   11. A chord of four different tones is called a _____ .
  *12. Explain closed chord position: _____
  *13-14. Analyze and harmonize: _____

I V I I   IV V I

  #*15. Melodic dictation:

  #*16. Rhythmic dictation:

IV. RECORD RECOGNITION: title   composer   period

    #*17. _____ _____ _____

    #*18. _____ _____ _____

    #*19. _____ _____ _____

    #*20. _____ _____ _____

V. RHYTHM:

    #*21. Write in the counting:

VI. COMPOSERS:

    #*22. Name the composer of Symphony No. 9 ("New World"): _____

VII. MUSICIANSHIP:

    #*23. Explain the value of solfege to performance: _____

VIII. AESTHETICS-PHILOSOPHY:

    #*24. What value does the concert band have in today's society? _____

DRUMS ONLY: How can a drummer get more involved musically? _____

CONCERT BAND QUIZ NO. 7
(Srs.—all; Jrs.—* only; Sophs.—# only; Bonus points if you do more)

I. MUSICAL TERMS:

    #*1. più mosso – _____

    *2. sostenuto – _____

    3. morendo – _____

II. MUSIC HISTORY:

    #*4. What period featured elaborate ornaments? _____

    *5. What period featured proportion, beauty? _____

    6. From what period are Stravinsky, Copland, & Bernstein? _____

    #*7. What two notes are flatted in a "blues" melody? _____

    #*8. Briefly explain the development of your instrument during the 19th century: _____

III. MUSIC THEORY, HARMONY, & MELODIC-RHYTHMIC DICTATION:

    #*9. Movement from an active tone to a rest tone is _____ .

    *10. The fifth note of a scale is called the _____ .

    11. The root of a chord is normally found in the _____ voice.

*12. List a short, normal chord progression: ___,___ , ___,___ .

*13. What note is most often doubled in a triad? _____

*14. Explain first inversion: _____

*15. Explain second inversion: _____

*16. The cadence V-I is called a _____ cadence.

*17. The cadence IV-I is called a _____ cadence.

#*18. Melodic dictation:

#*19. Rhythmic dictation:

#*20. Construct a major scale on the note B♮.

#*21. Identify the scales and chords played:

　　　a. _____ b. _____ c. _____ d. _____

IV. RECORD RECOGNITION:　　title　　　　　composer　　　　　period

　　#*22. _____　　_____　　_____

　　#*23. _____　　_____　　_____

　　#*24. _____　　_____　　_____

　　#*25. _____　　_____　　_____

V. RHYTHM:

　　#*26. Write in the counting:

VI. COMPOSERS:

　　#*27. Name the composer of "Psalm for Band": _____

VII. MUSICIANSHIP:

　　#*28. Explain the value of ensembles and recitals: _____
　　_____

VIII. AESTHETICS-PHILOSOPHY:

　　#*29. How can you become more intelligent listeners of music? _____
　　_____
　　_____

DRUMS ONLY: What is the lowest tone on each of our two timpani: _____ , _____ .

CONCERT BAND FINAL EXAM

I. TERMS: (Choose the phrase from the second column that best defines the term in the first column and put the letter of this answer in front of the number. Answers can only be used once.)

_____ 1. D.C.   a. sweetly, song-like
_____ 2. poco più mosso   b. marked, with emphasis
_____ 3. rit.   c. go back to the sign and play to Fine
_____ 4. dolce   d. go back to the beginning and play to Fine
_____ 5. allegro   e. gradually slow down
_____ 6. marcato   f. a little more motion
_____ 7. sostenuto   g. a little less motion
_____ 8. andante   h. fast, lively
_____ 9. crescendo   i. moderately slow, walking tempo
_____ 10. accel.   j. to sustain
   k. gradually get louder
   l. gradually get softer
   m. gradually get faster
   n. to detach

II. MUSIC HISTORY: (Matching directions as above.)

_____ 11. Baroque   a. 1830 to early 20th century
_____ 12. Classical   b. Today plus previous 60 years
_____ 13. Romantic   c. 1600-1750
_____ 14. Contemporary   d. 1750-1830

_____ 15. Baroque   a. Bach and Handel
_____ 16. Classical   b. Brahms and Beethoven
_____ 17. Romantic   c. Mozart and Haydn
_____ 18. Contemporary   d. Stravinsky and Schoenberg

_____ 19. Baroque   a. feelings and emotions
_____ 20. Classical   b. atonal, polytonal; polyrhythmical
_____ 21. Romantic   c. beauty and proportion
_____ 22. Contemporary   d. elaborate and ornamented

MUSIC 100 (Music History through audio-visual materials)
What word or words best complete the following?:

_____ 23. What kind of music is associated with the worship of the early church?
_____ 24. A very important early keyboard instrument was the
_____ 25. How many instrumental groups are used in a concerto grosso?
_____ 26. What musical instrument is particularly associated with J. S. Bach?
_____ 27. What form in music is especially associated with the music of Bach?
_____ 28. Handel was noted for what famous composition?
_____ 29. Haydn is credited with adding what movement to the symphony?
_____ 30. What instrument did Mozart introduce into the orchestra?
_____ 31. In one or two words, describe Mozart's melodies.
_____ 32. Name one special quality normally found in Beethoven's music?
_____ 33. What historical figure was a contemporary of Beethoven?
_____ 34. During what music history period did the following occur?: opera was established, the symphonic form was developed, the concerto was used extensively.
_____ 35. What musical form is especially associated with the name Rossini?
_____ 36. What is the correct name for a solo sung in an opera?

_____ 37. Who composed the Overture to "A Midsummer Night's Dream"?

_____ 38. What composer of the Romantic period wrote almost exclusively for piano?

_____ 39. Liszt is famous for having created the symphonic _____ .

_____ 40. Who composed "La Traviata"?

_____ 41. What composer called his operas music dramas?

_____ 42. Name the famous Russian composer of "1812 Overture" and "Marche Slave."

_____ 43. Name the famous Russian composer of "A Night on Bald Mountain" and "Coronation Scene" from _Boris Godunov._

_____ 44. Name the famous Bohemian composer of the "New World Symphony."

_____ 45. Name one of Ravel's most famous compositions.

_____ 46. Impressionism is the term applied to the music of what French composer?

_____ 47. Some principal ingredients in contemporary music are atonality, ostinato, and _____ .

_____ 48. What is atonality?

_____ 49. What is the Schoenberg system of composition called?

_____ 50. What was one of the main ingredients in Gershwin's music?

_____ 51. Name Gershwin's famous folk opera.

_____ 52. What contemporary Russian composer combined humor and moderate dissonance?

_____ 53. Name a famous Brazilian composer of the 20th century.

_____ 54. Name an American contemporary composers famous for "Rodeo."

_____ 55. "Rodeo" was written for what artistic form?

_____ 56. Varese, Cage, Stockhausen are famous composers of what type of music?

HISTORY OF INSTRUMENT:

_____ 57. Briefly describe the history of your instrument from its very beginning to the present:

_____

_____

_____

_____

_____

_____

_____

_____

III. THEORY: (Multiple choice items. Select the best answer and place the letter in front of the number.)

_____ 58. Identify the interval played (a. P5 b. P4 c. M6).

_____ 59. Identify the interval played (a. m2 b. M2 c. m3)

_____ 60. Identify the interval played (a. M3 b. m3 c. octave).

_____ 61. Identify the scale played (a. major b. relative minor c. harmonic minor).

_____ 62. Identify the chord played (a. major b. diminished c. seventh).

_____ 63. To move from key to another is called (a. modulation b. suspension c. motion).

_____ 64. Quality of tone is referred to as (a. vibration b. timbre c. sweet).

_____ 65. Movement from an active tone to a rest tone is called (a. suspension b. modulation c. resolution).

_____ 66. A dissonance caused by suspending a tone is called a (a. modulation b. suspension c. resolution).

_____ 67. A bass line that is repetitious is called an (a. ostinato b. revolving c. normal).

_____ 68. The form A-B-A-C-A is called (a. sonata allegro b. ronde c. suite).

_____ 69. The form A-B-A is called (a. sonata allegro b. rondo c. suite).

_____ 70. Modes refer to (a. harmony b. scales c. rhythm).

_____ 71. A round in music is like a (a. suite b. symphony c. fugue).

_____ 72. A sentence in music is called a (a. phrase b. movement c. period).

_____ 73. Symphonies normally contain how many movements (a. 3 b. 4 c. 5).

_____ 74. Suites in music are made of several (a. rhythms b. pitches c. movements).

———— 75. The fifth tone of a scale is called the (a. tonic b. dominant c. sub-dominant).

———— 76. In what minor scale do you raise the seventh? (a. relative b. harmonic c. melodic).

———— 77. The tone that a chord is built on is called the (a. tonic b. root c. dominant).

———— 78. C♯ and D♭ are called (a. active b. rest c. enharmonic).

———— 79. Spell the IV chord in the key of C major (a. FACF b. CECC c. GBDG).

———— 80. Spell the V7 chord in the key of F major (a. FACE b. CEGB♭ c. FACE♭).

———— 81. In the key of D major, DF♯AD is the (a. super-tonic b. dominant c. tonic).

———— 82. What does a sharp do to a note? (a. Lowers b. Cancels c. Raises) it ½ step.

———— 83. The first note of a scale is called the (a. tonic b. dominant c. root).

———— 84. The key of F major has (a. 1 sharp b. 1 flat c. no flats or sharps).

———— 85. The key of D major has (a. 2 sharps b. 5 sharps c. 5 flats).

———— 86. The key of 4 flats is (a. B♭ major b. A♭ major c. G♭ major).

———— 87. The key with 6 sharps is (a. F♯ major b. B major c. C♯ major).

———— 88. The half steps in the major scale are (a. 2-3 & 5-6 b. 3-4 & 7-8 c. 2-3 & 7-8).

———— 89. The half steps in the relative minor scale are (a. 2-3 & 5-6 b. 3-4 & 7-8 c. 2-3 & 7-8).

———— 90. A third clef often used by trombones and bassoons is (a. neume b. tenor c. alto).

———— 91. A dot after a note (a. adds one beat b. adds half the value of the note c. shortens it).

———— 92. The bottom number of a time signature tells (a. the number of beats per measure b. a certain tempo c. the kind of note that gets one beat).

———— 93. The abbreviation 𝅘𝅥 means play (a. four 8th notes b. four 16th notes c. four quarter notes.

———— 94. 𝅗𝅥 = 60 indicates a (a. fast tempo b. 60 beats per measure c. slow tempo).

———— 95. Chords with three different tones are triads, while chords with four different tones are (a. sevenths b. ninths c. quadrants).

———— 96. If a major interval is flatted, it becomes (a. major b. minor c. diminished).

———— 97. A typical chord progression is (a. I-III-II-I b. I-IV-V-I c. VI-VII-I).

———— 98. What note is most often doubled in a chord? (a. third b. root c. fifth).

———— 99. First inversion chords place what note in the bass? (a. third b. root c. fifth).

———— 100. The cadence V-I is called (a. plagal b. perfect c. imperfect).

———— 101. The cadence IV-I is called (a. plagal b. perfect c. imperfect).

———— 102. Construct a major scale on each given note:

103-109. Analyze the following and place the chord symbols below each chord:

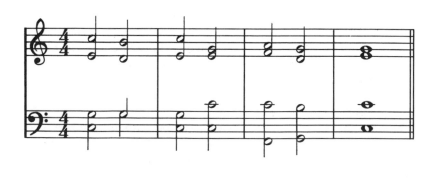

110-116. Harmonize the following soprano line, using the chords given:

I   V   I   I   IV   V   I

IV. RHYTHMIC DICTATION: (The exercise will be played four times)
117.

V. MELODIC DICTATION: (Each melodic exercise will be played four times)
118.

VI. COUNTING RHYTHMS: Write in the counting for each rhythm pattern.

119.

120.

121.

122.

279

VII. MUSICIANSHIP & STYLE:

123. Describe the style of a march: _____ .

124. Describe the style of a chorale: _____ .

125. Explain the value of solfege to performance: _____ .

VIII. COMPOSERS:

126-129. Name four major orchestral composers: _____

_____

130-133. Name four major composers of original band literature: _____

_____

IX. AESTHETICS-PHILOSOPHY: (Essay question)

134. Briefly explain what you have learned in concert band this year that has proved most valuable musically; and/or what you have learned that will prove valuable to you in adult life.

_____

_____

_____

_____

_____

_____

_____

_____

_____

_____

X. RECORD RECOGNITION: (Only one possible correct answer per number)

_____ 135.
    a. BAROQUE: "Toccata and Fugue in Dm" — J. S. Bach
    b. BAROQUE: Brandenburg Concerto No. 2, F Major — J. S. Bach

_____ 136.
    c. BAROQUE: "The Water Music" — G. F. Handel
    d. BAROQUE: "Royal Fireworks" — G. F. Handel

_____ 137.
    e. CLASSICAL: Symphony No. 40 in G minor — Mozart
    f. CLASSICAL: Symphony No. 29 — Mozart

_____ 138.
    g. CLASSICAL: Symphony No. 94, "Surprise" — Haydn
    h. CLASSICAL: Symphony No. 100, "Military" — Haydn

_____ 139.
    i. ROMANTIC: Symphony No. 3, "Eroica" — Beethoven
    j. ROMANTIC: Symphony No. 9, "New World" —Dvorak

_____ 140.
    k. ROMANTIC: Symphony No. 6, "Pathetique" — Tchaikovsky
    l. ROMANTIC: Symphony No. 3 — Brahms

_____ 141.
    m. CONTEMPORARY: "Rodeo" —Copland
    n. CONTEMPORARY: Symphony No. 5 — Shostakovich

_____ 142.
    o. CONTEMPORARY: "Firebird Suite" — Stravinsky
    p. CONTEMPORARY: "The Unanswered Question" — Charles Ives

_____ 143.
    q. ELECTRONIC MUSIC: Cage

_____ 144.
    r. CONCERT BAND: "Chorale and Alleluia" — Howard Hanson
    s. CONCERT BAND: First Suite in E♭ — G. Holst

_____ 145.
    t. CONCERT BAND: "Stars and Stripes Forever" — J. P. Sousa
    u. CONCERT BAND: "Psalm for Band" — V. Persichetti

_____ 146.
    v. CONCERT BAND: "La Fiesta Mexicana" — H. O. Reed

DRUMS ONLY:

———— 1. Name rudiment:

L R L L R L R R

———— 2. Name rudiment:

———— 3. Name rudiment:

———— 4. What stroke roll in 4/4?

———— 5. What stroke roll in 4/4?

———— 6. What stroke roll in 6/8?

———— 7. What position of the sticks is important for proper drum tone?
———— 8. What should be done with the sticks to draw the tone out of the drum properly?
———— 9. Where must the eyes be when performing?
———— 10. Name the lowest tone on each of the timpani.
———— 11. Must a drummer learn the mallet instruments to become a full percussionist and musician?

MUSICAL GROWTH EXERCISES: #1
Brooklyn Center High School — Minneapolis, Minnesota

Being a band member for four to eight years should involve more than technical progress on an instrument. Utilize your head and heart to discover what music can mean to you as an individual.

(Seniors=% Juniors=* Sophomores=# Frosh=$)

Name _____

I. MUSICAL TERMS:
% cantabile — _____

* sostenuto — _____

con moto — _____

$ rit. — _____

ALL BANDSMEN list one term, its meaning, and the title of the composition in which it was found during rehearsal this week: _____

_____

II. MUSIC HISTORY:
% Period with polytonality, polyrhythms, experimentalism, electronic music: _____

* Period with feelings and emotion dominating, large orchestras: _____

Period=precise, light, delicate; beauty, proportion, elegance: _____

$ Period=ornaments, terrace dynamics, driving runs, elaborate: _____

ALL BANDSMEN give one example of a composition rehearsed this week which would fit one of the above music history period descriptions. List title, composer, and period: _____

_____

III. MUSIC THEORY:
% Chord quality of the VII chord: _____

* Chord name and quality of the V chord: _____

Explain a time signature: _____

$ What is the function of key signatures? _____

ALL BANDSMEN give one example of music theory you used in rehearsal this week:

IV. RHYTHM: Write in the counting.

ALL BANDSMEN write out an unusual rhythmic pattern encountered in rehearsal this week:

V. COMPOSERS:
ALL BANDSMEN list the composer who appealed most to you this week in rehearsal. _____

VI. EAR-TRAINING: Melodic and rhythmic dictation.

Melodic

Rhythmic

VII. LISTENING:
ALL BANDSMEN listen to the record played and descrive the MELODY. (Optional: also describe the harmony, rhythm, form, timbre, style, period, composer, instruments, etc.) _____

MUSICAL GROWTH EXERCISES: #2

Name _____

I. Write four measures of your own melody, starting and ending on the tonic in the key of F major. Try to keep it playable and singable.

II. Write four measures of your own melody in 4/4 time and write in the counting below:

III. Name the following notes:

IV. Define *hemiola* and list an example of it from the concert folder: _____

_____

V. In what period of music history was *hemiola* prominent? _____

_____

VI. EAR-TRAINING: Melodic and rhythmic dictation.

Melodic

Rhythmic

VII. LISTENING: Describe the RHYTHM of the record played. (Optional: also describe the melody, harmony, form, timbre, style, period, composer, instruments, etc.) _____

_____

_____

_____

_____

MUSICAL GROWTH EXERCISES: #3

Name_____

I. Explain what a suspension is in music, and give an example of it from the concert folder:

_____

Put an example of a suspension on the staff below. Give the title of the composition where it is found.

II. INSTRUMENTAL TECHNIQUE PROBLEM: (Analyze the exercise for your instrument, practice it, and play it for your section leader on FRIDAY. Watch for alternate fingerings, etc.)

Clarinets

Oboes
+vibrato

Flutes
+vibrato

Saxes
+vibrato

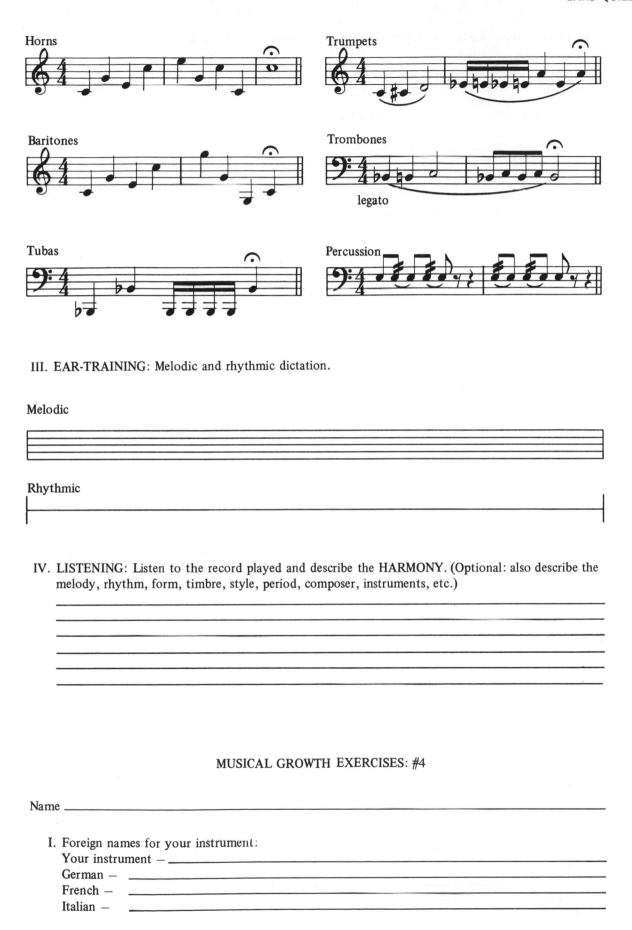

Horns

Trumpets

Baritones

Trombones

legato

Tubas

Percussion

III. EAR-TRAINING: Melodic and rhythmic dictation.

Melodic

Rhythmic

IV. LISTENING: Listen to the record played and describe the HARMONY. (Optional: also describe the melody, rhythm, form, timbre, style, period, composer, instruments, etc.)

MUSICAL GROWTH EXERCISES: #4

Name _____

I. Foreign names for your instrument:
Your instrument — _____
German — _____
French — _____
Italian — _____

II. Describe the historical development of your instrument. _____

_____

III. Find one or more measures in each of three concert folder numbers involving a special or alternate fingering on your instrument — or — involving a specialized technique on your instrument. Write the measures below, and illustrate your method for solving them:

IV. EAR-TRAINING: Melodic and rhythmic dictation.

Melodic

Rhythmic

V. LISTENING: Listen to the record played and describe the FORM. (Optional: also describe the melody, rhythm, timbre, style, period, composer, instruments, etc.) _____

_____

_____

_____

MUSICAL GROWTH EXERCISES: #5

Name _____

List one or more new music terms found this week during rehearsal. Give their meanings. _____

_____

List one composition read in rehearsal this week in the Baroque style, and give the title, composer and a few words describing its style: _____

_____

_____

  I. What is timbre? _____

 II. How does a composer utilize timbre? _____

III. What timbre(s) does the composer Nelhybel utilize most often? _____

IV. What timbre(s) is missing in a band? _____

 V. How does this effect the sound of a band? _____

VI. List a combination of timbres that might create a new sound: _____

_____

_____

_____

VII. EAR-TRAINING: Melodic-rhythmic dictation.

Melodic

Rhythmic

VIII. LISTENING: Listen to the record played and describe the timbres used. (Optional: also describe the melody, rhythm, harmony, form, etc.) _____

_____

_____

_____

_____

_____

MUSICAL GROWTH EXERCISES: #6

Name _____

MUSICAL FORM — Structure of Music

I. What is a fugue? _____
_____

II. What composer is known as the "Master of the Fugue"? _____

III. Write out a two-part fugue of your own or from the concert folder:

IV. List a new music term and its meaning from the music read during rehearsal this week: _____
_____

_____

V. List the title and composer of a number in the Classical style read during rehearsal this week. Describe the style. _____

_____

_____

VI. EAR-TRAINING: Melodic and rhythmic dictation.

Melodic

Rhythmic

VII. LISTENING: Listen to the record and describe the INSTRUMENTS. (Optional: also describe the melody, rhythm, harmony, form, timbre, style, period, composer, etc.) _____
_____
_____
_____
_____

MUSICAL GROWTH EXERCISES: #7

Name _____

AESTHETICS

I. Define the aesthetics of music: _____
_____
_____
_____

II. What number in the concert folder would bring out the aesthetics of music for you?
title _____ composer _____ period _____

III. Why does this number cause an aesthetic experience for you? _____
_____
_____

IV. What record have you heard recently that caused an aesthetic experience for you? _____

V. Why did it cause this experience? _____
_____

VI. Any other recent aesthetic experiences, music or otherwise? _____
_____

VII. Give title and composer of a number read this week in band that was in a church style, and describe what made it so: _____
_____
_____
_____

VIII. Any new or unusual music terms this week? (Give term & meaning.) _____

IX. EAR-TRAINING: Melodic & rhythmic dictation.

Melodic

Rhythmic

X. LISTENING: Describe any musical element that is prominent to you. _____
_____
_____
_____

MUSICAL GROWTH EXERCISES: #8

Name _____

1. Evaluate the "Pops" Concert — good, bad, add, drop, etc.: _____
_____
_____
_____
_____
_____

2. What educational value does the "Pops" Concert have for you? _____

3. What new educational experiences do you obtain, if any, from participating in the "Pops" Concert every year — or — should it cease to be an annual event if no new experiences are gained? _____
_____

4. Give your reactions, good and/or bad to the following:
   a. Weekly musical growth exercise sheets — _____
   b. No lectures — _____
   c. No quizzes — _____
   d. _____

5. List items to add or drop from next year's concert band curriculum: _____
   a. Add: _____
      Why add the above? _____
   b. Drop: _____
      Why drop the above? _____

6. List major performances to add or drop from the band's list of appearances: _____
   a. Add (Why?): _____
   _____
   b. Drop (Why?): _____
   _____

MUSICAL GROWTH EXERCISES: #9

Name _____

MUSIC THEORY

1. List one new music term and its meaning as found in rehearsal music: _____
   _____

2. Give the title, composer, and style of a number read during rehearsal this week that was in the Baroque style: _____
   _____

3. What is music theory? _____
   _____

4. Where have you used music theory in the last few weeks of band rehearsal? _____
   _____

5. SENIORS — Do you plan to continue to play your instrument after graduation and the marching band trip? _____
   If not, why? _____
   _____

6. ALL — Most band members do not continue to play their instruments after high school. Briefly explain why you feel this happens and if you feel that it is good or bad. Also explain how we might change this situation if you feel we should. _____
   _____
   _____
   _____

7. EAR-TRAINING: Melodic and rhythmic dictation.

   Melodic

   Rhythmic

8. LISTENING: Listen to the record and describe anything that is prominent to you, if you like it or not, and why: _____
   _____
   _____
   _____

**SENIORS — List any suggestions for graduation: _____
_____
_____
_____
_____
_____

DAILY REPORT

Jordan Vocational School
Columbus, Georgia
Band Department

Name	Reason
Absentees	
Rehearsal Infractions	
Sectional Absentees	

Date

Secretary

DETENTION ASSIGNMENT CHART FOR WEEK OF _____

Spencer, Iowa

NAME	REASON FOR DETENTION	DATE	TIME STUDENT CHECKED IN	TIME STUDENT CHECKED OUT

BAND ROOM INSPECTION

Jordan Vocational School
Columbus, Georgia

Rehearsal Room: _____
_____
_____
_____

Instrument Room: _____
_____
_____
_____

Cubbyholes: _____
_____
_____

Drum Area: _____
_____
_____

Bass Area: _____
_____
_____

Date _____ Officer _____

PERCUSSION SECTION CHECK LIST

Jordan Vocational School
Columbus, Georgia

_____ Marching drums stacked on top of lockers.
_____ Covers on timpani.
_____ All equipment put away in cabinet.
_____ Folders in place on rack.
_____ All paper and trash cleaned up.
_____ Drum cabinet locked.
_____ Air conditioning room locked.
_____ Door to stage locked.
_____ Keys returned to director.

I certify that all the above items have been completed.

Date _____ Signature _____

Turn this sheet in to the director at the conclusion of each rehearsal and wait until section has been inspected.

RECOMMENDATION FOR GIGS

Ft. Lauderdale, Florida

Name _____ is hereby recommended for a gig(s)* for

the following reason(s): _____
_____
_____

Date _____

Area of Involvement:
_____ General Band Procedures   _____ Field Work
_____ Turn-out   _____ Other (specify)

Dept. _____ Dept. member _____ Date_____

Director _____

Number of gigs given: _____

*Also known as demerits in some schools

UNJUSTIFIED GIG FORM

Ft. Lauderdale, Florida

I, _____ , feel that the gig(s) received at _____
    (name)   (event)

_____ on _____ was unjustified for the following reason(s): _____
_____
_____
_____
_____

(Student's signature)

Accepted _____
Rejected _____

Comment: _____
_____
_____
_____

Director _____

AWARD SYSTEM POINT CARD
Lenoir High School Band
Lenoir, N.C.

Name _____ Address _____ Phone _____

Grade _____ Parent's Name _____

		M T W T F	M T W T F	M T W T F	M T W T F	M T W T F	M T W T F	Total
I.	Marching Band							
II.	Appearances Outside	1 2 3	4 5 6	7 8 9	10 11 12	13 14 15	16 17 18	
III.	Practice Period							
IV.	Solo and Ensemble	1 2 3	4 5 6	7 8 9	10 11 12	13 14 15	16 17 18	
V.	Concert Band							
VI.	Extra Rehearsals	1 2 3	4 5 6	7 8 9	10 11 12	13 14 15	16 17 18	
VII. Perfect Attendance	Marching							
	Practice							
	Concert							
VIII. No Tardies	Practice							
	Marching							
	Concert							
IX.	Extra Individual Practice	1 2 3	4 5 6	7 8 9	10 11 12	13 14 15	16 17 18	

X. Instrument	**XI.** Year	**XII.** Semester	Total	
			Preceding Credits	
			Grand Total To Date	

1. 3300 points per school year are needed for band award.
2. Each hour of practice earns five points (three if tardy — 0 if absent).
3. 25 bonus points if not absent and 20 bonus points if not tardy during each grading period.
4. Any scheduled event offers points pro-rated on time involved.

CHECK LIST FOR IMPROVEMENT
Tucson, Arizona
Public Schools

Student's Name _____ School _____ Classroom Teacher _____

Grading Periods

	1.	2.	3.	4.	5.	6.

1. Needs to do more practicing either at home or at school (suggest a *minimum* of 30 minutes daily).

2. Needs to pay special attention to fingerings.

3. Needs to learn the names of notes (at least those covered to date in class sessions).

4. Has trouble getting the right pitches (usually too high; too low).

5. Instrument is in poor condition (sticky valves; leaking pads; keys sticking).

6. Needs to keep good reeds on hand. You cannot play well on a chipped or split reed!

7. Needs to keep instrument clean (valves; slides; key holes; other _____).

8. ABSENT FROM CLASS TOO OFTEN.

9. Embouchure (lip and mouth position) is poor and needs strengthening. (Feel free to call for instructions).

10. Needs to drill on counting note and rest values.

11. Rhythm is unsteady and weak: needs to count aloud and/or keep beat (count) going with foot.

12. Intonation is weak: plays consistently out of tune — sharp (too high) flat (too low).

13. Has a poor attitude in class.

14. Does not seem to be interested in improving musical performance.

15. Does not seem to be able to concentrate in class.

16. Forgets to bring instrument and/or music to class: frequently; all the time.

17. Needs private instruction.

18. Needs to pay special attention to the proper position of holding the instrument and of the _____ while playing.

19. NEEDS SUPERVISION IN HOME PRACTICE.

20 Other suggestions:

INSTRUMENTAL MUSIC GRADE

Parent's signature:

1. _____ 4. _____

2. _____ 5. _____

3. _____ 6. _____

Tucson Public Schools
Music Department

Woodwind, Brass & Percussion Sheet   Music instructor's name   Telephone

INSTRUMENTAL MUSIC IMPROVEMENT CHECK LIST
Tucson, Arizona

INSTRUMENT _____ STUDENT _____

GRADE _____ SCHOOL _____

PARENTS: Please read and sign.   STUDENTS: Return to instructor in one week.

INSTRUMENT
____ Needs reeds (strength _____)
____ Leaking or missing pads
____ Bent keys
____ Instrument dirty
____ Sticky or bent valves
____ Needs valve or slide oil
____ Needs cork grease
____ Needs mouthpiece pulled
____ Needs slide(s) pulled
____ Needs slide straightened (trombone)
____ Needs water key repaired
____ Needs key adjustment
____ Generally adequate/Excellent

ATTITUDE
____ Does not seem interested in improving
____ Does not seem able to concentrate in class
____ Seems to forget instrument frequently
____ Talks excessively
____ Plays out of turn during class time
____ Shows leadership
____ Attitude Outstanding

ATTENDANCE
____ Absent too often
____ Tardy too often
____ Excellent

EMBOUCHURE
____ Should not puff out cheeks
____ Chin not flat
____ Mouthpiece not centered
____ Generally adequate/Excellent
____ Suggest a private instructor.
____ Needs supervision in home practice. (Parents, encourage a practice schedule.)
    Rx for Practice: Beginners — Ten minutes three times a day.
            Advanced — At least 30 minutes daily practice.

BREATH CONTROL
____ Needs to work on diaphragmatic breathing
____ Breathes too often
____ Generally adequate/Excellent

RHYTHM
____ Needs to tap foot
____ Needs to learn how to count time with good rhythm
____ Generally adequate/Excellent

PITCH
____ Plays incorrect pitches (high/low)
____ Plays flat (low) sharp (high)
____ Needs to learn how to sit and/or stand correctly
____ Needs to learn how to hold instrument correctly
____ Generally adequate/Excellent

DRUMS ONLY
____ Needs proper drum sticks (_____)
____ Needs practice pad
____ Needs to learn correct method of holding sticks
____ Generally adequate/Excellent

SUGGESTED GRADE ACHIEVEMENT
____ Superior
____ Excellent
____ Good
____ Poor

Parent's Signature_____ Band Director _____

(Comments may be written on reverse side)

ELEMENTARY INSTRUMENTAL MUSIC REPORT
Ann Arbor Public Schools
Ann Arbor, Michigan

Name _____ Date _____ 19 _____

School _____ Classroom Teacher _____

Grade _____ Class: Beginning _____ Advanced _____

MUSICIANSHIP

The check in the first line of squares indicates the student's performance in relation to the entire class. The check in the second line shows the teacher's estimate of the student's ability in music. The check in the third line shows the student's progress in relation to this estimate of his musical ability.

Comparative Performance	☐ Poor	☐ Fair	☐ Average	☐ Good	☐ Superior
Estimate of Ability	☐ Poor	☐ Fair	☐ Average	☐ Good	☐ Superior
Performance vs. Ability	☐ Poor	☐ Fair	☐ Average	☐ Good	☐ Superior

For each ability used in playing an instrument a letter shows the student's achievement in relation to his own musical capacity: G (good) for achievement at the level of his capacity, F (fair) for achievement somewhat below his capacity, P (poor) for achievement seriously below his capacity.

_____ Tone quality   _____ Sense of pitch

_____ Knowledge of fingerings   _____ Breath control

_____ Reading of note names   _____ Playing position (position of hands, instrument, embouchure, posture)

_____ Sense of rhythm

CITIZENSHIP

The comments below indicate the student's attitudes and cooperation in instrumental music.

_____ Preparation of lessons   _____ Courtesy

_____ Attention in class   _____ Cooperation

_____ Response to instruction   _____ Promptness

_____ Care of equipment   _____ Attendance with instrument, music

A conference with the parent
is always welcomed.

_____
Instrumental Music Teacher

Phone: _____

Additional comments, if any, on reverse side.

GRADE SCHOOL BAND REPORT

Brooklyn Center High School
Minneapolis, Minnesota

This is an effort on the part of the Instrumental Music Department to give you parents a more comprehensive picture of the progress of your child on his chosen instrument. The letter grade can be better understood in terms of progress if you follow the check marks and become familiar with the information they represent. A pupil is not graded by comparison to others, but on the manner in which he develops his individual ability to perform on his chosen instrument.

Your assistance at home can be most helpful in assuring your child's success in the instrumental music program at our school. With help and encouragement at home we work *together* in giving your child the best musical education. Feel free to come in or call to discuss any questions you might have.

"Since Music has so much to do with the molding of Character, it is necessary that we teach it to our children." — Aristotle

- -

Student _____ Class _____

1. Outstanding   2. Excellent   3. Very Good
4. Good   5. Average   6. Below Average

	1st Qtr.	2nd Qtr.	3rd Qtr.	4th Qtr.
Attendance				
Required Practice Time (30 minutes daily)				
Attitude				
Work or Progress				

Parent's Signature

1. _____   3. _____

2. _____   4. _____

PARENT'S COMMENTS

1st Quarter   3rd Quarter

2nd Quarter   4th Quarter

(Continued)

x — Work needed　　　　xx — Much work needed　　　　xxx — Very poor, much work needed

		1st Qtr.	2nd Qtr.	3rd Qtr.	4th Qtr.
Playing position and embouchure					
Finger position	DRUMS				
Posture	Stick & Hand position				
Breathing	Counting rhythms				
Tone	Tapping time correctly				
Tonguing	Keeping steady time				
Naming notes	Long roll				
Note values	Speed on rudiments				
Tapping and counting time	Other:				
Fingerings for notes					
Scales					
Lesson assignments					
Solfeggio (singing intervals)					
Other:					

A — Superior:　This grade is reserved for the pupil who can play his part well and who shows evidence of practicing.

B — Good:　This grade indicates that the pupil plays his part well and does some practicing.

C — Average:　This pupil experiences trouble playing his part at times because he cannot read the music and cannot finger the notes properly. He probably needs parental help in planning his practice time and in being encouraged to improve.

Below C:　This grade is given to the pupil who does not play well, but who may be capable of doing average, good or superior work. This pupil tends to slow the band's progress because of the extra time he must be given.

Band Director's Comments:

Band Grade _____

INSTRUMENTAL MUSIC REPORT FORM
Sapulpa Public Schools
Sapulpa, Oklahoma

School _____ Date _____

Teacher _____

Grade _____

Dear Parent:

The following is an analysis of the work of _____ in instrumental music, with suggestions for his assistance (and yours) in making future improvement. Any additional comments will be on the reverse side of this form.

I. Attendance

II. Attitude & Cooperation
_____ Does not listen
_____ Talks too much
_____ Wastes time
_____ Posture
_____ Forgets assignment

III. Equipment Needs
_____ Pencil
_____ Note book
_____ Instrument
_____ Music
_____ Music stand
_____ Reeds
_____ Oil

IV. Articulation
_____ Tongues between teeth
_____ Not using tongue
_____ Tongues too heavy
_____ Slurs improperly
_____ Ends tone with tongue or lips
_____ Moves lips when tonguing or breathing

V. Preparation
_____ Needs to count rhythms & rests out loud
_____ Needs to learn note names
_____ Needs 30 min. daily practice
_____ Needs to learn fingerings
_____ Plays too loud
_____ Plays too soft
_____ Needs to use more air
_____ Improper hand position

VI. Embouchure
_____ Lips too tight
_____ Lips too open
_____ Teeth too close together
_____ Needs to move jaw forward
_____ Needs more mouthpiece in mouth
_____ Too much mouthpiece in mouth
_____ Puffs cheeks
_____ Breathes improperly
_____ Chin not down

Considering all factors involved, your child has made (satisfactory) (unsatisfactory) progress and it (is) (is not) advisable that he continue his study of this instrument. A conference with the parent is always welcomed.

A — Excellent progress
B — Above average
C — Average
D — Poor work
F — Unsatisfactory

Sincerely yours,

_____
Teacher

PARENT REPORT FORM
Brooklyn Center Independent School District No. 286
Minneapolis, Minnesota
Instrumental Music Department

To the Parents of _____
(name of band student)

The success of the instrumental music program is very dependent upon each student doing his particular task well. If one or two fall behind, the progress of the whole group suffers. We ask, therefore, that you cooperate in urging that your child accept the full share of responsibility he/she assumed in joining the instrumental music program.

Students occasionally run into difficulties which may be easily solved with a little understanding on the part of parent and teacher. We have checked below what we believe to be the apparent source of the difficulty which at present seems to be holding up your child's progress. If you wish to consult with us, you may do so by appointment.

1. _____ Insufficient Practice (30 minutes daily minimum)

2. _____ Poor attendance at (rehearsals, lessons)

3. _____ Technical difficulties (_____)

COMMENTS

_____
Band Director

SPECIAL REPORT
Temple High School
Temple, Texas

Date _____

TO THE PARENTS:

_____ is doing unsatisfactory work in my _____ class. I have indicated on this sheet some of the reasons which I believe are responsible for the inferior work. I think he will improve if the recommendations given are carefully followed. If you care to discuss the matter further, you may call at my room No. _____ at _____ .

Sincerely yours,

_____

REASONS FOR UNSATISFACTORY WORK		REMARKS:
Excessive absence		
Failure to make up work after absence		
Lack of adequate daily preparation		
Inattention in class		
Failure to complete work fully and on time		
Lack of participation in class activities		
Poor attitude		
Subject too difficult		
Other:		

SIX WEEKS' REPORT – SIXTH GRADE
North Little Rock, Arkansas
Instrumental Music Dept.

Student _____

School _____

Grading Periods

	1	2	3	4	5	6
Lesson preparation						
Attendance						
Attitude and Conduct						
Practice						
Posture						
Breath control						
Care of instrument						

Regular practice and *good playing habits* are necessary for good musical development. Parents are urged to check periodically to see that students observe these points.

_____

Teacher's signature

INSTRUMENT CHECK-OUT FORM
Lenoir High School Band
North Carolina, Caldwell County

The undersigned student hereby acknowledges receipt of the band property of the Lenoir High School Band, which is listed below.

In consideration for said property being thus issued to me, I do hereby agree:

(1) To fully pay the said Lenoir High School Band for any loss or damage to said property so issued, and for which I am responsible.

(2) To keep said property in good and proper repair, and in playing condition, as may be determined by the Band Director.

(3) To surrender to said Lenoir High School Band any property issued to me, as herein provided, at any time, upon notice to me, either by the Band Director or his assistants.

As a further consideration for said property being loaned to me, I do hereby agree to attend band rehearsals regularly, and to faithfully discharge all duties required as a requisite to being a member of said band. I understand thoroughly that all the musical instruments and other property connected with the said musical organization belong to said Lenoir High School Band, and same are subject to recall at any time, and that I hold my position in this organization on probation, and that violation of the rules and a lack of faithful and diligent discharge of the work assigned, on my part, subjects me to suspension, and withdrawal of the property assigned.

_____with case; No. _____

Lenoir, North Carolina, _____ , 19_____ .

_____ Student

I guarantee the above agreement on the part of the student.

_____ Parent or Guardian

Witness _____

INSTRUMENT CHECK-OUT CARD
Music Department
Springfield Public Schools
Springfield, Oregon
RECEIPT AND BOND FOR BAND AND
ORCHESTRA INSTRUMENTS

I hereby agree to hold myself personally responsible for the following instrument(s) while in my possession. I agree that no person other than myself will be allowed to use the instrument, and that I will return it to the school when requested by the music director.

School _____   Pupil _____ Grade _____

Instrument _____   Parent _____

No. _____ Bow No. _____   Address _____

Date _____   Phone _____

Approved by _____
Instructor

303

INSTRUMENT CHECK-OUT FORM
Oakwood High School
Dayton, Ohio
Department of Instrumental Music

ISSUANCE OF BAND INSTRUMENT AND PROPERTY

I have received the following school-owned property from the Oakwood Schools:

DESCRIPTION OF PROPERTY

MAKE _____ VALUE $ _____

FACTORY SERIAL NO. _____ STYLE _____

SCHOOL NO. _____ FINISH _____

Instrument is equipped with following accessories:

CASE _____ LIGATURE _____ LYRE _____

COVER _____ BOCAL _____ STICKS _____

MOUTHPIECE _____ CLEANING ROD _____ STRAP _____

CAP _____ SWAB _____ Other _____

　　　Remarks:

I hereby agree to hold myself personally responsible for any damage which may come to the instrument and the property while it is in my care. I agree that no person other than myself will be allowed to use the instrument, and that I will return it to the school when requested by the Director.

PUPIL _____ GRADE _____

PARENT _____

ADDRESS _____

PHONE NUMBER _____ DATE _____

APPROVED _____

_____ Director

DATE _____

INSTRUMENT INVENTORY FORM
Hutchinson Public Schools
Hutchinson, Kansas

Instrument _____ Make _____

Amount Insured For _____ Serial No. _____

Finish _____ Condition of Instrument _____

When Purchased _____ Purchased From _____

Purchase Price _____ Value _____

ACCESSORIES

Case _____ Extra Slide _____ Ligature _____

Lyre _____ Mouthpiece _____ Mouthpiece Cap _____

RECORD OF REPAIRS

Date	Nature of Repair	Cost

RECORD OF STUDENTS USING INSTRUMENT

Date	Issued to	Ret'd.	Date	Issued to	Ret'd

INSTRUMENT INVENTORY CARD
Oakwood Band
Dayton, Ohio

Instrument _____		Student	Out	In

Make _____ Serial No. _____

Model _____ Value $ _____

Description _____

School Number _____

Obtained _____

Reconditioned _____

Case _____ Mouthpiece _____

Crooks _____ Rod _____

Cap _____ Ligature _____

Strap _____ Sticks _____

Other _____

INSTRUMENT INVENTORY CARD
Westside High School
Omaha, Nebraska

				1	2	3	4	5	6	7	8	9	10	OVER 10
SERIAL NO.	ARTICLE	MAKE	YEAR	NUMBER OF YEARS IN USE										

	LOCATION		MAINTENANCE CONTRACTS			
	DATE	STORE OR DEPT.	SERVICE CO.	DATED	EXPIRES	COST
MODEL						
SIZE						
OTHER IDENTIFICATION:						
DATE PURCHASED						
PURCHASE PRICE						
PUR. ORDER NO.						
PUR. FROM						

			MAINTENANCE CALLS						
ACCT.									
DEPRECIATION FOR YEARS	DATE	REPAIR	CONTRACT SERVICE	DATE	REPAIR	CONTRACT SERVICE	DATE	REPAIR	CONTRACT SERVICE
DATE DISCARDED									
SALVAGE VALUE									
DISPOSITION									
REMARKS:									

NOTICE OF LOSS OR DAMAGE
Hutchinson, Kansas
Musical Instruments

Date _____ , 19 _____

Date of loss _____ A.M./P.M.
       Day   Month   Year   Time

Amount of insurance _____

Name of owner _____

Address _____

Probable Amount of Entire Loss $ _____

Portion of Loss Covered by Insurance $ _____

Item or Items Involved _____
                                 (Describe fully)

Kind of Loss _____
        (State whether Fire, Windstorm, Explosion, etc.)

Did loss originate on insured's premises: _____

If Fire or Explosion, state origin: _____

REMARKS:

Signed _____
                            (Owner)

INSTRUMENT RENTAL SCHEDULE
La Salle-Peru Township High School
La Salle, Illinois

TO: Parents of Students in Instrumental Music   Date _____

FROM: La Salle-Peru Township High School Instrumental Music Department

The following rental schedule has been approved and adopted by the La Salle-Peru Township High School Board of Education. This is a semester fee.

	Value	Fee		Value	Fee
Piccolo			Mellophone		
Oboe			Alto Horn		
Bassoon			Baritone		
Alto Clar.			Sousaphone		
Bass Clar.			Concert Tuba		
Contra Bass Clar.			Snare Drum		
Tenor Sax			Bass Drum		
Baritone Sax			Timpani		
Bass Sax			Bells & Xylophone		
Double Fr. Horn			Misc.		

These rental fees are payable each semester. We trust you realize it is necessary to make an assessment to help defray the costs of repairing and maintaining the school-owned instruments.

Sincerely yours,

_____
Director of Instrumental Music

REPORT OF ACCIDENT OR THEFT
Tucson Public Schools
Tucson, Arizona
School-Owned Instruments

Music Department

Prepare in TRIPLICATE. Send ALL copies to Music Dept. as soon as accident or theft occurs.

ACCIDENT

Name of Instrument _____ Make _____ Ser. No _____

School _____ Date of Accident _____

To be repaired by _____ Approx. Cost of Repair _____

Damage done to instrument _____

Describe what happened. _____

_____

_____

_____

INSTRUCTOR: In your opinion was the damage deliberate? _____ Accidental? _____
In your opinion can the parents afford to pay for this repair? _____

When you submit this form, please also attach regular Repair Form
properly made out.

_____
Signature of Instructor

LOSS or POSSIBLE THEFT

Name of Instrument _____ Make _____ Ser. No _____

School _____ Date found missing _____

By whom _____ Reported to Police _____
Date

By whom _____ What evidence of burglary or theft beyond
(Name of Teacher, Principal or Parent)

the disappearance of property? _____

_____

_____

_____
Signature of Instructor

(Music Office to complete)   Depreciated Value of Instrument as listed on inv. $ _____
Actual Cost of Instrument as listed on inventory $ _____
Date Purchased _____

The above was REPAIRED _____ REPLACED _____
Date   Date

INSTRUMENT REPAIR AUTHORIZATION

Independent School District of Boise City, Idaho
Music Department

Date _____ , 19_____

Pursuant to my obligation as stated in RECEIPT AND BOND FOR MUSIC INSTRUMENTS, I hereby make application to have the following instrument repaired:

Instrument _____ Make _____ Value $ _____

Style _____ Finish _____ Factory Serial No. _____ School No. ___

Replace the following ATTACHMENTS (Please indicate make)

Case _____ Oil _____ Bow _____ Cap _____ Screwdriver _____ Key _____ Strap ___ Swab _____

Ligature _____ Reed Case _____ Crooks _____ Mouthpiece ___ Piston Wiper ___ Lyre _____

Grease _____ Cleaning Rod _____ Sticks _____ Bits _____ Key_____

Other

Repairman or Dealer: _____

Name _____ Address _____

I understand that the cost of the above is to be billed to and paid by me.

Student _____ Parent _____

Address _____ Phone _____

APPROVED:

Music Instructor _____ Principal _____

INSTRUMENT CHECK-IN CARD

Instrumental Music Department, Norman, Oklahoma

Students using school owned instruments are to fill out this tag completely, attach it to the case handle, and remove old tags from the case prior to instrument check-in. Needed repairs should be cited by the student on the reverse side of this tag.

Instrument _____ Brand _____

Serial Number _____

Student Returning Instrument _____

Address _____ Telephone _____

I wish to use this instrument again.   Yes _____ No _____

NORTH LITTLE ROCK PUBLIC SCHOOLS

Transfer of Instrument - Card

INSTRUMENT _____ SERIAL No. _____

Transferred from: _____ School _____

To: _____ School _____

Date of transfer: _____

_____

Signature of Director making transfer

NORTH LITTLE ROCK PUBLIC SCHOOLS
INSTRUMENT DATA CARD

School_____

Instrument_____ Make_____

Serial No._____ Purchase date_____ From_____

School Number_____

Check-out date	Name	Date Returned	Condition

(These cards are to be printed back to back.)

INSTRUMENT DATA CARD
NORTH LITTLE ROCK PUBLIC SCHOOLS

Date	Type of Repair	Repair Shop	Condition

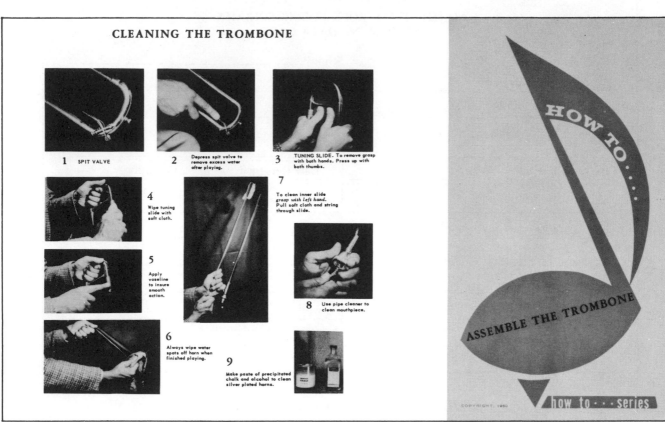

CLEANING THE TROMBONE

1 SPIT VALVE

2 Depress spit valve to remove excess water after playing.

3 TUNING SLIDE. To remove grasp with both hands. Press up with both thumbs.

4 Wipe tuning slide with soft cloth.

5 Apply vaseline to insure smooth action.

6 Always wipe water spots off horn when finished playing.

7 To clean inner slide grasp with left hand. Pull soft cloth and string through slide.

8 Use pipe cleaner to clean mouthpiece.

9 Make paste of precipitated chalk and alcohol to clean silver plated horns.

HOW TO . . . . ASSEMBLE THE TROMBONE

how to . . . series

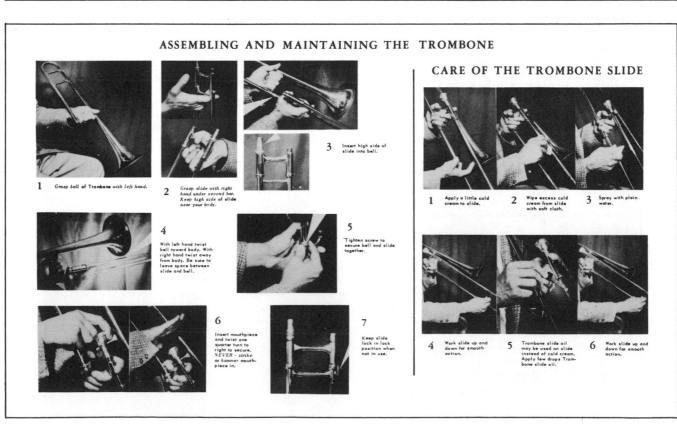

ASSEMBLING AND MAINTAINING THE TROMBONE

1 Grasp bell of Trombone with left hand.

2 Grasp slide with right hand under second bar. Keep high side of slide near your body.

3 Insert high side of slide into bell.

4 With left hand twist bell toward body. With right hand twist away from body. Be sure to leave space between slide and bell.

5 Tighten screw to secure bell and slide together.

6 Insert mouthpiece and twist one quarter turn to right to secure. NEVER · strike or hammer mouthpiece in.

7 Keep slide lock in lock position when not in use.

CARE OF THE TROMBONE SLIDE

1 Apply a little cold cream to slide.

2 Wipe excess cold cream from slide with soft cloth.

3 Spray with plain water.

4 Work slide up and down for smooth action.

5 Trombone slide oil may be used on slide instead of cold cream. Apply few drops Trombone slide oil.

6 Work slide up and down for smooth action.

Used by permission.

Additional brochures of the "HOW TO. . . SERIES" which describe the proper assembling, cleaning, and maintaining of musical instruments (see sample on previous page) are available for the following instruments:

Flute

Oboe

Bassoon

Clarinet

Bass and Alto Clarinet

Saxophone

Trumpet

French Horn and Baritone

Tuba, Sousaphone, and Bass

Write to: HOW-TO-COMPANY
8130 Surrey Lane
Oakland, California 94605

COMPOSER CATALOGUE CARD
Western Illinois University Bands

Composer/Arranger   Name of Composition

File Number _____ Publisher _____ Character _____

Date first acquisitioned into library _____ Performance time _____

Dates Performed: _____
_____
_____
_____
_____
_____

TITLE CATALOGUE CARD
Western Illinois University Bands

Name of Composition   Composer/Arranger

File Number _____ Publisher _____ Character _____

Date first acquisitioned into library _____ Performance time _____

Dates Performed: _____
_____
_____
_____
_____
_____

MARCH FOLIO CHECK–OUT FORM

Western Illinois University Bands

March Folio No. _____

Instrument _____

    I understand that this folder and its contents of music belong to the Western Illinois University Band and that its total value is $4.00. It is my intention in signing for the use of this folder and its contents to use extreme care in its use and upkeep. I agree to pay for the loss of the folder and any of its contents at the rate of 25¢ per march.

Date Checked Out _____ Signature of Student _____

Date Checked In _____ Shortages _____ Damages Paid _____

CONCERT FOLIO CHECK-OUT FORM

Western Illinois University Bands

Ensemble _____

Folio _____

I, the undersigned, do hereby agree to take all responsibility to see that the music and folio from which this card was taken are turned in at the library desk at least 10 minutes before the next rehearsal.

Date Taken Out	Name	Date Taken Out	Name

BAND QUESTIONNAIRE

Ninth Grade

Temple High School, Temple, Texas

Name _____ Instrument _____

Name of Parents: _____

Address _____ Telephone _____

1. Check one or all below:

    A. If your score is superior, will you accept assignment in the Varsity Band? _____

    B. If your score is average, will you accept assignment in the Junior Varsity Band? _____

    C. If your score is below average, will you accept assignment in the Cadet Band? _____

    (Students who do not wish to accept assignment based on entrance score will be dropped from further Band classes).

2. If you make a good score and are assigned to the Varsity Band and if there is a vacancy for your instrument, would you like to take Orchestra also? _____

3. If you make a superior score, and if there is a vacancy for your instrument, would you like to audition (tryout) for Highlighters? _____

BAND QUESTIONNAIRE

Temple High School, Temple, Texas

Name _____

1. Do you plan definitely to be enrolled in H.S. Band next year? _____

2. For present members of Orchestra only: Do you plan to be enrolled in Orchestra next year? _____

3. For present members of Highlighters only: Do you plan to be enrolled in Highlighters next year? _____

4. For prospective members of Orchestra: If a vacancy exists for your instrument, do you wish to be considered for Orchestra next year? _____

5. For prospective members of Highlighters: If a vacancy exists for your instrument, do you wish to tryout for Highlighters next year? _____

6. If taking Band, do you wish to keep the same uniform next year? _____

7. If football player on A team, please indicate so you will not be assigned a marching spot for halftime shows. _____

Please sign your name here: _____

BAND ENROLLMENT CARD
Mandan High School
Mandan, N.D.

Name _____ Grade _____ Age _____

Home Address _____ Phone _____

Father's Full Name _____ Occupation and Employer _____

Mother's Name _____ Occupation and Employer _____

Personal Instrument: Name _____ Make _____ Serial No. _____

School Instrument: Fee _____ Name _____ Make _____ Serial No. _____

Uniform: Fee _____ Coat _____ Overlay _____ Trouser _____ Shako _____

             Gloves _____ Tie _____ Spats _____ Cord _____ Bag _____

Organizations: Marching Band _____ Wind Ensemble _____ Concert Band _____

             Varsity Band _____ Stage Band _____

(Check-Out System and Class Schedule on Reverse Side.)

CHECK-OUT

Item	Out	In	Insp.

CLASS SCHEDULE

	Class	Room No.	Teacher
8			
1			
2			
3			
N			
1			
2			
3			
4			

INFORMATION FORM
LaSalle-Peru, Illinois
INFORMATION FOR PERMANENT RECORDS

FRESHMEN: Answer ALL questions.
SOPHOMORES, JUNIORS, SENIORS: Answer from No. 6 on.
Be accurate; write clearly.

1. Name and address: _____

_____

2. Parent's name: _____

3. Instrument, make, and serial number: _____

_____

4. Grade school: _____

5. Date entered band: _____

6. Years: Marching Band _____

       Concert Band _____

       Varsity Band _____

       Grade School _____

7. Seating (at end of school year): _____

8. Solos: _____

9. Awards: _____

10. Ensembles: _____

11. Activities: _____

INFORMATION FORM
Brooklyn Center High School Band Department
Minneapolis, Minnesota

Name _____ Parent or Guardian _____

Address _____ Phone _____ Grade in School _____

Study Hall or Free Period: 1 2 3 4 5 6   Lunch Period   1 2 3 4

Instrument _____ School No. _____

      If own, Serial No. _____ Brand _____ Value $ _____

Instrument Shelf No. _____ Pep Folio No. _____

Uniform No. _____ (need own white shoes, white sox, black shoes, black sox, black
                     bow tie and white shirt and maybe white gloves)

FEES DUE: Instrument Rental _____

              Uniform Rental _____

              Misc. (reeds, etc.) _____

ITEMS DUE: Solos/Ensembles signed out _____

              Records, books, etc. signed out _____

Date started on instrument _____

Any piano lessons? _____ How long? _____

Scholastic Grade Average _____

Director's Comments: _____

_____

_____

_____

_____

_____

PERMANENT RECORD FORM
Grades 10, 11, 12
Spencer, Iowa

Your Name _____

               Last   First

Parent _____

               Last   First

Address _____ Grade _____ Telephone _____

Note: In addition to band you are required to take one of the following:

       A. Private lessons outside of school time.
       B. 15-minute lessons on school time.
       C. Sectionals.

         (Circle one of the above choices.)

On the schedule given below, please list only your study halls or free time.

TIME	MON.	TUES.	WED.	THURS.	FRI.
8:00–8:55					
9:00–9:55					
10:00–10:55					
11:00–11:55					
1st Lunch 12:00					
2nd Lunch 12:26					
3rd Lunch 12:52					
1:25–2:20					
2:25–3:20					

Those who do not have time for lessons during the school day and who will not be studying privately will have to be assigned time between 3:20 and 4:00 P.M.

PRACTICE ROOM SCHEDULE
Temple High School, Temple, Texas

Period ———————————————— Date ————————————————

Room 1 ————————————————————————

Room 2 ————————————————————————

Room 3 ————————————————————————

Room 4 ————————————————————————

Room 5 ————————————————————————

Room 6 ————————————————————————

Room 7 ————————————————————————

Room 8 ————————————————————————

Room 9 ————————————————————————

Upstairs ———————————————————————

PRACTICE CONFIRMATION

The signature of a parent is requested on the appropriate line below.

First Nine Weeks

1. _____
2. _____
3. _____
4. _____
5. _____
6. _____
7. _____
8. _____
9. _____
10. _____

Third Nine Weeks

1. _____
2. _____
3. _____
4. _____
5. _____
6. _____
7. _____
8. _____
9. _____
10. _____

Second Nine Weeks

1. _____
2. _____
3. _____
4. _____
5. _____
6. _____
7. _____
8. _____
9. _____
10. _____

Fourth Nine Weeks

1. _____
2. _____
3. _____
4. _____
5. _____
6. _____
7. _____
8. _____
9. _____
10. _____

Weekly Practice Requirements for Practice Grades:

6 hours, A+; 4 hours, A; 3 hours, B; 2 hours, C; 1 hour, D. One-half of these hourly requirements may be reported for piano lesson practice. One hour credit may be reported for each director-approved private lesson taken on a band or orchestral instrument. One hour credit may be listed for each concert attended (specifically designated by the director).

INSTRUMENTAL MUSIC DEPARTMENT
Norman, Oklahoma Public Schools

PRACTICE REPORT CARD

This practice report card is intended to provide the student, parent, and instructor, a definite, systematic record of the effort expended in practice. The interest and concern of the parent in the progress and development of musical skills is extremely vital. Practice reports are due each Monday. The signature of the parent each week on the back of this report confirms the practice for our records. Your help and consideration are appreciated.

Instrumental Staff

Name of Student _____ Grade _____

Address _____ Ph. _____

Name of School _____

Instrument _____

Homeroom Teacher _____

(Daily practice record on reverse side.)

322

STUDENT'S NAME _____

Practice report cards are due each Monday. Late reports, except for excused absences, lose a letter grade per day. Practice should be recorded daily in whole hours, halves, or quarters. Total the weekly practice before handing in each report.

PRACTICE AIDS

Regular daily practice is much more effective in developing playing skill than irregular practice. Keep your band instrument clean and properly cared for. Control practice conditions: use a good music rack, maintain correct posture and hand position.

First Nine Weeks

WK	M	T	W	TH	FR	SA	SU	Total	Grade
1									
2									
3									
4									
5									
6									
7									
8									
9									
10									

Third Nine Weeks

WK	M	T	W	TH	FR	SA	SU	Total	Grade
1									
2									
3									
4									
5									
6									
7									
8									
9									
10									

Second Nine Weeks

1									
2									
3									
4									
5									
6									
7									
8									
9									
10									

Fourth Nine Weeks

1									
2									
3									
4									
5									
6									
7									
8									
9									
10									

DAILY PRACTICE RECORD
Oakland, California Public Schools
Music Department

Pupil's Name _____   _____ Semester, 19_____

Note: Success in the playing of a musical instrument is determined by the amount of practice. Daily home study of 30 minutes or more will insure satisfactory progress. In the spaces below, kindly fill in the number of minutes practiced each day. Parent must verify the week's practice with his or her signature. Thank you for your cooperation.

_____
Music Instructor

Week	Sun.	Mon.	Tues.	Wed.	Thurs.	Fri.	Sat.	Total	Parent's Signature	Practice Grade

PRACTICE CARD
Walla Walla High School
Walla Walla, Washington

Student's Name _____

Symbols used for director's rating
E - Excellent
S - Satisfactory
N - Insufficient Practice Time

WK	M	T	W	TH	FR	SA	SU	Director's Rating	Parent's Initial
1									
2									
3									
4									
5									
6									
7									

PRACTICE RECORD
Memphis High School
Memphis, Tennessee

BAND
Sr., Sr.II, Jr.

Student's Name _____

Address _____

Phone _____

WEEKS	FOLIO	METHOD BOOKS	SOLO and ENSEMBLE	OTHER MATERIAL	TOTAL HOURS
1.					
2.					
3.					
4.					
5.					
6.					
7.					
8.					
9.					
10.					
11.					
12.					
13.					
14.					
15.					

PRACTICE RECORD SUPPLEMENT
"THE MUSICAL PARTNERSHIP"
(Joliet, Illinois)

Parents and Home Practice Are an Integral Part of Success

There is scarcely a more neglected area in the field of instrumental music than that of parent-teacher relationships. The successful and superior student is invariably backed up by enlightened and progressive parents.

Music study is a three-way partnership composed of teacher, student, and parents. Each member of the partnership has a responsibility. Most parents are eager to be active members of the musical partnership, but need guidance and definition.

Parents' Responsibilities

What are the parents' responsibilities in the musical partnership?

1. *Patience* in repeatedly reminding the student to do his daily stint at his instrument, and doing this kindly but firmly.
2. *Encouragement* when the going is rough. Some things in music are learned easily; others require intensive and repeated application. Parental sympathy and understanding are important.
3. *Imagination* in creating a musical atmosphere in the home by tuning in interesting musical programs on radio and TV; inviting friends who also play into the home, and making playing for one another a part of the occasion; adding an attractive recording to the record collection at frequent intervals.
4. *Common Sense* in avoiding undue stress on musical work. All healthy children want and need a considerable daily portion of vigorous physical activity. Trying for a balanced schedule of interests into which music practice fits as a natural and compensating element will pay big musical dividends.

Favorable Practice Conditions

As a young person advances in his music study and is presented with increasingly difficult problems in thinking and playing, the regularity and quality of his preparation become more and more important. Regularity and quality can be promoted if parents will assume the responsibility for seeing that favorable practice conditions are assured. Here are some suggestions as to how this can be achieved:

1. Schedule a regular time for practice. Mornings are best, when minds and bodies are fresh and receptive.
2. See that proper physical conditions prevail: a quiet room, adequate lighting on the music stand, sufficient ventilation, comfortable temperature.
3. Keep instruments well tuned and in first-rate mechanical condition. Nothing is more discouraging than an out-of-tune piano, a clarinet key that sticks, or a saxophone reed that is defective.
4. Praise work well done. A congratulatory remark may be interjected during a practice session, or a complimentary comment made later during mealtime.
5. *Never* use practice as punishment. It is advisable occasionally to reschedule a practice period to allow for important conflicting school events, but avoid giving preference to any and all activities conflicting with the practice schedule.

Parental Help

1. Remind him to practice new work first.
2. When wrong notes and hesitations keep recurring, suggest:
   a. Practicing in short sections, a few measures at a time.
   b. Practicing more slowly.
   c. Checking the written notes carefully to make sure they have been read accurately.

Parents *can* and *must* have the firmness to insist on what they know is best in the long view, regardless of the frequency, length and volume of resistance. Sustaining interest is a real and difficult problem, and it is perhaps in this aspect of music study where parental action is most important.

Written by Charles S. Peters

PRACTICE RECORD— LETTER TO PARENTS
HUTCHINSON PUBLIC SCHOOLS
Department of Music
Hutchinson, Kansas

Dear Interested Parents:

When your child brings his band or orchestra instrument home for the first time, start right then to ENCOURAGE him! "I'm too busy," some Dads may say. "I don't have time to listen to squeaks and squawks. I have to keep my mind on my business. After all, I've got to pay for this horn."

Mom, you may voice this complaint: "Now son. . . learn to play your instrument at school. That's what your director is for, to teach you at school. I can't stand that spewing and sputtering. . . just leave your instrument in the music room." (Don't even *think* it, Mom, because your child will read it in your face.)

What can we conclude from these true situations? Basically, that somewhere in the learning process, probably during the first 4 to 6 weeks, most any youngster is apt to say: "Aw shucks, learning an instrument is too hard. I'm gonna try something easier." They need encouragement from *us* — their PARENTS.

Here are a few specific ways we Dads and Moms can keep our children happily engaged in this marvelous learning process, particularly when discouragement gathers on the horizon.

1. PRACTICE PERIOD. First of all, call it "music period," "rehearsal time," "swing time," or "playing period." The word practice just doesn't sound pleasant. Help your child establish a *regular* music period each day for at least 20 to 30 minutes. Mornings before school is an excellent time.

2. PHYSICAL CONDITIONS. Keep temperature and ventilation at the best level for alert instrumental playing. Try having a quiet period in the house when your child plays his instrument. Radio and TV are apt to distract.

3. MUSIC STAND. So important, so inexpensive (about $5.00), so needed by every musician. Get one for your child.

4. Above all, the most important thing you can do is to *be interested parents*. Remember, NO beginner plays his instrument beautifully. Expect only gradual improvement. Compliment some phase of his playing, i.e., his tone, rhythm, range, quality, dynamics (his ability to play loud or soft at will), his choice of exercises, etc. Sit by him and tap your foot while he plays.

Congratulations in your judgment and good taste in encouraging your youngster to become an important part of our instrumental music program.

The rewards of music are immeasurably greater than the cost in time and money. Let's sow the seeds of future satisfaction and accomplishment by encouraging our youngsters to KEEP ON PLAYING.

Respectfully yours,

_____

Instrumental Music Staff

PRACTICE RECORD SUPPLEMENT
Brooklyn Center High School
Minneapolis, Minnesota

"SO YOUR CHILD WON'T PRACTICE?"

The last round of applause could still be heard in the small concert hall where three boys were putting away their instruments. "Gosh, we did alright," said Stan, the thirteen-year-old, to his brothers. "Fun, too," said Gale, a year younger, as he tossed his music in a folder. "And now for something to eat," said Roy, snapping his instrument case shut.

The program for the local Sunday Evening Club was over. My husband and I were being surrounded. The gentlemen nearest my husband beamed. "I bet you never have to make those boys practice," he said. "Indeed we do," replied my husband. The pleasure on the man's face changed to surprise and curiosity. "But the way they play, I thought—." "They're regular boys and practicing doesn't come any more natural to them than washing their ears," answered my husband, "but both are part of their daily schedule."

Others crowded in, congratulating us on our three sons' performance as if it had been something spectacular. I couldn't understand. Was our family concert so unusual— playing music together and in solo? This could have happened in our living room most any evening. "How do you get your boys to practice?" The question seemed to come from several people. I looked up at them, wondering how to answer, when my husband spoke. "We teach them to practice. Our children are no exception." "But they play as if they enjoy it," said the woman at my left. "They do. After all, it's a form of self-expression. And playing for others gives them an added sense of achievement. But that doesn't mean they like to practice. It's our job to see that they do practice. We help them." "How?" came the blunt question. I thought of how hard it would be for a child to read and write by himself. Only through daily help and practice does it become easy and natural for him. Music is no different. But there are Ways to motivate his daily practice. So . . .

"First of all," I said, "we establish a regulation: one-half hour of practice each day, to be finished before 7:30 pm. I feel that if children know what is expected of them, what they may or may not do, they have something to hold on to. It gives them a feeling of security, which is essential to their happiness. Each of our boys has different hours of working best. With Gale, the one who played piano for you, it's early morning. As soon as his breakfast is finished, he practices until school time, getting most of it done then. He doesn't like to practice, but good music grades bring reward. This year it will be some special fishing tackle.

"With Roy, the ten-year-old, a half-hour practice session is too long. Two fifteen-minute periods for him. We sometimes have to help him, and each week of good practicing brings an extra privilege— a new ball, a movie or an afternoon picnic.

"Stan, the thirteen-year-old, has many after-school sports. He practices best after dinner. Radio and television are his to see only after his practice is finished. A solo or number mastered merits a Saturday movie, hamburgers for the gang, or a new baseball bat."

"Do they watch the clock while they practice?" came the question. "We have no clock in the living room. They check the time when they start, and after fifteen or twenty minutes, they call out, 'What time is it, Mom?' If they waste time, I simply add an extra five minutes and tell them it has been added. After the first few weeks, it seldom happens."

"But I thought children should never be forced to practice. It might kill their love for music," said a feminine voice in the group. "Let us look at it this way. Children are not mature in their judgment. We, as parents, must enforce what is right for them. If you review the early life of Haydn, Mozart, Beethoven and many others, you will find their training was part of their daily schedule, and not because they chose it to be. Free choice, in most things, is not for children. We know our boys are not genius material. They're normal, mischievous youngsters, full of energy and curiosity. And we want to give them preparation for experiences ahead by taking them by the hand and leading them. And one of those doors leads to the enjoyment of music.

(Practice Record Supplement continued on next page.)

"Music, a language of the feelings, goes beyond the printed or spoken word. It holds no barrier of race, creed or nationality. One of the finest forms of self-expression for all ages, music is relaxing, uplifting, and always teaches children that it requires patience and daily supervision. The latter is our job, as parents— just as it is our job to enforce a reasonable bedtime, whether they approve or not. Yet, many parents indulge in the belief that it is wrong to hold a child to a daily practice period. If he wants music, he must do his practicing on his own. Or is it because they, as parents, are content to take the path of least resistance?

"Let's look at it objectively. In a recent survey of our penal institutions, it was found that only a scattered few among the thousands of criminals had ever received any regular musical instruction or participated in a band, orchestra or chorus during their childhood. Music and delinquency seldom mix."

To make the daily practice period more enjoyable and worthwhile to both pupils and parents, here are some suggestions we hope you will find helpful:

FIVE KEYS THAT WILL OPEN THE DOOR TO MUSIC

1. Assist your child with his practicing.
2. Be generous with your interest and praise.
3. Credit each achievement with some form of recognition.
4. Develop the habit of daily practice.
5. Encourage note-reading, rather than playing by ear.

It may take all five keys to unlock the practice problem, but try them all before giving up. MUSIC IS ONE THING YOUR CHILD WILL NEVER THANK YOU FOR NOT GIVING HIM!!

BEGINNING INSTRUMENTAL MUSIC CLASS ANNOUNCEMENT
Tucson Public Schools Music Department
Tucson, Arizona

Date _____

Dear Parent:

Instrumental music classes are now being organized in your child's school. Free instruction in the band and orchestra instruments is a part of the regular program in the Tucson Public Schools. This is a wonderful opportunity for your child to discover himself and his talents. It will help him become a part of a group that will make its influence felt, not only for the rest of his school days, but for his entire life.

Participation in musical group activities provides an opportunity for talent to come to life which otherwise might be undiscovered and unappreciated. Most important, however, is the fact that music provides young people with a means of purposeful recreation that can be of life-long value.

Instruments may be purchased from local music stores or individuals, and should meet approval of the instructor. If rented from a music store on the basis of a four month's trial period, the rental may be applied toward purchase. One of the principal causes of pupil failure is an inferior instrument. If the instrument has a poor or dull tone, there is no pleasure to be gained from playing and youngsters soon give it up.

Class instruction, starting at the 4th-grade level, is offered on violin, viola, cello and string bass. Starting at the 5th grade, TPS No. 1 offers instruction on B-flat clarinet, saxophone, flute, trombone, baritone, trumpet or cornet. Snare drum will be taught to a limited number of 6th graders who furnish an orchestra type snare drum, drum pad, sticks, book and rack.

Students enrolling in instrumental music classes should understand that daily practice at home is expected of them. Unless parent conferences are arranged, students will be expected to stay enrolled for at least one full semester.

All students must supply their own method book and a folding music stand.

Instrumental demonstrations will be presented in each elementary school sometime during the 2nd full week of school in the fall. Class lessons start the 3rd week of school. Call the elementary school in your neighborhood for specific hours and dates.

If you have further questions, please do not hesitate to call the instructor at the school.

Sincerely,

_____
Instrumental Instructor

If you are interested in having your child become a part of the Instrumental Program, please fill out the following form and have your child return it to school immediately.

- -

Name_____ Grade_____ Room _____

Address_____ Telephone_____

School _____ Teacher _____

Instrument _____

Beginner _____ Second Year _____ Third Year _____

Years of Private Study_____ Can you rent an instrument?_____

_____
Signature of Parent

BEGINNER RECRUITMENT PROCEDURES
Oakland, California

The success of a school instrumental music program depends in large part upon how well student interest in instrumental music can be created and maintained. To assist the teacher in creating and maintaining this interest, several techniques and aids have been devised.

Key: (E) = Elementary
(JH) = Junior High
(SH) = Senior High
(A) = All levels

A. RECOMMENDATIONS AND SUGGESTIONS FOR PROMOTION AND MOTIVATION

1. Demonstration techniques

   a. Room-to-room canvass (E). This should be made at the beginning of a new semester. The teacher, or proficient students, should take a few basic instruments and perform on them for the students. If only a little tune is played on each instrument, it will suffice. A talk should be given on the instrumental program — what is offered, and how students can join. The suggestion can be made that possibly some relative may have an old instrument stored away which may be repaired and put to use. The instrument rental plan as offered by local music stores should be explained, and appropriate promotional bulletins should be distributed. The music promotional bulletin and rental letter should be distributed to *all* students in each classroom. These forms should be taken home by students and discussed with parents.

   b. Demonstration assembly (E). Such an assembly should be held at the end of the semester for P.T.A., Dads Club, and school assemblies, grades three to six. All students who take lessons, including song flutes, should perform either as a group or as soloists. Even the simplest exercise well done will spark the program. Insofar as possible, the assembly should be made progressive, starting with beginners, then intermediate, and ending with advanced classes or orchestra. This will show both parents and students the natural progress which can be made with steady practice. This should be followed with an informative talk to parents about the program.

   c. Classroom solos (E). Classroom teachers should be encouraged to have students play solos for classmates whenever possible. Teachers should have an "amateur" hour occasionally in which instrumental students have opportunity to participate. Advanced instrumentalists should be utilized to accompany class singing or choral groups.

   d. Assemblies (E). Music assemblies should be held at the beginning and end of the term. (The teacher should determine grades from which he wished to draw.) Either teacher or student should demonstrate the instruments, and the demonstration should be followed with complete information about the program. It would be worthwhile to show a film or filmstrip on music. An appropriate promotional bulletin and rental letter should be issued.

   e. Instrument display (A). Parents and children should be invited to see instruments. All types of instruments to be taught should be displayed and performed on so that children may hear them and ask questions about them. The rental-purchase plan should be explained. A promotional bulletin and rental letter should be distrubuted.

   f. Upper level school band or orchestra assembly (A). Teachers should ask instructor at the school into which he feeds to have the band or orchestra perform at his school, and also invite neighboring instrumental groups, colleges, etc., to perform.

In addition to the above suggested techniques, it has proved valuable in many instances to invite the parent to visit the class while it is in progress. As a result of the visit, the parent is better equipped to supervise home practice intelligently.

2. Films and filmstrips (A)

Motion pictures or filmstrips pertinent to instrumental music should be shown to students at an assembly. The program should be explained and the instruments demonstrated. A promotional bulletin and rental letter should be issued. Be careful to use audio-visual material appropriate to the grade level.

3. Musical performances (JH and SH)
   a. Assemblies
      1. Orchestras or bands in combined performances
      2. Solos and ensembles
      3. Exchange assemblies with other schools
      4. Visiting groups (college, military, or professional organizations)
      5. Talent shows
   b. Public performances
      1. Concerts
      2. Musical shows
      3. Variety and talent shows
      4. P.T.A. and Dads Club
      5. Appearances at professional music education meetings
      6. Athletic events
      7. Graduation
      8. Bay Area festivals, California Music Educators Association
      9. Parades
      10. City-wide festivals

4. Song flute program (E)

As a result of a conference with principal and classroom teacher, one or more rooms will be selected for the song flute program. At the end of each semester an appropriate promotional bulletin should be sent home with recommended students. Students should be tested and parents notified of an appropriate instrument for the child. The song flute program is a good way to find musical talent.

5. Talks (A)

The teacher should attend social gatherings, open house, P.T.A., Dads Club, etc., and explain benefits and values, and how the instrumental program functions in the school.

6. Posters (A)

Good, attractive-looking posters will catch the eye of every student and will create interest in the department. The cooperation of the art department should be enlisted. Thought should be given to making the room attractive with current music news, pictures, etc.

7. Parades and community activities (A)

Cooperation with civic groups will assist greatly in building community spirit and support and will stimulate interest in the school music program. Such cooperation should be given whenever possible.

8. Newspaper publicity (A)

Publicity in school and local newspapers is valuable. Explain the program— be brief and to the point. Present a publicity plan to the principal and request that he contact the Office of Publications and Public Information for arrangements regarding pictures and story.

9. Counselor contact (JH and SH)

The counselors should be kept informed at all times regarding the overall value and content of the instrumental program of the school.

10. Participation in Summer Music-Recreation Program

The Music-Recreation Program, established in 1959, is sponsored by the Music Section of the Oakland Education Association and the Oakland Recreation Department in cooperation with the Oakland Public Schools. This program is available to all students, fourth grade through ninth grade, in the Oakland Public Schools, parochial schools, and schools outside of Oakland. This is a nonprofit, self-supporting program which is completely dependent upon fees and scholarship contributions for its operation. Specific details and additional information are given in the annual brochure which is available following the spring vacation.

The supervisor of instrumental music is the permanent director of the program in cooperation with the Board of Directors, Music Section of the Oakland Education Association.

All Oakland Public School music teachers are invited to apply for summer employment. Responsibility of appointment rests with the director of the program and the Board of Directors.

B. MAINTAINING INTEREST

1. Awards

It is advisable to set up an award system to fit the individual school situation.

2. Public performance as suggested in previous recommendations

3. School visits

Instrumental music students receive stimulation from visits to upper-level school rehearsals and concerts.

4. Attendance at concerts

The student should be encouraged to attend school functions and professional performances as often as possible.

5. Music clubs

Supplementary lectures, materials, and discussions will elevate and motivate those who are interested.

6. Special group participation

Special groups provide a challenge to the more advanced student and an incentive for all to improve on their individual instruments in order to gain admission to these advanced organizations.

a. All-Conference Bands and Orchestras
b. All-City Bands and Orchestras
c. Honor Bands and Orchestras

7. Festival participation (A)

a. Elementary Solo and Ensemble Festival
b. Junior High Solo and Ensemble Festival
c. Junior High Spring Music Festival
d. R.O.T.C. Band Competition
e. Music Educators Association Solo and Ensemble Festivals
f. Music Educators Association Band and Orchestra Festivals
g. Music Educators Association Stage Band Festivals

8. Summer music activities (A)

a. Summer Music-Recreation Program
b. Music Camps

9. Practice cards (E)

The use of these cards is excellent for the motivation of home practice. DAILY PRACTICE RECORD cards are available.

10. Private study (A)

The student should be encouraged to study privately whenever possible. Use letter for parental contact.

11. Warning notice to parents

It is the responsibility of the instrumental teacher to inform the parent in cases of insufficient progress being made by the student. Before dropping a student from class, a notice must be sent home. It is imperative that the principal be notified when this notice is sent home as well as when a final decision is made to drop the student from class.

C. CONTINUITY OF PARTICIPATION BY INSTRUMENTAL STUDENTS

1. Coordination of Instrumental Enrollment Blanks (Elementary School to Junior High School only).

These blanks must be completed according to directions. It is recommended that teachers involved confer with each other for further clarification of ratings. This will insure proper scheduling and prevent further problems.

2. Visitations by upper-level school instrumental director to feeder schools for conferences with incoming instrumental students.

3. The junior high school director must confer with 9th grade counselor to insure programming of students on the senior high school level.

4. It is the responsibility of the secondary instrumental director to confer with the principal and all counselors regarding the continued participation of instrumental students.

These are a few suggestions. The resourceful teacher will try many approved methods and use the ones which work best for him.

LETTER TO PARENTS (Song Flute)
Oakland, California Public Schools
Music Department

_____ School   _____19_____

_____ Principal

Dear Parents:

As you know, your child's class has been studying the song flute for the past _____ . It is with a great deal of pleasure that I inform you of your child's progress. _____ has demonstrated that _____ has more than average musical ability and should continue the study of a band or orchestra instrument next semester. May I urge strongly that you investigate the possibility of obtaining an instrument for your child. I shall be happy to discuss this matter with you at your convenience.

Sincerely yours,

Telephone_____

_____
Music Instructor

LETTER TO PARENTS (Private Lessons)
Oakland, California Public Schools
Music Department

Dear Parents:

Your child has been participating in the instrumental music program and thus far has demonstrated more than average ability. The class lessons offered at school are satisfactory, but I feel that private study would be extremely beneficial in order to further develop (his) (her) technique and to allow progress commensurate with this ability. It has been proven that students who study privately derive a great deal more benefit from participating in and listening to music in addition to broadening and enriching their future cultural lives.

The Music Department has a listing of many fine private teachers. Please feel free to call me or make an appointment before or after school or during my conference period in order that we may discuss this further and that I may recommend teachers in your area.

Sincerely yours,

_____
Music Instructor

_____
Telephone

_____
School Principal

INSTRUMENT RENTAL FORM
Oakland, California Schools
Music Department

Date_____

Dear Parents:

The Oakland Unified School District provides each elementary school in the system with a basic allotment of instruments. The purposes of the instruments are for talent exploration and to determine the aptitude and ability of the individual student. After a trial period, which is generally one school semester in length, it is desirable for the child to have his or her own instrument.

Your child has proven very definitely that (he) (she) has more than adequate ability which would justify obtaining (his) (her) individual instrument. I shall be most happy to confer with you relative to the choice and selection of the proper instrument. My telephone number is_____ and I shall be happy to have you call me for an appointment.

Sincerely,

_____
Instrumental Teacher

School_____

Principal_____

LETTER TO PARENTS (promotional)
Oakland, California Public Schools
Music Department

_____ School   _____ 19__

_____ Principal

Dear Parents:

We wish to call your attention to one of the most valued activities promoted by our school— our instrumental music program. Pupils from the fourth grade up may enroll for instruction in classes now being formed. Instruction is offered on all band and orchestra instruments with the exception of piano. This instruction is a part of the regular school program and is given without charge. The classes will meet at regular periods during school hours. Instruments should be provided by the pupil; however, there are a few school instruments available.

For those who do not have instruments of their own, through the cooperation of local music dealers your child can have the instrument of his or her choice for a trial period for a nominal rental fee. If at the end of that period you desire to have your child continue, you may apply the rental fee on the purchase of an instrument.

It must be understood that your child has the responsibility of putting forth the necessary amount of effort required to progress in this program. This means adequate home practice, punctuality, maintenance of all equipment, and regular attendance with instrument.

If you wish your child to take advantage of this opportunity, please fill in the blank at the bottom of the page and return it to me immediately.

Sincerely yours,

Telephone _____

_____
Music Instructor

- -

I am interested in having _____ , _____ , _____ , enrolled for
                                         Child's Name   Room   Grade

instruction on _____ .
                        Name of Instrument

Please check:

We have our own instrument for our child's lessons. _____   _____
                                                          yes   no

We shall rent an instrument from a local music store. _____   _____
                                                             yes   no

My child has played a musical instrument. _____   _____
                                                  yes   no

The instrument is _____

Length of time: _____

_____   _____   _____
Parent's Signature   Address   Telephone

CLASSROOM TEACHER EVALUATION FORM
Oakland, California Public Schools
Music Department
(Elementary)

_____ 19 ___

Classroom Teacher _____ :

The following students have asked to begin the study of instrumental music. I would appreciate an evaluation of each applicant's abilities.

Use a rating scale of 1 to 5 (superior - poor).

Pupil	Reading Ability	General Intel.	Study Habits	Perse-verance	Conduct	Depend-ability	Singing Ability

Thank you for your cooperation.

Instrumental Teacher _____

Please add any names of pupils you feel should take advantage of this opportunity.

INSTRUMENT DEMONSTRATION ANNOUNCEMENT
Spencer High School
Spencer, Iowa

NOTICE: PARENTS AND STUDENTS

There will be a Music Instrument Demonstration in the senior high school bandroom on _____ , at _____ . All students who wish to begin music lessons on a band instrument (this summer or in the fall) and the parents of those students are asked to attend.

Included in the demonstration will be a brief description of each instrument and its use in the band. Examples of the sound and character of each instrument will be provided by an instrument demonstration team composed of top performers from the senior high school band. Also present will be a representative from _____ who will provide information pertaining to the rental or purchase of band instruments. At the conclusion of the demonstration the band directors will meet with parents and students for personal interviews to determine the instrument best suited to each student. (All 3rd, 4th, 5th, and 6th grade students have taken a standardized music aptitude test to help determine musical promise. Scores on that test will be availble at the personal interview upon the parent's request.)

Summer classes for elementary instrumental music students will begin on _____ . The summer schedule will be for an eight week period with classes held week-day mornings between _____and _____ . All classes and rehearsals will be held in the music rooms at the senior high school building. Students are instructed to bring their instruments, music racks and books.

SUMMER BAND ANNOUNCEMENT
Spencer High School
Spencer, Iowa

In addition to the free summer music classes for all beginning instrumental music students, plus the elementary and junior high bands, PRIVATE MUSIC LESSONS will be available commencing with the _____ week in _____ and ending on _____ . The following teachers will be available:

_____ Lessons on all band instruments.

_____ Lessons on all band instruments.

_____ Lessons on all band instruments.

_____ Specializes on woodwinds with emphasis on clarinet and saxophone.

_____ Specializes on oboe.

_____ Specializes on flute.

Cost of Lessons: _____ per half hour.

Location of Lessons: Each teacher will let you know where his or her students will take lessons at the time you sign up.

LETTER TO PARENTS (Test)
Hutchinson, Kansas Public Schools
Department of Music

_____ 19 _____

Dear Parents:

Recently we have given a music adaptability test to the students in the Hutchinson Schools. The test is a measure of natural ability and gives an indication of the probable success of the student in the field of music. Your child has placed in the upper percent of his class on this test.

Most normal persons can become successful amateur musicians. Important factors to consider are: the desire to play, willingness to work, the encouragement given the child at home, and the physical adaptation of the child to the instrument.

Knowing that most parents want to give their child every opportunity to develop his innate abilities, we feel that it is our responsibility to advise you of your child's high aptitude in music.

The Hutchinson Public Schools offer free lessons each year to beginning band and orchestra students in the fourth grade. It is recommended that those students who are interested attend exploratory classes beginning next week. The classes are designed to discover a pupil's natural aptitude and interest for a specific instrument. Physical limitations play an important part in the choice of the instrument best suited to a particular child. Your child will have the opportunity to play various instruments in order to determine the most suitable instrument for a successful experience in instrumental music.

If you have any further questions feel free to call me at your convenience.

Sincerely,

_____
Music Instructor

LETTER TO PARENTS (Beginning Classes)
Hutchinson, Kansas Public Schools
Department of Music

——————— 19 ———

Dear Parents:

The Hutchinson Schools offer free class lessons each year to beginning instrumental students in the fourth and fifth grades.

It is recommended that interested students attend exploratory classes beginning next week. The classes are designed to discover natural aptitude for and interest in a specific instrument. Physical limitations play an important part in the choice of the instrument best suited to a particular child. Your child will have the opportunity to play various instruments in order to determine the most suitable instrument for a successful experience in instrumental music.

If you have any further questions feel free to call me at your convenience.

Sincerely,

_____
Music Instructor

GENERAL INFORMATION ABOUT BEGINNING CLASS INSTRUCTION

Is there a charge for this instruction?

No, the instruction is free. Students furnish their own method books at a cost of about one dollar ($1.00).

Are students required to furnish their own instruments?

Some instruments are owned by the public schools and are rented, when available, for a nominal fee. These include the larger and more expensive instruments.

Our music stores have instruments which you may rent for a period of three months. Under this trial rental plan you have the option of returning the instrument at the end of the rental period or purchasing the instrument, in which case, your rental fee is applied.

What instruments are included in the band and orchestra?

You may choose for your child any of the following instruments: flute, oboe, B-flat clarinet, alto and tenor saxophone, cornet, trumpet, French horn, trombone, baritone, tuba, drums, violin, viola, cello, string bass. Instruction is not provided for harmonica, accordian, fretted instruments or piano.

How can I tell which instrument is best?

The exploratory class is designed to help you decide which instrument is best for your child. Please feel free to contact the instrumental music instructor if there are any questions.

Are private lessons required?

Private lessons are not required. But they are recommended, because students who take them progress more rapidly.

Is home practice required?

A minimum of thirty minutes home practice a day is recommended if the child is to make normal progress.

How often do classes meet?

Elementary instrumental classes meet twice a week during school time (two half-hour periods).

LETTER TO PARENTS (Instrument Rental)
Hutchinson, Kansas Public Schools
Department of Music

_____ 19 _____

Dear Parents:

The Hutchinson Schools offer free class lessons to beginning instrumental students. These classes are open to fourth and fifth grade students. Some instruments are owned by the public schools and are rented (if available) to students for a small fee. These include the larger and more expensive instruments.

Our music stores have instruments which you may rent for a period of three months. Under this trial rental plan you have the option of returning the instrument at the end of the rental period or purchasing the instrument, in which case, your rental fee is applied. Your child's chance for success will be much better if you secure a new instrument or one in excellent condition. If you are in doubt, call or see me.

You may choose for your child any of the following instruments: flute, oboe, B-flat clarinet, alto and tenor saxophone, cornet, trumpet, French horn, trombone, baritone, tuba, drums, violin, viola, cello, and string bass. When choosing an instrument it is advisable to consider correct physical adaptation, which will enable the child to progress faster and easier. The choice of the correct instrument will be an important factor in his success in instrumental music.

Your child seems to adapt best to the following instruments:

Feel free to call me about any questions you might have.

Phone _____

Sincerely,

_____
Music Instructor

LETTER TO PARENTS (Instrument Insurance)
Hutchinson Kansas Public Schools
Department of Music

_____ 19 _____

Dear Parents:

It is now possible for all band and orchestra students to have their instruments insured at a very low rate because of the larger number of instruments which can be placed on one blanket policy. This insurance covers all risk of loss or damage, except by deterioration, moths or vermin, or inherent vice.

The rates are _____ per one hundred dollars ($100.00) value for one (1) year. This will furnish coverage from _____ to _____ .

If you are interested in having this insurance will you please complete the form below and return this letter, with the proper amount of money, to _____ no later than _____.

Sincerely,

_____
Supervisor of Music

- -

Name of Instrument _____ Make of Instrument _____

Serial Number _____

Value of Instrument _____ Amount remitted _____

Name of Student _____

Name of Parent _____

Address _____ Phone _____

BEGINNING INSTRUMENTAL CLASS ANNOUNCEMENT
Missoula, Montana Public Grade Schools

To Fifth Grade Parents:

Commencing with the week of November 13th, we will be organizing Pre-instrument Classes in the schools for prospective band and orchestra beginners. These classes will meet in each school twice weekly.

Pre-instrument Classes are open to fifth grade students who . . .

1. Are average or better than average students (this is important because they will be leaving the classroom to attend Pre-instrument Classes and, later, beginning band or orchestra classes).
2. Have the desire to learn to play an instrument and become a member of the Missoula Grade School Orchestra or Band.
3. Have some degree of natural music talent (the enclosed Musical Aptitude Profile for your child is quite an accurate appraisal of his degree of talent).

PLEASE NOTE: The Musical Aptitude (Talent) Profile, a nationally standardized test recently administered at the fifth grade level in all grade schools, may be interpreted in this manner:

90–99, VERY HIGH; 75–90, HIGH; 50–75, ABOVE AVERAGE; 25–50, LOW AVERAGE; AND 0–25, LOW DEGREE OF NATURAL MUSIC TALENT.

If your child scores HIGH, you can be quite sure that he has a talent for music. However, should he score LOW, one must keep in mind that he might have had a bad day, wasn't feeling well or was distracted during the test (particularly where you find two high and one low score). In some cases, the testing environment was not the most desirable due to a crowded class or outside noises.

Pre-instrument Classes are of an exploratory/instructional nature and do not obligate you or your child to the instrumental music program in any way; their purpose is threefold: (1) To acquaint the youngsters with some of the fundamentals necessary to reading music; (2) To acquaint them with the band and orchestra instruments; and (3) To determine what instrument(s), if any, they are best suited to play. At the close of the pre-instrument period (third week in January), we will send a report to the parents of all who take part in this program with our recommendation for their child. Also, we will schedule a parent meeting for the purpose of describing the instrumental music program in general, and the beginning program in particular.

If you would like to enroll your child in the Pre-instrument Program, kindly complete the attached Enrollment Blank and have your child bring it to his first scheduled Pre-instrument Class. Also, he should bring a notebook and pencil to each class.

Very cordially yours,

_____

Director

(Letter continued on next page.)

We wish to enroll our child (full name): _____ in the grade school Pre-instrument Program. We understand that we are not obligated to provide an instrument for him at this time, and that we will receive a recommendation for our child at the close of this program in January. We understand that this report will indicate whether or not he should begin on an instrument, and if so, what instrument(s) he is best suited to play.

Student: _____ Parents: _____

Mailing Address: _____ Teacher: _____

School: _____ Home Phone: _____

PRE-INSTRUMENT CLASS SCHEDULE

CENTRAL SCHOOL . . . . . . Each MONDAY   12:50– 1:30   and WEDNESDAY 12:50– 1:30
COLD SPRINGS SCHOOL . . . Each WEDNESDAY 10:50–11:30   and FRIDAY   10:50–11:30

Due to lack of rehearsal space, students from the Cold Springs School will walk to and from the Meadow Hill School for these classes. Allow five minutes walking time before/after time indicated above.

DICKINSON SCHOOL . . . . . Each TUESDAY   1:45– 2:25   and THURSDAY   1:45– 2:25
FRANKLIN SCHOOL . . . . . Each MONDAY   1:45– 2:25   and THURSDAY   1:45– 2:25
HAWTHORNE SCHOOL . . . . Each TUESDAY   12:50– 1:30   and THURSDAY   12:50– 1:30
JEFFERSON SCHOOL. . . . . Each TUESDAY   12:50– 1:30   and THURSDAY   12:50– 1:30
LEWIS & CLARK SCHOOL . . Each MONDAY   12:50– 1:30   and WEDNESDAY 12:50– 1:30
PAXSON SCHOOL . . . . Each TUESDAY   10:10–10:50   and THURSDAY   10:10–10:50
C.S. PORTER SCHOOL . . . . Each TUESDAY   10:10–10:50   and THURSDAY   10:10–10:50
PRESCOTT SCHOOL . . . . . Each TUESDAY   10:50–11:30   and THURSDAY   10:50–11:30
RATTLESNAKE SCHOOL . . . Each WEDNESDAY 10:10–10:50   and FRIDAY   10:10–10:50
ROOSEVELT SCHOOL . . . . . Each TUESDAY   12:50– 1:30   and THURSDAY   12:50– 1:30

Due to lack of rehearsal space, students from the Roosevelt School will walk to and from the administration building for these classes. Allow five minutes walking time before/after time indicated above.

RUSSELL SCHOOL. . . . . . . Each TUESDAY   10:50–11:30   and THURSDAY   10:50–11:30
WASHINGTON SCHOOL . . . . Each TUESDAY   12:50– 1:30   and THURSDAY   12:50– 1:30
LOWELL SCHOOL . . . . Each WEDNESDAY 9:00– 9:40   and FRIDAY   9:00– 9:40
WHITTIER SCHOOL . . . . . . Each WEDNESDAY 9:00– 9:40   and FRIDAY   9:00– 9:40
WILLARD SCHOOL . . . . Each WEDNESDAY 9:00– 9:40   and FRIDAY   9:00– 9:40

UNIFORM AND INSTRUMENT CHECK-OUT FORM
Jordan Vocational High School
Columbus, Georgia
BAND DEPARTMENT

UNIFORM

_____ Coat No.	_____ Grey Belt	_____ Shoulder Knots
_____ Trouser No.	_____ Belt Buckle	_____ Drum Major Uniform
_____ Cape No.	_____ White Cross Belt	_____ Drum Major Hat
_____ Shield No.	_____ Breast Plate	_____ Majorette Uniform
_____ Cap	_____ Breast Cord	_____ Majorette Hat

INSTRUMENT

INSTRUMENT _____ MAKE _____ SER. NO. _____

CONDITION _____ CASE CONDITION _____

VALUE _____ SCHOOL NO. _____

_____ Swab	_____ Lyre	_____ Ligature
_____ Bocal	_____ Mouthpiece	_____ Reed Cap
_____ Strap	_____ Sticks	_____ Mute No.
_____ Reed Case	_____ Bow	

List Additional Equipment

AGREEMENT

I acknowledge the receipt of the above checked items. I will be responsible for any damage or loss that might occur while in my care. I agree to keep all items in the best possible condition and to return them at the request of the director.

Student's Signature _____ Parent's Signature _____

Address _____ Phone _____

UNIFORM CHECK-OUT FORM
Lenoir High School Band
Lenoir, North Carolina

UNIFORM AND ACCESSORIES RECEIPT

Received from the Lenoir High School Band the following property. I agree to pay for any loss or damage to this property as determined by the Band Director and also for the cost of keeping it in repair. I agree to return it promptly upon graduation or leaving the band for any other cause, or at any other time upon notice to do so from the Band Director.

As a further consideration for said property being loaned to me, I do hereby agree to attend band rehearsals regularly, and to faithfully discharge all duties required as a requisite to being a member of said band. I understand thoroughly that all the musical instruments and other property connected with the said musical organization belong to said Lenoir High School Band, and same are subject to recall at any time, and that I hold my position in this organization on probation, and that violation of the rules and a lack of faithful and diligent discharge of the work assigned, on my part, subjects me to suspension, and withdrawal of the property assigned.

Cap Number _____   Citation Cord _____

Overcoat Number _____   Robe Number _____

Belt Number _____   Chevrons _____

Coat Number _____   Trousers _____

Shako _____   Cross Belt _____

Other Band Property _____

Date _____

_____   _____
Parent's Name   Student's Name

UNIFORM CHECK-OUT CARD
Springfield, Oregon

UNIFORM RECORD

Year _____

Name _____

Coat No. _____ Dance Band Jacket _____

Pants No. _____

Overlay No. _____ Comments _____

Hat No. _____ _____

Plume No. _____ _____

Spats No. _____ _____

Alterations made on uniform _____

(Student data on reverse side.)

BAND STUDENT RECORD

Year _____

Name _____
    (Last)   (First)   (Middle)

Address _____ City _____ Zip _____

Telephone _____ Year in school _____

Parent's Name _____

Instrument(s) _____ Years in music _____

Age _____ Special Interests _____

Plans after high school _____

_____

Remarks _____

_____

ELIGIBILITY CONFIRMATION
Temple High School, Temple, Texas
Classroom Teacher's Report of Grades, Attitude and Attendance

Student's Name: _____ Date _____

Each band and orchestra student who represents Temple High School in an Interscholastic League Concert and Sight-reading Contest will submit this blank to all of his teachers approximately 30 days prior to the contest.

After each teacher has signed this blank, the student should turn it in to the Band Office. Grades are to be indicated by writing in "passing" or "failing." Attitude should be indicated as excellent, good, average or poor. Attendance should be given for study hall periods.

Subject	Grade	Attitude	Attendance	Teacher's Signature

NOTES TO CONTEST SOLOISTS AND ENSEMBLES
Brooklyn Center High School
Minneapolis, Minn.

1. Arrange for a piano accompanist early and practice together often.
2. Time your solo down to 3-1/2 to 4 minutes, no more.
3. Practice: How you practice the solo is most important!
   a. Practice standing (except French horns, bass clarinets, bassoons, etc.). Trumpets especially — stand up and hold horns up! (Elbows out slightly.)
   b. First work out little passages that prove difficult for you and go over these passages until they can be played perfectly ten times.
   c. Then go on to the next difficult part in the solo and do the same there. Practice over and over until it can be played perfectly ten times.
   d. Breathe in the same places as you practiced. Mark breaths in pencil so you are not forced to break phrases at the contest.
   e. Now after you have worked out all the hard spots in your solo, go back and play the entire solo from the beginning once with no stops.
   f. Now put the solo away for the day, but remember the places you had trouble with and practice these spots again the next day.
4. KNOW SOLO INSIDE AND OUT: Work out all technical difficulties in advance of the contest.
5. MEMORIZE: You'll play much better if you don't depend on music.
6. TONE: Constantly work for a better tone. Watch your intonation at all times. Strive for good balance of tone and for better quality at all times.
7. PHRASES: Be sure your solo is played with good musical phrasing and meaning. You will need good breath control for this.
8. INTERPRETATION: Give the solo meaning for yourself as well as the listener. Watch the tempo, rhythm, and overall expression of the solo. Let the listener be able to say, "That soloist said something to me with his music."
9. TECHNIQUE: Work for accuracy, good phrasing and the special instrumental techniques of your solo.
10. TEN TIMES THROUGH PERFECTLY before it is ready for the contest or public.
11. TUNE UP: Do this slowly; take lots of time. Flutes tune to B♭ concert and C concert; clarinets and all others to B♭ and F concert. (Tune to B♭ concert and pull middle joint if needed, also bell if needed. Tune F concert, pull barrel if needed. Tune High B♭ concert. Re-tune B♭ concert!)
12. HAVE CONFIDENCE in yourself and your solo. Play with authority.
13. APPEARANCE: Stand tall, erect, have confidence, relax and play to the best of your ability. Hold your instrument properly.
14. ANNOUNCE YOUR SOLO TITLE AND COMPOSER. This will aid in relaxing you.
15. NERVOUS? Try biting your tongue lightly and take big, deep breaths.
16. MUSICIANSHIP: This comes from experience and years, so be thinking about it at all times.
17. RATINGS: Remember not everyone will get an "A" rating. Go into the contest with the thought of obtaining a musical experience, some constructive criticism and valuable information in furthering your musical education.

DRUM MAJOR TRYOUT FORM
Ft. Lauderdale, Florida

I. POSTURE (4 points) _____
   a. Head up
   b. Back straight
   c. Baton position

II. DRILL FUNDAMENTALS (4 points) _____
   a. Attention
   b. Parade rest
   c. At ease
   d. Left face
   e. Right face
   f. About face
   g. Left flank
   h. Right flank

III. COMMAND (4 points) _____
   a. Bearing
   b. Decisiveness
   c. Clarity
   d. Speed

IV. VOICE (4 points) _____
   a. Volume
   b. Quality
   c. Clarity of diction

CANDIDATE'S NAME _____ GRADE _____

TWIRLING TRYOUT FORM
Temple High School, Temple, Texas

Academic ability: _____ Musical ability: _____ Suitability (figure): _____

Ability to get along with other students: _____ Personality: _____

Classification _____

Fundamentals: Finger twirls (both hands) _____
             Time tosses   (both hands) _____
             Wrist twirl   (both hands) _____
             Figure eight (both hands) _____
             Little Joe Flip   _____
             Front two-hand spin   _____
             Aerial work   _____

Strutting (Poise, co-ordination, in-tempo, etc.): _____

Special Routine: _____ Rating: _____

Comments: _____
_____
_____

_____
(Judge)

FINANCIAL OBLIGATION FORM
Ft. Lauderdale, Fla.

Name _____ Date _____

The following financial obligation is to be entered on the above person's financial record. $ _____
Amount

for:

Lost Music _____ _____

Solo Purchase _____ _____

Ensemble Purchase _____ _____

Technic Book _____ _____

Record _____ _____

Instrument Fee _____ _____

Uniform Fee _____ _____

Other _____ _____

Authorized by: _____

LETTER TO VISITING GROUPS (Football Marching Band)
Temple, Texas

FOR VISITING BANDS AND DRILL GROUPS:

Welcome to Temple! If we may be of assistance, please let us know. As our guests you are requested to perform first at halftime. Please be ready to move on the field as soon as the first half gun sounds and the players leave the field. The time allotted for your performance (on and off field) is 7 minutes.

At _____ p.m., the Temple High School Band will play the National Anthem. This is followed by a prayer. Subsequently, you may play your school song at any time convenient to entry of your team, etc. Try not to wait any later than _____ . This will allow us to play our Alma Mater just prior to kick-off.

If you have a script, please send copies to the Radio Stations and the P.A. booth. If you have your own announcer, ask him to be ready in the booth.

We will drop by to see you at the conclusion of halftime.

_____
Director, Temple High School Band
Temple, Texas

HONORARY CONDUCTOR CERTIFICATE
Jefferson City, Missouri

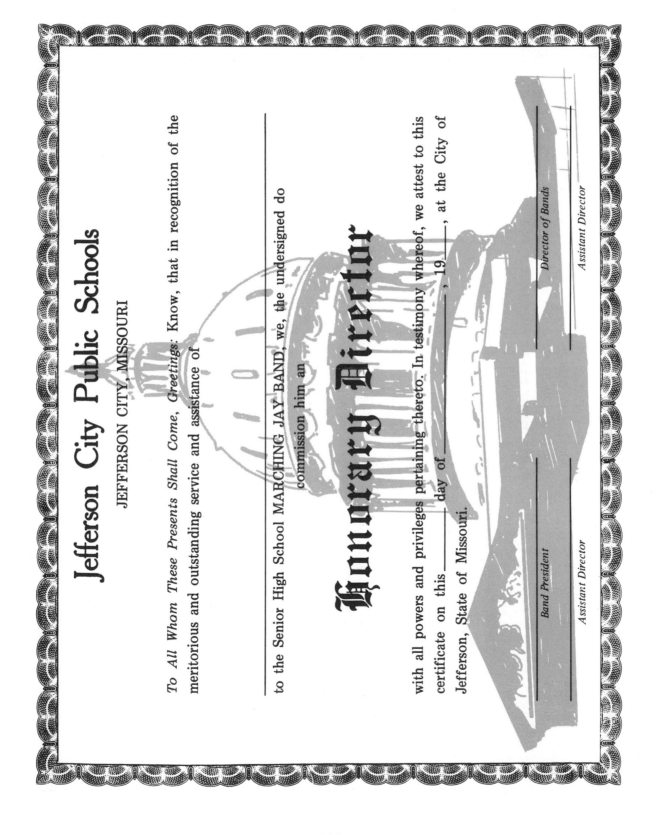

Jefferson City Public Schools

JEFFERSON CITY, MISSOURI

To All Whom These Presents Shall Come, Greetings: Know, that in recognition of the meritorious and outstanding service and assistance of

to the Senior High School MARCHING JAY BAND, we, the undersigned do commission him an

Honorary Director

with all powers and privileges pertaining thereto. In testimony whereof, we attest to this certificate on this _____ day of _____, 19_____, at the City of Jefferson, State of Missouri.

_____
Director of Bands

_____
Assistant Director

_____
Band President

_____
Assistant Director

HONORARY CONDUCTOR CERTIFICATE
Norman, Oklahoma

TO ALL WHOM THESE PRESENTS SHALL COME, GREETINGS:

Know ye, that

has been commissioned an

HONORARY CONDUCTOR

of the Instrumental Music Department, West Junior High School, Norman, Oklahoma, with all the honors, rights and privileges belonging thereto. In testimony whereof, we have caused the hand of the Director to attest to this certificate, at the City of Norman

on

DIRECTOR OF INSTRUMENTAL MUSIC

West
jr. high school
instrumental
music dept.
1919 west boyd street
norman, oklahoma

PETITION FOR APPOINTED OFFICES
Temple High School Band and Orchestra
Temple, Texas

APPOINTED OFFICES: Drum Major and Assistant Drum Major, Majorettes, Librarians, Managers, Office
Secretary

I, _____ , petition for the office of _____
_____ for the school year 19 ___–19 ___ . I certify that I have read and
understand the duties and qualifications as outlined in the Handbook. I further certify that during this
past year I have no grade average lower than C in any subject. (List any additional qualifications here,
such as past experience, etc.):_____

_____

_____

_____

_____

The following students signed this petition in my behalf:

1. _____   13. _____

2. _____   14. _____

3. _____   15. _____

4. _____   16. _____

5. _____   17. _____

6. _____   18. _____

7. _____   19. _____

8. _____   20. _____

9. _____   21. _____

10. _____   22. _____

11. _____   23. _____

12. _____   24. _____

25. _____

OFFICER RESPONSIBILITIES
Jordan Vocational High School
Columbus, Ga.

Band officers will include the following:

> Captain
> First Lieutenant
> Second Lieutenant
> Secretary
> Drum Major

Officers will be nominated by a committee appointed by the band director. All nominees must have the approval of the band director, based on their previous demonstration of leadership and assumption of responsibility. Election of officers will be held during the first regular week of school.

CAPTAIN

Captain is the highest ranking officer of the band. He must be a senior boy and should be an outstanding member of his class. He should be prepared to spend an hour each day in the band room.

Duties of Captain:
1. Preside at all band meetings and Band Council meetings.
2. Uphold the highest traditions and spirit of the band.
3. Hold inspections before marching performances.
4. Serve as a bus chairman on each trip.
5. Maintain discipline in the band room each day before rehearsal and after school.
6. Check band room after each concert performance.

FIRST LIEUTENANT

First Lieutenant is the second ranking officer of the band. He must be a senior boy.

Duties of First Lieutenant:
1. Preside at band meetings and Band Council meetings in the absence of Captain.
2. Serve as the band social chairman.
3. Collect band dues and keep records of the Band Social Fund.
4. Be in charge of band spirit and morale.
5. Serve as bus loading chairman on trips.
6. Serve as a bus chairman on each trip.

SECOND LIEUTENANT

Second Lieutenant is the third ranking officer of the band and must be a junior boy.

Duties of Second Lieutenant:
1. Serve as rehearsal hall monitor.
2. Issue and check in band equipment and uniforms.
3. Inspect band lockers and cubbyholes.
4. Serve as a bus chairman on each trip.
5. Check all uniform accessories after each performance.
6. Set up a system of cleaning band room after each rehearsal.

DRUM MAJOR

Drum Major is the only appointed officer and may come from any class. He is the ranking officer of the Marching Band and the fourth ranking officer of the concert band.

Duties of the Drum Major:
1. Act as field leader of the marching band.
2. Instruct in basic marching fundamentals.
3. Assist in maintaining good discipline in the marching band.
4. Hold inspections before marching performances.
5. Check the band room after every marching performance.
6. Serve as a bus chairman on each trip.
7. Be in charge of the field crew.

SECRETARY

The secretary is the fifth ranking officer and must be a senior girl. She must be proficient in typing and be available to work an hour each day in the band room.

Duties of the Secretary:
1. Record attendance at all band rehearsals.
2. Handle all band correspondence.
3. Send thank you notes to chaperones and others.
4. Secure chaperones for each trip.
5. Secure a pastor to give the invocation at home football games.
6. Send sympathy cards and get-well cards.
7. Record the minutes of Band Council meetings.
8. Record practice hours when required.

* * * * * * * *

In addition to the above officers, an advisory council composed of one boy and one girl from each class will be elected. This group will be a sounding board for band spirit, discipline and procedure.

MUSIC GROUPS AVAILABLE FOR PUBLIC PERFORMANCE (Announcement)
Walla Walla, Washington High School

Date _____

Type of Ensemble _____ Name _____ Group Size _____
(or soloist)
School _____ Instructor _____ Phone No. _____

When Available _____

Program Prepared _____

_____

_____

_____

_____

_____

_____

MUSIC PERFORMANCE REPORT FORM
Walla Walla, Washington High School

Group (or individual) Performing _____

Date _____ Time _____ Type of Audience _____

Estimated Size of Audience _____ Comments _____

_____

_____

_____

_____

_____

_____

_____
Teacher

RECITAL FORM
Tucson Public Schools
Tucson, Arizona

SEND THIS FORM signed by instructor to the Recital Chairman, Music Education Dept. Please complete accurately and legibly. Submit at least one week in advance of desired appearance.

TITLE OF COMPOSITION _____
        (Include key and opus or K. number if appropriate)

FULL NAME OF COMPOSER _____ Min. ___ Sec. ___
                                                            Performance Time

TITLES OR TEMPO MARKINGS of movements to be performed:

Performers (full names)	Instrument*	School and Organization	Division

*Vocalists indicate voice; accompanists should be listed as such.
Desired date of appearance _____ INSTRUCTOR _____

APPLICATION FOR BAND SCHOLARSHIP
Temple High School, Temple, Texas

                                           Date _____

Do you plan to participate in a college music organization, such as band or orchestra, upon entering college? Yes _____ No _____

Which college do you plan to attend? _____

What will be your major? _____ Minor? _____

Have you already been accepted by a college music group? _____

Are you now maintaining an average grade of C or above in all subjects? Yes _____ No _____

Number of children in your family _____

Number in college at present time _____

(Have three of your present or past high school teachers sign the following statement)

I believe _____ is capable of successfully carrying a normal college work load.
               Name of Student

                     Teacher's signatures: 1. _____

                                     2. _____

                                     3. _____

List your achievements in music: _____

_____

_____

                     Signature of applicant: _____

SQUAD LEADER PLAN — VARSITY BAND
Temple High School
Temple, Texas

1. Squad leader selection will be based on the quotas shown below:
   1 from trombone rank
   1 from baritone horns & alto saxes
   1 from French horns and baritone sax
   1 from bass clarinet and tenor sax
   2 from cornets
   1 from percussion
   2 from bass and flutes
   3 from clarinets and oboes
2. Each eligible applicant will submit a "Petition for Appointed Office" signed by at least 10 fellow students. (Get blank petition from band secretary.)
3. Upon receipt of Petition, the director will give applicant a training guide for drill. This will be followed by drill instruction and guidance in military commands.
4. Each applicant will choose 4 students to train and drill in tryouts.
5. Tryouts will be held after school, _____ .
6. The Director will judge the tryouts. Selection will be based on leadership ability as exhibited by applicant during tryouts, general musicianship and citizenship.
7. Following final appointment to the position of Squad Leader, the director may remove any appointee who fails to measure up to standards.
8. The Squad Leader will:
   a. Serve as right guide for his rank.
   b. Be held responsible for complete training of his rank in the execution of drill fundamentals.
   c. Direct all movement and chart reading for halftime shows.
   d. Meet with all other squad leaders prior to drills to check movement and placement of ranks.
   e. Be responsible for discipline and control of his rank.
9. Deadline for Petitions will be _____ .

SUMMER BAND CAMP SCHOLARSHIP CERTIFICATE
Jefferson City, Missouri

Jefferson City Public Schools

Jefferson City, Missouri

In recognition for superior performance and service in the

JAY BAND

is hereby presented this

Summer Band Camp Scholarship

This award for _____ *is provided*

by _____

_____
Month, Day, Year

_____
Director of Bands

_____
Assistant Director